CH00923504

'It never snows in September'

'IT NEVER SNOWS IN SEPTEMBER'

The German View
of MARKET-GARDEN
and The Battle of Arnhem,
September 1944

Robert J. Kershaw

SARPEDON
New York

First published 1990 by The Crowood Press
First published 1994 by Ian Allan Publishing Ltd
Reprinted 1996
This impression 1999

ISBN 0 7110 2167 8

© Robert J. Kershaw 1990

Published by Ian Allan Publishing

an imprint of Ian Allan Publishing Ltd, Terminal House,
Shepperton, Surrey TW17 8AS.
Printed by Ian Allan Printing Ltd, Riverdene Business Park,
Hersham, Surrey KT12 4RG.

Code: 9905/3

Published in the United States by Sarpedon publishers,
166 Fifth Avenue, New York, NY 10010

ISBN 1-885119-31-3

Please note: For an overview of the situation in September 1944, there are
eight colour maps in a section between pages 192 and 193.

Picture Credits
All maps by Claire Upsdale-Jones
The front of jacket photographs are from the following sources (clockwise,
from top left): author, author, author, Imperial War Museum, Imperial War
Museum, Kabel-Kracht, author, Imperial War Museum, author. The
photographs on the back of the jacket were supplied by (left) Imperial War
Museum, and (right) Enthammer.

Dedication
For my wife Lynn

Contents

Preface

During a recent British Army of the Rhine exercise, three parachute infantry companies attacked and captured a bridge held by a substantial enemy force. An exercise 'pause' was declared after sixty minutes by the battalion commander who wished to extract the relevant tactical lessons. One independent observer invited to attend this debrief found it difficult to establish, as each company commander spoke, who was defending and who had attacked. Military historians face similar problems. If intelligent individuals are unable accurately to recall what has happened barely one hour before, what hope is there in recreating a picture of events that occurred in southern Holland nearly forty-seven years ago?

Combat is an intensely personal, emotional and confusing experience. Events can often be misinterpreted, often by the individuals who enacted them. The approach attempted here is one expressed by Christopher Isherwood when he wrote of his experiences in Germany in *Goodbye to Berlin* in 1945:

'I am a camera with its shutter open, quite passive, recording not thinking . . . Some day, all this will have to be developed, carefully printed, fixed.'

In this instance, the battles fought in southern Holland in September 1944 as part of MARKET-GARDEN are seen through a human prism, reflecting the sights and experience of the ordinary German soldier. German documents for this period are incomplete. Recourse has therefore often been made to contemporary eye-witness accounts. Interviews were conducted using maps and photographs to stimulate distant memories. They are a personal exchange between the witness and the author, occasionally producing stress for the former. It soon became apparent to the author that an urgent need 'to tell it as it was', sometimes in uncompromising terms, was driven by a belief that their misfortunes should never be visited upon a future hapless generation.

All judgements and opinions concerning the present-day relevance of MARKET-GARDEN historical lessons to NATO are those of the author, and should in no way be construed as the official policy of the British Ministry of Defence.

Much of this book is concerned with individual experiences. My grateful thanks go to all those who assisted in a difficult and confusing area of research. The project would never have come to fruition without the unselfish assistance provided by Herbert Fuerbringer, Jost W. Schneider, and Rudolf Donth, who opened up the archives of the *Bund der Europaische Fallschirmjaeger* and the 9SS and 10SS Panzer Division Associations to my research. In so doing, they paved the way for many subsequent interviews.

In conception the material was to aid the Camberley Staff College battlefield tour of Arnhem. After much encouragement, in particular from Geoffrey Powell, I decided to go to book form, stimulated by the quality of the material I had been sent. These stories simply had to be told.

Many former serving veterans of the 9SS and 10SS Panzer Divisions and the Fallschirmjaeger Association offered diaries and unpublished personal accounts for perusal. In the absence of official records these did much to paint a realistic scene – for once from a different perspective – through the eyes of the German soldier. Where practical, I have told the story in their own words, attempting in translation to capture the manner in which they delivered it. Particular thanks are due to Hans Moeller, Wilfried Schwarz, Joseph Enthammer, Erich Hensel, Heinz Damaske, Wolfgang Dombrowski, Alfred Ziegler, Rudolf Trapp, Karl-Heinz Euling, Karl-Heinz Kabel, Paul Mueller and Rudolf Lindemann for interviews and the use of personal correspondence. All these gentlemen offered time and advice and occasionally expense to produce the material presented here. Heinz Harmel, the former commander of the 10SS was still able, with a few gestures of hand and cigar over map, to give one of the most lucid accounts of the German perspective of the battles for Nijmegen and Arnhem I had ever heard.

Every effort has been made to trace the source and copyright holders of the maps and illustrations appearing in the text, and these are acknowledged where possible.

Similarly, the author wishes to thank those publishers who have permitted the quotation of extracts from their books. Quotation sources are annotated in the notes that follow the text.

Special thanks are also due to Herr H. Nilges of the photographic department of the *Bundesarchiv* in Koblenz, John Harding from the historical branch of the Ministry of Defence, and Dr Adrian Groeneweg from the Hartenstein Airborne Museum in Oosterbeek. The Freiburg Military Archive in Germany and the National Archive in Washington were helpful in providing many important documents.

Marlitt Boettcher, who assisted in my initial research, receives a particular thank you, for without her I would never have been able to trace the many first-hand accounts that appear in this book for the first time. She and my mother assisted in some awkward colloquial translations.

Finally, this book would never have been written if my wife Lynn had not been able to keep our young boys at bay as patiently as she did during the crucial formative stage in the writing. As ever, she had an unerring eye for detail during the proof reading. Her husband has now returned from the streets of Arnhem.

Church Crookham
May 1989

At 1400 hours local time on 17 September 1944, Lieutenant Joseph Enthammer, a Wehrmacht artillery officer, was gazing in the direction of Oosterbeek when he detected what appeared to be white snowflakes hanging in the air. 'That cannot be,' he wondered; 'it never snows in September! They must be parachutists!'

They were. It certainly does not snow in September. The war had reached the Reich. The blow, moreover, had come as a total surprise.

CHAPTER I
The French Odyssey

We believed that once we got over the German border it would all be over.

SS-Corporal

Cambrai, 2 September 1944 . . .

SS Gunners feverishly prepared their positions, digging and improvising cover in the growing light of early morning along the western approach roads to Cambrai. The 9SS 'Hohenstaufen' had only 18 heavy 88mm flak guns left. These were intermingled with the remaining 37mm anti-tank guns mounted on half-tracks and sited in depth along the main routes from Arras and Bapaume. A number of outposts were forward in Douai, to the right, watching for enemy movement. Panzer-grenadier infantry secured the flanks. All the bridges over the surrounding network of canals and ditches were blocked by obstacles and guarded. By 0900 positions reported they were ready for action. Rearguard was the task. Buy sufficient time to allow the rest of the division mixed up with other fleeing columns to break clean.

Tension gripped the crews. There were no friendly tanks left. Many suspected that this might therefore be their last great tank battle. Only the flak, as so often before, was of sufficient calibre to repel an armoured attack. Gun crews were repeatedly briefed on the priorities for opening fire. Not too soon, the aim was to surprise or ambush targets. Nerves were on edge. Engagements like this had been fought scores of times during the preceding

months. Great care was taken to select safe withdrawal routes. They had only to win a breathing space. Few had any illusions; to withdraw in contact is the most difficult phase of war. By midday outposts were withdrawing, reporting enemy progress. SS-Lieutenant-Colonel Walther Harzer, the 32-year-old acting† divisional commander of the Kampfgruppe Hohenstaufen,

SS-Lieutenant-Colonel Walther Harzer, Commander of the Kampfgruppe 9SS 'Hohenstaufen'. (Fuerbringer Collection)

---

†Stadler the divisional commander had been wounded earlier in the retreat.

The advance was monitored from Harzer's tactical command post.
(Fuerbringer Collection)

monitored the advance from his tactical command post, a collection of camouflaged vehicles dispersed in the Bois-de-Bourlon. This small wood west of Cambrai, between the Arras and Bapaume roads, was in the depth of the main defensive position. Down these roads came 200 enemy tanks accompanied by infantry. It was 19 Corps, the spearhead of General Hodge's 1st (US) Army.

The characteristic high-pitched dry bark of the 88mm flak guns heralded the opening of the engagement at 3,000 metres. Following a flat trajectory, shell tracer bases languidly curved toward targets, ending abruptly with a flash and, following a short pause, a discernible 'plunk', as they tore through the lead tanks. Clouds of inky black smoke boiled skyward, ejected by jets of flame, and began to obscure the battlefield. Each succeeding report whipped up more dust and scattered camouflage foliage, as crews, open-mouthed, hands on ears, sought to relieve the concussive effect of rounds tearing out of the muzzle. Ahead the advancing tanks and infantry paused and split into assault formations. Opening fire at long range was a cheap method of buying time. Infantry, obliged to take cover as mortar and artillery bursts mushroomed around them, became separated from tanks. More time was needed to co-ordinate a response, a further gain for the defence. By late midday of 2 September the battle was in full swing.

The divisional staff of the 9SS Hohenstaufen was cut off in the Bois-de-Bourlon. (Bundesarchiv)

Noise and smoke assaulted the senses, making it difficult to distinguish the course of the battle. By 1500 there were, according to reports, 40 enemy tanks in flames, but some guns had already been knocked out or their crews disabled by counter battery fire. The odds began to tell as groups of tanks isolated single guns and overwhelmed them in multiple engagements. Gradually picking off the German defence, a breakthrough was achieved by Neuville on the outskirts of Cambrai. Having pierced the flak girdle enemy bridge layers attempted to force a crossing of the Escaut Canal. SS panzer-grenadiers succeeded, however, in blunting the effort, disabling a number by shooting them up with *Panzerschrecks* (bazookas) at close range.

A further penetration south of the belt convinced Harzer he would achieve no more. Units ordered to withdraw disengaged where they were able and streamed northwards, hotly pursued by the enemy. 37mm anti-tank guns mounted on half-tracks, contemptuously referred to as 'door-knockers' by their crews, attempted to cover the retreat. Fighting an unequal battle against the pursuing armour, they were destroyed one after the other, while their comrades streamed through Cambrai, held open by the 4th Flak battery, guarding against *Maquis* ambushes. Fully preoccupied directing the battle, Harzer was suddenly bypassed by American tank platoons exploiting the breakthrough. A twenty-four-hour delay had been achieved, but the divisional staff of the 9SS Hohenstaufen had been cut off in the Bois-de-Bourlon.

The Odyssey begins . . .

Germany had suffered a catastrophic defeat. Allied armies had broken out of the invasion bridgehead and worn down two armies in the battle of Normandy. Between 6 June and 31 August 1944 the Westheer lost 23,019 dead, 198,616 soldiers missing or taken prisoner, and 67,240 wounded. On 29 August Supreme Headquarters West had fielded 50 infantry and 12 panzer divisions, this had been reduced to 24 infantry and 11 panzer, all skeletal formations barely intact. Newly-appointed Field Marshal Walther Model, commanding the vanquished Army Group B, felt that from 11 divisions intact in name, he might be able to form four full infantry divisions. Panzer divisions had been reduced to regimental-size armoured combat groups, fielding on average only 5 to 10 tanks each.[1]

These shattered formations, hotly pursued by the enemy, set off on their various odysseys, striving to reach the homeland. Among them was a 19-year-old artillery lieutenant, Joseph Enthammer. He had been on the technical staff of the largest V2 rocket installation in Europe, based in Marie-sur-Oise. His vehicle convoy had been on the road since 24 August, when the base had been blown up to prevent its capture by the Americans. Despite chaos on the roads, his unit remained, and was still travelling as a cohesive whole. The priority accorded the strategic 'wonder weapons' had aided their progress northwards via Belgium into Holland. Their destination was Germany, where it was

These shattered formations set off on their various Odysseys, striving to reach the homeland. (Bundesarchiv)

The 19-year-old artillery Lieutenant Joseph Enthammer. (Enthammer)

hoped they might continue to operate with fewer interruptions.

Vehicles were constantly strafed by 'Jabos' or fighter bombers *en route*, and losses were replaced by requisitioning civilian alternatives. Enthammer's group was eventually obliged to seize a rubbish collection lorry. Its driver, frantic to ensure its safe return, even offered to drive them to Germany himself, but he was taken from the cab. Near Lille it was rammed by a *Luftwaffe* car also anxious to escape, and tipped from the road, where it turned over. Seven of the twelve occupants were killed, and Enthammer himself was left lying unconscious by the roadside. First aid was administered but he had to be left behind in the hands of a friendly farmer. A message

was left for when he woke up: 'Unit collection point Nijmegen.'

Realising despite his injuries, that his own life and that of the farmer would be endangered if they were discovered by partisans, the lieutenant decided to press on and regain contact with his unit. Against the farmer's advice he set off again. Stealing a horse, he made good progress, riding only by night. When the opportunity arose to replace it with a moped, he tied the horse to the spot as a half-hearted gesture of compensation. He now made good time all the way to Nijmegen, refuelled *en route* by passing German tanks.

Arriving at the bustling collection point he was redirected to a small 'well-to-do' village on the outskirts of Arnhem called Oosterbeek. Shortly after, his V2 rocket unit was moved into a school in the north-western suburbs of Arnhem itself. Holland was a new experience:

'France had been a desert for us
Germans, while here the inhabitants
appeared very friendly. Why was this?
That was certainly not the case in
France where it had always been
difficult to procure food and drink. In
Holland you could buy cheese,
tomatoes – everything!'[2]

Hanna Roesch, a Wehrmacht *Nachrichtenhelferin* of the signals staff of Supreme Headquarters West, was also on the run. Following the French Resistance uprising she and her colleagues had fled the George V Hotel in Paris and joined a large convoy driving for Holland.

'By day we were attacked by low-
flying fighters and by night by
partisans. It was a huge column of
vehicles, painstakingly stopping and
starting. During fighter attacks we
scrambled from the lorries and flung
ourselves down in the neighbouring

fields. Here and there Wehrmacht vehicles were hit many times, exploding within the column. But I was lucky. After a short pause in Waterloo we drove on further to Deventer in Holland. From there we girls were transported further on to the Homeland, on the 10 September, shortly before the British airlandings.'[3]

The exhausted Kampfgruppe Hohenstaufen, employed as rear-guard at Cambrai, had been in action without a break or reinforcements since 29 June, more than two months. Its operations officer (G3) SS-Captain Wilfried Schwarz wistfully recalled his impressions as he watched the division entrain in Russia shortly before it was redeployed to the west:

'When we entrained for Normandy we were a proud fighting division – a force to be reckoned with – complete with all our vehicles, tanks and artillery. We were 18,000 men strong.'[4]

An SS panzer division then included 170 tanks, 21 self-propelled (SP) tank destroyers, 287 armoured half-track personnel carriers, 16 armoured cars, 18 armoured SP artillery pieces and 3,670 other vehicles of varying types. Reduced by enemy action to a combat group before Cambrai the Kampfgruppe Hohenstaufen numbered under 3,500 men, with a handful of armoured vehicles of all descriptions.

The Hohenstaufen had been retreating westwards for two weeks. It barely escaped encirclement at Falaise and was harassed by fighter bombers and the French Resistance all the way. Serviceable vehicles often towed two disabled ones. Columns were constantly reduced to a snail's pace, negotiating wreckage littering roadsides. The armoured engineer battalion was driving up the rear of the retreating division. Its 41-year-old commander, SS-Captain Hans Moeller, recalled the situation, having crossed the Seine river at Duclair. He lost two more vehicles to 'Jabos' in the wooded collection area near Barentin on the other side. These constant and unpredictable losses demonstrated how

' . . . the situation could change by the hour. Every second was vital and called for quick decisions. The engineer battalion was last in the divisional column, and had to look after itself; we had lost radio contact. Should we be struck off as lost already? The weather at this moment was favourable. It had rained and low cloud was hindering enemy air sorties. Our move north over Totes to Neufchatel progressed faster than anticipated. Then on to Poix. Air activity now noticeably picked up. Not wanting to lose any more vehicles and certainly not risk any more men, we moved into some accommodation east of Poix, and waited in good cover for the onset of dusk . . . '

Progress was good, and, despite the privations normally accompanying a retreat, they were well supplied. Nevertheless they felt uneasy. The main problem was

' . . . the unknown. One was dependent upon hearsay and rumours. Radios only rarely worked. There was always a feeling of uncertainty. Although not admitting it openly, everyone was preoccupied with the thought that chance or the fortunes of war may yet change. I kept my thoughts to myself, but I knew all these sleeping forms exhausted wrapped in blankets and tents were thinking the same. We were all absolutely worn out.'

Chance nevertheless remained on their side, at least until reaching Arnhem. Night moves were delayed by aircraft dropping flares, but the main hindrance had been the need to wind their way through mazes of wrecked vehicles. By 6 September they reached the accommodation earmarked for them north-east of Arnhem.

Moeller's journey provided a stark contrast to the situation faced by the divisional command group, whose 15 vehicles were stranded in the Bois-de-Bourlon, screened by trees, as American tanks thundered by 300 metres away. Thirty kilometres further on the remnants of the Hohenstaufen's rear-guard waited, constantly scanning the Cambrai road for signs of the missing group. On the following day, having paused as long as they dare, they continued the march on through Mons into southern Holland.

Harzer's group waited until darkness and then drove out through the streets of Cambrai guided by sympathetic civilians. Exploiting the night, the SS column proceeded to drive along the junction between the 1st US Army to the south and 2nd British Army moving in the north. When it became necessary to cross the American line of march, the SS *Feldgendarmerie* (military police) travelling with the column waved lights and cold-bloodedly flagged down an enemy convoy. Both sides ignored each other. Dust and exhaustion cloaked the scene with a protective mantle of anonymity. At dawn on 3 September Harzer decided to lie up and wait for darkness again.

During the day vehicles were festooned with battlefield booty, flags, and other souvenir insignia to cover their drive through an enemy-occupied village *en route*. Victory celebrations were in full swing in a lighted bar as the half-tracks and vehicles nosed their way through narrow streets. Unattended jeeps outside the pub were plundered by SS-troopers clambering over bonnets to remove any carelessly-left articles of equipment, weapons or supplies. They had no idea how long their journey would take, or indeed if they would even reach their own lines; anything picked up on the way was therefore a bonus.

On 5 September Harzer's group crossed the main Allied approach route to Brussels, and slipped in behind the leading enemy tanks. Maintaining a discreet distance, the SS column tagged on to the advance. German stragglers picked up *en route* could hardly believe their eyes, when having been overtaken by the British advance guard, they were offered lifts by this cheeky German 'rear-guard' sweeping up behind it. Eventually contact was made with the German Brussels garrison which had just evacuated the city, and Harzer's group was directed on to the division. Losses in men and material during the march had been nil. Indeed, they had added to their strength, picking up stragglers and an abandoned German Field hospital with 20 wounded. Even in the face of disaster the fortunes of war could occasionally smile.

Others were not so fortunate. The Kampfverband Schulz from the 10SS Frundsberg, the sister division in IISS Corps, had been condemned to fight a last-stand rear-guard in Albert, to allow the 9SS and others to break clean through Cambrai. As the Hohenstaufen recced its positions for the Cambrai battle, SS-Lieutenant-Colonel Schulz was engaged in bitter street fighting which continued all night, until his battle group ceased to exist as an effective force. Schulz himself was killed alongside his staff officers. A few survivors broke out during the early morning of 2 September and moved eastwards to join the remainder of the Frundsberg.

Partisans meanwhile harassed the retreat wherever they were able. Roads to Mons were littered with nails and upturned tins, designed to catch the unwary. A cutting device was attached to the lead vehicles of the Hohenstaufen's radio company to prevent crews being decapitated by cables strung across roads. Despatch riders often disappeared without trace. Single vehicles were frequently fired upon.

One 9SS column was ambushed seeking to use a northern route via Valenciennes over the bridge crossing the Scarpe canal. The hapless group seeking a through route was shot up in the middle of St Amand les Eaux by the *Maquis*, assisted by an American advance guard. Troops exhausted on the line of march, or misunderstanding Resistance calls to surrender, were shot down at the least sign of hesitation. Up to 50 soldiers were killed in this location alone. Survivors recall the devotion of a French English-German speaking doctor who, despite the ferocity of these skirmishes, offered comfort and treated the German wounded. Mercy was often neither offered nor given, by both sides, during these clashes. A wounded SS-trooper Ortmann asked the doctor if he could at least recover the ID discs the numerous German dead were wearing. The doctor's formal and correct response was that 'they would be passed on to the Geneva Red Cross'.

Many soldiers disappeared without trace during the tortuous retreat, as in the case of the Hohenstaufen's 'optics' platoon. This was a specialist unit attached to the tank recovery company, and was the first of its type in the Army group. Carrying something like 15,000 spare parts, its technicians repaired tank optics and dials. Its absence was not appreciated until the roll was called in Arnhem. They never reappeared, having doubtless fallen victim to a *Maquis* ambush somewhere in France or Belgium.

Motorised units like the IISS Panzer Corps fared a lot better than their infantry cousins. General der Fallschirmtruppen Eugen Meindl, the commander of II Fallschirmjaeger (Parachute) Corps had barely managed to fight his way out of the Falaise

pocket. The corps had distinguished itself during the bitter 'hedgerow' defensive battles around St Lo in Normandy, and had been badly mauled trying to escape Falaise. On 28 August Meindl received welcome news – remnants of his corps were to be reconstituted in Nancy. Having been in action since 12 June, his heavy weapons were all gone, and his manpower was so low that there were barely enough survivors to form a cadre to retain a unit identity on reconstitution. However, this order was countermanded when the 3rd Fallschirmjaeger Division, originally feared lost, reappeared again after fighting its way

General der Fallschirmtruppen Eugen Meindl (left) *Commander of II Fallschirmjaeger Corps, with his Chief of Staff Lieutenant-Colonel Blauensteiner* (right) *contemplate the enormity of their defeat in Normandy.*

through, only to be nominated again as rear-guard to the surviving motorised elements of 5th and 7th Armies. Meindl was scandalised at the callousness of the directive:

'Why? Due to the cowardice of other troops unprepared to fight on? The parachute arm was now to be sacrificed in France . . . Tank and panzer-grenadier divisions are always able to retreat faster. The infantry cannot cover these bounds on foot, and were eventually surrounded by enemy tanks, making escape impossible. On 4 September the greater part of the 3rd Division was taken prisoner. Only a few managed to escape. Hopefully we shall see them again some day – *Auf Wiedersehen*.

'A tragedy. I had meanwhile been ordered to Hitler's headquarters to receive the oak leaves to the Knight's Cross for the battle of Normandy. I had not then been aware of the loss of the 3rd Division, otherwise I would have taken the opportunity to comment upon this "brilliant" order.'[5]

The rest of II Fallschirmjaeger Corps were pulled out of the line to be refurbished east of Cologne.

Fallschirmjaeger Regiment 6, commanded by Major von der Heydte, was similarly battered. It had been in action continuously since 6 June, spearheading the first promising attacks on the American Utah invasion bridgehead. One of the regiment's bicycle companies, numbering only 20 men, supported by a single Mark IV tank from the 2nd SS 'Das Reich' division, captured a complete American battalion, taking 13 officers and 600 soldiers prisoner. Caught up in the vortex of the American breakthrough at St Lo, the regiment fought its way out of the Coutances pocket. Cut off, von der Heydte led his regiment in single file stealthily along secondary roads and paths as American tanks roared past on the main roads alongside them. Only 60 men were left standing when they re-established contact with the German 353 Division. When they caught up with their sick and wounded at Lisieux they numbered 1,007 men. From this one regiment alone 3,000 officers and men had been killed or declared missing in action.[6] Survivors were transported to Guestrow–Mecklenberg in Germany, to form the cadre for a newly-reconstituted Fallschirmjaeger Regiment 6.

Nothing could withstand the Allied advance. Attempts to hold on the Seine or Somme rivers were simply brushed aside. Hard-fought rear-guard actions, such as those fought by the 9SS in front of Cambrai, warrant barely a mention in American unit histories. There were insufficient German forces to hold at any point. A regimental commander of the Herman Goering Division, Lieutenant-Colonel Fritz Fullriede wrote cryptically in his diary:

'31 August. The whole west front has collapsed, and the other side is marching about at will; and what a big mouth we had over the Atlantic Wall.'[7]

Newly-raised anti-tank companies, belonging to the Hohenstaufen's tank-destroyer battalion Panzerjaeger Abt 9, arrived on the unloading ramps at Mons from East Prussia just in time to be spirited off to a number of hastily-fought rear-guard actions. These piecemeal reinforcements were simply swept along by the tide of events. 'Jabos', or fighter-bombers, paralysed all road and rail movement by day. Alfred Ziegler, a 19-year-old despatch rider on the staff of Panzerjaeger Abt 9, recalled the situation just before reaching Mons:

'The first company was caught in a very heavy fighter-bomber attack during which our company commander von Brocke was killed. We all fired our machine guns so that no bombs scored a direct hit on the train. Subsequent strafing runs did however cause some damage to the tank destroyers (Panzerjaeger mark IV SP guns) and vehicles, and wounded about 10 men. Later we detrained and joined the third company which had already been in the West for some time.

'But now the enemy started to chase us.'

The companies regrouped in battalion strength barely in time before being committed to a rear-guard action near Mons. It was a fiasco. SS-Captain von Allworden, the battalion commander, was separated from his unit, but the situation was past saving from the beginning. Three hundred Fallschirmjaeger commanded by a major joined in what rapidly became a running battle with no leader to co-ordinate it.

Only two SPs survived the journey to Arnhem. The rest were lost in battle, integrated into other units, or blown up for lack of petrol.[8]

The German army in the west appeared finished. Wolfgang Dombrowski, an SS-corporal in Moeller's engineer battalion, became separated from his company in the Falaise pocket. He managed to get out with a Wehrmacht unit and was fortunate enough to relocate his battalion three or four days later. Like his comrades, Dombrowski had been shaken by events.

'The division was virtually burnt out in the Normandy fighting . . . We felt that once we got over the German border it would all be over. Many soldiers were lost in the withdrawal. The situation moreover in Holland when we arrived was desperate. It seemed impossible that a front could be built out of these disparate fleeing elements.'[9]

CHAPTER II
Stand and Fight

A captured document indicates that the degree of control exercised over the regrouping and collecting of the apparently scattered remnants of a beaten army [was] little short of remarkable. Furthermore the fighting capacity of the new Battle Groups formed from the remnants of battered divisions seems unimpaired.

G2 (Intelligence Officer) 82nd US Airborne Division, 13 Sep 44[1]

A crust begins to form . . .

Covering hundreds of miles in a week, the tanks of the Second British Army swept across northern France into Belgium. Antwerp fell on 4 September and opened a huge hole in the German western front, stretching 120km (75 miles) from the North Sea by Antwerp to Maastricht. Only one division, the 719 Infantry under command of Generalleutnant Karl Sievers, remained to bar the way. It was the sole remaining division of General der Infanterie Hans Reinhard's LXXXVIII Corps, who had commanded the German army in Holland between July 1942 and September 1944. Supplemented by one Dutch SS battalion and a few *Luftwaffe* detachments, 719 Infantry was a 'fortress' division that had been guarding the coast of the Netherlands since 1940. Mainly elderly soldiers, they had never heard a shot fired in anger.

Consternation and shock greeted the fall of Antwerp in the 'Wolfchancellory', Hitler's headquarters in Rastenburg, east Prussia. Previously preoccupied by the collapse and 'cannae' of Army Group Centre on the Russian front, the parallel disintegration of the western Army Group B now attracted its full attention.

Generaloberst Kurt Student, Supreme Commander of the Fallschirmjaeger arm, was working with a meagre staff in his rear headquarters in Berlin-Wannsea, busy planning the formation of new parachute units. Shortly after midday on 4 September he received a personal telephone call from Generaloberst Jodl, the chief of the Armed Forces Operations Staff, direct from Hitler's headquarters. 'Collect all available units together and build a new front on the Albert Canal,' he was told. 'This new front is to be held at all costs!' As Student recalled, the new formation was given the 'high-sounding' title of 'First Parachute (Fallschirmjaeger) Army'. At this stage, however, it was a paper formation. Its kern consisted of units spread all over Germany between Gustrow in Mecklenburg and Bitsch in Lothringen – regiments either in the process of forming up, or remnants cadred by the survivors of previously burnt-out formations, supplemented by untrained personnel. Nevertheless, the German penchant for organisation and improvisation, even in the face of disaster, coupled with a professionally effective staff network, began to make itself felt. General der Flieger Friedrich Christiansen, the Wehrmacht Supreme Commander of the Netherlands, filled the immediate vacuum by pushing a thin security screen made up of Luftwaffe fortress personnel forward to the Albert canal.

Both at the front and in the rear, effective leadership and initiative, supported by a

*Generaloberst Kurt Student, Commander
1st Fallschirmjaeger Army.*

staff system geared to the needs of the combat soldier, steadily and persistently began to organise order from chaos. Unbeknown to the Germans, the Allied armies in the west had all but outrun their logistic support. 'Mad Tuesday', 5 September, following the fall of Antwerp, marked the climax of the panic-stricken flight; an appropriate term accorded by Dutch historians. A breathing space was to emerge unexpectedly. As the exhausted Allies replenished and debated whether a 'broad front' or 'single thrust' was required to finish off the Reich, German commanders frantically improvised and exploited any means at their disposal to blunt it. A crust began to form.

On 4 September Sievers 719 Division began to dig themselves in on the north bank of the Albert Canal, and on the same day Horrock's advance south of the water line practically came to a standstill. 176 Infantry Division, a 'Kranken Division', was entraining at that moment, on its way from West Germany. These so-called 'eyes and ears battalions' consisted of soldiers with disabilities which had until now prevented them from serving. It appeared an untenable situation, until help appeared from an unexpected quarter.

Generalleutenant Kurt Chill had suffered heavy losses with his 85 Division in France. Retreating northwards with the remnants of his division, he picked up scattered units of the 84 and 89 Divisions *en route*. Arriving at Turnhout, north Belgium, on 4 September, his troops were ordered to the Rhineland for rest and reinforcement. The fall of Brussels, however, prompted him to disregard this order. Instead, on his own initiative, he disposed his troops along the northern bank of the Albert canal between Massenhoven and Kwaadmechelen. Reception centres were set up at the bridges between his sectors to pick up small groups of German soldiers fleeing northwards. By the following day he had informed 719 Division of his dispositions, and placed himself under command of Reinhard's LXXXVIII Corps, who detached a further regiment from Sievers division to Chill. Now more or less a cohesive battle group, the new formation became known as 'Kampfgruppe Chill'. It was sufficiently strong to repel the first British forays against the canal.

Some semblance of order was now beginning to emerge. On 7 September the promised 176 Kranken Division, commanded by Oberst (Colonel) Christian Landau, arrived from Aachen, where it had been manning the Siegfried Line, and was placed under Student's orders. Similarly, elements of the newly-formed First Fallschirmjaeger Army began to appear on 6 and 7 September.

On 5 September, Student, galvanised by his orders, had flown from Berlin to see Field Marshal Model, the Commander in Chief of Army Group B, to whom First Fallschirmjaeger Army was responsible. Student's force at this stage consisted of Lieutenant-Colonel von der Heydte's Fallschirmjaeger Regiment 6, the First Battalion of Fallschirmjaeger Regiment 2, and five other newly-raised Parachute Regiments. Three of these were formed into the 7 Fallschirmjaeger Division under General Erdmann. Moreover, during his discussion with the Fuhrer's Headquarters, Student had managed to have a collection of 20 heavy, medium and light anti-air batteries allotted to him. An army anti-tank battle group consisting of a mix of 25 self-propelled assault guns and tank-destroyers gave the improvised formation a little more substance. However, it was in essence foot-borne, with few vehicles, and therefore tactically immobile.[2]

Model was disappointed that the whole Fallschirmjaeger Army amounted so far to only 20,000 men. Nevertheless, he allotted Student the area running from the North Sea to Maastricht, a front of 120km (75 miles). To enable this insufficient force to cope, Reinhardt's LXXXVIII Corps, already in position, was also placed under First Fallschirmjaeger Army's command. The end result was a fully stretched front of 32 battalions, supported by weak artillery, equipped with only light infantry weapons. An effective anti-tank network could, however, be built around the large number of 88mm flak guns now available in terrain particularly suited to defence.

Improvisation and astonishingly accurate staff work enabled the developments charted on the map on page 34 to take place. Within 48 to 72 hours of being called out, the widely-dispersed regiments of First Fallschirmjaeger Army, equipped for training only, began to arrive at the front. Weapons and stores were collected at the railway stations from where they were transported to their various rail heads. A prodigy of organisation enabled units to be equipped *en route*. Major Oswald Finzel's 1st Battalion Fallschirmjaeger Regiment 2 had been re-formed after heavy casualties on the eastern front in the Flak barracks at Ahrbrueck at the end of August and beginning of September. It was re-armed and equipped from material salvaged from units that had retreated from the west.[3] As the locomotive carrying the battalion steamed out from Roermond on 6 September, its soldiers considered themselves well supplied with weapons, lorries and bicycles. Arriving at Hechtel-Beringen it was placed under command of the Kampfgruppe Chill.

General von Zangen, commander of Fifteenth Army, was seeking, like the remainder of the defeated Army Group B, to retreat and hold somewhere in the east. His own six original divisions had been joined by the remnants of a further five retreating from Normandy. Bottled up against the Channel coast by the swiftly-moving Allied armies, his slowly moving force of almost 100,000 men was attempting to withdraw to the north-east. As von Zangen recalled:

'When we retired from the Somme about 1 September I planned slowly to fight my way back to Brussels and Antwerp and then take up a line in Holland. I had no fear that Antwerp would be taken since it was far behind the front line, and there was a special staff to defend it. When I heard on 4 September that it had been captured it came as a stunning surprise . . . instead of an army on my left flank there was an empty gap.'[4]

Von Zangen was ordered to make preparations for the evacuation of his army across the Scheldt to the islands of Walcheren and South Beveland. So long as the road through here and the mainland remained in German hands the plan was feasible. General Eugen Felix Schwalbe was given the responsibility for directing the evacuation of Fifteenth Army across the Scheldt. In 16 days nine shattered infantry divisions – 59, 70, 245, 331, 334, 17 Luftwaffe Field, 346, 711 and 712 – were evacuated. The task was complete by 21 September. In the process 65,000 men, 225 guns, 750 trucks and wagons, and 1,000 horses were saved. No serious attempt was made throughout this period by the Allies to push on beyond Antwerp and cut the base of the Beveland Isthmus, to deprive Fifteenth Army of its only reasonable escape route.

As a result two badly battered and poorly armed divisions of these troops became available, appearing in Brabant on 16 and 17 September: the 245 Division under Colonel Gerhard Kegler and the 59th under Generalleutnant Walter Poppe. The latter, for example, still retained up to 1,000 good infantry men, a few engineers, a field replacement battalion, 18 anti-tank guns and about thirty 105mm and 150mm howitzers.[5] They were to play an important role in future operations.

Erich Hensel, a 23-year-old Feldwebel (Sgt) in a divisional 'Nachrichten' (signals) company, retreated from Normandy to Belgium at the beginning of September. His unit, commanded by a lieutenant, himself and one other sergeant, numbered about 30 men. Well-trained and armed, the unit had thus far managed to keep together. Self-sufficiency had been the key. Air defence was provided by a twin 20mm lorry-borne anti-aircraft cannon. Casualties in Normandy had been light, although Hensel had been 'heartbroken' by the loss of a friend, a corporal, to a low-flying 'Jabo'. Following Fifteenth Army's escape route, the journey to the Scheldt proved to be perilous. Civilians were not friendly. A Belgian priest had to be coerced into decently burying the corporal. On another occasion, when briefed to check the demolition of a bridge

by his company commander, Hensel returned to find a British tank astride it, and victory celebrations in full swing. Isolated by cheering Belgian civilians he only escaped the mêlée by threatening to open fire. His officer from Duesberg was a good commander and kept the unit together. They were a close-knit band, as Hensel commented: 'In Normandy we learned that we would survive only if we kept together.' Joining the Fifteenth Army evacuation process, the signals company was loaded on to one of the many ferries to be taken across the Scheldt Estuary.

> 'On the Sheldt an army Lieutenant-Colonel arrived with a truck filled with booty, champagne and two women. "Give me that boat!" he demanded. The corporal skippering retorted indignantly: "You're staying there!", and off we sailed. Our company commander, a decent man, was ashamed that we should witness such a scene. He had previously told us about the assassination plot against Hitler in terms of "Thanks to God he wasn't killed". I was not so certain I could go so far as to agree with that!'

Hensel, despite his youth, was already regarded as one of the *Alte* or veterans. He had already fought on the Russian front. Normandy, however, had opened his eyes:

> 'Discipline was normally very good. The retreat from France was the first time I had ever seen demoralised German units.'

Their troubles, even on crossing the Scheldt, were not over. Some of the company marched on foot, whilst heavy equipments were carried on the lorry. Suffering from a grenade shrapnel leg wound, Hensel had to ride one of the bicycles. There were constant delays *en route*. After crossing the

Erich Hensel: 'We learned that we would survive only if we kept together.' Fifteenth Army on the retreat marching through Goes in Zeeland. They have all kept their weapons.

river, an 88mm gun ahead of them rolled over in the road. Partisans had spread soap on the road surface. Constant checks by the so-called *Kettenhunde*† halted stragglers and formed them up into 'march units'. Due to the company's technical expertise, and the fact that it was a complete unit, they were allowed to proceed. At Vught they received papers incorporating them into First Fallschirmjaeger Army Headquarters, with instructions to continue on to Wesel in Germany. Prospects of a home posting hastened the unit's pace, 'before anything else could go wrong'.[6]

During the fortnight following the creation of First Fallschirmjaeger Army, renewed British probes against the Albert canal met stiffening resistance. A British bridgehead was created at Beeringen by the Guards Armoured Division on 7 September. By the following week they had pressed forward a further 20 miles and gained two bridgeheads across the Meuse-Escaut canal. The main bridgehead was at De Groote Barrier on the Hechtel-Eindhoven Road, the so-called 'Neerpelt bridgehead', established on 12 September. This represented the high tide of the British

†German military police; referred to as 'chain-dogs' because of their distinctive metal plate insignia worn on the chest, suspended by a chain, when on duty.

advance. A tenuous German defence line was now discernible along the final water barrier before Holland, and that line was holding.

These British achievements were in the teeth of desperate if inadequate German resistance. Formations were flung into action, whatever their training state, to buy time at any cost. To soldiers fighting with limited or no knowledge of the big picture, the measures employed appeared senseless. They were kept together by officers becoming increasingly cynical of the point of it all. Lieutenant-Colonel Fritz Fullriede, a veteran holder of the Knight's Cross, recorded his diary impressions of the human cost it took to form the crust of this opposition. Commanding dispersed combat teams (*Abteilungen*) of the Hermann Goering Division scattered over Holland he wrote:

'8 Sep. The enemy is already over the Albert canal at Beeringen. On order from General Student's Para High Command that all air force troops were to be taken under command, I despatched the II Abteilung on the road before Harderwijk post-haste to Eindhoven.'

Forty-eight hours later he was bitterly to record:

'10 Sep. The II Abteilung following a successful attack, after being inserted in the wrong place, and stabbed in the back by its neighbours, was surrounded by strong forces in Hechtel and following a three-day battle practically wiped out, only a few stragglers and tanks returned. Almost all the tanks, armoured artillery, anti-tank and flak elements were lost. All due to the mistakes of our joke of a high command.'

Relentlessly the Allies were wearing down these scattered German reserves.

'11 Sep. The I Abteilung and III Abteilung [combat teams], and the entire artillery and flak were despatched to Eindhoven on orders from 1st Para Army HQ. These orders are sending them all to the devil. Discussion with the Netherlands High Command. Even the recruits are to be sent in. Otherwise there is nothing more available.'

From east to west on 13 September First Fallschirmjaeger Army was lined up in the following order of battle. From Antwerp to the junction of the Albert and Meuse-Escaut canals was General Siever's 719 Division. Opposing the two British bridge-heads beyond the Meuse-Escaut canal were 'Kampfgruppe Chill', supported now by a newly-formed unit, the 'Kampfgruppe Walther'. All these troops were under General Reinhard's LXXXVIII Corps. From the bridgehead on the Eindhoven-Valkenswaard-Hechtel road to the boundary with the Seventh Army near Maastricht were two divisions directly under General Student's control: the Division Erdmann and 176 Division.

Improvisation of resources – the formation of the Kampfgruppe Walther . . .

Improvisation and not systematic planning was the main factor thickening the crust of the German defence. Personal initiatives could be and were supported by effective and accurate staff work. *Ad hoc* formations were created by the pressure of events and thrust into the front line. One such battle group, the 'Kampfgruppe Walther', provides a typical example of the 'poor man's' war the German army was obliged to fight at this time. Its formation and early operations provide a glimpse of what was expected from such small units hastily formed on the eve of operation MARKET-GARDEN.

On 12 September a few tanks of the British Guards Armoured Division stormed the bridge over the Maas-Scheldt canal west of Neerpelt. This was the last water barrier separating Belgium from Holland. First Fallschirmjaeger Army Headquarters received the news around 0800, and despatched motorised reconnaissance elements to investigate. Light enemy resistance was encountered at the Dutch-Belgian border astride the Valkenswaard to Hechtel road. Thereupon, Fallschirmjaeger Regiment 'Hoffmann', which had just arrived in the vicinity of Goirle south of Tilburg, was alerted. The sequence of events leading to the creation of the Kampfgruppe Walther were now set in motion. Existing for only one month, the battle group was to play a leading part in subsequent MARKET-GARDEN operations. Comprising elements of all three services of the Wehrmacht, its composition was to change continuously, governed as ever by operational necessity.

Colonel von Hoffmann, the Regimental Commander, was given the task of containing any further enemy advances along the Hechtel-Valkenswaard Road. There was sufficient motor transport to move two companies up immediately, until the remainder of the regiment arrived. When this happened, the bridgehead was to be eliminated.

Formed a mere three weeks before at Halberstadt, the Regiment von Hoffmann was a personnel-holding reinforcement unit – a training depot. It was organised into a regimental headquarters, three battalions and an anti-tank company with eight 75mm anti-tank guns. Lieutenant Heinz Volz was the adjutant of the 1st battalion commanded by Major Helmut Kerutt. Commenting on the readiness of the battalion six days prior to committal, he wrote:

'The Regiment at this point in time had no uniform issue of parachute smocks and practically no weapons.'

These it received two days later on the way to its initial assembly area near Tilburg. No time had been available for individual or collective training, nor had weapons been zeroed. The regimental commander, two of the acting battalion commanders, as well as the majority of the company commanders, had no combat experience. Of the non-commissioned officers and enlisted men, 90 per cent came from Luftwaffe ground units. Volz commented further upon arrival in Udenhout on 10 September that his battalion during the previous period . . .

'. . . had done everything possible in the three available days to equip ourselves appropriately for the coming operations. Above all we tried to get at least the majority of soldiers equipped with bicycles in order to make the unit more mobile. There was insufficient fuel for the few motorcycles at our disposal. This improved when considerable quantities of petrol were discovered . . . at an abandoned airfield.'[7]

At the same time, Fallschirmjaeger Regiment 6, commanded by a newly-promoted Lieutenant-Colonel von der Heydte, had incurred casualties occupying a blocking position north-west of Beverloo. He was to fall back northward across the Meuse-Scheldt canal. Although badly mauled in the Normandy fighting, the regiment had already been reconstituted and reinserted into combat. Despite being bulked out with untrained replacements, its combat effectiveness was rated highly, because of its highly experienced veteran cadre and good armament. Von der Heydte was also ordered to attack the Neerpelt bridgehead – from the north-west on 13 September.

Kerutt's 1st Battalion of the Fallschirmjaeger Training Regiment von Hoffmann arrived amongst the customs buildings on the Hechtel-Valkenswaard road during the evening of 12 September. A fire fight broke out with the enemy in the inky blackness. Kerutt, a combat-experienced officer, hastily established a security screen. His flanks were covered by the boggy pastures north of La Colonie and north-west of Neerpelt. Enemy tanks, engines idling, were identified in La Colonie.

On the same day, Student sent a General Staff Officer, Major Schacht, on a fact-finding mission from his headquarters to get a feel for the situation emanating from confusing reports coming out of the Neerpelt bridgehead. Feeling that Kerutt had done all he could in the circumstances, Schacht was not impressed with the readiness of the 2nd and 3rd battalions as he passed these and regimental headquarters on the road forward. He advised Student accordingly, and on his own initiative cancelled the attack planned for the 13th. In any case a blocking force from the 10SS 'Frundsberg' division had also been earmarked by Army Group B for use in this threatened sector. Further co-ordination was necessary.

Based on Schacht's orientation of the situation, General Student decided to charge a certain Colonel Walther with the command of all units to be employed against the Neerpelt bridgehead. No counter-attack was to be attempted until more combat-effective troops arrived.

This then was the nemesis of the Kampfgruppe Walther, a unit created by the urgency of a particular operational situation, whose equipments and organisation were dependent virtually upon the sequence of arrival of combat-ready troops in the area of operations. Four more units arrived during the evening of 13 September. Von der Heydte's Fallschirmjaeger Regiment 6 now totalled four infantry battalions, numbering between 150 to 200 men each. Its well-equipped heavy 4th battalion held an 81mm mortar company, a motorised anti-tank company with 125mm guns, an air defence machine gun company, and five 20mm quadruple guns, in addition to recce and engineer companies. IISS Panzer Corps had provided the 'Blocking Force Heinke', numbering two SS Panzergrenadier battalions: 'Segler' from the Hohenstaufen, and 'Krause' from the Frundsberg panzer division. Elements from the SS Tank-Destroyer Battalion 'Panzerjaeger Abteilung 10', commanded by SS-Captain Roestel, complemented the force with 15 Jagdpanzer IVs armed with the long-barrelled 75mm gun. A motorised battery of six 105mm field howitzers from the Frundsberg's Artillery Regiment 10 had already reinforced Kerutt during the course of the day. Luftwaffe Penal Battalion 6 also arrived. Its four rifle companies of infantry were to prove ineffective. Earmarked for 'special assignments', and newly arrived from Italy, its unfortunate soldiers were still wearing tropical uniforms. An air defence task force was the final element to report. Its two 88mm flak guns and platoon of three 20mm guns were to be sited in the depth of the unit position.

These forces joined the Regiment von Hoffmann already on the ground. Colonel Walther arrived at Valkenswaard in the early morning hours of 13 September and assumed command. He had commanded Fallschirmjaeger Regiment 4 for several years, and was destined to become a division commander, a post he now, by virtue of the forces at his disposal, took on. Von Hoffmann exchanged places with him in the reserve pool of commanders of First Fallschirmjaeger Army Headquarters;

whereupon he was appointed 'Stadtkommandant' of Eindhoven. Walther's Kampfgruppe headquarters was built around von Hoffmann's original regimental organisation, reinforced with additional radio and telephone maintenance teams. A section of despatch riders and some limited motor transport were to follow.

'D' Day for the attack on the Neerpelt bridgehead was fixed for the early morning of 15 September. Barely 24 to 36 hours separated the arrival of units before they were to be committed to battle. Von der Heydte was to spearhead the attack from the west, and began to form up south-east of Luyksgestel. His objective: secure La Colonie, and advance across the Heunel Heath to seize the bridge site. Kerutt's 1st battalion and Segler's SS battalion were to mount a diversionary 'recce in force', whilst the light field howitzer battery and two 88mm flak guns were placed in direct support.

As preparations were mounted, rainy weather limited enemy air interference. British artillery observers, however, rewarded the detection of any movement with regimental-level artillery strikes. Lieutenant Volz's 1st battalion headquarters in Luyksgestel attracted just such a salvo, as units gathered for the planned assault:

'The battalion suffered its first losses here. Lieutenant Hansbach was killed on 13 or 14 September by a direct artillery strike in his trench. A member of the staff was torn to pieces as a shell splinter set off the hand grenades he was carrying. At the same time a Feldwebel fell before the door of the command post, killed by a mortar burst. Unfortunately I cannot remember his name. Another of these persistent strikes, probably due to the fact the enemy had identified our headquarters, landed when

Lieutenant-Colonel von der Heydte happened to be present. With an elegant leap he disappeared through the ground floor window. I – with splinters flying around, covered in plaster and dust – got further under the table. The insanely jangling telephone slowly got on my nerves. I could not reach the receiver, which in this storm of buzzing splinters would have meant suicide. During a short fire pause, Major Schacht on the staff of First Parachute Army explained he was not used to being made to wait on the telephone, without at least some information on the immediate situation – as military protocol demanded.'

The reinforced Fallschirmjaeger Regiment 6 started its attack under cloudy skies and light drizzle at 0800 hours on 15 September. Enemy outposts in the meadows north-west of La Colonie were at first dislodged. The pick-pock of small arms fire became punctuated by the shouts of men, interspersed by the ripping sound of rapid-firing German machine guns, and the slower thump-thumping of British bren guns. At 0830 the shriek of heavy artillery, accompanied by crackling bursts of heavy detonations, signalled the arrival of enemy supporting fire, directed on attacking spearheads and the forming-up place. Roestel's SS tank-destroyers moved ahead desperately slowly, slipping and lurching in the slightly boggy terrain. By the middle of the afternoon the attack was bogged down in the middle of La Colonie. Enemy counter-attacks supported by tanks came in against the diversionary forces. Several were knocked out. Von der Heydte's laconic evaluation of the crisis summed up the reason for failure: 'this attack failed as it had to be conducted without artillery support.'[8] It was impossible to advance beyond La Colonie. Two or three of Roes-

The view from the British line during the Kampfgruppe Walther's abortive attack on the Neerpelt bridgehead. Two of SS-Captain Roestel's SPs are blazing fiercely. (Imperial War Museum)

tel's committed assault guns had been lost, and personnel losses were considerable.

Colonel Walther now devoted his attention to reinforcing his defences in the northern sector of the bridgehead. His Kampfgruppe was firmly established astride the Hechtel to Valkenswaard road. Adjacent and to the right was the 85th Infantry Division, on the left the Parachute Division Erdmann. Around the bridgehead bulge itself was Fallschirmjaeger Regiment 6 on the west, Luftwaffe Penal Battalion 6, with the Regiment von Hoffmann reinforced by an SS engineer company from Heinke in the north astride the road. On the other side to the east were two SS Panzer-grenadier battalions: 'Segler' and 'Richter'.

During the evening of 16 September, First Fallschirmjaeger Headquarters ordered the attacks to be continued. As it was becoming increasingly apparent that the bridgehead was being reinforced by the British, the order was received with scant enthusiasm. Colonel Walther decided to compromise and only launch a few local probes westward from the north. If anything they were dissipating their strength in attacks which were unlikely to succeed, while the enemy was obviously going to resume his advance in the very near future. But where. . ?

Where will the impending blow fall. . . ?

Concurrent with these desperate *ad hoc* measures shoring up the front came increasing apprehension by the staff of Army Group B over the 'constant stream' of reinforcements concentrating behind the right wing of Second British Army. From 9 to 14 September Model's intelligence officer issued daily warnings of an imminent British offensive, probably to be launched in the direction of Nijmegen, Arnhem and Wesel. The objective was the Ruhr. Intelligence was further convinced that airborne troops would be used, as they had in Sicily and in the invasion of Normandy. Perhaps in the area of the Siegfried Line, north of Aachen, or as part of an American thrust in the Saar. Projecting himself as an imaginary General Eisenhower, the Army Group B G2 Intelligence Officer wrote his report in the form of a mythical order:

'. . . the Second British Army [he imagined the Supreme Allied Commander to say] will assemble its units at the Maas-Scheldt and Albert canals. On its right wing it will concentrate an attack force, mainly composed of armoured units, and after forcing a Maas crossing, will launch operations to break through to the Rhenish-Westphalian industrial area [Ruhr] with the main effort via Roermond. To cover the northern flank, the left wing of the [Second British] Army will close to the Waal at Nijmegen, and thus create the basic conditions necessary to cut off the German Forces committed in the Dutch coastal areas [The Fifteenth Army].' [9]

Not surprisingly, the whole balance and direction of the German defence effort reflected these assumptions. Four days before this estimate the outline plan for the forthcoming Allied offensive MARKET-GARDEN had been accepted. It was issued

The enemy was obviously going to resume his advance in the very near future. But where . . . ? (Bundesarchiv)

in directive form by 14 September. MAR-KET, the air plan, required that three and a half airborne divisions were to be dropped in the vicinity of Grave, Nijmegen and Arnhem to seize bridges over several canals and the Maas, Waal and Neder Rijn (lower Rhine) rivers. They were to open an 'airborne corridor' more than 50 miles long leading from Eindhoven northward. As soon as an adequate landing field could be secured, an air portable division was to be flown in as reinforcement.

Its companion piece GARDEN, the ground plan, required land forces of the Second British Army to push from the Dutch-Belgian border to the Ijsselmeer (Zuider Zee), a total distance of 99 miles. The main effort of the ground attack was to be made by XXX Corps from its bridge-head at Neerpelt across the Maas-Scheldt canal a few miles south of Eindhoven on the Dutch-Belgian frontier. On either flank VIII and XXII Corps were to launch supporting attacks.

Operation MARKET-GARDEN's major objective was to get Allied troops across the Rhine, thereby creating a bridgehead from which subsequent operations could be directed against the Ruhr. Three major advantages were expected to accrue: cutting the land exit of Fifteenth Army remaining in Western Holland; out-flanking the 'West Wall'; and providing the means for a final thrust into Germany along the north German Plain, which might shorten the war.

The German forecast was therefore totally mistaken. There would be no advance from the Neerpelt bridgehead merely to provide a covering force via Eindhoven, hinging on Nijmegen. Rather, this was to be the point of main effort, directly north and beyond to Arnhem, not at a tangent via Roermond and thence through the Siegfried Line to Dusseldorf and Duesberg. Airborne forces were not poised to drop in the vicinity of the Ruhr, they were going to parachute *en masse* into the rear combat zone of Army Group B. Axis for the XXX Corps advance was to be the Hechtel-Valkenswaard-Eindhoven Road. The main blow was to fall on the sector of front manned by the Kampfgruppe Chill, Walther, and Erdmann's Parachute Division.

How well disposed were German forces to react?

CHAPTER III
All Quiet on the Western Front

We believed the war was probably over. But you must realise that we lower ranks were only 18 to 19 years old. Our officers were aged between 24 to 29. Still youngsters! Life's deeper issues did not concern us too much. We were prepared to fight on.

SS-Corporal [1]

Despite stiffening resistance, the Allies believed that one more good push after the débâcle in Normandy would bring the whole crumbling German defence edifice down. Due to the 90-mile ground dash required to relieve the planned three-divisional airborne 'carpet', Allied planners began to take stock of the likely resistance they might encounter. XXX Corps, spearheading the assault, estimated in its intelligence summary at the beginning of the second week in September that:

' . . . further back in the area of the river Waal, about 200 88mm guns could probably be switched from an anti-aircraft to a ground role. And a Dutch resistance report of battered Panzer formations sent to Holland to refit might be true . . .

'The enemy made no attempt at divisional organisation in this period; transport, signals and heavy equipment were almost non-existent. Battle groups were formed from regiments or from stragglers and were named after their commanding officers; they varied in strength from 100 to 3,000. Many went into battle so quickly that the men did not know the name of their battle group. Food and

ammunition were short, but some of these groups fought with great and at times fanatical determination.'[2]

A microcosm of the situation in the Kampfgruppe Walther. Not unusually, Second British Army's intelligence at this time was coming from the interrogation of captured prisoners. Information about Arnhem, 55 miles beyond the German front line, could therefore be expected to be fragmentary. First British Airbornes' intelligence summary issued on 14 September, produced from information compiled by 21 Army Group and XXX Corps, stated:

'Such reinforcements as have been made available have been put in to thicken up the line, and there is still no direct evidence that the area Arnhem-Nijmegen is manned by much more than the considerable flak defences already known to exist.'[3]

The message that reached the troops who were to conduct the operation is summed up by Private James Sims of the 2nd Battalion the Parachute Regiment, soon to be fighting on the Arnhem bridge:

'Intelligence told us we had nothing to worry about. There was no armour in

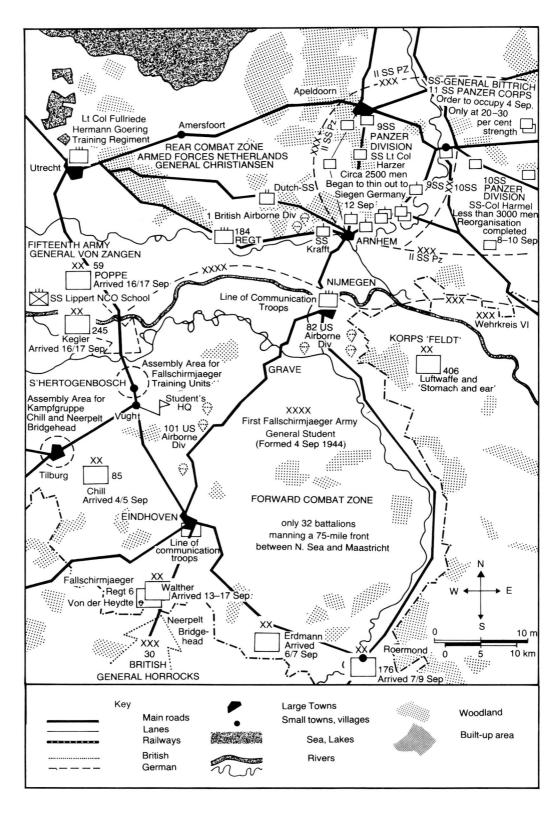

the area and only second-rate line-of-communication troops and Luftwaffe personnel – a piece of cake in fact.'[4]

Based purely on what one would expect to find in the rear combat zone following a major defeat, this is not an unreasonable assertion. It was reasonably accurate, apart from the deduction process. The people sifting the intelligence jigsaw, despite the facts, missed a major formation, and mis-interpreted how fragmented units could recuperate enough power to invalidate a series of otherwise logical estimates.

The situation in the rear areas . . .

Both Fifteen and First Fallschirmjaeger Armies formed the front line in Holland. They were subordinate to Field Marshal Model's Army Group B, which also controlled the remnants of Seventh Army now manning the Siegfried Line on its left flank. Responsibility for the rear combat zone in Holland was vested in the Armed Forces Command Netherlands, commanded by General der Flieger Friedrich Christiansen. His duties were to represent the interests of the Wehrmacht with the civilian administration, to safeguard the organisation and guard military installations such as railways, roads and supply dumps. In addition he was to co-ordinate and provide combat support for all Wehrmacht branches in his territory, as required. For tactical purposes his forces were also under Model's control.

The rearward demarcation line was the Maas and Waal rivers. Christiansen was charged with defending all territory north of that line. Because MARKET-GARDEN involved a penetration deep into this area, Christiansen's troops would be embroiled in the fighting every bit as much as the field armies. Their structure and organisation were effected by their sequence of arrival, which, because of the defeat in Normandy, was inevitably haphazard. Along the Maas and Waal rivers, reception screens were set up to intercept the remnants of demoralised divisions retreating in forced marches to the north. Set up originally at the end of August, by mid-September a hodgepodge of units from every branch of the German Armed Forces had been gathered into a mixed regimental organisation.

The screen on the Waal river for example, commanded by Generalleutenant Hans von Tettau, included the 'SS Unteroffizierschule Arnheim'. This SS NCO school, led by the experienced SS-Colonel Lippert, was one of the few effective units at Christiansen's disposal. Most of its soldiers had already completed one year's service and virtually all had served on the Russian front; although 20-year-old Rolf Lindemann, an SS-*Junker* (officer-cadet) in the unit, recalls, 'a soldier with one year's service is not really experienced'. Nevertheless, trainee NCOs all had leadership potential. Lindemann was serving as an instructor at the school, and remembers its skeletal organisation. Two companies of three platoons of infantry and a fourth heavy weapons platoon had been formed.

(Preceding page) THE DISPOSITION OF GERMAN TROOPS IN THE 'MARKET-GARDEN' AREA OF OPERATIONS, ON THE EVE OF THE AIRBORNE ASSAULT ON 17 SEPTEMBER 1944.
First Fallschirmjaeger Army was holding a thin 32 battalion front forward between Antwerp and Maastricht. Many units had still not arrived. The Allied airborne assault was to split the rear combat zone into two. Fifteenth Army was beginning to arrive across the Scheldt from the west, while the weakened II Panzer Corps refitting near Arnhem was within easy striking distance of the proposed British landing-zones.

Lindemann was in charge of one of the mortar sections. Heavy fire power was provided by some 20mm cannon. Despite its size, and using the leadership resources available, the NCO school had the potential to be rapidly expanded to regimental size. Colonel Lippert, Lindemann remembers, was 'a father-type, admired and respected by the soldiers'. The latter had been selected from the best recruit intakes, served at the front and then been referred to the NCO school. As SS they were aggressive, proud of their elite arm, but not as Lindemann recalls 'necessarily fanatical National Socialists – Himmler was not loved at all by the Waffen SS'. In addition to sweeping up stragglers, the school was constructing field defences along the Waal at Gorinchen.[5]

In Arnhem, the SS Panzer-grenadier Depot and Reserve Battalion 16, commanded by SS-Captain Sepp Krafft, was another potentially effective unit. Originally taken from positions on the coast, it had been brought under von Tettau's control as a 'Divisional Reserve' in the Oosterbeek area west of Arnhem. Consisting of two infantry and a third heavy weapons company, it was supplemented by trench mortar, anti-tank, flak, flame-thrower and heavy mortar sections. With its 12 officers, 65 NCOs and 229 soldiers, it represented a well-integrated and balanced force on paper. However, it was still under training. Of the force, forty per cent were graded 'not yet fit for action'. Nevertheless, they were reasonably fit 17- to 19-year-olds. Krafft himself, although a committed National Socialist, was a professional and capable officer.[6]

Luftwaffe ground staffs that had been picked up by the reception screens were grouped into 'Fliegerhorst' battalions. These men had provided the ground personnel for the abandoned airfields in France, and the majority had no combat experience whatsoever, and only a rudimentary knowledge of infantry weapons

and training. A large number had also been drafted into the newly-raised regiments of Student's First Fallschirmjaeger Army. All these units were now undergoing training, scattered in various rear locations throughout Holland.

German naval personnel were similarly grouped into *Schiffstammabteilung* (naval manning divisions) and trained as infantry. Outflanked by the Allied armies as they had manned the 'Atlantic Wall' they comprised the non-seagoing older navy classes and garrison artillery units. An injection of infantry-trained NCOs was required if they were to function effectively in combat. Some skills were, however, inter-operable. Heavy weapons could sometimes be crewed by these ex-'sailors', and a number were also well-trained artillery observers.

In Holland there were a number of locally-raised forces, mainly consisting of Dutch-German nationals that could also be employed in an emergency. An SS-Dutch surveillance battalion, 'Wach Battalion 3', was stationed in Amersfoort north of Arnhem. Four companies strong, with some limited support weapons, it had originally been formed to guard the concentration camp established near the same town. Apart from some German nationals, the rest of its soldiers had been recruited from Dutchmen wishing to avoid *Arbeitsatz* in Germany, or petty criminals from a detention camp. There were, of course, a few genuinely committed National Socialists in its ranks, but like everyone else, they were becoming increasingly aware of the proximity of the Allied armies, and the likely retribution 'liberation' would bring. Thus far its operational experience had merely been to provide quick-reaction forces *Alarmeinheiten*, which were sent out in requisitioned lorries to track down shot-down Allied air crews. The battalion commander, 46-year-old SS-Captain Paul Anton Helle, possessed no combat experience, being totally reliant upon his adjutant SS-Lieutenant Albert

Naumann for advice on military affairs. The latter, 21 years old, had already been wounded on the Russian front, and had a permanently disabled right arm. When fully mustered, the battalion approached 600 strong, but was currently dispersed over several locations. Its reliability in combat would prove questionable.[7]

Units under training were a prime option for reinforcement at times of crisis. A number of these were stationed within or near the proposed Allied airborne drop zones. Captain Breedman was training a collection of artillery gunners in Wageningen west of Oosterbeek-Arnhem. On 11 September this training formation Artillery Regiment 184 received factory-new 105mm artillery pieces, still covered in protective grease. Crews were trained in their rudimentary use and then passed on to other formations. Twelve guns with crews departed for Doesberg the same week for additional training.

To summarise, units scattered around northern Holland numbered a few SS and 'Hermann Goering' Division depot battalions, supplemented by navy and airforce units. All were organised as light infantry, were at this stage inadequately trained, and were devoid of heavy support weapons and equipment. Troops were nevertheless still generally well motivated. Evidence further points to a number of anti-aircraft battalions, several police battalions and three battalions of Georgian and Caucasian volunteers, recruited from the eastern front. Most were dispersed in separate company locations throughout the rear combat zone.

Because the Allied landing–zones at Nijmegen and Arnhem were only a few miles from the German border, troops and headquarters of another rear area unit could become involved. This was Military District (Wehrkreis) VI. As in the case of Armed Forces Command Netherlands, Wehrkreis VI was an administrative command, responsible for training replacements, organising

new units and channelling material as required to Wehrmacht units. It embraced almost the whole of the province of Westphalia. The replacement training units it had already instructed – the whole point of its function – had already been removed to man the West Wall north of Aachen. 406 (Landesschuetzen) Division was the sole administrative unit left under command, and was also so earmarked. Its geographical location was to give it some significance as a threat to the right flank of the proposed Allied airborne 'corridor'. An *ad hoc* corps staff had already been formed to lead it, and the other elements of armoured replacement, quick-reaction 'alarm' units, 'stomach and ear', and Fliegerhorst and Luftwaffe NCO training schools, attached to it. Commanded by the General der Kavallerie Kurt Feldt, the new force became known simply as 'Korps Feldt.'

This was the paper situation in the rear areas prior to the Allied airborne assault. Lieutenant-Colonel Fritz Fullriede's diary account offers another survey of the situation in areas held by regiments from the division 'Hermann Goering'. Remnants of the combat teams under his command had been pulled out of the line, and were resting and replenishing behind Chill's 85 Division. Travelling between his base headquarters in Utrecht and the front, Fullriede was in a unique position as a roving correspondent to comment upon morale and preparedness in a zone that was to be split in two by the airborne landings four days later. He wrote in his travel log on 13 September:

'Drive between Ede-Arnhem and Nijmegen etc. 21st NCO Anw. Company [probably an NCO training school] are securing the bridges at Nijmegen and Grave with totally inadequate forces. The bridges have not even been correctly prepared for demolition. It's criminal.

'Hertogenbosch-Tilburg then to Loon op Zand the 1st battalion, and then to the 3rd battalion at Udenhout, parts of which have already arrived suffering losses from air attack *en route*. Continued on to First Para HQ at Vught. Its unbelievable how by Spurk, following the loss of so many soldiers that troops can still laugh and crack jokes.

'On to the rest of my 2nd battalion at Loon north of Eindhoven. From there once again to a conference in Vught, then Zaltbommel and over the bridge to Utrecht.

'In unlit Utrecht I came across a sad platoon of Dutch National Socialists being evacuated to Germany, to flee the wrath of the native Dutch. Lots of women and children. That evening first Lieutenant Raden reported, having escaped out of the Hechtel pocket with a few people by swimming the canal. They had fought in the pocket until Tuesday evening, fully motivated by their task; but our jinx of a Higher Command had simply stabbed these valiant chaps in the back. The wounded officers and men who wanted to give themselves up were for the most part – to the discredit of the British – shot by the Belgians.

'After their officers had fallen, some of the poorly trained recruits ran senselessly into the fire of tanks. Just as well our people in Germany do not know how their youngsters are senselessly and irresponsibly sacrificed. All one hears from Germany, even here, is gloomy news about bombed-out towns etc.'[8]

A mobile reaction force. The arrival of IISS Panzer Corps . . .

During the evening of 4 September, the remnants of 10SS Panzer Division 'Frundsberg' were ordered by the commander of IISS Panzer Corps, Wilhelm Bittrich, to establish yet another rear-guard bridgehead west of Maastricht. Its commander, the 38-year-old SS-Colonel Heinz Harmel, was a wily veteran, fully aware that, despite the retreat, his unit would be required to fight another day. Despite the withdrawal Harmel's artillery resources were stronger than they had ever been. A train had been discovered in Arras with no guards on it. 'Loaded aboard were 40 artillery pieces in factory mint condition!' he recalled. 'We took as many pieces as we wanted.'[9] As other units from beaten divisions began to cross the bridge at Maastricht, the 'Frundsberg' commandeered leaderless vehicles and heavy weapons to supplement its own equipment. The following night Bittrich ordered the division to refit and replenish east of Arnhem. Breaking clean and encountering no enemy resistance, the Kampfgruppe Harmel reached its new assembly area on 7 September.

The 9SS Panzer Division 'Hohenstaufen', its sister unit, had meanwhile been collecting in the area of Sittard north of Maastricht. On 7 September it was ordered to detach a Kampfgruppe, including a battalion of infantry and a battery of artillery under SS-Captain Dr Segler, to Valkenswaard, where it subsequently fought under the Kampfgruppe Walther. The rest of the divisional battle group drove through Venlo and Nijmegen to its prepared assembly areas north and east of Arnhem.

The corps was in urgent need of reorganisation. At this stage the true extent of losses were unknown. Both divisions had probably been reduced to a corps total of 6,000 or 7,000 men;[10] that is approximately

20 to 30 per cent of their original strength. They had been in action without pause or reinforcements since the end of June. Losses in officers and NCOs had been especially high. Most of the logistic elements and baggage had already arrived at the beginning of September. As the teeth arm elements arrived they kept their 'battle group' organisations.

Model's original intention had been to replenish both divisions at the front and thereby quickly form an Army Group reserve. Material would have been directly transported from the Reich. Personnel losses, however, had been so great that it was decided to replenish one division – the 10SS – on the spot, and the 9SS in Siegen Germany. As this replenishment process was unlikely in view of the operational situation to be allowed to continue undisturbed, the 'Hohenstaufen' was instructed to hand all its heavy equipments over to the 'Frundsberg'. This order was received with mixed feelings. Wolfgang Dombrowski in Moeller's engineer battalion stated simply: 'Our heavy equipments had to be passed on to the Frundsberg. This was given over freely enough, as we knew we were to receive fresh kit in Germany.' However, veteran officers and NCOs were reluctant to hand over weapons and equipment when the situation could still unpredictably change. Many of the vehicles had been carefully husbanded throughout the retreat from Normandy. Dombrowski's battalion commander took appropriate action, as did a number of other prudent commanders in the Hohenstaufen. As SS-Captain Moeller explained:

'On the 6th September we reached our accommodation north-east of Arnhem . . . Here SS-Sergeant Bicking had already done a lot of work to raise our state of readiness. Where the crafty old fox had managed to get all the parts to produce two usable lorries

and three armoured half-tracks on the road was a surprise to me. In any case I was more than satisfied with my first troop . . . We ought [however] to give our five remaining half-tracks to the 10th Division. Karl Bicking complained, and my case, presented to the division, was to no avail. Right then – we gave up three APCs. The remaining two were "out of order" and "unroadworthy".'[11]

Events were to prove that Moeller's fears had not been groundless. The reorganisation process continued. 'Frundsberg' was chosen to remain in Arnhem because its first tank battalion was about to be equipped with new Panther tanks. Harmel, however, remembers them not arriving until after the battle of Arnhem, stating: 'There was only the Panzer Mark IV Abteilung and the tank-destroyer battalion. The only other tanks were those in Arnhem under repair.' Although the Jagdpanzer IV assault guns had arrived, many of them were already despatched under their commander Roestel to Neerpelt, as was also the 'Kampfgruppe Heinke'. Corps had ordered Harmel to have battle groups standing by to deal with crises. Heinke was therefore despatched on 10 September with SS Panzer-grenadier Battalion 21, a battery of artillery, and reconnaissance and engineer companies.

Realising that his strength was dissipating faster than reinforcements might arrive, and that the reorganisation process was unlikely to remain undisturbed, Harmel embarked upon a basic reorganisation of his battle group. The aim was to pool available equipments, to create balanced combat teams able to deal with most eventualities. This process, followed through between 8 and 10 September, exemplifies the seriousness of the losses suffered in Normandy. The Panzer-grenadier Regiment 'Frundsberg', the only infantry group

The 9SS Hohenstaufen Division began to entrain for Siegen Germany.
Moeller declared that 'understandably the move into the Reich was the
number-one talking point.' (Bundesarchiv)

remaining, was ordered to form an anti-tank company of 12 guns within its own organisation, four of which were to be motorised. All experienced anti-tank gunners from the other units were drafted into this new company. Self-propelled gun drivers in the artillery regiment were attached to the division's tank regiment. Armoured half-tracks held by the Panzer-grenadier Regiment and the armoured engineer company were to be given to the reconnaissance battalion – whether they were serviceable or not. (The 'Hohenstaufen's devious if prudent interpretation of corps orders had not gone unnoticed.) Remaining flak guns were to be concentrated in the division's Flak Regiment. These measures represented a thorough overhaul and regrouping of the division's resources. At the end the 10SS battle group resembled a modern weak brigade, consisting of a staff and divisional 'slice' at Ruurlo, three Panzer-grenadier battalion equivalents at Deventer, Diepensen and Rheden, and a tank headquarters with some armour – Pz Mark IVs – in

Vorden, and artillery in Dieren. Henceforth referred to as the 'Kampfgruppe Frundsberg', in recognition of its reduced strength, it probably numbered less than 3,000 men on the eve of MARKET-GARDEN.

On 12 September the advance parties, quartermasters and technical personnel of the 9SS 'Hohenstaufen' Division began to entrain for Siegen Germany. The troops were delighted. As Moeller declared: 'Understandably the move into the Reich was the number one talking point!'

On 14 September Montgomery's Operation Order M525 was issued. The biggest airborne operation of the Second World War was thereby set in motion.

Two days before, First British Airborne Division had announced during an orders group that the enemy would not be able to muster any mobile force exceeding a brigade, with a few tanks and guns, before their relief by XXX Corps. This was despite the fact that divisional intelligence had already recorded a message that one depleted Panzer

Division had been sent back to the area north of Arnhem for rest and refit. XXX Corps mentions a similar report, but Second Army appears not to have believed it. On 15 September a Dutch Resistance report reached London giving the location of 9SS as being along the river Ijssel. First Airborne Division received this information four days into the battle of Arnhem.[12] A 'betrayal legend' arose after the war, but it has been conclusively proved that IISS Corps moved into the area surrounding Arnhem before the MARKET-GARDEN order was issued. The speed of the German reaction was to be a factor more of geographical distribution rather than an early warning.

The 'dress rehearsal' for Arnhem. Dispositions of the Kampfgruppe 'Hohenstaufen'…

By 17 September the 'Kampfgruppe Hohenstaufen' had also been reduced to a weak brigade, with less equipment than the 'Frundsberg', as most had already been handed over, or loaded on trains for the journey back to the Reich. Model, wary of an airborne attack, had ordered that the division's fighting units were to depart last. Meanwhile, battalions were formed into *Alarmeinheiten* in order to combat any such eventuality. On paper the Hohenstaufen could muster 19 quick reaction or equivalent company strength groups, spread over 12 locations, numbering an approximate total of 2,500 men. The maximum distance over which these units would be required to react to landings west of Arnhem was 23km. An average was 10 to 15km; that is, two hours heavily laden on foot, or 30 minutes by vehicle.

Apart from being veteran panzer formations, both the Frundsberg and Hohenstaufen had been specifically trained for an anti-airborne role. Indeed the IISS Panzer Corps had from birth been formed to deal with an anticipated invasion of the west. Under the expert tutelage of the then Commander-in-Chief Panzertruppen West General Geyr von Schweppenburg, both divisions had trained to repel airborne landings, while awaiting the delivery of its heavy equipments. During the summer of 1943, invasion 'alarms' had practised all units. In September of the same year, the Hohenstaufen had undergone a testing anti-airborne exercise that was pronounced a success.

Month-long exercises dealt with practical night and live firing manoeuvres. Aggressive reactions were instilled into commanders, who were taught to attack direct from the line of march, and bring every weapon immediately to bear – one had to 'drive into the teeth of an airborne landing in order to defeat it'. Companies were practised in repelling raids and engaging in anti-partisan operations. The enemy had to be hit at his weakest point, on landing, before he had a chance to assemble. Numerically stronger forces in such a scenario should be engaged. Harmel summed up the impact such training had upon his division:

> 'The whole IISS Corps was especially trained over the previous fifteen months via classroom and radio exercises – all directed to countering a landing supported by airborne forces in Normandy. This training benefited us enormously during the Arnhem operation. At the lower end, NCOs and officers were taught to react quickly and make their own decisions. NCOs were taught not to wait until an order came, but to decide for themselves what to do. This happened during the fighting all the time.'[13]

The fragmented distribution of battalions and companies, organised as quick-reaction

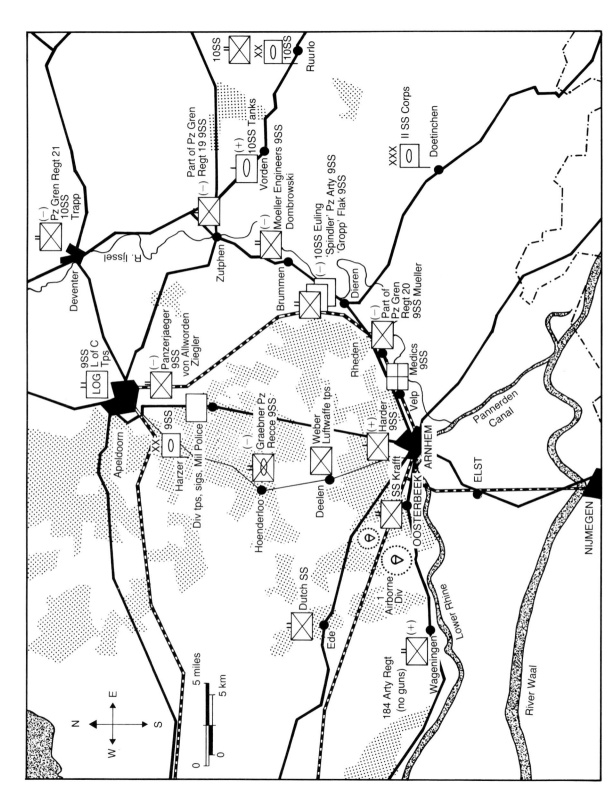

10SS

XX

10SS

Ruurlo

Part of Pz Gren Regt 19 9SS

10SS Tanks

Vorden

Moeller Engineers 9SS
Dombrowski

II SS Corps

Doetinchen

Pz Gren Regt 21
10SS
Trapp

Zutphen

R. IJssel

Deventer

Brummen

Dieren

10SS Euling
'Spindler' Pz Arty 9SS
'Gropp' Flak 9SS

Part of
Pz Gren
Regt 20
9SS Mueller

Rheden

Medics
9SS

Velp

Panzerjaeger
9SS
von Allworden
Ziegler

9SS L of C
Tps

LOG

9SS

Harzer

Div tps, sigs, Mil Police

Graebner Pz
Recce 9SS

Weber
Luftwaffe tps

Harder
9SS

Pannerden
Canal

Apeldoorn

XX

9SS

Hoenderloo

Deelen

SS Krafft

ARNHEM

ELST

Oosterbeek

Dutch SS

1 Airborne
Div

Lower Rhine

NIJMEGEN

Ede

184 Arty Regt
(no guns)

Wageningen

River Waal

N
W — E
S

0   5 miles

0   5 km

groups, was not therefore regarded as a particularly unusual or disadvantageous tactic by the corps now manned by veteran soldiers. Locations were picked to capitalise upon the numerous good roads in the Arnhem area. Most units were billeted in villages along the Arnhem-Velp-Zutphen road, and in those south of Apeldoorn. Experience suggested the avoidance of large towns, like Arnhem itself, as uprisings by the Resistance, already encountered in Paris and Brussels, could pin down large numbers of troops.

First British Airborne was about to leap into a hornets' nest. Far from the worse-case scenario of a mobile brigade group building up gradually over three days – if at all – it was to confront one within 12 hours of landing.

The front. Hechtel-Valkenswaard road, 15-16 September . . .

With the failure of the attack against the Neerpelt bridgehead on 15 September, the Kampfgruppe Walther settled into a defensive routine. The bridgehead was (at least apparently) being contained by a half-circle of nearly three infantry regiments and supporting arms.

Unexpected guests arrived at the command post (CP) of the SS-Kampfgruppe 'Richter' during the afternoon following the attack. They were a naval frogman team. SS-Captain Friedrich Richter had been tasked by the 10SS to reinforce this sector of the front with his battalion from

Panzer-grenadier Regiment 21 of the Frundsberg. He had already been there a week before the welcome arrival of the Kampfgruppe Walther, under whose command he was taken. Now he was tasked to support this strange team who had been briefed by High Command to blow the bridge over the Maas-Scheldt canal. Richter's adjutant, 23-year-old SS-Lieutenant Heinz Damaske, remembered the 'heavy equipment', possibly a 500-kg underwater mine, they brought with them. After darkness the team was driven by lorry to a farm in the vicinity of the canal, where it was attempted with a few available signallers from the command post to get the naval team into the water. Everything went wrong – the darkness, the inability to speak so near the enemy, and the weight of the mine all caused unavoidable problems. The canal shoulder was two to three metres high. Eventually the bumpings, scrapings and murmurings attracted the enemy's attention even before the swimmers could enter the water.

> 'The British began to heavily mortar our section of the front. With all our exertions trying to get this explosive "colossus" into the water without a sound – it did not bear thinking what would happen should it be struck by a mortar round. This is precisely what occurred to the naval team as well. Their task they decided was impossible under these prevailing conditions, and they left us alone with their "package".'

(Preceding page) DISPOSITION OF IISS PANZER CORPS PM 17 SEPTEMBER 1944. The corps consisted of some 5,500 infantry with some armoured vehicles on the eve of MARKET-GARDEN. The geographical distribution of the refitting units did much to aid the speed of the German reaction to the British landings near Arnhem. The 9SS Hohenstaufen were the nearest with a total of 19 companies poised to react within 30 minutes by vehicle or up to 2 hours on foot. If the British had landed nearer the Arnhem bridge, these reaction times would have been much reduced. First British Airborne Division jumped literally into a 'hornets' nest.

All along the front, tell-tale signs of increasing enemy activity were picked up. (Bundesarchiv)

British reinforcements cross 'Joe's Bridge' across the Maas-Scheldt canal, the target for the abortive underwater frogman attack mounted from the SS-Kampfgruppe Richter's sector during the night of 15–16 September.

The bridge could not be blown. Richter's men were not only aware of the alertness of the British, but there appeared to be a reason for it. Heavy columns of traffic could be heard moving up the road towards them from Hechtel beyond. Rising and falling in the night, the traffic sounds were a sinister harbinger of what must come; 'occasionally dimmed headlights could be made out'.[14]

All along the front, tell-tale signs of increasing enemy activity were picked up. 719 Infantry Division announced 'continuous enemy motorised movement from west to east on the roads south of the Albert canal' in its daily report on 16 September. Kampfgruppe Chill (85 Infantry Division) passed on High Command's estimate in its daily situation report that 'the big attack would be forthcoming as soon as the British manage to concentrate stronger tank forces on the north bank of the canal'. Kampfgruppe Walther reported 'heavy enemy supply traffic with headlights at full beam was observed south of the canal during the night of 15–16 September, indicating offensive intentions'. During the following night 'engine noise in the bridge-head itself indicated that new armoured units were moved up'.[15] As indeed they were. British Irish Guards group spear-heading the Guards Armoured Division, and elements of the 50th Northumbrian British Infantry Division were occupying their jump-off positions, prior to the advance on the 17th.

Constricted tactically to moving up a single isolated road, these advance elements of XXX Corps were justifiably nervous of the reception they were bound to attract. Intelligence estimated that:

'. . . about six battalions of infantry with 20 armoured vehicles of 559 Anti-Tank Battalion were still available to contest the corps advance on 17 September from the bridgehead

All appeared to be quiet on the Western Front . . .

on the Eindhoven road. Artillery support would probably not be great as few guns appeared to have been withdrawn from the anti-tank defences of Arnhem and Nijmegen to support the forward troops. The rumoured Panzer formation appears to have been considered non-existent or too weak for action as no use had been made of it in the forward area during this period.'[16]

In fact, approximately 10 weak battalions of infantry with limited artillery but some anti-tank weapons, and, more importantly, about 12 self-propelled (SP) tank-destroyers would be in a position to contest the Valkenswaard road.

Kerutt's 1st Battalion of the Regiment

von Hoffman was suddenly switched into reserve positions in depth along the Valkenswaard road on 15 or 16 September. This battalion would therefore contest the leading Irish Guards element coming up the road toward Eindhoven. Its CP was located 1½ kilometres east of the road in Achter de Brug. Companies were dispersed in well-camouflaged positions in the small woods on either side of the main road.

Captain Brocke's anti-tank company sited its factory-new 76mm 'Pak' guns left and right of the road. There were no cross-country vehicles available to tow them, so the best positions – off the road with superior arcs of fire and better cover – could not be chosen. Without exception the guns were placed only a few metres off the road on either side. This was to have catastrophic consequences later.

To secure the road further along, a tank ambush was established 2½ kilometres behind the line, manned by Kerutt's headquarters defence platoon. Fox holes were dug along the edge of the road utilising overhead cover. Inside, panzerfaust gunners occupied a number of positions, intimately supported by intermingled machine gunners. Once a tank was disabled its crew would be engaged by the machine gun, whose subsidiary task was to protect the panzerfausts. Thirty men were placed here to block any armoured breakthroughs.

On 16 September Luftwaffe Penal Battalion 6 was stricken by a succession of artillery and mortar strikes. Intermittent salvoes worked their way up and down the woods on either side of the road. Delayed-action fuses produced tree bursts, stripping cover and exposing trenches without overhead cover to even more punishment. Cowering in their trenches these ex-airforce reduced-in-rank NCOs and officers were totally unprepared for life at the front. Major Veith, the battalion commander, and his adjutant were both killed. The unit was leaderless 24 hours before GARDEN was due to begin.

Lieutenant Heinz Volz remembers one scant comfort:

> 'Enemy air activity was not particularly unusual these days. The German Luftwaffe never appeared. A single night air attack on the enemy's positions and assembly areas [therefore] came as a pleasant surprise.'[17]

Nothing much appeared to be happening. It was all quiet on the Western Front.

CHAPTER IV

Portrait of the German soldier in Holland, September 1944

We are in a hell of a fine place . . .

Feldwebel 712 Infantry Division

Pause to take stock . . .

The apparent pause in the Allied advance was inexplicable to the average German soldier. But he made the most of it. Alfred Ziegler, an SS despatch rider with the anti-tank battalion of the Hohenstaufen, animatedly recalled the period of respite before the battle of Arnhem:

> 'The eight-day break we had after the shambles in France and Belgium was decisive. During this time we regrouped and re-equipped. I managed for example to get my motorcycle repaired. It had received a bullet straight through the engine block from a low-flying 'Jabo'. I had to be towed in.'[1]

Moeller's 9SS Engineer Battalion similarly prepared itself for future operations. Reorganised now as an infantry 'alarm' company, it numbered 80 to 90 men. Every section received an MG 42, an improvement upon the older MG 34 machine gun, which greatly increased their dismounted fire power. Explosives, defence materials, and even some bridging material and engineer stores were provided through Moeller's contacts at Corps. Moeller was particularly grateful to his contact 'for procuring two

flame-throwers, which were to prove particularly useful a few days later'.

SS-Corporal Wolfgang Dombrowski took equal stock of the battalion. He had been with it since its inception and basic instruction the year before. 'By this time there were only seven men left in the battalion who had completed the year-long instruction in Dresden; and naturally the replacements were not so well trained.' Nevertheless things could be worse:

> 'We were accommodated in Brummen, and despite the occasional grumbling of artillery fire in the distance, we were happily living in virtual peace-time conditions.'[2]

South-west of Arnhem SS-Colonel Hans Michael Lippert, the 47-year-old commander of the 'SS Unteroffizierschule Arnheim', was directing defensive preparations on the Waal between the ferry at Gorinchem and the road bridge at Zaltbommel. General Christiansen, C-in-C Netherlands, had just visited and thanked Lippert for his actions in stabilising the situation in his part of the rear combat zone. A torrent of retreating troops had now reduced to a trickle. Lippert shuddered to think what may have happened barely a week ago, if the British had continued the advance beyond the Albert canal. Only a few battalions had barred the way to the Ruhr. 'What I experienced then amongst this surge of retreating German troops brought back personal memories of November 1918. It became evident to me that the only way of overcoming this situation was to tackle it head on, until it was mastered.'

His task was aided by the fact he had only two bridges to control. There was no alternative to crossing the river here because of its width, depth and the fast-flowing current. The bridges were monitored and regulated by just one platoon apiece.

Lippert recalls:

'At both these crossing points the torrent of German soldiers dammed up, then pushed and shoved across. A shambles of innumerable vehicles, carrying every conceivable load – and not always military supplies – exacerbated the situation.'

Lippert's NCOs checked the papers of all civilian and military personnel who wished to cross. Within two days 3,000 unattached stragglers had been assembled in Woudenburg. Integrated into 'march battalions', they were passed on to the Netherlands High Command, responsible for administering and controlling the rear combat zone.

Lippert was, as one of his section commanders SS-Officer Cadet Lindemann recalls, a 'real fair, gentleman-officer type'. He lined up the apprehended soldiers one Sunday morning in the market place in Thiel and attempted to remonstrate with them. Given the chance to explain themselves, a cross-section of opinion emerged covering the whole spectrum of units fleeing Holland at that time. When asked why they had fled, several soldiers replied that:

'. . . they had been obliged to hold positions at the front without their officers, or had been advised to throw down their weapons because further fighting and dying was senseless. Here and there the same reasons for flight emerged, but could not be checked in detail. I could not blame them, I had already experienced officers trying to cross the Waal bridges. The assembled soldiers were passed on to the Netherlands High Command, where a number of officers would be required to give an account of themselves before a court-martial.'[3]

These *ad hoc* march battalions were immediately passed on as recruits for the *ersatz* or replacement training battalions. The front in Holland was composed of battle groups formed from the reorganised remnants of the retreating defeated divisions, supplemented by these rapidly retrained replacements.

First Fallschirmjaeger Army . . .

First Fallschirmjaeger Army was born from Goering's unexpected announcement to Hitler that the Luftwaffe was suddenly able to offer a pool of 20,000 men to alleviate the acute manpower shortage problem. Recruited primarily into the Luftwaffe-controlled Fallschirmjaeger regiments, they were the potential pilots, observers, navigators and signallers who were emptied from the now redundant Luftwaffe training schools in Germany. Although completely untrained for their role, they were to fight tenaciously, making up for inexperience with courage and zeal. This collection of fresh youth, picked from among the best manpower in Germany, had yet to experience the carnage and disillusionment of combat as infantry soldiers. Until they did, they were to prove formidable opponents. But first of all they had to be trained.

Lieutenant Heinz Volz offers an illuminating account of the state of training of these Fallschirmjaeger 48 hours before being committed to the Neerpelt bridgehead. The 1st Battalion Regiment von Hoffman was preparing for battle in its assembly area near Tilburg. All the ammunition yet to be distributed was stacked in a barn next to the battalion CP.

'A significant amount of high-explosive material was stored in this place. One morning I came across the armoury NCO who wished to prepare the panzerfausts for firing. Pointing out to me that he was completely unfamiliar with the weapon – as he had come from either the airforce or Signals Corps – he requested an explanation of its handling and firing procedures. Meanwhile another interested junior NCO had also turned up. I made the already armed panzerfaust safe in order to demonstrate how to arm it again (whereby I had clearly indicated the significance of the red release button), when to my complete surprise, one of them activated it. The result was correspondingly what one would anticipate. We saw only smoke and flame and the warhead flying toward the barn door at 5 metres distance. Only a split second we reckoned now remained of our lives. The projectile struck the door – and dropped to the ground like a stone. Nothing happened. Luckily the armourer had inserted the detonator and explosive charge in the wrong place. He had thereby not only saved our lives, but received a salutory demonstration on how effective his prepared panzerfausts would have been against enemy tanks.'[4]

Major Finzel's 1st Battalion of Fallschirmjaeger Regiment 2 was a similarly hastily-formed unit. It was in action against the Beringen bridgehead on 8 September, shortly after the British had stormed the Albert canal. Formed only three weeks before, its other two sister battalions were cut off and fighting for their survival in the fortress of Brest. Only 10 per cent of its originally trained parachute personnel remained. These veterans, who had participated in airborne assaults in Holland, Corinth and Crete earlier in the war, now formed the kern of the new regiments. Most had either been wounded or were returning having served in other units. Replacements were green 17- to 18-year-olds. Leadership in the 1st battalion was provided by a smattering of these experienced men reinforced by 26 officer cadets, sergeant-majors and senior NCOs transferred from the Reich Air Ministry Staff. None of the latter had any front experience.[5]

Lieutenant-Colonel von der Heydte, the Commander of Fallschirmjaeger Regiment 6, was not convinced, despite the official view, that the residue of veterans surviving in his unit was sufficient to swing the balance of the survival chances of his replacements. Committed far too prematurely in southern Holland at the beginning of September, having been reduced to 60 fit men in Normandy a few weeks before, he felt that:

' . . . the combat-effectiveness of the regiment was low. It had not yet developed any cohesion; and the young replacements which made up 75 per cent of the unit had received little or no training. Hundreds of the soldiers in this regiment had never even held a rifle in their hands before, and fired the first shot of their lives in battle! Moreover, several members of the officer corps were unable to perform what is expected of an officer.'

He was particularly scathing in his criticism of the Luftwaffe Penal Battalion 6, also serving with the Kampfgruppe Walther. 'Its personnel was largely made up of degraded officers. Its commanding officers were incapable and their equipment was the worst imaginable. The men still wore tropical uniforms!'[6]

Nevertheless, unit commanders, as in the example of the Regiment von Hoffman, did what they could in the scant time available. During the few days it formed up around Tilburg, before being committed to the Kampfgruppe Walther, they were well equipped with light anti-tank weapons, particularly panzerfausts. Problems arose over who was to conduct the necessary training, as many of the officers and NCOs, like the recruits, had only just been detached from airforce staffs, signals, flak-artillery or from airfields. Only the few veterans available were in a position to impart at least a rudimentary infantry training before they departed to the front.

The Wehrmacht . . .

Meanwhile, the front line was still being held by remnants of depleted Wehrmacht units. Although ostensibly quiet, Allied thrusts attempted to improve local tactical positions, and deprive the weary German troops of any chance of rest in the line. A *Feldwebel* (Sergeant) of the 712 Infantry Division west of Antwerp wrote in his diary on 13 September, a static time in the campaign:

'Near Bath a convoy has been shot up by fighter bombers. We bandaged the wounded and send them back. We have to leave the dead lying in the street, for with fighter-bombers overhead any unnecessary movement may be fatal. Some of the dead are so mutilated as to be unrecognisable.

The results of a fighter bomber attack. 'Some of the dead are so mutilated as to be unrecognisable,' wrote a sergeant from 712 Infantry Division. (Bundesarchiv)

One of our mates commits suicide by hanging. During the night British aircraft drop flares and attack, with fighter bombers. We are in a hell of a fine place . . .'[7]

The structure and psychological outlook of the Wehrmacht units defending southern Holland in September 1944 had undergone a transformation from the armies that had manned the Atlantic Wall in June. A number of different 'types' could be identified among the rank and file. Firstly, and occupying paramount place, were the veterans or *alte Hasen* (literally 'old salts'). Many had been previously wounded, a proportion

Occupying paramount place were the veterans or alte Hasen. *Digging in on the Neerpelt bridgehead.* (Bundesarchiv)

formation that was to have any staying power.

A second element were the young and inexperienced soldiers, born between 1924–26, now beginning to arrive in waves as replacements. Before the invasion battles in June and July they may have received 12 weeks' training; now, few could boast as many days. Most were highly-motivated volunteers, convinced by their National Socialist education that they might achieve final victory. Disciplined and willing, their conception of heroic service was to prove a bitter disappointment.

Older age groups were also appearing for the first time. Fathers of families of up to 40 years old were mixed with previous exemptions from service – the non-essential factory workers, small shop-keepers and petty officials who had hoped to remain in the Reich until the end of the war. After a short training they fitted in, often looking after the youngsters in their units with the same fatherly concern they might have shown their own offspring, but for the accident of war.

The real problem was the pressed or physically disabled elements which made up the fourth group. Pressed recruits were virtually useless. 'Hiwis' or *Hilfswillige* were Poles, Czechs or Alsace Germans often employed in logistic units. They were not suitable for combat, and often deserted at the first available opportunity.

The difficulty, as with First Fallschirmjaeger Army, was to quickly train and assimilate all these elements entering service in September 1944. Experience suggested that only unconditional obedience to orders enabled units to survive when engaged in protracted combat. Discipline was therefore harsh, even draconian, whilst concepts of soldierly 'duty and order' were extracted with no compromises. Some varieties of unit, particularly the physically disabled, were beyond all this. To qualify for admission into an 'ear' battalion, a

for the third or fourth time. These soldiers preferred after convalescence to return to their previous haunts; preferably in the same unit, where they could reunite with friends and serve under known officers. Although small in number, the returnees were always greeted with pleasure. They were the most worthwhile reinforcements. Veterans developed their own peculiar 'front atmosphere'; a sense of established cameraderie intensified by danger. They worked within the accepted duty framework but gave it a human face, contributing the flexibility required to make an otherwise harsh and uncompromising system work. As such they could generate the sense of 'belonging' and 'unit pride' essential to any combat

The difficulty was to quickly train and assimilate all these elements entering service in September 1944. Relaxing in southern Holland. (Bundesarchiv)

recruit had to prove he was deaf, had one or two ears missing or badly damaged, together with an additional minor disability such as a missing finger or rheumatism. The consequences at the front could be practically insurmountable:

'Verbal orders could only be given by a frantic series of gestures. Inspecting the guard at night was a nerve-wracking and hazardous task since the men on duty could not hear anyone approach. Thus when suddenly confronted in the dark they fired first and attempted to find out who it was later. In one ear battalion, two sergeants of the guard

had been killed this way shortly after the unit went into action. Casualties from artillery fire were also inordinately high because the men could not hear the sound of approaching shells and therefore took to shelter much too late.'[8]

Members of this, the 176 Infantry Division, were manning the line to the left of Erdmann's Parachute Division. Another unit soon to be embroiled in the MARKET-GARDEN battles was of similar quality. One of its newly-recruited 24-year-old soldiers caustically commented upon his arrival in his diary:

'Today I was transferred to the 42 MG Fortress Battalion, as a messenger. Destination West Wall. This battalion is composed of Home Guard soldiers half crippled – I found many among them quite obviously off mentally. Some had their arms amputated, others had one leg short, etc – a sad sight. "V2, V3" they jokingly call themselves "a bunch of fools".'[9]

Beliefs and concerns

What motivated these disparate and untrained elements in the German army in September 1944 – Wehrmacht, SS, Fallschirmjaeger, Luftwaffe, Navy, 'stomach and ear' – to fight on, when the war at this stage had so clearly been lost?

Alfred Ziegler remembers the atmosphere within the SS Panzerjaeger Abteilung 9 of the Hohenstaufen, now reorganised as an infantry quick-reaction company on the eve of MARKET-GARDEN.

'Morale was good but we were under no illusions that the war was not already over. The joke when we were sent to Tarnepol Russia had been "we are on our way to pick up a little wooden hut in Siberia". Things improved with the invasion of Normandy, now we were more likely to end up in a logging camp in Canada! One of my best friends confided in me: "Don't be a hero," he said. "The war is lost".'

SS-Corporal Wolfgang Dombrowski, now part of the Engineer 'Kampfgruppe Moeller' another Hohenstaufen 'Alarmeinheit', was more philosophical but in a practical sense:

'We believed the war was probably over. But you must realise that we lower ranks were only 18 to 19 years old. Our officers were 24 to 29. Still youngsters! Life's deeper issues did not concern us too much. We were prepared to fight on.'[10]

The catastrophic reverses experienced by the Wehrmacht, both in the east and west in the summer of 1944 served to emphasise the main factor holding it together until the end: an increasing awareness that the Homeland was now in danger. This factor alone probably encouraged a will to resist more than the whole sum of National Socialist propaganda. Fears that the war may be lost were seldom stated openly, and certainly not mentioned by officers and NCOs to lower ranks. Doubts about a happy outcome would have weakened resistance. The only conceivable happy outcome at this stage might be to defend the frontiers of the Reich, and negotiate for the pre-war status quo, assisted by the new 'wonder weapons', the V1 and V2. Nobody could imagine the consequences of a total defeat. Even in the shambles of the Falaise pocket in Normandy, a corporal had written to his wife on 18 August:

'We had to retreat in a great hurry. All the other units pulled out without firing a shot and we were left to cover them . . . I wonder what will become of us. The pocket is nearly closed, and the enemy is already at Rouen. I don't think I shall ever see my home again. However we are fighting for Germany and our children, and what happens to us matters not. I close with the hope that a miracle will happen soon and that I shall see my home again.'[11]

A soldier in any case never benefited from the peace and solitude necessary to gloss over the course of the war. His immediate concern was survival. A universal worry was not death, but worse – that one may not come out of the war sound in mind and limb. Nobody wanted to die a hero's death or suffer mutilation at this stage. For most, and particularly the veterans, the nerve-racking period was waiting in assembly areas prior to going into battle. The green replacements were blissfully ignorant, the dubious distinction of battle experience would come in its time.

Survival was, therefore, a more important theme at the front than politics and party. Occasionally there were complaints about the 'brown big-shots' at home. When important party member scandals were commented upon in letters from families, the response was 'just wait until we get home, and then we will see . . .'. But such statements were rarely taken seriously by superior officers. Scant notice was taken of such outbursts. It was after all the prerogative of the front-line soldier to moan. Letting off steam did more good than harm. Significantly, complaints about party hacks always fell short of criticising the Führer – perhaps an element of trust or blind faith still remained. One battalion commander voicing the opinion of his men wrote after the war:

'We did not know how tense or hopeless the situation on the front was, and knew nothing of the negative impact differences between Hitler and his commanders had upon operational decisions'.[12]

It was inevitable that the sudden influx of medically unfit and badly trained personnel would bring about a serious deterioration of morale in the German forces in Holland. But soldiers were still dependent upon radio broadcasts, front newspapers, correspondence and orders for knowledge of the general overall situation. What a soldier personally saw had an impact, and the retreat from France had been an eye-opener for many, yet no organised mass opposition to conditions could be expected to develop.

Discipline was too ingrained. Soldiers welcomed the organisation and control measures instituted at the various reception screen centres. The horrors of the retreat bespoke a potential collapse that few could imagine or even wished subconsciously to contemplate.

The 'system' in effect held them together. The formation of a defensive crust along the Albert canal at the beginning of September was a demonstrative example of the recuperative ability of the German General Staff to stave off total defeat. Martin van Creveld[13] has produced material suggesting that the German Army inflicted more casualties per head upon its enemies than did all its Allied adversaries during the Second World War. This was achieved by evolving a military infrastructure dedicated almost exclusively to operations. Built around the operational, social and psychological needs of the fighting man, it produced a higher concentration of 'fighting power' per unit than in any other Allied army. Playing a key role in all this was the German General Staff. Sound, accurate staff work, from headquarters that continued to function despite the annihilation of combat formations, played a key role in restoring order among commanders overwhelmed by local crises on the ground. German soldiers craved order, and fought better within its confines.

At the lower level, bonds of comradeship also held them together. Mutually shared privation resulted in close friendships which meant more than an identification with Führer and Reich when it came to fighting and dying. Characteristically, the Field Army took these bonds into account in structuring the training system that supported it on active service. Divisions were responsible for training their own conscripts in Replacement or Feldersatz battalions, whose three companies directly paralleled and fed the three regiments forming the division. On completion of training, recruits were formed into 'march battalions', which were self-contained units that could be committed as a reinforcement at any stage during its journey to the front, should the local situation warrant it. This was the system adapted by the reception centres set up behind the front line in southern Holland. 'March units' here were often committed of necessity, before they had the chance to form a unit identity. One method of introducing identity was to name the unit after its commanding officer; for example, the Kampfgruppen 'Walther', 'Chill', or 'Moeller', and so on. Headquarters generally knew the personalities of the officers concerned, and soldiers in time could feel some sense of association with new commanders. The system was preferable to allocating a unit with a number, which, apart from being impersonal, served to confuse headquarters into believing formations were more complete than they actually were. A 'Kampfgruppe' such as the 'Frundsberg' or 'Hohenstaufen' was recognised for what the term implied – the remnants of a major unit now at battle group strength.

Personal contact with families at home also had an impact upon fighting morale at the front. Despite restrictions, letters from home did not necessarily conform to officially released bulletins. This could be unsettling for some. However, the main worry for front soldiers was the welfare of families at home exposed to the full rigours of the Allied bombing campaign.

Doris Dantscher was 71 when she was 'bombed out' in Munich. Her letter written on 20 July to her children is typical of hundreds received by troops at the front. She had just been evacuated to Muennerstadt in lower Francony.

'Since Thursday we no longer have a roof over our heads, we have lost everything. It happened so quickly, that we were unable to save anything; only what was left in the cellar remained, as it held up . . . The house is completely burnt out . . . Father shovelled backwards and freed the entrance to the cellar. It is impossible to go inside from the street, one must go via Zentnerstrasse through the garden and into the cellar . . . Johanna took me out of this hell on Monday, and took me to Muennerstadt. Father is still in Munich, and it greatly worries me as he has to stay and sleep in the cellar . . . Hopefully he is still alive, as from the 18th to the 19th there were more heavy attacks in Munich . . . I cannot yet grasp that we no longer own a home. We are lucky in our misfortune to have Auntie Johanna, with whom we have managed to recover. Who would have thought as you left your parent's home the last time, that this would be a departure for good. Everything that was loved and dear to us must be abandoned . . . We did not get out of our clothes for five days. There was no water, no light and no gas. We were glad to be able to wash in Muennerstadt.'[14]

Similar letters, often delayed, had a particularly negative effect upon the morale of those concerned. On occasion such news was not even passed on. When it was, superior officers would try and mediate through close comrades first. Reactions varied but generally dwelt upon 'the pointlessness of fighting if our families are killed at home', or 'it's no use listening to speeches about wonder weapons when the Luftwaffe is unable to shoot down any more enemy bombers!' Soldiers from the West German provinces worried constantly about relatives until they were evacuated.

News of atrocities in eastern Prussia at the hands of the Red Army, and continuing tragedies caused by the bombing offensive, created the so-called *verruckte Helmuts* or 'crazy Helmuts'. 'Every platoon had one', reported one Fallschirmjaeger veteran. Despite inadequate training, men who had lost everything – families, sweethearts, homes – became depersonalised by despair. They had nothing further to look forward to, except perhaps to fight and expend their lives dearly in order to extract revenge. Such unpredictable individuals became deadly adversaries to the enemy, but their fanatical recklessness had to be closely monitored by unit commanders.

All these factors had a collective impact upon fighting quality at the front. Not often admitted was perhaps the prime emotion motivating German tenacity at this stage of the war. It was bound up with a desire to protect the Homeland and families against the very excesses that had been committed by the German armies in their own campaigns to date. A dreadful realisation that they may soon be fighting the war in their own streets and gardens began to grip German soldiers. It would be inaccurate to term this realisation 'war guilt', as the full implication of the systematic slaughter of the Jews and 'undesirables' was only gradually beginning to emerge publicly. Most Germans were, as they claim, unaware of the depredations being committed in the twilight zone administered by the political arm of the SS. But there was sufficient evidence at hand to make many uneasy. This produced a type of fatalistic resignation; an awareness that the Reich had probably 'burnt its boats' and the only recourse was to fight on. As yet, it was not a motive apparent to the fighting man, more than pressured by events. A feeling of unease was coming to the fore, hinted at, but indefinable. Lieutenant-Colonel Fritz Fullriede's diary, so often critical of the conduct of operations during this period, remains unemotional. What he chooses not to say in some respects is more significant than what he does say. Discussing the situa-

tion with colleagues in the officers' mess in Utrecht on 2 September, he writes in his diary:

'The West Front is finished, the enemy is already in Belgium and on the German Frontier; Romania, Bulgaria, Slovakia and Finland are pleading for peace. It is exactly like 1918.'

The year 1918 to his generation was the equivalent of the year zero. Everything had to start over again from scratch. But he does not take the statement any further. He ends by simply recording:

' . . . in the evening I was in a very nice night club, but I appeared to be the only German.'[15]

The Wehrmacht and the Waffen SS were not totally blind to the excesses that had already been committed by itself by 1944. Divisions which had campaigned on the eastern front – the majority by this time – had witnessed the treatment meted out to partisans and Soviet prisoners of war. Little mercy was therefore anticipated from the Allies as a whole, and none from the Russians. Of 5.7 million Soviet POWs, 3.3 million perished in German captivity; and those Germans unfortunate enough to have been encircled by the Soviets after the collapse of Army Group Centre were receiving the same treatment.

Partisans were referred to as 'bandits' in German official reports. There was no place in the ordered German military mind or tactical doctrine to deal with civilian irregulars. This had historically been the case since the Franco-Prussian war of 1879, and through the First and now into the Second World War. Failure to understand the 'guerrilla' mentality accounted for the Wehrmacht inability to deal with large-scale Resistance uprisings by any means other than counter-terror. Thousands of

'Enjoy the war while you can because the peace will be terrible.' SS soldiers during the retreat across the Belgian-Dutch border. (Bundesarchiv)

troops had been tied up on the eastern front policing rear areas. Unable to deal with the same phenomenon on the western front, atrocities occurred, as at Vercors and Oradour-sur-Glane. Dutch partisans, suspected, caught, or otherwise, were often shot out of hand. Executions had taken place near Arnhem shortly before the airborne landings.

Defeat was staring the German army in the face in Holland in 1944. Even if there had been doubts concerning the Führer's leadership after the débâcles both in east and west in the summer of 1944, the Allied call for 'unconditional surrender' confirmed a gut reaction that there was no recourse but to fight on. It blurred the distinction between Nazi and anti-Nazi. An Allied survey of German POWs[16] revealed that in a typical unit, fanatical Nazis, apoliticals and anti-Nazis were roughly on a par with each other. Nazis were considerably more numerous amongst NCOs and junior officers, and, as the mainstay, they chose to fight on. Their sardonic response, couched in black humour, was: 'Enjoy the war while you can, because the peace will be terrible.'[17]

CHAPTER V
The Landings

'What an absolute swine! There are two parachute divisions on top of us!'

Model's Chief of Staff

Lieutenant Heinz Volz, in the Neerpelt bridgehead with the Fallschirmjaeger Regiment von Hoffmann, remembers that '17 September began like any other day before, a beautiful autumn Sunday, sunny and warm'. Activity at the front was uneventful. General Reinhard, Commander of LXXXVIII Corps, visited the headquarters of both 719 and 85 Divisions, as was his normal routine. Air activity was mentioned in passing in the daily reports of all formations, but occupied no more space than the weather, and elicited no comment.

Meanwhile, 435 British and 983 American aircraft began the preliminary bombardment of flak positions and the landing zone areas for the airborne assault. Attacks continued throughout the morning but were not regarded as being particularly unusual. Heavy bomber swarms flying toward Germany were a daily occurrence.

At about 1130 the sirens wailed at Deelen airfield north west of Arnhem: *'Flieger Alarm!'* A savage air attack reduced flak positions and Luftwaffe accommodation to rubble. Clouds of black smoke belched up in and around Arnhem. On the Wilhelmsplein the well-known Café Royale was soon in flames. The Wilhelmskaserne barracks was straddled by heavy calibre bombs. Air pressure from the blast ripped out some of the walls and fire destroyed the rest, burying many soldiers within. Other Wehrmacht barracks were also hit: the Menno-von-Coehoorn and Sachsen-Weimar barracks on the north road leading

to Apeldoorn. The latter had provided accommodation for the 'SS-Unteroffizierschule Arnheim' before it had been moved to the coast. Munition dumps began to explode. Chaos temporarily reigned in the town centre; a number of trams were abandoned in the streets. Wehrmacht garages in Bloemstraat, as well as the magazine in

As seen from the German front line: heavy bomber swarms flying towards Germany were a daily occurrence. (Bundesarchiv)

The Wilhelmskaserne blazes after the raid on 17 September.

Beekstraat, the station and other locations, were all damaged. Smoke could be seen rising from the direction of Wolfheze as an ammunition dump near the lunatic asylum exploded, and the old peoples' home was set on fire by fighters strafing the Ede-Arnhem railway. Much clearance and rescue work was required. SS-Captain Sepp Krafft, gazing at the scenes of desolation appearing around him, decided to 'stand to' his troops – Panzer-grenadier Training and Replacement Battalion 16 – and moved to the protection offered by the woods west of Arnhem.

At 1200 the German barracks at Ede were bombed. SS-Lieutenant Labahn, commanding headquarter company of the SS Training and Replacement Battalion 4, was despatched to assist:

'As the fires were being put out a second bombing pattern fell on Stevin barracks, and on the air raid trenches outside the barrack complex. The company immediately sustained 11 dead and 30 wounded through this attack. Shortly after recovering the dead and transporting the wounded to hospital in Arnhem the next attack came in. Again the bombing pattern was through the middle of the barrack installations as far as Beeckmann barracks. Losses during this onslaught could only be guessed at, as the greater part of the wounded had to be immediately taken to aid posts and treated. An accurate registration was therefore impossible.'[1]

As shocking as these casualties were, this simply paralleled what had already happened in Normandy weeks before. Nobody considered it bizarre should nervous colleagues leap into ditches at the

59

sound of approaching aircraft. It was not significant. In any case, life throughout the other unaffected parts of the rear combat zone in Holland remained quiet. Unit daily reports concerned themselves almost exclusively with routine and administrative matters. There was much checking and counter-checking in the 'Korps Feldt' over who was responsible for bridge demolitions in their area, and what their states of readiness should be. General Student requested Wehrkreis VI to provide him with a map of all its unit locations east of the Maas river. Unit areas of responsibility were being tied up in normal staff routine.

To the west the first rays of the sun broke through as the aerial armada moved into the Channel. A broad ray of sunlight appeared, then a second and third as it grew progressively lighter. Flying now into clear skies, the extent of the armada became apparent. The outlines of aircraft and gliders blended with one another into a single mass. Hundreds and hundreds stretched away towards the clouds in the west. Dozens of Dakotas with twin engines and uptilted wings flew in 'Victory V' formations of three, followed by further groups of Halifaxes with gliders in tow, wallowing from side to side. It was an aerial layer cake. Transport planes flew in the middle with fighter cover flying at three different heights.

A force of 1,545 transport planes and 478 gliders had taken off that day from airfields around Swindon, Newbury and Grantham. They were escorted by 1,131 fighters. The stream was 16km wide and 150km in length. Nothing like it had ever been seen before.

SS-Lieutenant-Colonel Walther Harzer, commander of the 9SS Hohenstaufen Panzer Division, was driving to Hoenderloo, accompanied by staff officers to decorate the commander of his reconnaissance battalion – Graebner – with the Knight's Cross. Graebner had won this distinction

in Normandy. Harzer's divisional Chief-of-Staff Schwarz had already departed for Siegen to oversee the future replenishment of the division. All thoughts were on the likelihood of leave in Germany. SS-Colonel Harmel, the commander of the 10SS Frundsberg Panzer Division, was in Berlin, personally negotiating for a speedier reconstitution of his own division.

The aircraft stream meanwhile droned on. All that marked the coastline of flooded Holland was a long ridge of land, not unlike the spine of some extinct prehistoric reptile. As they flew inland the water gradually gave way to ribbons of soil, and then whole fields, canals and forests glistened in the sun. There appeared to be no trace of human communities. After the juicy green of an English landscape, the green of the Continent seemed a little grey to those on board, as though covered in dust or rather withered.

Soldiers manning flak batteries were not too concerned as the first dots approached from the west. They had been under attack before. Indeed, all morning intense air activity had kept them fully preoccupied. There was to be no break. The dots multiplied and thickened as the swarm approached. Its oncoming was heralded by a sinister, low-pitched hum that developed into a roar as the skies above them filled with aircraft. A crescendo of sound ebbed and pulsated as each successive wave passed over. Behind the transport aircraft came the silent gliders, with the slender cables between sometimes flashing in the sun.

Soldiers from the Training and Replacement Regiment Hermann Goering were relaxing in the sun next to coastal positions near Katwick an Zee. Herbert Kessler, a young NCO, recalled it was

'a Sunday of wonderful sunshine, appearing to be one of a series of charming but uneventful autumn days. At least until the afternoon . . .

Suddenly the air was filled with the noise of engines, the air defence guns nearby fired from all ports, and the soldiers looked at each other full of amazement when they realised that the engine-powered planes had gliders in tow.'[2]

In Arnhem Wolfgang Dombrowski, the SS Engineer Corporal in Moeller's battalion, was enjoying 'a wonderful day'. He had heard the bombing in the morning and thought Deelen airfield had been attacked. Even so:

'Nobody had thought something might come at us from the air. From the ground maybe, but not from the air. We realised the Allies had logistic problems.'

The pattern established in Normandy had been initial ground contacts followed by a timely withdrawal to avoid the inevitable massive bombing carpet. There was a gigantic column of smoke over Arnhem, but so what? An attack was not expected.

Alfred Ziegler, a young despatch rider serving in the 9SS anti-tank battalion 'Panzerjaeger 9', liked Arnhem. After the carnage of Normandy, 'Arnhem and Oosterbeek were amazing sights'. After his experiences, tranquil surroundings were the exception rather than the rule.

'I was astonished to see such a beautiful town and village. So different from my home surroundings. There were wealthy-looking homes with gardens and houses neatly laid out. Even its little tracks were cobbled or tarmaced. Bicycle tracks ran alongside the roads. These were useful to drive along because they afforded better cover from the air.'[3]

Ziegler was looking forward to leave that afternoon but did not get it. Defaulted on parade by his first sergeant, he had to sew the corner of the double seat of his camouflage suit trousers before he would be released.

Others did not even get the chance of leave. SS-Captain Sepp Krafft, having avoided the morning bombings by deploying his Training and Replacement Battalion 16 in the woods, was now exercising west of Arnhem with two of his three companies. In the fields nearby luckier German soldiers were entertaining Dutch girlfriends or indulging in pleasant bicycle rides. Everyone remarked upon the beautiful weather.

Having crossed the coast, both the northern and southern aircraft streams altered course and flew toward their ultimate objectives. From the ground below coloured smoke suddenly belched up, and the whole of the southern armada banked to the left. Hardly an aircraft was out of position. Inside jumpmasters ordered: 'Stand up . . . hook up . . . action stations!'

SS-Captain Viktor Graebner, the 30-year-old commander of the 9SS Recce Battalion Hohenstaufen, was on parade at Hoenderloo, 10 miles north of Arnhem. His unit, 400 strong, was formed up on the square flanked by armoured half-tracks. There was no music. Harzer, his divisional commander, recollected:

'I made a speech in which I referred again to the bravery of the troops and their commander Graebner, in Normandy. Then I pinned the Knights Cross on his breast.'

The cameras clicked, freezing his image for perpetuity. In less than 24 hours Graebner would be dead.

At the same time the southern aircraft stream crossed the British XXX Corps bridgehead. Startled German infantry

SS-Lieutenant Colonel Harzer (left) *and SS-Captain Graebner* (next right) *were on parade in Hoenderloo. A previous picture taken in Belgium.* (Fuerbringer Collection)

gazed skywards. Lieutenant Heinz Volz, whose Fallschirmjaeger Regiment von Hoffmann was in the line with the Kampfgruppe Walther, recalled:

'At about midday we suddenly discerned an unearthly droning noise coming out of the air. A huge stream of transport aircraft and gliders approached out of the enemy hinterland, flying at an unusually low altitude. This enormous swarm was escorted by countless fighters, in particular Lightnings. These could observe everything moving on the ground and covered our defence area in minute detail, engaging anything they could see. Our own anti-air did not react. Only in the hinterland did flak open up.'[4]

Lieutenant Martin, commanding a platoon in Fliegerhorst Battalion 3, was occupying a road crossing between Breda and Tilburg

Within 24 hours of this photograph being taken, SS-Captain Graebner was dead.

behind 719 Division as the northern aircraft stream flew past. He and his three infantry sections gaped at an incredibly large number of planes towing gliders overhead. It 'lasted two hours', during which his platoon downed one glider. Inside they found a bren gun carrier which was salvaged. On the glider fuselage they deciphered a cryptic message: 'Is this trip really necessary?'[5]

The stream continued on, flying past Vught, the headquarters of 1st Fallschirmjaeger Army. Generaloberst Kurt Student, its commander, had left his study window open in order to carry on with his paper work undisturbed by the heat. His command post was near S'Hertogenbosch

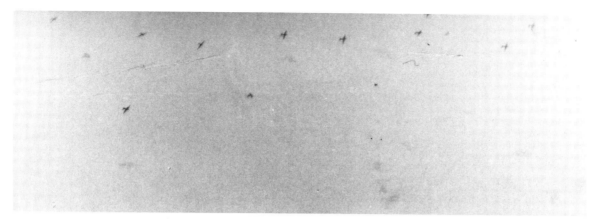

Lieutenant Volz: 'Only in the hinterland did flak open up.' Aircraft swarms broken up by German flak over the front line. (Bundesarchiv)

south of Vught. Detectable at first as a low sinister whisper, the fly-past of the northern stream, carrying the British 1st and American 82nd Airborne Divisions, developed into a pulsating roar:

'I stepped out on the balcony, and wherever I looked I could see aircraft-troop transports and aircraft towing gliders – flying quite low over our house. They came in groups and as one disappeared into the distance another one followed – flight after flight. It was a spectacle which impressed me deeply. At that particular moment I had no thought of the dangers it foreshadowed; I was only thinking of my own airborne operations in earlier days. If ever I had such resources at my disposal!

'I went up on to the flat roof of the house with my Chief of Staff Colonel Reinhard to see where the aircraft were going. There was still an immense stream of them passing overhead and some flew so low that we ducked our heads.

'There was quite a lot of shooting going on by this time. Our clerks, drivers, batmen and the signal section had grabbed their rifles and were shooting at the low-flying aircraft.'[6]

The massive nature of this airborne onslaught gradually became apparent in radio messages from the front to the subsidiary commands in the rear areas. Lieutenant-Colonel Schuster, the Chief of Staff of the Battle Group Chill (85 Infantry Division), reported to LXXXVIII Army Corps at 1400 that 40 transport aircraft had flown over their positions at 1340. One had been shot down. Similarly, the Korps Feldt received information from the Division Scherbening (406 Infantry Division) ten minutes later that 500 to 2,000 enemy paratroopers and 30 gliders had landed in the Nijmegen, Groesbeek and Mook areas at about 1345.[7] H. Sitter, a German paratrooper belonging to the 1st Battalion Fallschirmjaeger Regiment 2, witnessed the passage of this stream, containing the 82 (US) Airborne Division south-west of S'Hertogenbosch. He later jotted down his impressions:

'Above us is the armada of airborne troops, and transport planes with gliders in tow. Our 88mm and tanks shoot many of them down. A huge pile of debris. We searched through the area, picking up many prisoners

'*Off to the rear with him.*' *Defiant members of the US 82nd Airborne Division taken prisoner.* (Bundesarchiv)

with hardly any resistance – only surprise. I took one POW to Ortmann [his company commander]. He had his pockets full of money, and handkerchiefs with overprinted maps, etc. He also had a Fallschirmjaeger's knife. He says he found it. We could have almost lynched him for it. Still – off to the rear with him.'[8]

With their doors open, the transport aircraft now began to descend to jump height for the final run into their respective parachute drop zones.

SS-Colonel Lippert, commander of the SS NCO School 'Arnheim', became aware of the approaching Arnhem stream:

'During the midday meal at my command post in Schooreward I heard a terrific droning noise from aircraft engines. It was about 1300. As I came outside to work out where the noise was coming from, I saw

hundreds of aircraft with escorts heading westwards. Looking through my binoculars, it was possible to make out that the doors were open, and that an airborne landing was about to take place. I immediately ordered 'stand to' and observed the aircraft further. There was a Luftwaffe air control station near me, but they had no information. After a short while it became clear that the aircraft were coming down, and large numbers of paratroopers were jumping out. I reckoned we were faced with a major airborne operation. The distance to the drop zones was estimated at something like 40 kilometres – the area of Ede-Wageningen and Arnhem.'[9]

Alfred Ziegler with the 9SS Panzerjaeger, having lost his leave, was wistfully regarding the landscape north of Arnhem. He was, as he claimed, 'an imaginative fellow,

SS-Colonel Lippert: 'As I came outside to work out where the noise was coming from, I saw hundreds of aircraft with escorts heading westwards.' The aerial armada sweeps across the Belgian border. (Imperial War Museum)

always contemplating things' (a characteristic which as a soldier often got him into trouble).

'Then I saw the twin-engined bombers [Mosquitoes] flying fast and low. I remarked to a colleague "something is up, now we are for it". "Don't be daft," was the rejoinder. "You're always imagining things." The Mosquitoes must have been forming up in the east because suddenly they returned and swooped down over our flak positions and shot them up. Nothing was left standing.'

At that moment transport planes lumbered into sight and began dropping parachutists.

Leave was now most certainly off. 'See that?' he jocularly remarked to his first Sergeant. 'They're dropping from the heavens, and it won't be long before we're up there and join them!'[10]

The armada, now at drop height, flew steadily north-eastwards disgorging its loads: the 101 (US) Airborne Division in the area of Son, Veghel and Eindhoven, the 82 (US) Airborne Division around Grave and Groesbeek, and 1st British Airborne Division east of Arnhem.

SS-Lieutenant-Colonel Harzer dismissed the parade at Hoenderloo. 'As the troops were moving off to their quarters and the officers and myself were making for the officers' mess for lunch, we saw the first British parachutes in the sky over Arnhem,'

SS-Captain Moeller: 'Without interruption, stick after stick, wave on wave, they came down noiselessly and peacefully, presenting a fascinating view.' 1st British Airborne Division Wolfheze-Heelsum near Arnhem. (Imperial War Museum)

he remembered. 'It could not be deduced at this stage that a large-scale operation was under-way and we sat down quietly to lunch.'[11]

Harzer was not the only individual to be misled. SS-Captain Hans Moeller, the commander of his engineer battalion, was out walking with his adjutant on 'a Sunday with a wonderful blue sky and cirrocumulus clouds above the western horizon'. He called to his companion to share his admir-

ation of such a beautiful spectacle. They were enjoying the stroll. However, as Moeller relates, the scene took on a more sinister hue. Screwing up their eyes the commander and the adjutant tried to focus on a strange phenomenon gradually taking shape in the distance.

'These can't be cirrocumulus clouds, these are parachutes! – No, flak bursts? But so many of them? Others stopped

Lieutenant Enthammer: 'That cannot be,' he wondered. 'It never snows in September! They must be parachutists!' Arnhem. (Imperial War Museum)

too, including civilians; everybody seemed captivated and gazed in that direction, where more and more "fluffy clouds" were appearing.

'"For Christ's sake, Grupp, these are parachutes!" Without interruption, stick after stick, wave on wave, they came down noiselessly and peacefully, presenting a fascinating view. But what was going on? The distance was about 20 kilometres. That was strange indeed. And still there was no end to it.

Stick came after stick. That meant danger! Paratroopers?
' "Let's get back, but fast!". '[12]

Field Marshal Model, the commander of Army Group B, was sitting down to lunch with his staff in the Hotel Tafelberg in Arnhem. At about 1400 his chief of staff Colonel von Tempelhoff excused himself to answer an urgent telephone call. As soon as he left a succession of explosions accompanied by a deafening roar led to a mad scramble to take cover beneath the dining table. After a second series of explosions further away, everyone ran outside to see what was happening. The sky was black with aircraft. Von Tempelhoff, dishevelled and evidently ruffled, shouted his report. 'What an absolute swine! There are one to two parachute divisions right on top of us!' The Field Marshal ordered: 'Right – everyone out, reporting place Terborg!' (the logistic headquarters). He departed immediately by road, leaving his staff to dismantle the headquarters.[13]

Lieutenant Joseph Enthammer was still temporarily based with his V2 rocket artillery unit in St Joseph's School in Arnhem. Exhausted after his experiences in France, he had slept late. Gazing in the direction of Oosterbeek he detected what appeared to be white 'snowflakes' hanging in the air. 'That cannot be' he wondered. 'It never snows in September! They must be parachutists!' His unit must depart for Emmerich in the Reich as soon as possible.[14]

The aircraft stream, having dropped, was now passing over Deventer prior to turning back for England. Deventer was a collection point for Panzer-grenadier Regiment 21 of the 10SS Frundsberg Panzer Division. Its 3rd Company trainees were receiving weapons instruction from its 19-year-old 'veterans', including SS-Corporal Rudolf Trapp, as the aircraft flew over. As Trapp relates, they were immediately ordered to 'stand to':

> 'The sky over us was black with aircraft. An armada, absolutely full with transport aircraft and bombers towing gliders. There was an immediate alarm. No time to eat. We did not know where the paratroopers had come from, only later did we hear that they had landed in Arnhem.'[15]

Emmerich, Enthammer's destination, was only 30 kilometres away, and it lay within the Reich. Operation MARKET-GARDEN was to transcend its western frontier for the first time. A policeman on the lookout tower in S'Heerenberger street in Emmerich was able, with the aid of a telescope, to witness the gigantic spectacle now unfolding in the skies over Nijmegen and Arnhem. Aircraft filled the sky. Some of them left a dense tangle of tiny dots – paratroopers – behind them, whilst others descended directly to earth as gliders, whereupon air-landed soldiers poured out.[16]

It certainly does not snow in September. The war had reached the Reich. The blow, moreover, had come as a total surprise.

CHAPTER VI

Drive into the Teeth

We knew from experience that the only way to draw the tooth of an airborne landing, with an inferior force, is to drive right into it.[1]

SS-Captain Krafft[1]

First Reactions . . .

During the first hour or two, German commanders could not even begin to estimate the size and scope of the Allied operation. SS-Captain Hans Moeller, driving frantically to his divisional headquarters, tried to collect his thoughts. 'What did the future have in store for us? What was going on?'[2]

The time was 1400 hours. A total of 331 British aircraft with 319 gliders and 1,150 American planes towing 106 gliders had laid an airborne 'carpet', concentrating over three zones between Eindhoven and Arnhem. Over a period of one hour and 20 minutes approximately 20,000 parachute and glider-borne infantry landed in good order far behind German lines. German troops at the front gazed anxiously at these massive aerial formations thundering across their rear areas. They did not want to be cut off. Lieutenant-Colonel Schuster, Kampfgruppe Chill's Chief of Staff, reported the return of these aircraft as they crossed the line again. Major Klemeier, the commander of Training Battalion I/6, was despatched by the Corps Feldt to lead a patrol to investigate the reported landings around Nijmegen, Krauenburg-Groesbeek and Mook. He failed to return.

Fragmentary reports added to the confusion. Flak Brigade 18, behind the Kampfgruppe Chill, reported 'advances by one or two enemy battalions toward Oedenrode

north-west of Best' and 'heavy artillery fire on the approaches to Son, where a heavy flak battery was engaged with an enemy force of approximately battalion strength'. Kampfgruppe Chill confirmed this picture, identifying 'two to three enemy parachute battalions in the Best-St Oedenrode-Son areas', and that 'the railway bridge south of Best has either been blown or is still held by us. Counter-attacks with hastily assembled units are being carried out.' Fighting was also reported on the Boxtel-Eindhoven Road.[3] Nobody could give a clear indication as to what was going on.

Lieutenant-Colonel Fritz Fullriede's diary reflects this atmosphere of confusion, rumour and counter-rumour reigning in the rear combat zone after the initial landings. His impressions of 17 September are jotted down in note form:

'Hertogenbosch-Vught-Tilburg-Aerondonk.
   'An unbroken stream of enemy transport aircraft and glider tug planes flying towards Nijmegen and Arnhem. The air is full of enemy fighters. Rethy-Pampfert. There I speak to the adjutant of the III Combat Team [*abteilung*]. The command post and the 16 Flak Battery is under constant heavy artillery fire. Captured American paratroopers from shot-down aircraft. Drive further to Casteele. The road is under enemy

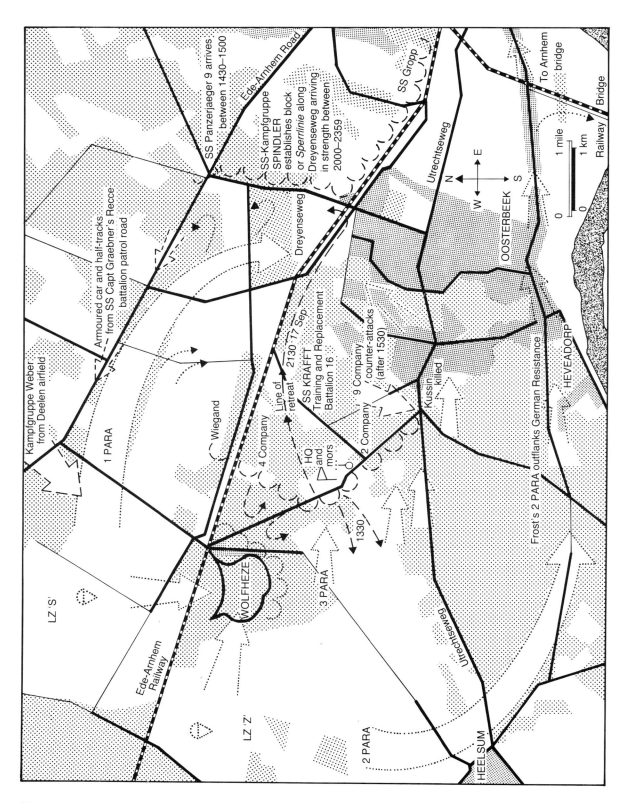

LZ 'S'

LZ 'Z'

Ede-Arnhem Railway

WOLFHEZE

2 PARA

3 PARA

1 PARA

HEELSUM

Wiegand

4 Company

Line of retreat 2130 17 Sep.

1330

HQ and mors

2 Company

SS KRAFFT
Training and Replacement
Battalion 16

9 Company
counter-attacks
(after 1530)

Kussin
killed

Utrechtseweg

HEVEADORP

Frost's 2 PARA outflanks German Resistance

OOSTERBEEK

Utrechtseweg

Dreyenseweg

Ede-Arnhem Road

Kampfgruppe Weber:
from Deelen airfield

Armoured car and half-tracks
from SS Capt Graebner's Recce
battalion patrol road

SS Panzerjaeger 9 arrives
between 1430–1500

SS-Kampfgruppe
SPINDLER
establishes block
or Sperrlinie along
Dreyenseweg arriving
in strength between
2000–2359

SS Gropp

To Arnhem
bridge

Railway Bridge

N
W — E
S

0 ____ 1 mile
0 ____ 1 km

fire. It is impossible to drive on. All around enemy parachutes. Up until now it appears paratroopers have landed in battalion strength around Veghel and Loon. Also by Grave, Nijmegen and Arnhem.'

'All the bridges there fell undamaged into enemy hands. That much was clear. It seems like sabotage.'

'I met a major from 1 Fallschirmjaeger headquarters in front of Eindhoven, he reported that the bridges at Zaltbommel and Gorinchem also appear to be in enemy hands. This was later found to be false, no enemy had landed there. Back to Valkenswaard but impossible to get through because of heavy artillery fire. In Helmond as everywhere else confusion reigns. Our engineers there are still being improperly led.'[4]

A Waco glider from the first wave was shot down near Student's headquarters in Vught. Sifting through the debris, a Feldwebel found a collection of documents of such importance that within hours they were on the General's desk. The papers were a set of orders for MARKET, the air plan. Sufficient material could be pieced together to enable the staff of LXXXVIII Corps to advise its commander the same evening that:

'101 American Airborne Division has been tasked to secure crossing points over the water obstacles, at Son-St Oedenrode and Veghel, and hold them until the attacking British ground forces – Guards Armoured Division, 50th Infantry and 43 Infantry Divisions – link up. The latter are assaulting toward Eindhoven.'[5]

General Student immediately grasped the full implication of the Allied plan. He himself had initiated and led a similar operation four years before. Then, the objective had been to lay an airborne carpet across the rivers and canals that formed 'Fortress Holland' in May 1940. This time it was the Allies attempting to establish a bridgehead across the lower Rhine, going the other way. Moreover, thus far it appeared to be succeeding.

The American 101 Airborne Division had dropped nearest to the ground link-up forces. Its task was to secure 15 miles of the 'corridor' between Eindhoven, Son, St Oedenrode and Veghel. By the end of the first day Son had been captured, but the bridge blown. The other two crossing points were captured intact.

In the middle of the corridor 82 (US) Airborne Division was to capture the bridges at Grave over the Maas, astride the Maas-Waal canal, and the huge road bridge

(Preceding page) THE INITIAL GERMAN REACTION WEST OF ARNHEM DURING THE AFTERNOON OF 17 SEPTEMBER 1944.
Krafft's SS Training and Replacement Battalion 16 provides a temporary block with three companies; while Weber's Luftwaffe Kampfgruppe attacks the landing-zones from Deelen airfield. Krafft's recce and probing attacks are repulsed, and he forms a defensive line which is eventually outflanked by 1 and 3 PARA by late afternoon. A more substantial blocking force has meanwhile begun to establish itself along the line of the Dreyenseweg and railway line. This is the SS Kampfgruppe Spindler thickening up between 2000 and 2359. Krafft retreats along the railway line and links up with Spindler. Frost's 2 PARA has bypassed this German resistance forming from north to south and advances at speed eastward along the line of the lower Rhine, and captures the northern end of the Arnhem road bridge. (Map compiled from Krafft's original report and maps.)

over the Waal at Nijmegen. The heights south-east of Nijmegen were to be secured in order to protect the Waal crossing from German counter-attacks that would probably form up in the Reichswald forest. 504 Parachute Infantry Regiment overwhelmed the Grave bridge garrison within three hours, and the Heumen bridge was taken over the Maas-Waal canal. The 505 and 508 Parachute Infantry Regiments occupied the high ground around Groesbeek, Wyler and Beek, and dug in. A reconnaissance patrol was despatched to report on the Nijmegen bridge.

First British Airborne Division had been ordered to secure the bridge at Arnhem and maintain a bridgehead north of the lower Rhine, sufficiently large for XXX Corps to push on to the Zuider-Zee. First Polish Parachute Brigade and another airportable division were to be flown in later to support this vanguard, the furthest from the GARDEN start line, and the last that could expect relief from the approaching ground columns.

Sepp Krafft's SS Training and Replacement Battalion 16 was the largest self-contained unit nearest to any of the Allied landing–zones. They had been exercising in the woods by Wolfheze, 2 to 3 kilometres east of the British landing–zone. At first the high trees obscured the extent and location of the parachute assault. Krafft's reaction was therefore based upon sketchy observer reports. It was a compromise of all available options. Two small patrols were immediately sent out to gain more information. Second Company (2 Kp) was ordered to attack toward the landing–zones, essentially conducting a reconnaissance in force. Fourth Company (4 Kp) began to establish a defence line in the vicinity of the Hotel Wolfheze, while his third company (9th Company) was summoned from Arnhem to create a battalion reserve.

Searching for the landing–zone, 2 Kp became disorientated by its passage

SS-Captain Sepp Krafft, Commander of SS Panzer-grenadier Depot and Reserve Battalion 16.

through the woods, and compromised its earlier intention to approach from the north by inadvertently emerging directly opposite the centre of the landing–zone. Its heavy machine gun section immediately engaged gliders still landing, reportedly seriously damaging four. Fearful of over-extending itself, the company quickly fell back and joined 4 Kp digging in the blocking positions established on the Wolfheze Road. Krafft correctly deduced that the Arnhem road bridge was the objective for these surprise landings. He therefore positioned himself astride the two main approach routes into Arnhem. These were the Ede-Arnhem railway cutting and the Wageningen-Arnhem road, both providing an east-west axis. This he blocked with two companies forward, effectively parrying the first advances by Brigadier Lathbury's 1st Parachute Brigade.

All afternoon Krafft's battalion inflicted considerable casualties upon the 1st and 3rd battalions of the Parachute Regiment attempting to pierce or outflank his line of 'hedgehog' outposts. By 1530 his force had swollen to 13 officers, 73 NCOs and 349 soldiers with the arrival of 9 Kp, which was immediately employed as a mobile reserve to overcome local crisis. Supported by mortars in the centre, and anti-tank guns on the main approaches, heavy and at times intense forest skirmishes continued, with the line holding more or less intact until 1800. Suspecting by then that he was being encircled, Krafft resolved to break out under the cover of darkness. The death, however, of the Stadtkommandant of Arnhem, General Kussin, killed returning to his headquarters following an on-the-spot situation brief by Krafft, was an indication, unrecognised at the time, that his battalion had already been bypassed.[6]

The only other force in a position directly to contest the British landings was the Kampfgruppe 'Weber', situated northwest of Krafft. It was formed from 'Teerose II', a Luftwaffe radar air-control network manned by a signals company from 213 Nachrichten (Signals) Regiment. Captain Willi Weber assembled a scratch force of 90 poorly armed signallers who attacked the landing-zone in the area of Reijer's compound and over the Amsterdamsweg road. It was a courageous gesture, demonstrating the extent to which lightly armed, inexperienced troops, if forcefully led, can hold up numerically and qualitatively superior forces when given an opportune tactical moment – here, the period of confusion that always follows an airborne landing. Achieving little of measurable consequence, Weber withdrew his force, and reoccupied his established defensive positions near Deelen airfield. Nevertheless, the sum result of all these delays was significant.

Of more consequence were the radio situation reports sent up the chain of command by the Luftwaffe troops. Third Fighter Division's air traffic control point was located near Deelen airfield. Protected by Weber's aggressive reaction, it was given time to withdraw, and radio the initial key reports that were to trigger the German reaction in the Arnhem area.[7]

General Bittrich, the Commander of IISS Panzer Corps, received the first enemy situation reports at 1330 and issued his first warning order at 1340. Both 9SS and 10SS division headquarters were given 'stand to'. IISS Corps' reaction to the crisis reads like a staff command and control exercise. Bittrich based in Doetinchem quickly and expertly deduced the likely enemy aim. Command and staff procedures began to function with the efficiency that was so much a hallmark of the German General Staff. Nijmegen and Arnhem were identified as the key objectives for this renewed Allied offensive. Airborne landings of considerable strength had been identified near both locations. Therefore, the 9SS were to recce Arnhem and Nijmegen, assemble, occupy the former and defeat the enemy landings west of Arnhem by Oosterbeek. This was to be achieved post-haste, and the Arnhem bridge secured. 10SS were to occupy the Nijmegen bridge and form a bridgehead south of it.

Harzer's staff at Beekbergen had already noticed that 'something was up' in Arnhem. Bittrich's warning order reached Harzer personally in Hoenderloo. Graebner's Reconnaissance Battalion was immediately set to work remounting weapons and replacing tracks on the armoured half-tracks that had been kept 'unroadworthy' to avoid passing them on to the 10SS. Within two hours a force of 40 armoured cars and personnel carriers was ready for action, the heaviest concentration of armour in the Hohenstaufen. By 1440 most of the 9SS 'alarm' quick-reaction companies had been notified and had declared themselves 'at action stations'.

On the Harskamp training area elements of Panzer-grenadier Regiment 20, belonging to the Hohenstaufen, were waiting to be transported back to Germany. Although ordered to 'stand by' following reports of airlandings, they were in no position to react as they had given up all their weapons and field equipment. Nineteen-year-old SS-Corporal Paul Mueller remembers that 'our luggage had already been assembled in a pile to be picked up by a lorry'. They were due to depart for Siegen by rail at 2000 hours.

'Now we immediately received weapons. Everyone got a rifle and 90 rounds of ammunition which was stuffed into our pockets or haversacks, because we no longer had our ammunition pouches, steel helmets or entrenching tools.'[8]

Their luggage would eventually be brought up on lorries. They had no food, and also, it appeared, little luck.

Influenced by experience and their anti-airborne training, and motivated by the innate aggressiveness of the Waffen SS, most units were moving, travelling toward the sound of the guns. SS-Captain Wilfried Schwarz has since recounted the prevailing atmosphere in this hour of crisis:

'These soldiers were thinking about their families, as everything had virtually been packed for the move to Siegen. The mood was a resigned – 'here we go again!' They were inevitably disappointed at first, but the officers and NCOs were able to overcome this and get the soldiers quickly into action.'

Schwarz had already arrived in Siegen. He was summoned by a short cryptic signal from Harzer: 'Get back, airborne landings.'[9]

Personal initiative, and the realisation that one must drive into the teeth of the landings before the parachutists could assemble was the main force driving officers and NCOs. Troops were ordered: 'Move now, orders an objective.' The hastily assembled Kampfgruppe von Allworden, the remnants of SS Panzerjaeger Battalion 9, reorganised as an infantry alarm company, sped off to Arnhem. It still had one or two Mark IV tank-destroyers and some towed 75mm PAK guns left. Alfred Ziegler recalls receiving the order to move between 1430 and 1500 hours:

'We set off elements of the Kampfgruppe straight away towards Arnhem. I was at the head of the column, carrying my commander on the motorcycle combination, with the assault guns clattering down the road behind us. Troops who had been on leave in Arnhem were streaming back, and I waved them off the road as we sped past.'[10]

There was total confusion. Nobody was certain what had happened. SS-Lieutenant Gropp's Hohenstaufen anti-aircraft battery Kampfgruppe rolled into Arnhem, 87 men strong. It had been called out in the middle of a tactical loading exercise. Only one 88mm flak and a 20mm cannon remained from the unit that had so effectively blocked the American advance on Cambrai 15 days before. They became involved in an exchange of fire along the Ede-Arnhem railway cutting and took up defensive positions. Convinced they were engaging Dutch terrorists, they had probably hit the leading elements of the 1st British Parachute battalion (1 PARA).

SS-Corporal Wolfgang Dombrowski bullied his section of eight to nine soldiers on to one of the lorries that were to take Moeller's engineer Kampfgruppe into Arnhem. No encouragement was required.

'We thought we were on our way back to Germany. It was simply "load up – and get to Arnhem!".' Totally unaware of what all the fuss was about, the four Opel Blitz lorries laden with assault pioneers drove through Arnhem's suburbs and out towards Oosterbeek. The time was 1630 hours. They had just cleared the outskirts of town

'. . . when we saw tracer bullets whizzing across the road. Idiots! We thought, they are on exercise! But then a Wehrmacht major called across and cried: "That's live ammunition – the Tommies have landed!" We stopped and the battalion commander spoke to us.'[11]

Moeller had already been notified by division that landings had occurred in the Renkum Heath-Heelsum area. He was not too concerned as 'I knew Arnhem and also Oosterbeek quite well, and had taken another look at it only a few days earlier'. History had turned a full circle, because in May 1940 Sergeant Moeller, then commanding an engineer platoon in the SS 'Der Fuhrer' Regiment, had forced a crossing of the Yssel near Arnhem, and had then cleared snipers along the Arnhem, Oosterbeek, Renkum route. He was now to do it again, and in the same direction. 'Well same old routine,' he claimed. 'And it really was like that, only a lot worse than the first time.' At least he was fighting on familiar terrain. Within the hour the first attack went in.

Counter-measures . . .

At 1500 Field Marshal Model appeared at Bittrich's headquarters at Doetinchem and began to put his personal stamp on the battle. Collecting his thoughts during the car journey from his logistic headquarters

SS-Captain Hans Moeller, Commander Pionier Battalion 9 'Hohenstaufen'. (Fuerbringer Collection)

at Terborg, he was ready on arrival to put immediate counter-measures into action.

The Arnhem 'legend' has cast Model in the mould of a monocle-sporting caricature of a German Staff Officer. Believing he had barely escaped capture at the hands of British parachutists while sitting down to lunch in the Hotel Tafelberg, his suitcase with personal belongings is alleged to have been scattered on the hotel steps as he made his breathless departure. Such a view does not accord with the facts.[12] Model may not have been a warm, approachable personality, but he was a sound commander. He did not survive the war and was therefore in no position to refute the more colourful aspects of the Arnhem legend painted by some who did live.

Model was a 'soldier's officer', he knew his men and played on their belief (shared by himself) that if the front could somehow be held, Hitler's 'wonder weapons' may yet achieve a miracle.

Model was regarded as a trouble-shooter – a man with steady nerves in a crisis. Hitler regarded him as the 'fireman of the eastern front'. It was Model's personal allegiance to his Führer that has attracted the odium that clouds a clear perception of his abilities as a military commander. Five times Model stabilised the front after defeats and retreats during his military career, at the Rshew salient in 1942, Orel in 1943, in the Baltic and Galicia in 1944, and on the western front in southern Holland in September 1944. He is alleged to have instilled *Kampf-willen* (resolve to fight) in his soldiers by

personal character and example at the front. Model was a soldiers' officer – he knew his men, and he played on their belief (shared by himself) that if the front could somehow be held, Hitler's 'wonder weapons' may yet achieve a miracle. Strongly attached to his family, and with no close personal friends, he was a very self-contained man, a private person. He destroyed all his personal papers prior to committing suicide in the Ruhr pocket in 1945. His approach to duty was Lutheran. Prussian sense of duty was allied to a strong religious conviction, and this produced an unshakeable self-confidence, whatever the ruin and chaos that surrounded him – in the end all would be God's will. Therefore, no crisis, however serious, could not be overcome. Such traits were unlikely to endear him to his subordinate commanders. Emotion in these instances was irrelevant. A crisis had arisen that required all his personal will and ability to master.[13]

Model confirmed Bittrich's measures, directed that headquarters IISS Corps command the counter-measures now to be enacted in the Arnhem-Nijmegen area, and took the corps directly under command of Army Group B. At 1730 the key operational order, subsequently to dictate the course of the battle of Arnhem, was issued from Bittrich's headquarters. IISS Corps was to attack the enemy immediately and destroy him. Clear divisions were laid down: 9SS were to advance through Arnhem-Oosterbeek and take on the British bridgehead established north of the lower Rhine. 10SS were to take and occupy the Nijmegen bridge, and secure a bridgehead south of the river Waal for subsequent offensive operations. Above all, any link-up between the enemy at Nijmegen and Arnhem was to be prevented.[14]

Model's future intentions to tackle the crisis in southern Holland at army group level now became apparent. Possibly as a result of the captured order, or the same

At 1500 Field Marshal Model appeared at Bittrich's headquarters at Doetinchem. Later photograph, left to right: *Model, Bittrich, Knaust and Harmel. Events were moving fast.*

geographical lines that influenced the Allies, Model divided the affected zone into three sectors, corresponding roughly to the areas of the three Allied divisions.

General Student and the First Parachute Army was given the dual mission of containing the British ground offensive opposite the Maas-Escaut bridgehead, and destroying the 101 Airborne Division now located in the vicinity of Eindhoven. Kampfgruppe Chill, already committed along the Maas-Escaut canal, was to oppose the British ground troops. To deal with the Americans, Model gave Student those elements of 59 Infantry Division (from 15th Army) fortuitously already in transit near Tilburg, and 107 Panzer Brigade. Commanded by Major Freiherr von Maltzahn, 107 Brigade was re-routed from its original task, which had been to oppose First US Army in Aachen.

The job of contesting the 82nd American Division at Nijmegen fell to Wehrkreis VI, the rear echelon German headquarters which controlled the Corps Feldt and 406 (Landesschuetzen) Division. These Wehrkreis units were ordered to destroy the airborne troops along the high ground south-east of Nijmegen, seize and hold the rail and road bridges across the Waal river at Nijmegen, and stand by for continued operations 'in a southerly direction', once the 10SS had arrived. That this was recognised as too big a task for the Corps Feldt alone was revealed by Model's further advice to Wehrkreis VI that he intended shifting corps troops and increments of Fallschirmjaeger troops to Nijmegen, under General der Fallschirmtruppen Eugen Meindl, commander of II Fallschirmjaeger Corps. This would not happen immediately, however, as Meindl's corps was currently re-fitting in the Cologne area.

Stronger forces were to be committed against the British at Arnhem, as IISS Corps was already at hand, and possibly because Model, on the spot, was intimately involved. General Christiansen, the Armed Forces Commander Netherlands, was, in addition to the IISS Corps thrust from the east, given the task of attacking Arnhem from the opposite direction, the north-west and north. 'Division' von Tettau, a collection of regional defence and training bat-

talions quickly thrown together under command of Generalleutnant Hans von Tettau, Christiansen's director of operations and training, was already at his disposal. Bittrich's IISS Corps was also to receive a motorised infantry battalion commandeered from Wehrkreis VI, and the 280th Assault Gun Brigade, re-routed from Aachen.

These intentions were translated into orders by 2315 that night, 17 September. Events were moving fast.

CHAPTER VII

Smashing through the Crust

The regiment . . . sought in vain to re-establish contact with German units in the north towards Eindhoven and in the west – but there was only a wide gap there.

Lieutenant-Colonel von der Heydte, 17 Sep 44

The Kampfgruppe Walther is split in two . . .

In the Neerpelt bridgehead there was wide-ranging comment among the German troops about overflying bomber and transport aircraft. They were uneasy. The fighter coverage had been so extensive that planes would peel off just to engage single despatch riders. Nothing was able to move. Lieutenant Heinz Volz, adjutant of the 1st Fallschirmjaeger Battalion of the Regiment von Hoffmann, described the maelstrom of fire that then unexpectedly descended:

'The front, which had been relatively quiet from about midday, suddenly erupted into a hell, as at 1400 an unearthly crescendo of artillery fire fell on the ring enclosing the bridgehead. For an hour the soil shook time and time again as the defenders were ground down. Captain Brockes was killed by a direct hit from a mortar round on his command post, in a house on the Valkenswaard road. A shell fragment from above penetrated his skull.'[1]

At the same time the Kampfgruppe Walther observed the arrival of strong twin-engined bomber formations which laid a bombing carpet down the Valkenswaard road. A ragged stream of bomb bursts, punctuated by larger calibre explosions, darted rapidly across the positions of the 1st and 3rd Battalions of the Regiment von Hoffmann, and over the village of Borkel where the anti-tank destroyers were hidden. Every single anti-tank gun commanded by the mortally wounded Brockes was knocked out in the initial barrage without firing a shot. Lack of gun tractors had meant that each gun, because it had to be manhandled, had been sited in a vulnerable position. The infantry anti-tank ambush, established as a reserve by the newly-relocated defence platoon, and Major Kerutt's other companies, escaped relatively lightly. Enemy batteries concentrated upon known positions. An SS light battery located rearwards of the Fallschirmjaeger positions was straddled time after time and heavily damaged.

One hour later, Volz recalls, at 1500, the armoured attack began. Attempting to link with the Allied paratroopers who had flown over earlier, armoured vehicles advanced down the road in closely echeloned columns. Lead tanks, tracks squealing, engines racing through rapid gear changes, nosed through the devastation wrought by the supporting fire, spewing clouds of blue-grey exhaust in the air. Shell holes still seeped acrid cordite smoke, as they passed the mutilated remains of Brocke's crews strewn around wrecked guns. The tanks

Lack of gun tractors had meant that each gun, because it had to be manhandled, had been sited in a vulnerable position. (Imperial War Museum)

drove on, steadily gaining momentum, unopposed, down the Valkenswaard road toward Eindhoven. Ahead lay the surviving elements of the Regiment von Hoffmann.

Major Kerutt, the 1st Battalion Commander, had by chance been visiting First Fallschirmjaeger Army headquarters and had been prevented by the air and artillery activity from rejoining his unit. He was not to reach his command post until the middle of the afternoon, just as the first tank attack started.

The Fallschirmjaeger, crouching in fox holes by the roadside, falsely believed they were up against Canadians. However, it made little difference as the leading tanks blundered into the first infantry tank ambushes. According to Lieutenant Volz:

'A large number were knocked out by panzerfausts [bazookas], firing from five to ten metres away. For the first time we were able to impose a decisive block, because the terrain left and right of the road was not suitable for tanks, being sandy and boggy, and probably also thought to be mined. It is certain that a large number of German soldiers were killed here, but unfortunately I do not know their names. Many of our comrades later declared missing also probably disappeared here. The fighting was extremely bitter, and a fox hole sheltering a wounded man can easily be collapsed by a waltzing tank.'

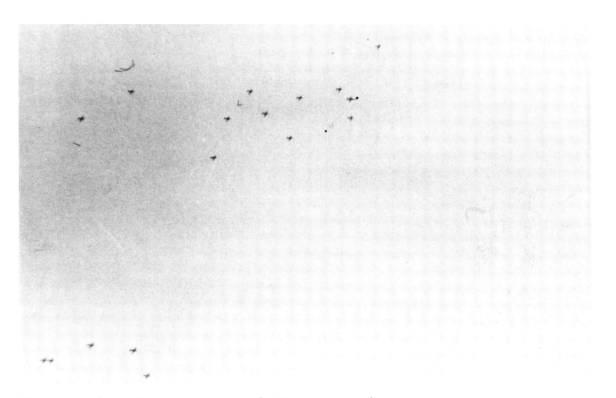

There was wide-ranging comment among the German troops about
overflying bomber and transport aircraft. It made them feel uneasy.
Allied reinforcements as seen from the German front line.
(Bundesarchiv)

The Fallschirmjaeger had struck the rear of the leading squadron of the Irish Guards group and the head of the second one. There was an instantaneous and devastating response. Tank machine guns sprayed the edges of woods and ditches with fire. Typhoon fighter-bomber aircraft were directed on to identified targets.

Even so, German survivors from the tank ambush turned up later at Kerutt's headquarters escorting the British tank crews which had baled out. Lieutenant Schulz's company, relocated when the air activity started, ambushed more British tanks further down the road. Eight tanks and two armoured cars were now fiercely-burning wrecks. Enemy progress was monitored, with columns reported reaching the area just south of Valkenswaard. Although a breakthrough had been achieved, Volz recalls 'the situation was gloomy but not yet hopeless'. Skirmishing continued throughout the night, with forays mounted by small groups of Fallschirmjaeger harassing columns lined up on the road to Valkenswaard. Flashes followed by detonations, shouts and heavy automatic fire punctuated the night, with an eerie glow here and there indicating success.

A few kilometres away, Lieutenant-Colonel von der Heydte, commanding Fallschirmjaeger Regiment 6, was seething. His unit was holding the western wing of the curve in the Neerpelt salient. He had

Major Kerutt was prevented by the air and artillery activity from rejoining his unit. An air sentry perched on the bonnet of a staff car anxiously scans the skies. (Bundesarchiv)

The leading tanks blundered into the first infantry tank ambushes. Here Fallschirmjaeger disable a British armoured car. (Bundesarchiv)

*Lieutenant Volz: 'For the first time we were able to impose a decisive
block . . . ' The damaged vehicles are checked for booty.*
(Bundesarchiv)

*' . . . the terrain left and right of the road was not suitable for tanks,
being sandy and boggy, and probably also thought to be mined.'*

Disabled tanks were pushed to the side of the road. The dead tank commander of '53' is hastily covered with a greatcoat. (Imperial War Museum)

anticipated an armoured breakthrough at this point all along. Bemoaning the Kampfgruppe Walther's lack of adequate signals equipment, and a non-existent logistics support organisation, he had complained to Major Schacht, the battle group's Chief of Staff, the day before:

> 'Instead of selecting the major highway to Valkenswaard as the main defence effort, it was designated as a boundary between units. Consequently nobody really wanted to feel responsible for this road.'

Which was precisely the main avenue of approach to Nijmegen and eventually Arnhem. Instead of co-ordinating responsibility through one agency, 'there were four independent commanders there who

Skirmishing continued throughout the night. A British Cromwell tank disabled, with the dead commander sprawled limply across the turret. (Imperial War Museum)

belonged to three different services of the armed forces'. Von der Heydte's damning condemnation was that if the situation did not change, 'the British armoured break-through simply had to succeed'. Neverthe-less, some depth and cohesion to the defence of the road had been achieved by juggling the relocation of Kerutt's 1st Bat-talion on 16 September.

Adding to von der Heydte's frustration was the total failure of communications with the Kampfgruppe Walther once the action started. Messengers reported that the command post had moved and was nowhere to be found. Fallschirmjaeger Regiment 6 was obliged to swing its left wing back to a forest 100 metres from the road after the British armour had broken through. It held its positions in the face of light probing attacks 'and sought in vain to re-establish contact with German units in the north towards Eindhoven and in the west – but there was only a wide gap there'. The crisis was deepening.[2]

On the other side of the salient, the SS Kampfgruppe 'Richter' witnessed 'the over-rolling' of the defence force on the road with dismay. The Fallschirmjaeger forces attached to them belonging to von Erdmann were also overwhelmed. This presented SS-Captain Richter with a dilemma. Should he attack the flank of the armoured vanguard that had broken through with his scant anti-tank resources, or retire eastwards to avoid being cut off by armoured spearheads already spotted bear-ing down on Hamont? Orders were received in any case to pull back a further bound eastwards to Budel. The mouth of the breakthrough point was enlarging. Streaming back through the woods, the SS-troopers were further depressed by the sight of even more heavy aircraft forma-tions flying over towards Eindhoven.

Richter's Kampfgruppe reached Budel in the late afternoon. 1st and 2nd Companies secured the village entry points, and 3rd Company, little more than a platoon strong, established itself as a reserve jointly located with the command post in the centre of the village. Having been denied rest for 38 hours, observing the steady build-up of Allied strength in the bridgehead, and exhausted and dismayed by their sudden retreat, all ranks snatched what rest they could. This lasted well beyond midnight, until suddenly, at 0430, four English tanks accompanied by infantry roared into the centre of the village, having slipped past the dozing security outposts. Fifteen other tanks bypassed the perimeter and took up positions on either side of the village. Tanks stood between the outlying companies and the command post and reserve. They were trapped. Machine guns and main tank armaments covered all the exit routes. There appeared to be no route out. SS-Lieutenant Heinz Damaske, Richter's adjutant, described the ensuing rout:

'Enemy night raids in such strength had until now been the exception rather than the rule. After the initial panic caused by the tank-shock "Willy's" desire to survive quickly surfaced. The commander and his adjutant as well as the signallers demonstrated by example how to destroy four Sherman tanks in close combat. The battalion was then able, albeit with heavy losses, to flee between and through houses, over walls and through hedges and gardens eastwards clear of Budel. This withdrawal in contact, which had to be conducted without anti-tank cover, lasted until 0930 the following day'.

Three kilometres east of Budel the survivors collected. Only 86 of the original 150 enter-ing the village managed to get away. It was a disaster. Chastened by their experience, the remnants of the Kampfgruppe formed up and retired in good order to Weert.[3]

Self-propelled guns supported by infantry would suddenly emerge and snipe at the Allied spearheads on the road. (Bundesarchiv)

By 1700 the British tank column had penetrated just south of Valkenswaard, here passing one of their number knocked out at the roadside. (Imperial War Museum)

By 1700 the British tank column had penetrated just south of Valkenswaard. The proximity of artillery fire indicated the extent of the advance to German observers. SS-Captain Roestel's assault guns, reduced to 8 Panzerjaeger IV, were still able occasionally, supported by infantry, suddenly to emerge and snipe at the armoured spearheads trundling down the road. Dense vegetation on either side of the road made it difficult for the British to take evasive action, as did ditches, boggy ground and, in places, steep embankments. The height of the trees effectively screened accurate observation for artillery shoots by both sides. Glutinous sandy soil made the off-road going difficult for all types of vehicle. 88-mm flak guns with no tractors fell easy prey to British tanks once they had compromised themselves firing from ambush. Unable to move, their crews were cut down by probing tank machine gun fire and the guns destroyed.

Losing control . . .

First Fallschirmjaeger Army headquarters slowly became aware of the gravity of the situation. Contact with von der Heydte was lost. Kampfgruppe Walther, informed about the magnitude of the airlandings to their rear, were told they could not expect any substantial reinforcement the next day. In the meantime they were ordered to organise a new line of resistance. Fortunately and 'incomprehensibly, the enemy remained relatively quiet south of Valkenswaard during the night of 17–18 September, restricting himself to patrolling'. Attempts were made to salvage something from the débâcle. 'Contact with the Division Erdmann (on the left flank) was to be maintained at all costs.' Von der Heydte re-emerged and established contact with the Kampfgruppe Chill, attempting to adjust and push his positions westward on his side of the breakthrough point. Chill took him

under command on 18 September.[4] Meanwhile, the initial focus of the enemy thrust had been recognised. Colonel von Hoffmann had already been charged with the defence of Eindhoven. This he proceeded now to organise using local *in situ* forces.

The nature of the fighting in and around the Neerpelt bridgehead alternated between savage and chivalrous. One Allied column was ambushed by Kerutt's Fallschirmjaeger in the small village of Schaft east of the Valkenswaard road, as it tried to bypass one of the other German companies defending Borkel nearby. In the ensuing skirmish a wounded English captain was taken prisoner. Later an English ambulance was allowed to approach the Fallschirmjaeger positions. An exchange was offered, the Englishman for a lightly wounded Lieutenant, who, it transpired, may have been from von der Heydte's Fallschirmjaeger Regiment 6. It was accepted. This represented a bargain to the German battalion which had lost so many of its leaders, and now received a welcome reinforcement.

Such chivalrous behaviour was not, however, a feature in the area of the line contested around Moll in the Kampfgruppe Chill's sector. Here Major Oswald Finzel's 1st Battalion Fallschirmjaeger Regiment 2 were being attacked by elements of XII Corps supporting GARDEN. A company messenger in Captain Ortmann's company, H. Sitter, vividly describes the scene as the 15th Scottish Infantry Division attacked their positions. His disjointed notes sent as a letter to Finzel after the war read like a series of film clips:

'Railway embankment with a signalman's cabin which changed hands several times during the course of the day. You Finzel, occupied the battalion command post in a farmhouse. Suddenly a strong enemy attack, you were cut off. Captain Ortmann sent me to you as a messenger. Received machine gun fire *en route*, dashed for cover in a hedgerow, can't get any further. Range to the machine gun is approximately 20 metres, am under continuous fire. Then a German tank rolls by. I hope that it has got you out. Afterwards I see eight to ten paratroopers walking towards the machine gun nest with their hands up, followed by Tommies or Canadians. A brief halt, the machine gun swings around and shoots up all the prisoners. I am powerless, having lost my machine pistol when I dashed for cover to the hedgerow. It is lying a few metres away. I went to reach for it slowly, suddenly " Hands up!" [in English]. I think that's it. Another mortar barrage. My captors take cover. I get my machine pistol. Short bursts of fire, a few enemy less, including the machine gun nest. Able to report back to Ortmann and also report on the killing of the prisoners. Ortmann informs me that you have made it back.'[5]

At 0415 on 18 September the Chiefs of Staff of both First Fallschirmjaeger Army and Army Group B were engaged in an animated telephone conversation. As the operational log of LXXXVIII Corps records, the comment was passed: 'There is no doubt about it, the enemy has broken through.'[6]

Not only was the enemy breaking through, command was losing control. There was contact with the Kampfgruppe Walther and also Heinke, now withdrawing to the eastern side of a corridor gradually taking shape. There was a feeling of helplessness, an inability to cope in the face of such an overwhelming blow. Fallschirmjaeger Regiment 6 withdrew on its own initiative, moving westwards until it made contact with 85 Infantry Division on that side of the corridor. Although the regiment's right

wing rested on the Maas-Scheldt canal, its left wing 'was still dangling in the air', as von der Heydte described it, near the Turnhout-Eindhoven road. Remnants of the Luftwaffe Penal Battalion and another battalion from the Regiment von Hoffmann, separated from the Kampfgruppe Walther, were taken under command. Von der Heydte was ruthless in dealing with some of their hapless commanders. It was the final straw, officers whom he considered incapable were despatched to the rear and replaced by those from his own regiment. Von der Heydte later expressed his reaction to the handling of the crisis, voicing the opinion of his own subordinate commanders.

'The enemy airlandings on 17 September and the breakthrough by the Guards Armoured Division seemed to spread panic among all higher headquarters up to Army level. Neither Corps nor Army were able to provide any information at all on the situation during the first few days; the only order which was repeated time and time again by Army headquarters was not to give up one foot of ground. Airlandings were reported to have occurred almost everywhere; communications and logistics appeared to be largely paralysed.'[7]

LXXXVIII Corps Commander spoke to General Chill at 0852 on 18 September and told him to grip the errant commander of Fallschirmjaeger Regiment 6, as the log reveals:

'The Regiment von der Heydte is to be taken firmly in hand. It was explicitly remarked that Colonel von der Heydte was not to be allowed to exercise any initiative when it came to withdrawing.'[8]

But it was already too late.

Lieutenant-Colonel von der Heydte, the Commander of Fallschirmjaeger Regiment 6.

kenswaard south of Aalst. At 1020 the Kampfgruppe Chill were informed that armoured columns were in front of the village. Around midday the enemy bumped the position. Distinctive crack-and-clunks rang out, as armour-piercing shells tore into the leading armoured cars and Shermans. Clouds of black smoke belched skyward, indicating the limit of the advance. Taking evasive action, following squadrons of tanks bypassed the blocking position. Kerutt's battalion withdrew, still fighting, but forced over on to the eastern side of the corridor. Once again, because of the lack of tow vehicles, the anti-tank guns and many of their crews were left behind.

The road to Eindhoven was now wide open. It fell in any case in the late afternoon of 18 September to American airborne forces. By 1900 the first tanks from the Guards Armoured Division drove on to its cobbled streets amidst the cheers of waving civilians. In the northern suburbs of Eindhoven two 88mm guns attempted to block the passage of the 2nd Battalion 506 Parachute Infantry Regiment from 101 Division. Kampfgruppe Koeppel of 18 Flak Brigade telephoned a running commentary of the last moments of the city's defence:

As this message was being relayed, Major Kerutt managed to form yet another blocking position along the southern edge of Aalst. All that was left were the survivors of the 1st and 3rd Battalions of the Regiment von Hoffmann, a 20mm anti-aircraft platoon, and eleven 75mm anti-tank guns with no tractors. This thin screen was all that barred the British from Eindhoven some 3km away. SS-Captain Roestel's remaining Panzerjaeger IVs were disposed along the flank of the approach from Leende to Val-

'Enemy has penetrated into the north of Eindhoven. Street fighting. Further contact with unit not now possible; the insertion of infantry reinforcements has been ruled out. Anti-tank group "Grunewald" requests further orders from Army . . . [the telephone message was cut off].'[9]

First Fallschirmjaeger Army had now been split in two.

CHAPTER VIII
March! Follow the Sounds of Shooting

We were told that the enemy was where we drew fire from.

SS Battalion Commander

Piercing the left flank . . .

Two brigades of infantry and divisional support troops had arrived with the initial lift of 1st British Airborne Division. Totalling some 8,000 men, half of the teeth arm element comprised 1st Airlanding Brigade, commanded by Brigadier Hicks. His task was to secure the drop-zones around Wolfheze and its environs for subsequent lifts. Lathbury's 1st Parachute Brigade had been ordered to capture the main road and pontoon bridges in Arnhem itself. His battalions, ready to move by 1500, began to leave their respective drop-zones within 1½–2 hours of landing. 1 and 3 PARA were soon confronted by Krafft's SS Battalion and Weber's Luftwaffe Kampfgruppe. Krafft could not be bypassed until late afternoon and early evening. By then some British company groups had penetrated the western suburbs of Arnhem itself.

Under Lieutenant-Colonel John Frost, 2 PARA made better progress. It had moved due south via Heelsum and Heaverdorp to the Lower Rhine. Meeting little opposition, and unaware of their good fortune, Frost's battalion maintained a punishing pace despite heavy loads. Its objective was the Arnhem bridge. Unbeknown to both the enemy and themselves, as they moved along the river they were turning the German left flank.

Other troops were also on the way to the Arnhem bridge. SS-Corporal Rudolf Trapp's weak company of about 50 'Frundsbergers' – 10SS – were pedalling furiously from Deventer to Arnhem. Bicy-

SS-Corporal Rudolf Trapp's company of Panzer-grenadier Regiment 21 of the 10SS cycled from Deventer to Arnhem. (Trapp)

cles had been purloined from the Dutch at pistol point. *'Es geht wieder los!'* ('Here we go again') had been the sigh upon receipt of the inevitable order to get going following the awesome fly-pass over Deventer. With adrenalin in their stomachs, they ate up the miles. As they progressed, their spirits soared; as Trapp remembers, they were young and therefore 'had less fear'. And what was more:

'It was wonderful weather, a sunny day. Morale was high. There were no "Jabos" like there were in Normandy – we felt we could win!'[1]

By the middle of the afternoon the dispersed quick-reaction 'alarm' companies of the 9SS began to collect together. They arrived on foot, bicycles, horse-drawn carts, or in ramshackle cars. Twenty lorries from the Hohenstaufen's transport resources operated a shuttle service, moving companies through Arnhem city centre and out into the western suburbs. They reacted to a simple slogan: 'Follow the sounds of shooting; that is where the front is!' SS-Captain Moeller's Kampfgruppe had arrived in the northern outskirts of Arnhem by 1630.

'There was a lot of confused shouting and running around. Nobody knew what was going on. We were told that the enemy was where we drew fire from.'[2]

SS-Corporal Dombrowski's assault pioneer section was already aware of this. Having passed the St Elizabeth's Hospital on the Utrechtseweg towards Oosterbeek, they had drawn such a volume of fire that they were obliged to take cover. Trucks and half-tracks pulled up sharply and became jammed in the road as the occupants baled out; some, struck by small arms fire, tumbled into the street. Between arrival and dusk the Kampfgruppe Moeller fought with com-

panies of 3 and 2 PARA attempting to fight their way through to the road bridge. Pinned down a few hundred metres west of the hospital in a park area, Den Brink, Moeller was anxious to proceed, but was destined to remain in these same houses for days as the battle for Arnhem raged around him. For the moment he tried to disperse his companies into assault formation and advance. Dombrowski's section, expanded now to 11 or 12 men, moved to the left of Utrechtseweg. As he recalled:

'This was just like a wild west shoot-out. There was no front. Sections and half-sections fought scattered actions against similar size, British groups. There was no discernible line on the English side either.'[3]

Further on, to the right, scores of English paratroopers lay dead in a harvested field, some still wearing parachute harnesses. Dombrowski did not know how they had got there. 'Maybe a glider broke up under fire, or they were more likely caught by German flak.' But he managed to pick up a Mark II sten-gun. 'I only had a pistol at this stage. I clutched at the sten frantically and thought "Thank God I've got a gun!".' It proved unfortunately unreliable during his first actual contact with the enemy, a surprise confrontation with a group of British paratroopers in a garage. Damaged by shell splinters, the cocking mechanism jammed. Luckily he was able to bluff his way. The British, equally aghast, dispirited and tired, surrendered. They were led off to the rear. He recalled the significance of the incident because

'. . . after two or three days it was no longer possible to identify friend or foe from the firing of weapons. Ours fired faster generally than the British. But both sides used each others.'

A German line of sorts belonging to the Kampfgruppe Spindler began to impregnate itself on the side roads leading off Utrechtseweg in Arnhem town centre. (Bundesarchiv)

Dombrowski later managed to secure a real prize – a Sten with a wooden handle. These were much sought after, in preference to their own Schmeisser machine pistol, because the side loading action enabled the weapon to be operated low in the prone position. Sniper head and chest wounds had been a common occurrence on the Russian front until veterans discovered this more favoured alternative. Dombrowski held on to his until almost the end of the war, until the time when ammunition supplies ran out.

Moeller's battalion was unable to advance, and neither could the British. The SS-Captain assessed the difficulties:

'We were deadlocked in this jungle of gardens and mansions, of hedgerows and fences, of flower gardens and vegetable patches, of terraces and pavilions. Utrechtseweg – wide with a deserted tram car – turned into a death zone.'

A German line of sorts impregnated itself on the side roads leading off Utrechtseweg just east of the Den Brink park. Moeller's battalion began to fan out, attempting to bypass the British positions blocking their way. Every initiative became pinned down as the British trying to penetrate his line did likewise. SS-Lieutenant Voss commanding

SS-Captain Moeller: 'There was a lot of confused shouting and running around. Nobody knew what was going on.' The scene directly opposite Arnhem railway station. (Bundesarchiv)

the right forward company extended his men further north until they established contact with the anti-aircraft Kampfgruppe north of the railway, commanded by SS-Lieutenant Gropp. On the left, or southern side, a reconnaissance patrol reached the lower Rhine but failed to detect any enemy.

Then, at about 1800 hours, when the situation appeared to be stabilising, Moeller was startled to hear

'. . . a huge detonation . . . from the banks of the Rhine, and everything shook under its pressure wave. It came from the direction of the railway bridge across the lower Rhine.'

General Bittrich, the Corps Commander, appeared at Moeller's command post shortly afterwards. By then information had been passed on that the railway bridge had been blown. 'But why?' Moeller asked. 'Bittrich had no idea of any plans to that effect either, and was quite concerned about what was going on in our rear!'

An empty train stood abandoned on the northern approach to the railway bridge. The embankment, already damaged by British bombers that morning at 1100, was further strafed by British fighters chasing away Dutch workers attempting to repair it at 1300 hours. Three 20mm cannon manned by a detachment of anti-aircraft gunners guarded the northern end. These men were *Reichsdeutsch*, Germans resident in Holland before the war, not naturalised, but later conscripted. They were nervous after the strafing, and uneasy following the awesome spectacle of the parachute descent now lost to them behind the trees. 'What next?' they thought. The demolition party, an NCO commander and ten men, were billeted in Dutch houses near the southern end. 'Why didn't they blow the bridge before it was too late?' wondered the gunners. But there were no signs of activity.

From Oosterbeek came the unmistakable popping sounds of small arms fire, interspersed with machine gun bursts and the crump of grenades. Small stay-behind groups of German soldiers were trying to delay the British advance. As the gunners continued to watch, three lorries drove by the road on the north side of the river, heading towards the Oosterbeek church. The trucks, carrying German infantry, were halted out of sight, and the occupants taken prisoner by A Company 2 PARA force-marching their way toward the bridge.

Suddenly more firing broke out around the northern railway embankment. Thirteen German stragglers dressed in camouflaged smocks, commanded by SS-Lance-Corporal Helmut Buttlar, burst into view, engaged in a running fight with the vanguard of 2 PARA. They were a mixture of infantry and anti-aircraft gunners from the 10SS Frundsberg Division. Cut off during the retreat from northern France, they were just about to rejoin their comrades, when they had been surprised at lunch by the airborne landings around Oosterbeek. Nine of them reached the railway embankment, having already delayed the British at Oosterbeek-Laag railway station.

Horrified, the German gunners already on the bridge observed almost the whole of Frost's battalion swing into view. With impressive flair and co-ordination a company detached itself from the main body and snaked out toward the bridge. Soon it was in assault formation. The others continued on. This was too much. After a brief exchange of fire the gunners were cut down or fled. As C Company 2 PARA, however, stepped on to the bridge, its main span curled up in the air and collapsed in on itself with a resounding crump. The demolition commander, aided by one of his soldiers, had fired the charge.

Disappointed, 2 PARA pressed on, with that same unhurried pace that misleadingly eats up the miles. 'From now on the real fighting began,' recounted one of its platoon commanders; 'it was a crutch-rot of a march.'[4] There were now only two chances of achieving their mission – get the pontoon bridge or seize the main prize, the Arnhem road bridge.

Buttlar's group withdrew into the park at Den Brink, trying to further delay the force. His section was subsequently wiped out in the fighting for the city, with Buttlar himself being severely wounded.[5]

A few hundred metres to the north, Moeller and Gropp were totally preoccupied with the immediate threat to their front. Down by the lower Rhine a long column of sweating, heavily-laden and determined parachute infantry pushed on, completely missed by the Germans. Eyes glazed with perspiration, they longed to see with every passing bend in the river their target, the Arnhem road bridge.

'The youngsters had not paid sufficient attention' . . . the capture of the Arnhem road bridge

Major General Kussin was responsible as *Stadtkommandant* for the defence of the Arnhem road bridge. Two narrow rivulets of blood had congealed on his gold

Major-General Kussin was responsible as Stadtkommandant *of Arnhem for co-ordinating the measures to secure the road bridge. But by 1730 hours on 17 September he was dead.* (Imperial War Museum)

epaulettes. Lying half-sprawled from his staff car, he had been hit several times in the chest and throat. The staff car, windscreen shattered, was riddled through and through like a sieve with bren-gun bullets. His leather-gloved right hand gripped a revolver, in his left was an unfinished cigarette. Soldiers from 3 PARA continuing the advance into Arnhem glanced curiously inside the car, at him and his two aides, who, as their grotesque attitudes in death suggested, had sought to hide behind each other to avoid the hail of fire. The time was 1730 on 17 September.

Harzer, the 9SS Kampfgruppe commander, had been at Kussin's headquarters thirty minutes before, to tie up defence measures for the bridge, and for his other units now pouring into Arnhem. The Stadtkommandant was not there. General Kussin, he was told, was out, advising and briefing other units. He would be back.

Kussin's Chief-of-Staff, Major Ernest Schliefenbaum, was tasked by Model directly as soon as he learned of the General's death. 'You are responsible that we hold Arnhem,' he told him on the telephone. Schliefenbaum wrote later that he 'felt giddy' at the thought, as the situation was 'a pretty thorough mess-up'.[6] There were two dozen elderly men and teenagers manning light flak around the road bridge, and only a few other security elements under command.

Harzer was understandably concerned. The rapid series of warning orders and counter-measures pushed out by Corps required time to enact. Time was not in generous supply. Graebner, he felt, would probably check the bridge out as he recced toward Nijmegen. He had in any case been promised reinforcements, which he would immediately dispose around the bridge. In the meantime, Kussin's measures would have to suffice. The British were still being held up on the western side of Arnhem. At least, that was what reports suggested.

At 1800, Graebner's Reconnaissance Battalion thundered across the Arnhem bridge, driving towards Nijmegen. The column of 30 armoured cars and half-tracks took some minutes to cross. Clouds of exhaust swirled around the bridge girders as the armoured vehicles, now totally fitted and cleared for action, rumbled past. This would have been an encouragement to the bridge guards, starved of news, – they could at least be visibly reassured that someone had the situation in hand and that counter-measures were being enacted. Graebner had one thought on his mind as he crossed – 'Nijmegen'. What would he find there? Parachute landings had been reported there as well. They had to move quickly. No time was taken to pause and brief the security elements on the bridge. In any case it was not their problem. The Stadtkommandant, having been briefed, would already have taken the necessary measures. But Kussin was dead.

With a few waves the column of camouflaged SS vehicles was across. Whose responsibility therefore was it to guard the bridge? There was a degree of confusion in the minds of all the responsible commanders concerned. An examination of IISS Corps directives, sent out at 1340 and 1730 to cope with the crisis on 17 September, is illuminating.[7] 9SS was initially given the overall responsibility to secure and reinforce the bridge, which, in the interim period, was the Stadtkommandant Arnhem's concern. However, Graebner's Reconnaissance Battalion, having craftily 'conserved' its vehicles, was the first armoured formation ready for action at the disposal of IISS Corps. Bittrich sent it immediately to Nijmegen, which he perceived to be his *Schwerpunkt*, or main focal point in the defence, as he felt the main threat lay with the advancing Allied ground forces in the south. The Frundsberg's Reconnaissance Battalion 10 was therefore offered to the 9SS as compensation for Graebner's removal to Nijmegen. It was formed into the Kampfgruppe 'Brinkmann' and ordered to secure the bridge. This would take longer as they had further to travel, but this was of no immediate consequence, because nobody realised how close Frost's battalion actually was. The responsible unit commanders therefore believed it was either somebody else's task to secure the Arnhem road bridge, or there was already somebody there who could be relieved in time. Frost was to fill this vacuum caused by misconjecture.

Other counter-measures further confused the situation. The Battalion 'Euling', formerly of the 9SS, had in the past week been transferred in its entirety to the 10SS. It was ordered to cross the Arnhem bridge in order to reinforce the Nijmegen garrison. Supplementary 'alarmed' quick-reaction forces, such as Trapp's 3rd Company of Panzergrenadier Regiment 21, were also racing for the Arnhem bridge. All these units, on arriving at different intervals at both ends of the bridge, were to encounter an unexpected British presence. The stultifying effect of these misdirected counter-measures was to ensure that Frost's 2 PARA was to be firmly established by morning.

Paradoxically, as soon as Graebner's column had cleared the bridge – its passage also observed by the approaching British – it appeared to be deserted. A Dutch police constable van Kuijk claims he strode across it at 1930 without seeing anybody.[8] This is not surprising, as the defenders listening to the sounds of approaching battle 2 kilometres away would have been at full battle readiness, manning their bunkered positions.

Karl Ziebrecht, the Commander of the 1st Company 10SS Reconnaissance Battalion, was on the move with his armoured cars – wheeled vehicles armed with 20mm cannon. His destination was the Arnhem bridge. Bittrich, the corps commander, had been shocked at the scale of the airborne landings. 'Christ!' he said, 'this is a huge airborne operation, we need to look further afield.' Otto Paetsch, acting commander of the 10SS in Harmel's absence, instructed SS-Captain Brinkmann to split his reconnaissance battalion initially, and cover the east side of the Rhine as well as Emmerich and Wesel. Ziebrecht's company received the order to recce the approaches to the Arnhem road bridge. He arrived at dusk, just as A Company 2 PARA attempted a *coup-de-main* attack. It was 2000 hours. Ziebrecht's armoured cars immediately came under fire. Uncertain what was going on, they returned fire, withdrew, and radioed Paetsch on what they had seen.

The bunker guards were suddenly jolted into action. As SS-Colonel Harmel later assessed: 'The youngsters had not paid sufficient attention. They had not expected Frost to get there so soon – and he surprised them.' Instead of regularly patrolling the bridge itself, the inexperienced guards had preferred the safety of their bunkers. This was to cost them their lives as the first PIAT projectiles bored home. Cocooned within, they had not been in a position to detect the angle of approach, down by the river, of Frost's vanguard force. Streets soon

began to echo with the sharp crack of small arms fire and the crash of explosions. 20mm cannon fire boomed out, reverberating around the surrounding buildings. Momentary flashes followed by bangs produced a din confusing to all. Nobody knew for certain who was firing and where it was coming from.

At the same time Euling's 10SS battalion arrived at the northern end of the bridge, intent on crossing to Nijmegen. His leading company immediately became embroiled in the fire fight. Totally perplexed, the troopers fought back, wondering what on earth was going on.

Rudolf Trapp's weak 3rd Company of the Frundsberg's Panzer-grenadier Regiment 21 also approached from the northwest. Having pedalled furiously on their bicycles all the way from Deventer, they arrived at dusk. 'We abandoned our bicycles on the northern outskirts of Arnhem, and made our way to the bridge on foot.' They soon realised they were moving directly behind a British unit – 2 PARA. Trapp recalls seeing 'scattered articles of British equipment with dead British and German soldiers as we approached'. Stealthily, his company moved toward the bridge along Ryn Kade on the lower Rhine road.

'It must have been about 2000, and it was getting dark. You could make out the outline of the bridge in the gathering dusk. We realised a front was forming as we approached. Carefully we advanced down the street, darting from house to house, using the facades as cover.'[9]

The first exchanges of fire occurred in the area of the church, 'which was later to catch fire'.

On the bridge British PIAT rounds finally silenced the bunker resisting at the northern end. A flame-thrower came into action, casting an eerie and diabolical light

Trapp recalls seeing 'scattered articles of British equipment with dead British and German soldiers' as they approached the Arnhem bridge, following 2 PARA's advance. (Bundesarchiv)

Lieutenant Joseph Enthammer, whose artillery 'V2' unit was based only a few thousand metres north of the bridge, was concerned. The situation since sighting the first 'snowflakes', signifying the arrival of the parachutists, was unclear. Troops had been hurriedly assembled and marched off in the direction of the landing–zones, but not his. 'We were not drawn into the fighting,' he remembers, 'because of the nature and importance of our specialist arm of the service.' Intermittent sounds of skirmishing, including machine gun fire, drew nearer. Between 1900 and 2000 hours the unit, numbering some 120 men, was ordered to retreat to Emmerich. Enthammer, placed in charge of a rear-guard group of 17 soldiers, was not able to depart until 2100. Setting off in a truck,

'. . . we couldn't have travelled more than 300 to 400 metres before British soldiers stepped out and halted the lorry in the street. What could we do? We were virtually unarmed except for a few rifles. It came as a complete surprise. The sergeant in charge of the paratroopers kicked open one of the doors of a terraced house and hastened us inside. We were taken to the first floor where we spent the first night. The Sergeant (who I later discovered came from Vienna, and could speak German) treated us well. "Consider yourselves lucky you were not captured by the Poles," he said. "A Polish battalion jumped with us and said they would not take any prisoners."'[10]

on the facades of the houses beneath the ramp. There was a huge explosion and screams on the main span, as an ammunition hut engulfed by cascades of flaming petrol disintegrated.

Trapp's men beneath the level of the bridge ramp were searching houses for their elusive enemy. He remembers 'being fired at from all directions'. They started to lose their first dead and wounded. Short of everything, 'we picked up weapons from the dead British'. This was going to be no easy task. 'The British had taken up positions in houses, and it was damned difficult to get them out of there.'

Enthammer did not consider himself lucky at all. After all, his unit had barely finished launching V2 rockets against London. He required little imagination to discern what the 'reaction would be if that leaked out'. 2 PARA had won the race to the bridge.

SS-Corporal Trapp was also beginning to realise the situation was far from rosy:

'There was a tram, either within or on the road leading into the Market Place, totally destroyed – shot to pieces. Here we recovered a badly injured woman, and some other civilians and British wounded. Later we received some panzerfausts and ammunition. Up until then we had had to replenish using British weapons and ammunition.'

German vehicles, unaware that the British were already firm at the north end of the bridge, attempted to cross during the night. Three lorries exploded on the northern ramp as they attempted to force a passage, after coming under fire. The occupants baled out, some, in flames, were cut down in the blinding light produced by the burning debris. Wreckage now blocked the bridge as the British fortified the houses around the northern ramp. The 10SS would have to find an alternative method of crossing the lower Rhine to reach Nijmegen.

All the German commanders had been aware of the significance of the Arnhem bridge. All assumed somebody else was dealing with it. Eventually so many different units became embroiled, that it was to take the entire night to sort out and co-ordinate measures for its recapture. SS-Colonel Heinz Harmel, the divisional commander of the 10SS, was to lament after the war:

'If only Graebner had left a few soldiers behind to reinforce the bridge security – then it would have been a different story! Graebner had been far too certain of himself. He was totally preoccupied with what he might find in Nijmegen.'[11]

This was to be the supreme irony of the battles for the two most important bridges to be secured during MARKET-GARDEN. Whoever gained one, in the moment of victory lost the other. Success in both in- stances was therefore transitory. In any case the future of 1st British Airborne Division was more dependent upon what happened on the Waal, rather than on the lower Rhine.

The race for the Waal bridges, Nijmegen, the night of 17–18 September . . .

As news spread in Nijmegen about air- borne landings south of the city, Colonel Henke, commanding a spare Fallschirm- jaeger Training Regiment staff head- quarters, was ordered to co-ordinate the necessary measures to safeguard the two bridges crossing the Waal in Nijmegen. Henke 'alarmed' all in situ local forces and took them under command. Kampfgruppe 'Henke', however, had neither the troops or equipment resources to defend the city satis- factorily. There were three companies of the Ersatz Battalion 6 from Wehrkreis VI, a company of the Hermann Goering Training Regiment – which had been in transit retreating northwards – and an NCO school which had already been positioned as bridge security. In addition there were Henke's regimental staff, some reservists and other troops who had been responsible for guard- ing the railway station and sidings. It was a force numbering some 750 men. Flak bat- teries sited to provide anti-air coverage were adjusted so that they could perform a dual anti-tank ground role.

Nijmegen was a city covering 5 to 6 km of urban sprawl. Only limited sectors could be covered. Henke decided therefore to con- centrate his forces in two bridgeheads south of the road and rail bridges. They were diffi- cult objectives to secure, because the Waal river is nearly 300 metres wide at this point.

A string of defended early-warning out- posts was established at the southern edge of the city, manned by small sections of 8 to 10 soldiers. Two traffic circles 1,000 metres south-east and south-west of the bridges – the Kaizer Karel Plein and Kaizer Lodewijk Plein – provided the initial focal points for the defence. Strong points were disposed around the bridges themselves, and established in the small village of Lent opposite on the north bank of the Waal, controlling access and providing observation over both bridges. Important buildings such as the Post Office were also occupied and fortified.

Henke's soldiers were understandably nervous. There was no firm information, apart from initially exaggerated reports of the geographical spread of the airborne landings. The Ersatz Battalion from Wehrkreis VI pessimistically radioed its headquarters at 406 Division that there had been

'. . . enemy airlandings around Zyfflich and Groesbeek. Nijmegen detachment surrounded, support urgently requested.'

Major Rasch, the adjutant to the commander of 406 Division, was completely taken aback. 'It hit us like a bombshell,' he later wrote, when further reports clarified the extent and strength of the airlandings. Rasch surmised 'the three companies in Nijmegen must be regarded as write-offs; no more reports were ever received'.[12]

During the afternoon and early evening of 17 September there were no contacts with enemy units in Nijmegen. The 82nd (US) Airborne Division, fully occupied with seizing its initial objectives, did not send a patrol into the city until 1830 hours, and this did not report until the following morning.[13] During the first afternoon Bittrich, the commander of IISS Corps, decided to send the bulk of the Kampfgruppe Frundsberg – a brigade strength battle group – to defend Nijmegen. This mission was his Schwerpunkt, or focal point of effort. Allied ground forces must

be prevented from moving up the corridor to link up with the British Airborne division at Arnhem. This could then be destroyed at leisure, as it had clearly overreached itself. Kampfgruppe 'Reinhold', with the 10SS Engineer Battalion attached, was to provide the vanguard. It was spearheaded by the Battalion Euling, which unexpectedly became enmeshed in the fighting to force a passage over the Arnhem bridge. Only its leading elements were, however, pinned down. SS-Captain Euling, its commander, well aware of the importance of his task to reach the Waal at best speed, displayed some initiative and turned his vehicles around. They drove east out of Arnhem, seeking an alternative route.

SS-Captain Viktor Graebner, the 30-year-old Commander of the Hohenstaufen's Reconnaissance Battalion, reached Elst, 9km north of Nijmegen, at about 1900 hours. In order to fulfil his mission of clearing Betuwe – the island – between Arnhem and Nijmegen, he dispersed his column on either side of the main road. Racing through villages and side roads, groups of armoured half-tracks sought out units of enemy airlanded forces, but found nothing. Graebner himself radioed back 2 kilometres south of the Arnhem bridge that there was no sign of enemy activity. The column re-formed and gathered speed, driving toward Nijmegen. To their relief the approaches to the bridges were already occupied by Henke's Kampfgruppe. Much of what subsequently happened is based upon conjecture supplemented by fragmentary reports.

Graebner left some half-tracks mounting 75mm anti-tank guns in Elst. These, in addition to security, provided a radio relay between 9SS Division in Arnhem and himself. He was, however, by command of Harmel's 10SS Division to whom he was attached, under orders to remain in Nijmegen. Graebner liked to use his initiative and could be impetuous. He had probably been briefed by Henke's men on the Nijmegen bridge that there had not as yet been contact with the enemy. At the same time, at 2000 hours, the 1st Company of the 10SS Reconnaissance Battalion was involved in a heavy exchange of fire on the Arnhem road bridge. They had radioed Paetsch – Harmel's deputy standing in during his absence – that the bunkers on the bridge had fallen, and the enemy was already firm in a strong position.[14] One of Graebner's half-track recce groups was also in action at the southern end of the bridge, denying Frost's 2 PARA the chance to cross.[15] Fire was being exchanged with houses along the northern bank. With a crisis developing in his rear, and nothing happening to his front in Nijmegen – apparently secured – Graebner turned back with the bulk of his column, and began his final drive toward Arnhem. The defence of the Waal bridges had inadvertently become Henke's sole responsibility again.

Nine hours after the airlandings around Groesbeek, the first burst of automatic fire shattered the eerie stillness of Nijmegen by night. It was 1000 hours. The fire had come from the area of the traffic circle nearest to the rail bridge, the Kaizer Karel Plein. Two companies of the 1st Battalion 508 Parachute Infantry Regiment from the 82nd (US) Airborne Division were conducting a reconnaissance 'in force' into Nijmegen's southern suburbs. A and B companies were trying against hope to seize the bridge by a coup de main attack, which Dutch Resistance members suggested may be possible, as they were only lightly defended. This was indeed the truth. But as A Company fanned out to attack, a motor-convoy screeched noisily to a halt on the other side of the traffic circle. Tailboards crashed down with a clatter, followed by urgent voices, bumps and scrapings as the SS-troopers in the back urgently dismounted, spurred on by the sounds of gunfire.[16] Lit by tracer rounds rapidly feeling across the circle, and by the flashes of grenades and automatic weapons, the camouflaged troopers fanned out and immediately and savagely counter-attacked. In the confusion and darkness and ear-splitting noise it became virtually impossible to distinguish friend from foe. Fire opened up from every conceivable direction. The American A Company, just on the point of retiring, was only able to stabilise its position when its sister B Company arrived.

About 400 metres north-east of the traffic circle stood the Post Office. According to Dutch civilian reports, it housed the main demolition mechanism for the bridge. Taking advantage of the darkness and confusion the building was reached and stormed by American paratroopers. Henke's men within fought back, but were overrun, enabling the 'control mechanism' to be destroyed. A fresh SS counter-attack, however, reoccupied the surrounding area, marooning the hapless paratroopers inside. They were to remain under siege for a further three days. The Americans, unable to push through and heavily engaged in a maze of unknown streets, withdrew in order to reorganise.

The German defenders took advantage of the lull and hurriedly attempted to improve their positions before dawn. They were revitalised. There was some hope. A new situation had emerged. 10SS Panzer Division had arrived – the race appeared to have been won.

CHAPTER IX

Arnhem. The Pendulum Swings

The British have not got us yet, and . . . if we have already gone under, then we won't make it too easy for them.

SS Battle Group Commander

The formation of the eastern block: the Kampfgruppe Spindler . . .

Krafft's SS Training and Replacement Battalion 16 began withdrawing through the woods east of Wolfheze, north-eastwards towards the Ede-Arnhem railway line. From there they followed a track alongside the railway line moving in an easterly direction towards Arnhem. It was dark, 2130 hours on 17 September. Lit by two blazing ammunition trucks, the convoy moved laboriously through the trees, attracting intermittent British fire. Krafft was well satisfied, having beaten back a number of attempts to penetrate his positions. He felt, as his later report indicates, that he had covered himself with glory.[1] Only light casualties were sustained by mortar rounds which sporadically burst in the trees at points near the column. His battalion had indeed temporarily blocked the progress of two British Parachute Battalions (1 and 3 PARA), but not for as long as he thought. Much of the historic credit for this particular action may have been prematurely ascribed to Krafft. Frost's 2 PARA had already slipped by on the left, and 3 PARA were already beyond and outflanking Krafft when he began his retreat. A more

substantial line, including some armoured vehicles, had stopped this growing stream of British units entering the western suburbs of Arnhem. This was the SS Kampfgruppe 'Spindler'.

Krafft noted in his report at 2230 hours: 'We meet the battle group "Spindler" from the SS Panzer Division "Hohenstaufen" on the Ede-Arnhem road.' This Kampfgruppe, formed only a few hours before, contributed more than any other identifiable formation to the defeat of the 1st British Airborne Division. Its full significance in the battle of Arnhem has yet to be fully assessed.

During the afternoon of 17 September SS-Lieutenant-Colonel Spindler was appointed commander of various 'alarm' or quick-reaction companies belonging to the 9SS. Its *ad hoc* organisation characterised all the German Kampfgruppen that fought in the battle of Arnhem.[2] Before the battle was finished, 16 separate units were to come under command at some time or other. At 34, Ludwig Spindler was the commander of the Hohenstaufen's armoured artillery regiment. He was an experienced officer, who led by example and was greatly respected by his men. Only a strong personality could have kept such a multi-various formation like his together with such impressive results. Spindler had been decorated with the Iron Cross in both

SS-Lieutenant-Colonel Spindler, at 34 and a hardened campaigner, was the Commander of the Hohenstaufen's Artillery Regiment. He was to lead the Kampfgruppe Spindler which played a decisive role in the battle of Arnhem. (Fuerbringer Collection)

the Polish and Russian campaigns, and was awarded the German Cross in Gold following Normandy. A hardened campaigner, he was to apply his talents to good effect.

At 1730 hours the newly-formed battle group was ordered to attack from east to west along the main thoroughfares from Arnhem town centre to Oosterbeek. On reaching the western edge of Arnhem, its task was to institute a block stretching from the pivot point in the north, manned by Krafft's SS battalion on the Ede-Arnhem road, south to the lower Rhine.

It is interesting to review the speed with which the disparate and dispersed elements of the Kampfgruppe came together. The initial core was provided by Spindler's own armoured artillery regiment, reduced by casualties in Normandy to two companies of infantry numbering some 120 men without guns. They were based in Dieren, 8 or 9 kilometres from Arnhem. Kampfgruppe command was based upon his own regimental headquarters. Gathering in widely scattered units presented problems. There was as yet no identifiable enemy front. Spindler's adjutant, SS-Lieutenant Steinbach, has described 'the thankless task of gathering small fighting groups and of establishing liaison'. Driving around looking for the commander of the Reconnaissance Battalion, Graebner, he 'parked in front of a large building with revolving doors'. Steinbach continued:

> 'SS-Corporal Mayer, who is accompanying me, gets off to see what's going on inside the building. Entering by the revolving doors, he flew out again in the same instant. "The lower floor is full of Englishmen!" he shouts, and leaps into the *Schwimmwagen* [an amphibious car]. My driver Oelschlaeger accelerates and we rush off.'[3]

Spindler's artillery companies joined those of the Kampfgruppe Moeller, the remnants of the Hohenstaufen's engineer battalion already fighting in the western outskirts of Arnhem. Here some 100 assault-pioneers, equipped with a few armoured half-tracks, were organised into three weak skeletal companies. Moeller related how,

> '. . . starting at dusk, the forces of the Artillery Regiment infiltrated forward into my sector and extended the line, particularly to the left, so that an almost seamless front line was

established to deny the enemy a further advance.'

Moeller had already linked up with the 87-man force of the anti-aircraft battery under SS-Lieutenant Gropp. By midnight Krafft's SS battalion, numbering 300 men, and some heavy weapons were also taken under command. Spindler was obliged to conduct a 'fight as you arrive' war. It was a broad, almost indistinguishable front line, formed by the 'no go' areas established between the mix of British and German fighting groups manœuvring to gain advantage. By the middle of the night Spindler had achieved the first part of his mission. An irregular block of strong points had been established, from Krafft on the Ede-Arnhem road in the north-west, through Gropp on the railway cutting, south via Moeller, from the railway junction to Utrechtseweg. Spindler's artillery companies covered the gap from here south to the lower Rhine. Additional units were used to reinforce and extend these focal points. These included some *Reichsarbeitsdienst* (pioneers) who arrived without weapons or equipment, and had to be armed from captured British stocks.

The influx of so many diverse and inexperienced platoons and companies meant that the Kampfgruppe had to be restructured. To achieve this, two more Kampfgruppen were formed from within Spindler's original orbit. One focused around the remnants of the Hohenstaufen's 'tank-destroyer' battalion, Panzerjaeger Abteilung 9. This was named after its commander SS-Captain Klaus von Allworden. The other was formed from the original Panzer Regiment 9, led by one of its previous company commanders, SS-Lieutenant Harder. Kampfgruppe Harder consisted of three infantry companies, one of dismounted tank-crewmen, another of fitters and logistic personnel, and the third from a hastily formed naval unit. There may also have been three 'Panther' Mark V

SS-Captain Klaus von Allworden, Commander of the Kampfgruppe von Allworden, infantry formed from the dismounted tank destroyer crews of Panzerjaeger Abt. 9 of the 9SS Hohenstaufen. (Fuerbringer Collection)

panzers, but these were quickly lost early in the fighting. It was a totally improvised fighting force.

Kampfgruppe von Allworden had 120 men, previously armoured self-propelled gun crews, supplemented by naval personnel sufficient to form three infantry companies. There were in addition two self-propelled (SP) guns and some 75mm towed PAK anti-tank guns. Von Allworden's 'Panzerjaeger' had been billeted the furthest away from the landing-zones – 21km, just south of Apeldoorn. Even so, part of it, including the two SPs were in action along the Dreyenseweg, north of Arnhem, during the late afternoon of 17 September. This force arrived in time to block 1 and 3 PARA trying to bypass Krafft. They were later taken under command of the Wehrmacht Kampfgruppe 'Bruhns' when it arrived at the same location.

SS-Corporal Alfred Ziegler, a despatch rider with von Allworden, remembers the initial success that the Kampfgruppe's blocking action had along the Dreyenseweg during the first afternoon following the landings:

'Do you remember the famous photograph of the dead paratroopers by the six-kilometre Arnhem stone?[4] They were killed by us lying in ambush in the woods. We were told first of all to let the British through, and then we opened up from all directions and cut the first lot down. There must have been 30 to 40 prisoners. They were so beaten and submissive that it only needed one man to march them off to the rear. We were not too impressed by this lot. They were completely surprised. I ask you, they came marching straight down the road in company file! What a nonsense! We were so few! They should have taken a route through the trees because it was a truly macabre mistake. Perhaps they were too arrogant or cocksure; maybe they

This photograph of the dead paratroopers lying by the six-kilometre Arnhem stone appeared in the German propaganda magazine Signal, *as part of an article describing 'as it really was'. The reporter, Ziegler believes, was subsequently killed in Oosterbeek.*

were determined to get to Arnhem first to demonstrate what they could do.'[5]

Attempting to exploit their success, the Panzerjaeger attacked down the Ede-Arnhem road towards the landing zones. The advance was supported by a towed 40mm gun and a Jagdpanzer IV SP mounting a 75mm gun. 'Practically every man in the unit had an MG 42,' Ziegler remembers, 'which we had picked up in the retreat from France. We possessed a terrific fire power as a result.' The attack petered out; but the line, periodically reinforced by some of Graebner's reconnaissance half-tracks, could not be pierced by the lightly-armed airborne troops.

In the centre of Arnhem a second German blocking line began to form, attempting to seal off the route already penetrated by Frost. This secondary obstacle, manned by the SS-Kampfgruppe Harder, supplemented the main front forming in the western suburbs of Arnhem, 2,000 metres further west. Harder used a natural north–south gap between buildings running from the railway station on the high ground in central Arnhem, south via the Nieuwe and Roermonds Plein, down to the lower Rhine. He was now able to deny access to the bridge 800 metres away to the east. Frost's 2 PARA was now completely cut off. Despite the thickening opposition, and ever-increasing casualties, 1st Parachute Brigade attempted to punch through.

The German blocking line, reinforced by heavily armed armoured half-tracks, could not be pierced by the lightly armed airborne troops. Here 20mm cannon engage paratroopers in the vicinity of the Dreyenseweg at point-blank range.

'His desperate attacks were repelled time after time.' The aftermath of such an engagement on the Dreyenseweg.

At 2400 hours on 17 September Spindler radioed divisional headquarters that he had reached the western edge of Arnhem town centre against strong resistance. Now he was going over to the defensive to block any further British advances. Liaison with Krafft, he announced, had been established, and his unit taken under command. A number of resistance nests had already been overcome, but the general situation was still unstable. Despatch riders were being shot off motorcycles, and messages needed armoured vehicles. British paratroopers, when beaten back, were not giving up, but simply melting away into the homes of the civilian population.

The main pressure was on the outer 'front' manned by the bulk of Spindler's forces. Moeller's Engineer Kampfgruppe in the centre formed a breakwater, around which successive British attacks ebbed and flowed during the night and early morning. Moeller observed how

'. . . again and again the enemy tried with great determination to break through our lines. His desperate attacks were repelled time after time with the same resolution that characterised the fighting that raged from house to house – from garden to garden, yes, even from flat to flat, man against man . . . The engineer battle group stood firm against all attacks. Around 1000 hours the paratroopers slackened their momentum. They had suffered great losses in men and material, and we had been shown we were up against a very strong and determined opponent. We permitted them the chance to recover their wounded as well as dead and wounded civilians. Then it was quiet in our sector.'

Moeller's men may well have gained a respite,

'. . . but it was not to take very long before it started further to the left with Spindler's men. It was quite obvious they were probing the front for a soft spot, but their attacks failed there also, withering in the well-aimed fire of the Waffen-SS. They had not succeeded in breaking through, much less, they had not even gained a single metre of ground. The fighting had been devastating on both sides – now the war was catching its breath.'[6]

The *Sperrlinie*, or blocking line, that the Kampfgruppe Spindler instituted on the western approaches into Arnhem during the night of 17–18 September was to affect the outcome of the battle of Arnhem decisively. The pendulum of success appeared to be swinging in the German favour. Eight hours before, the unit had not even existed. By dawn eight separate formations had already come under command with more to follow.[7] All the other scattered units in the locality were taken up and included in the line. Spindler's Kampfgruppe was now the focus of resistance, with the task of preventing further reinforcements from reaching Frost's 2 PARA on the Arnhem road bridge.

Western forces. The formation of the Kampfgruppe von Tettau . . .

As SS-Colonel Hans Lippert gazed open-mouthed at the aircraft stream thundering toward Arnhem during that first afternoon, he 'knew then with certainty that the SS NCO School "Arnheim" would be employed against the airlanded enemy'. He waited hours for information and the anticipated call to action. Every conceivable type of Dutch vehicle, including bicycles, was impounded for the expected move. But nothing happened. Companies had been ordered to 'stand to', but still they received no call to action. Lippert was seething with impatience.

'I waited constantly for our committal through the High Command Netherlands. Still the stream of aircraft continued without interruption. Everybody certainly knows that the success of an airborne landing is decided in the first 24 hours!'

By 1800 he had given up hope of any likely committal. Then at 1900, six hours after the first landings, he received word to report with his unit to von Tettau's headquarters at Grebbeberg. His first impression on arrival 'of this improvised staff was of an unholy cock-up, with panic reigning'. General-leutnant von Tettau greeted him with the words: 'Now we're in the shit, we're finished.' Lippert's response was: 'Herr General, firstly the British have not got us yet, secondly, if we have gone under, then we won't make it too easy for them.'[8]

Lippert was being slightly unkind. General Hans von Tettau, the 56-year-old Commander Training in the Netherlands, was not totally inexperienced, having already commanded the 24th Infantry Division in

SS-Colonel Hans Lippert gazed open-mouthed as the aircraft stream thundered toward Arnhem during that first afternoon. (Imperial War Museum)

Russia. He had neither the forces or operational staff and resources available to handle this crisis that had been suddenly thrown into his lap. Tettau's conduct of operations over the next few days were to reveal that he might lack charisma and the personal touch with soldiers, but he was able to weld together a more disparate command than Spindler's, operating on the opposite side of Arnhem. The General did display some antipathy towards SS units under his command.[9] It is possible he already felt the war was lost, putting himself immediately into conflict with committed National Socialists like Lippert who were energetically seeking counter-measures.

(Interestingly, after the battle, SS-Captain Krafft was to bypass his superior von Tettau, when he submitted his glowing post-combat report directly to Himmler.) The failure of the July plot against Hitler had created some peripheral difficulties between the Wehrmacht and SS, although these were generally personal enmities between commanders, rather than between the rank-and-file in the field.

Von Tettau had been commanding the equivalent of seven 'scratch' battalion formations in a screen along the river Waal when the call to action came.[10] These consisted of SS training units, *Schiffstamm*, or naval manning companies, and *Fliegerhorst*,

General Hans von Tettau, Commander of the Kampfgruppe von Tettau, advancing on Arnhem from the west.

eventually delayed reaching Arnhem. Consequently, little was done until reconnaissance could offer a clear picture. Krafft's SS battalion was under command and already in action, but disappeared shortly from the order of battle when its location dictated it should sensibly come under command of the 9SS Kampfgruppe.

The Dutch SS-Surveillance Battalion 3, commanded by the 46-year-old SS-Captain Paul Anton Helle, was the first unit under command of von Tettau to make effective contact with the British on the western side of the landing zones. They were also one of the more incompetent and inexperienced. Initial probes were little more than a charade. In the past the band had generally been the battalion quick-response unit, 'crashed out' to pick up shot-down Allied airmen. It arrived first in commandeered lorries at about 1700 and proceeded to recce the western woods bordering Ginkel heath on the Ede-Arnhem road. Waiting in ambush was a platoon of the 7th Kings Own Scottish Borders (KOSB). Drum-major Sakkel commanding the bandsmen was the first to be cut down; he fell, mortally wounded. Having encountered a larger force than expected, the shocked musicians fled, many of the young Dutchmen taking the opportunity to desert *en route*. 4th Company, commanded by Bartsch, then arrived, having grabbed the battalion's transport resources before the other companies had assembled. At 2100 they moved off. They too were allowed to approach close to the British positions in the dark before being suddenly silhouetted by flares and mercilessly flailed by KOSB gunfire. These British glider troops were responsible for securing the Ginkel heath drop-zone. 3rd Company, commanded by SS-Lieutenant Hink, was simply inserted to the right of Bartsch on arrival and suffered the same fate. The piecemeal and uncoordinated committal of Helle's battalion was a complete failure. In total darkness, over unreconnoitred ground,

converted Luftwaffe infantry battalions, as well as some artillery men operating as infantry without guns.

As in most other locations, total confusion reigned after the landings around Wolfheze and Oosterbeek. Numerous incoming reports 'told of further enemy airlandings at Eindhoven and Nijmegen, but also Dordrecht, Tiel, Utrecht and Veenendaal'.[11] As there were no reserves, the geographical spread of the reported landings confounded a decisive or logical response to the threat. Some units, such as the 2nd Battalion Sicherheits Regiment 26, upon being moved to counter the phantom – yet reported – landing at Veenendaal were the Germans could do little more than await the onset of daylight.

As von Tettau was subsequently to record in his post-combat report, it soon became clear that the reports of airlandings at Utrecht, Tiel, Dordrecht and Veenendaal were wrong. 'These places had only been flown over.'[12] IISS Corps had already identified the main landing areas at Nijmegen and Arnhem. Army Group B directed von Tettau to attack from the 'west and north'.[13] The General realised that 'countermeasures could now concentrate solely on the airlandings north-west of Arnhem'. To achieve this strong forces were removed from the Waal screen front and moved to Arnhem, and some demolition guards were left at bridges and ferry sites. Lippert's SS NCO School had now been expanded to regimental size. One of its battalions, commanded by SS-Captain Schulz, was ordered to Grebbeburg; the remaining two, led by SS-Captains Mattusch and Oelkers, were to follow as soon as practical. Naval Manning 'Schiffssturmabteilung' 10, reinforced by other naval detachments from Battalions 6 and 14, and an artillery battalion acting as infantry (formed from Artillery Regiment 184) were ordered to begin clearing the forests and woods east of Wageningen, bordering the landing-zones. Warning orders were issued and reconnaissance undertaken in preparation for a west to east advance beginning at dawn.

At 0400 on 18 September High Command Netherlands promised further units to reinforce those already withdrawn from the Waal line. Six further Kampfgruppen, brought together from a hastily formed reserve of four to five battalions, were assembled and despatched – stiffened with an additional company of tanks. They included only one effective veteran unit, the SS combat group 'Eberwein'; others included the Training and Replacement Regiment 'Hermann Goering', and a Police-School battalion provided by Waffen-SS High Command.[14]

On paper the measures appeared effective; on the ground reality did not present such a well-organised picture. SS-Officer-Cadet 'Rolf' Lindemann, a Leningrad veteran, commanding a mortar section in Lippert's Regiment, vividly recalled the move to Oosterbeek, via Leerdam-Rhenen and Wageningen:

'We didn't see the drop, but we were "alarmed" – called out. It took two days for the company to arrive and assemble complete in Oosterbeek and Arnhem. Transport was sparse. At

SS-Junker 'Rolf' Lindemann commanding a section in the SS Unteroffizierschule 'Arnheim', who likened the advance of German reinforcements on Arnhem to Napoleon's retreat from Moscow. (Lindemann)

first we had a couple of wood-burning trucks which we requisitioned from civilians. These soon broke down because nobody knew how to operate them.'

They got moving, but not without problems. He observed with a wry sense of humour that

'. . . on Sunday we took over two fire brigade tenders in the village of Leerdam. One was large complete with ladders, the other smaller. This became the transport for the support weapons platoon, the rest moved by bicycle. Some of the company were already in action when we arrived perched on these fire brigade vehicles. We came under fire as we unloaded, but not effectively. I then had to travel back and pick up the rest. The mortar ammunition vehicle and the bicycles had gone missing. When I approached our start point I found they were on horse-drawn carts which they had taken from farmers.'

Confusion reigned. Many of these battle-hardened NCOs from Lippert's SS school were professional soldiers. They were not impressed by the conduct of this particular battle. Lindemann complained:

'It was really depressing to witness the march to Arnhem – a ridiculous event! More like Napoleon's retreat from Moscow than a military operation.'

He and his comrades were more perplexed than frightened:

'Stupid as it may sound, only the company and platoon commanders had a map. I did not get to see one during the entire fighting. We could not even imagine we would be

successful! The British we knew were in a pocket, but nobody was aware of what was going on inside or around it.'[15]

Herbert Kessler, the young 19-year-old NCO whose 'Hermann Goering' Training and Replacement Regiment had been surprised by the Allied overflight in Katwick an Zee, was undergoing a similarly hectic experience:

'Alarm! The ensuing hurry and flurry was a clear indication of the urgency of the situation. The company did not have any armoured personnel carriers. Bicycles were the only means of transportation. Daylight movement was out of the question because of the activities of low-flying aircraft. Therefore our departure time was set for dusk.
'Before the march towards Arnhem began the battalion assembled in a forest concealed from aerial observation. The acting battalion commander gave a pep talk: "Comrades, the time has come . . . I demand an unrelenting commitment until this operation proves a complete success. I know that I can rely on you . . .etc." Promotions that were due were then awarded, and after nightfall the battalion moved out.'

It was not easy to keep bicycle companies together; Lindemann had already experienced this. However, units stopped to reassemble during regular breaks. 'Some soldiers even travelled by day to re-establish contact with their unit.'[16]

During the night of 17–18 September the hastily assembled Kampfgruppen of the 'Division' von Tettau began to form up in their holding areas on the eastern edge of the Wageningen forest. Even now confusing last-minute changes and *ad hoc* measures had to be instituted to ensure a degree of combat effectiveness. Kapitanleutnant Zaubzer, the commander of Naval Manning Battalion 10, asked Lippert if he could provide a small cadre of veteran officers and NCOs to provide combat experience and stiffen his unit.

The plan of attack for the general advance at dawn was relatively simple. In the north, Helle's surveillance 'Wach' Battalion 3 was to advance to the right of the Ede-Arnhem road, moving east, with the eventual intention of swinging south to encircle the landing zone. Eberwein's SS-Kampfgruppe, due to arrive at 1030, was to attack from Bennekom in a north-westerly direction to the Arnhem railway, then follow this along, acting as a central wedge, in order to split the landing zones in two. In the middle was a large gap, taken up to some extent by a Fliegerhorst battalion that would try and maintain a link with the southern force, attacking eastwards toward Renkum and Hilversum along the Wageningen-Arnhem road. Left of this road would be the SS-Battalion Schulz from Lippert's Regiment, supported on the right of it by Naval Manning Battalion 10, beefed up with elements from two other naval detachments. In reserve, supporting the southern force, was the infantry converted Artillery Regiment 184. Von Tettau was in effect advancing over an 8-kilometre front with six battalions. A pitchfork thrust with the northern prong – Helle and Eberwein – acting in concert with a southern force commanded by Lippert, consisting of SS and naval soldiers. In between and providing a tenuous link was the Luftwaffe Fliegerhorst Battalion.

At 0500 the southern prong struck Renkum. Schulz's SS Battalion managed to clear the town and the terrain north of it by 0700. These were the more experienced troops. On their right, however, sounds of heavy firing indicated that the naval battalion was not gaining ground. An assault on the brickworks and paper factory south

of the Wageningen-Arnhem road was repulsed with heavy casualties. As Lippert laconically remarked, 'confusion and panic reigned'. Mortars and heavy machine guns had to be brought up before, at 0900, the factories could be stormed. By 1000 Schulz had taken Heelsum west. To the north Helle's four Dutch-SS companies were across Ginkel heath and engaging the glider troops protecting the landing zones around Wolfheze. By 1500 the naval unit, paying bitterly all the way for its inexperience had captured the brickworks in the south and reached the eastern edge of Heelsum. The more experienced SS-NCO school troops were flushing out groups of paratroopers who fell back quickly to the landing zones. SS-Officer-Cadet Lindemann recalls:

'The fighting was not hard at all for the first few days. We advanced from each covered position to the next, not really in contact at all.'[17]

By 1500 on the afternoon of 18 September it appeared the advance was going broadly to plan. The Germans smelled success. Helle's battalion would soon, by wheeling right, be in a position to influence operations in the south. If Eberwein's SS Battalion maintained momentum, the encirclement of the drop zones could be completed. Lippert, well forward with his leading elements, felt optimistic:

'In the Heelsum-Wolfheze-Ede triangle covering the Renkum and Ginkel heaths were several hundred parachutes lying on the ground amongst landed gliders and considerable quantities of combat supplies. All the time men and materials were moving off the drop zones. We had reached the airborne and logistic resupply landing area for the 1st British Airborne Division. It was to be bitterly defended by the British.'[18]

It was theirs for the taking. Only a degree of re-grouping would be required. On the western horizon, however, came a familiar sound. A menacing whisper that gradually rose to an unearthly droning noise. Specks were just discernible, and the droning changed pitch to an escalating roar as ever-more parachute transport aircraft hove into view, decelerating as they descended to drop height. The second lift had arrived.

CHAPTER X
Scraping the Barrel

Our sector, we were told, was to be along the Maas from Venlo to Nijmegen, which we were to occupy with troops which did not yet exist.

Adjutant to Commander 406 Division

Fifteen miles through 'Indian territory'... 101 Airborne Division

Major-General Maxwell Taylor's 101 Airborne Division had the task of protecting 15 miles of road at strategic intervals between Eindhoven and Grave. He likened the task to protecting the 'railroad' against Indian attacks in the days of the American western frontier. Because of the dispersion of objectives priority was given to infantry and mortars in the first parachute lift in order to protect the road. Artillery and heavy equipments would follow later. Just under 7,000 paratroopers landed on the first day. Splitting his division only made sense, however, if they were going to be quickly relieved by the British ground column. But the 'Indians', even at this early stage, knew the plan. The information was soon to result in this stretch of macadam being nicknamed 'Hell's Highway'.

The papers recovered from the American Waco glider did not reveal the full MARKET-GARDEN plan to General Student, but it did outline the role expected of 101 Division. Army Group B was able to announce at 2330 hours on 17 September that

'...101 Airborne Division has the task, according to captured papers and interrogations of prisoners, of occupying the roads and bridges

between Veghel-Oedenrode and Son. These are to be kept open for British troops – XXX Corps – who are to attack through Holland and Germany. Details to follow.'[1]

An outline order of battle for both XXX Corps and 101 Airborne Division was included. Further deductions based upon events in the Arnhem area, supplemented by further prisoner interrogations, enabled a full picture to emerge within 24 hours. Student immediately exploited this intelligence windfall in his planned counter-measures. A veteran of Holland and Crete, he commented, 'I knew more than anybody else that an airborne landing is at its weakest in the first few hours, and must be sorted out quickly and determinedly'. He began personally to direct and co-ordinate operations against the 101 Division.[2]

Knowledge of the enemy's intentions was not matched by the availability of forces to carry out the necessary counter-measures. Reserves were not at hand. First Parachute Army was a 'paper' formation, it had barely formed up, and had now been literally as well as metaphorically torn in two. Forces were required, not only to clear the rear combat zone, but to shore up the crumbling front. It was a question of scraping the barrel. In Hertogenbosch there were several thousand Fallschirmjaeger in training units. Two 'march battalions' were formed. One, the Fallschirmjaeger Battalion

'Ewald', was committed against St Oeden-rode via Schijndel, the second against Veghel.

Fortunately for Student, the first elements of 15th Army began to arrive, having been inexplicably allowed to escape by the British, across the river Scheldt. This was an unexpected development that was to contribute in some measure towards the future fate of 1st British Airborne Division. Lieutenant-General Poppe's 59th Division was directed toward Boxtel and Tilburg where they began to detrain. Its first available regiment was ordered to attack Son via Best, and attempt to recapture the most southerly of the bridges in the corridor. They began to arrive by afternoon and late evening of 17 September.

Flak Abteilung 424, part of Flak Brigade 18, was engaged in a heavy fire fight with members of the American 502 Regiment at a road junction east of Best on the edge of the Son Forest. Rallied by the commander and his staff, and supported by a 20mm cannon, the junction was cleared. They were helped in the nick of time by several lorry loads of infantry and more cannon from Hertogenbosch. By 2014 hours, Abteilung 24, having checked the area, reported the Boxtel-Eindhoven road clear of enemy. 'American paratroopers' they observed 'signal each other using red towels.'[3] General Poppe's 59 Division had arrived.

As more units appeared they were immediately inserted into the savage

As more units of General Poppe's 59 Division arrived, they were immediately inserted into the savage fighting that now developed in the Son Forest and around Best. A cautious advance somewhere in southern Holland. (Bundesarchiv)

fighting that now developed over the next two days in the Son Forest and around Best. In addition, three companies of infantry, reinforced by two training replacement battalions and a police battalion, were tasked to cut the road at St Oedenrode.

An examination of a myriad of conflicting snippets of information reported in the rear of Chill's 85 Division and passed on to LXXXVIII Corps captures the atmosphere reigning in the German headquarters at this time, trying to cope with the American 101 Division astride 'Hell's Highway'. Higher command may have had an inkling of Allied intentions, but troops on the ground did not have a clue what was going on. Taken off troop trains, sometimes re-armed and often reorganised, they were thrown piecemeal into battle, in part formations against veteran airborne troops. The Americans were elite troops, operating within their normal order of battle.

Confusion reigned over the destruction or capture of bridges. An experienced Kampfgruppe from the Training Regiment 'Hermann Goering' managed to hold on to the Son bridge in the teeth of an attack from the American 506 Regiment, until it could be blown. However, other bridges targeted by 101 Division fell easily, due to the inexperience of security guards. General Student bemoaned this deficiency in his area of responsibility. If he had only possessed an 'intact defence' he wrote then, 'the Allied airborne troops would have been confronted everywhere with just rubble from blown bridges!'[4] Orders were based upon ignorance of the true situation. The commander of LXXXVIII Corps ordered the commanders of the bridges over the Wilhelmina canal at Oirschott and another north of Best 'to be blown only following written permission from High Command'. This was at 1745. 'They are to be defended,' he ordered 'to the last man.' They were blown at 1300 the next day.

It was a bizarre and confusing situation.

General Chill summarised the situation in his own rear area during the evening of 17 September:

'At least two to three enemy parachute battalions have jumped into the Son heath area Best-St Oedenrode and Son. The canal and railway bridge south of Best has been blown, or is occupied by our own forces. Counter-attacks are being mounted with hastily gathered and inserted units.'[5]

More of 59 Division's units were now arriving by train, but were hardly combat-effective. A transport arrived at 1145 on 18 September and dropped off an infantry regiment. They were foot-borne and had no heavy weapons. Artillery was expected to detrain in the afternoon but possessed virtually no ammunition.

A constant and depressing flow of reports of further American airborne reinforcements was received. At 1415 aerial formations were observed pouring in over 719 Infantry Division's front. 'Three hundred gliders were sighted flying in an easterly direction along the canal,' LXXXVIII Corps were informed. 'They were in waves up to 50 strong.' More still were reported at 1600. Corps felt they were losing control of the situation.

Kampfgruppe 'Rink', a mixture of trainee infantry, police and flak forces, was actually pressed back after assaulting Best in the afternoon of 18 September. General Reinhard, the Corps commander, castigated the luckless unit:

'First Parachute Army Headquarters is to be formally informed that the deputy commander of the Kampfgruppe Rink is exhibiting a defeatist attitude. The battle group is commanded to hold its present position regardless of conditions, even against superior enemy attacks. They are to take part in the 59 Infantry Division attack, under whose command they are appointed. I will court-martial any officer who thinks of retreat.'[6]

Rink's subsequent attack was unsuccessful, as was also the attack of the Fallschirmjaeger Battalion 'Ewald' against St Oedenrode. Contact with the other battle group, which overran an American resupply drop zone near Casteel in its drive on Veghel, was lost.

By the end of 18 September, only a succession of weak attacks had been mounted against the 101 Division. At 1900 the leading elements of Guards Armoured Division made its first contact with the American airborne troops on the outskirts of Eindhoven. 59 Division was still being inserted piecemeal, yet its attacks were growing stronger in proportion to the arrival of each rail transport. Numbers alone were not enough. Ammunition was scarce, as much of 15th Army's had by necessity been left behind on the other side of the Scheldt. LXXXVIII Corps had little to offer. Only two days' infantry small arms ammunition, and a quarter of a day's worth each of mortar and artillery rounds were held. Across the various Kampfgruppen the equipment state was only 75 per cent of what it should have been. Divisions were down to three-quarters of a day for petrol, which could not be supplemented because there simply was no more. Rations were sufficient for only seven days, again with no hope of resupply. Units were operating on a shoestring.[7]

A self-contained battle group, sufficiently strong to affect the situation decisively, had yet to arrive. Although the Allied plan was known, there was nothing substantial to oppose it. Only two battalions were, for example, manning a defence line 19km long enclosing the western side of the corridor around Best. 'An observer line rather than a defensive front,' observed LXXXVIII Corps. It further commented that the only units as yet uncommitted again to battle – the 'Hermann Goering' Training Regiment, Fallschirmjaeger Regiment 6, and Grenadier Regiment 723 – 'had been so reduced by casualties over the past 13 days, that their combat value is very low.'[8]

107 Panzer Brigade, re-routed from Aachen, was on the march. After detraining, it moved in clattering, exhaust-shrouded columns toward Helmond. The brigade was totally armoured and motorised. Built around a battalion of Mark V 'Panther' tanks, it possessed a Panzergrenadier infantry battalion mounted in armoured half-tracks, further supplemented

Panzer Brigade 107 was on the move. As it was to be employed against lightly armed airborne troops there was more than a fair expectation of victory. (Bundesarchiv)

by a self-propelled assault gun company, an engineer half-track company, as well as supply and transport detachments. The whole force moved under its own effective anti-aircraft umbrella, also mounted on tracks. Having just completed a re-equipment programme, the brigade had been due to load on rail transports bound for the eastern front. The crisis in the west had changed all that. Now it was to be employed against lightly armed airborne troops. Its commanders did not foresee any great problems. Indeed, it would be a welcome change to be deployed with more than a fair expectation of victory. Moving by night to avoid air attack, villages *en route* were awakened by this mass of armour thundering through narrow streets, shaking walls and deafening all. Kerb corners were smashed on tight bends as, tracks squealing, engines racing, drivers mercilessly pushed their vehicles, anxious to reach their jump-off points before dawn. Commanders checked their watches in the half-light of crew compartments illuminated by masked lamps. 'H' hour should be some time after first light on 19 September. Gloved fists jabbed skywards – *Marsch! Marsch!*

Securing the heights above Nijmegen . . . 82 Airborne Division

Resistance to Brigadier-General James M. Gavin's 82nd Airborne Division drop was negligible – 7,277 paratroopers and 48 gliders were successfully landed. One of the main prizes, the bridge over the Maas at Grave, was secured within three hours, and the Heumen bridge over the Maas-Waal canal within six. Of particular tactical importance to the division was a successful occupation of the hill mass south-east of Nijmegen. This feature, triangular in shape, is roughly 300 feet high, 8 miles long, and

the only pronounced high ground for miles. It provided a natural escarpment, covering possible German approaches from the Reich border on its eastern slope, and in particular from the Reichswald. Allied intelligence had suggested this forest area might conceal a mass of German forces forming up. Occupation of this high ground therefore took precedence even over the capture of the main Waal bridges in Nijmegen. The feature, once taken, was occupied by two American regimental groups. Right forward, or south, was 505 Regiment sited on the high ground and woods west of Groesbeek as far south as Mook. On the left, or north, 508 Regiment occupied the heights up to Berg-en-Dal and overlooking Beek. Possession of this feature controlled the main roads converging on Nijmegen from Cleve and Mook. Because of the priority accorded to this operation, only company-size forays were mounted – unsuccessfully – against the Waal bridges in Nijmegen between 17–18 September.

The Germans had nothing immediately available to contest this force that had landed so far and unexpectedly in the rear combat zone. Generalleutnant Scherbening, commanding 406 Division, which at that time consisted only of his headquarters and the cadres of a number of training units, telephoned his adjutant Major Rasch at 2100 hours on 17 September, seven hours after the landings. Rasch was told to assemble the staff on his return. 'He had something important to tell us,' the Major recalled. 'Having served the General as adjutant for some time, I realised from the pitch of his voice that it must be something particularly significant.' At 0200 he arrived and ordered the Headquarters to make itself sufficiently mobile for immediate operations at the front. They were to depart at 0800 to a destination as yet unconfirmed. Rasch could immediately foresee problems. 'Only an expert in such matters can appreciate what it means to change from a barracks-based staff organisation, with no equipment or vehicles, and turn it into a mobile field headquarters, all in the space of six hours.' Rasch, however, confounded himself by achieving the deadline. This was not the end of the problem. When they arrived at their proposed headquarters site in Geldern, they were faced with a similar task, but on a grander scale. The instructions were to

'. . . form an *ad hoc* Division using forces and resources already *in situ*. That was not quite what we had expected. Certainly we felt we would be sent to the front in France, and take over a division – and now? Where in fact was the front? Our sector, we were told, was to be along the Maas from Venlo to Nijmegen, which we were to occupy with troops which did not yet exist.'[9]

General Feldt immediately transferred the tactical headquarters of 406 Division to Kruegers-Gut on the Kranenburg-Nijmegen road. A number of 'alarm' units of Wehrkreis VI headquarters were immediately made available to it. Manpower came from the 'Juelich' Wehrkreis NCO school, numerous replacement and training battalions, 'stomach and ear' battalions, and a few Luftwaffe battalions formed from recently-closed air force NCO schools. There were virtually no heavy infantry support weapons or artillery. None of the troops were infantry trained, vehicles were scarce, field kitchens non-existent, and there was no signals communication equipments, not even for the artillery.[10]

The division had somehow to form its own transport 'columns' to move ammunition, rations and evacuate the wounded. Major Rasch outlined the staff solution to the problem:

'As our commander was the supreme authority in our sector, we simply

sited units on all crossroads. Within a short time, all serviceable vehicles – lorries, cars and other types – not already in Wehrmacht hands, were picked up, and directed with their drivers to our collection points. In this fashion the transport problem was quickly, if not particularly correctly, solved, and we slowly became self-sufficient for movement.'

406 Division gradually increased in strength as more reinforcements arrived. Firstly, three more Luftwaffe 'fortress' battalions, then finally artillery. It was a piecemeal

406 Division gradually increased in strength, as Rasch describes, 'albeit ad hoc' it 'was gathered together, and directed to our sector where it was then disposed and sited'. (Bundesarchiv)

process. Commanders and gun crews turned up, then a collection of captured Russian 143mm howitzers. As Rasch summarised:

'Eventually another division, albeit *ad hoc*, was gathered together, and directed to our sector, where it was then disposed and sited.'

The Commander of the Corps 'Feldt' tasked the division to prevent an enemy advance using all the formations west of Kleve, to hold a line east of Nijmegen stretching across Zyfflich, Wyler and the eastern edge of Groesbeek. Another Kampfgruppe, made up from the Wehrkreis NCO school from Kempton and an engineer battalion from Roermond, was placed under the command of a colonel, and deployed at the south-western tip of the Reichswald, just short of Mook. Its task was to prevent enemy advances in this direction. By dawn on 18 September the equivalent of about four battalions split into various combat teams, and three batteries of artillery had been assembled in the Groesbeek-Zyfflich area. All these forces were assigned to 406 Division, which received the order to assault the airborne bridgeheads starting at 0630, and throw them back across the Maas. General Feldt, having issued the executive order, has since confided:

'I had no confidence in this attack, since it was almost an impossible task for 406 Division to attack picked troops with its motley crowd. But it was necessary to risk the attack in order to forestall an enemy advance to the east, and to deceive him in regard to our strength.'[11]

In any case the attack was in accordance with Model's intentions. Army Group B had promised Feldt the 3rd and 5th Fallschirmjaeger Divisions. They were expected

The attack by three Kampfgruppen belonging to the Corps Feldt against the Groesbeek area 'to our surprise', Feldt relates, 'made slow progress everywhere' on 18 September 1944.

to have assembled west of Cleve, and be at his disposal by the afternoon of the same day.

Starting at 0630 three Kampfgruppen – 'Stargaard', 'Fuerstenberg' and 'Greschick' (named after their commanders, and roughly battalion strength) – each attacked on a broad front from the Cleve-Kranenburg area towards Beek, Wyler and Groesbeek. The main direction of attack was west and north-west, across the landing zones, toward the high ground shielding Nijmegen. Numbering some 2,300 men, light armoured support was provided from within Captain Freiherr von Fuerstenberg's

Kampfgruppe – namely five armoured cars and three half-tracks mounting flak guns. A fourth Kampfgruppe, 'Goebel', supported by the battalion south-east of Mook, moved off from the south, heading north-west with a further 350 men. Including units securing a thin line behind the advance, a force totalling some 3,400 men was hastily assembled and flung into the attack – 24 mortars, 130 light and heavy machine guns in addition to small detachments of flak were intermingled with them and supported the effort.[12]

Any American complacency or concern over the relatively muted reaction of the German defence in 82 Division's area was soon shattered by the arrival of this force. Feldt himself remarked 'to our surprise, at the beginning, the attack made slow progress everywhere. The results south-east of Mook were remarkable.'[13] Yet there was no disguising the problems of the attackers, they were pressed amateurs, untrained conscripts, up against seasoned veterans fighting their third campaign. Difficulties soon developed. Major Rasch, observing the main attacks toward Groesbeek with General Scherbening, saw that their own 'soldiers were armed only with Czechoslovak machine guns'. One of the replacement battalions forward of their location radioed the divisional commander and reported they were unable to continue their advance due to flanking fire. Scherbening, knowing his adjutant was infantry trained, turned to him, having quickly made up his mind and exclaimed: 'Take over his task. If we don't get Groesbeek inside half an hour, the whole attack will have had it!'

Rasch moved forward, having detached a machine gun section from the staff for additional protection, and took over Captain Gruenenklee's battalion. When he arrived he found the battalion pinned down on the edge of a wood. He quickly assessed the situation:

'Remarkable' progress was initially made by three hastily gathered Kampfgruppen of untrained conscripts. The village of Mook was penetrated. (Bundesarchiv)

'These were all old boys lying here, veterans of the First World War, who had just been called up to relieve the younger soldiers manning POW camp battalions. Now they too had been put into the front line. Somebody in the line called out to me "Captain, we've already stormed the Craoneer Heights in 1914!" "*Ja*," I was able to answer. "Can't you see that it's up to us old boys to run the whole show again; and we will do it exactly as we did then. First of all we have got to get Tommy [they thought they were fighting the English] on the run, then we've cracked it!".'

After 'a quick morale boost', Rasch got the troops moving again within the attack schedule. This was achieved 'practically without loss, because "Tommy" had become nervous and was shooting too high'. At that moment he was abruptly recalled to headquarters, where Field Marshal Model had appeared on the scene. Rasch recalled: 'He was always feared, because he constantly demanded precise reports over the situation, available manpower, wounded, units involved and so on – everything the Adjutant was expected to know.' So he started to move back. Control was handed back to Captain Gruenenklee, who in any case was 'normally a good officer'.

82nd Airborne Division was able to contain these attacks, but they were under pressure. An American company was surrounded and cut off in Wyler. The situation at some local points was serious. Of particular importance was the need to secure drop zones which had been overrun. Aircraft with reinforcements had already taken off from England at 1000 hours, and were expected by 1300. Companies were extracted from available reserves, and further American soldiers detached from Nijmegen to overcome this crisis. Orders were given to clear both the northern and southern landing zones.

Rasch, hurrying back to the rear, was looking for his vehicle in the woods, when suddenly:

'There! . . . First of all a droning, a buzzing in the ears which developed, rattling and crackling, into a thunderous rumble. Enemy aircraft formations covered the entire sky. Their crew machine guns swept the entire area with fire. Bombs exploded in between, it was as though all hell had broken loose. Then gliders came

down at every conceivable place. The Americans† had predicted the attack and its likely success, and were now throwing new airborne troops into the fight without respite . . . gliders were landing as if on a normal airfield.'[14]

The impact of new airlandings, matched with the sudden insertion of ground reinforcements taken from other locations, shattered the German advance. A battalion of the American 505 Regiment attacked at the same time, dashing downhill straight across the northern drop zone in the teeth of flak and German small arms fire. The arrival of the airlift was the final straw. A panic-stricken rout ensued. Caught up in the mêlée was General Feldt. Having moved forward he was surprised at the suddenness of the renewed landings, which, he said, 'caused a panic among the attackers'. As the troops fled, the Corps commander, who had by then joined the commander of 406 Division, remarked: 'It was with the greatest difficulty that General Scherbenning and I succeeded in halting our troops in the original jump-off positions.' He had been fortunate because 'on this occasion I just managed to avoid being taken prisoner myself in the area of Papen Hill'.[15]

German commanders strove desperately to stabilise the situation. A group of gliders landing in the Bruck-Horst area were shot up by the Replacement Battalion 1/E6 in positions supported by a flak gun. American survivors who managed to scramble out fled towards Groesbeek. One of Rasch's NCOs, a Corporal Kronenberg, managed to salvage a brand-new jeep from the glider and drove it on to Wasserburg. Gleefully demonstrating this newly acquired booty to comrades, he was killed when he lost control and collided with a bus. Rasch himself was able to observe the devastating effect of the airlandings upon

†Rasch incorrectly believed them to be English [author's note].

now dispersed troops before reporting to headquarters. Many soldiers, in particular the Viennese Luftwaffe 'fortress' battalions, had fled well back before they could be collected again. Replacement Battalion 39, he found, had retreated right back to the edge of the Reichswald. Everything gained during the successful phase of the advance was lost. On the northern drop zone alone, some 20mm cannon, 50 dead and 150 prisoners were abandoned. American casualties that day had been light; Rasch summed up the prevailing mood among the survivors:

> 'The amount of ground lost in the middle part of the assault was significant. This was caused mainly by the unease attendant upon "landings in the rear". A new attack with these troops would not be possible.'

During the afternoon, following the débâcle on the landing zones, General Feldt drove to Emmerich hoping to speed up the transit of reinforcements. Major Karl-Heinz Becker reported to him there the arrival of the remnants of the 3rd and 5th Fallschirmjaeger 'Divisions'. These were in essence the vanguard of II Fallschirmjaeger Corps. But there was only one weak battalion to represent each division, formed primarily from logistic troops who had survived the battle of Normandy. There were virtually no heavy weapons. At least, and this was the only saving grace, they had not suffered any casualties *en route* from air attacks.

On returning to his command post at Kruegers-Gut, General Feldt met both Field Marshal Model and General Meindl, the Commander of II Fallschirmjaeger Corps. He expressed 'astonishment to the former at the condition of the 3rd and 5th Fallschirmjaeger Divisions, which the army group had called fully available for commitment'. This did not, however, alter the facts; the Field Marshal insisted another attack would have to go in the next day. Major Becker's 3rd Fallschirmjaeger Division contingent would be organised into a Kampfgruppe, supported by another formed from the 5th, commanded by a Captain Hermann, and committed to an assault in the Zyfflich-Wyler sector. Model wanted this the next morning, and along the whole front. Meindl and Feldt managed to change his mind. More time was required. Model prevaricated, arguing fiercely, but was obliged eventually to concede to logic. The attack time was fixed to start on 20 September. With that – as Rasch wryly observed – 'crash, bang, wallop! Out and away went the Field Marshal', in his normal fashion. Once again it had not proved possible to finalise effective and concerted counter-measures. By this time Model was fuming with impatience.

CHAPTER XI

Take the Arnhem Bridge

Suppose they'll send a hearse next.

Paratrooper, Frost's battalion

From the east . . .

The situation at the Arnhem bridge was still confused during the early hours of darkness, before dawn on 18 September. IISS Corps mistakenly informed Army Group B by telephone that the 'bridge has been cleared once again of enemy and is passable'. Much later this had to be corrected: 'According to a telephone call just received, the Arnhem bridge is not in our hands. The enemy is holding a strong bridgehead on the northern bank from within fortified houses. Strength approximately 120 men.'[1] In fact, the British strength was more like 500 to 600.

During the remaining hours of darkness efforts were made to co-ordinate the measures required to wrest control of the bridge back from the British. Brinkmann's 10SS Kampfgruppe, under command of the 9SS, had been given the task of clearing the northern ramp by Bittrich, the Corps Commander, the evening before. Part of SS Panzer-grenadier Regiment 21 (3rd Company) was already fighting in the houses due west of the bridge and around the market place near Eusebius-Plein. Euling's 10SS Battalion, trying to drive across the bridge to Nijmegen, also had its lead company fully committed around the northern ramp. At 0400[2] Major Hans-Peter Knaust, the 38-year-old commander of the Panzer-grenadier Training and Replacement Battalion 'Bocholt', reported for orders. Knaust's battalion had been provided by

Wehrkreis VI. With him came eight panzer Mark III and IV tanks from the 6th Panzer Replacement Regiment 'Bielefeld'. These tanks had been used for driver training. Knaust's Wehrmacht force included four companies of infantry. They were made up

Major Hans-Peter Knaust, the 38-year-old Commander of the Panzer-grenadier Training and Replacement Battalion 'Bocholt'. (Fuerbringer Collection)

of 'reconvalescents' who were rated as 'not quite fit yet' for front-line service. Knaust reported to the Hohenstaufen's command post, where he was placed under Brinkmann's Kampfgruppe command. His immediate task on arrival was to relieve Euling's men at the northern ramp, so that they could continue on to Nijmegen. Knaust, invalided with a wooden leg on the Russian front, was a charismatic figure. His unit was to fight with distinction. Whilst this concurrent activity took place, it was decided Brinkmann's unit would provide the *schwerpunkt*, or main effort, for the dawn attacks. This advance was to hit the houses surrounding the northern ramp from the marshalling yards and factory buildings east of the bridge.

As these forces got into position, pressure was still being maintained on the British enclave from the west. SS-Corporal Rudolf Trapp, a machine gunner serving with the Frundsberg's 3rd Company Panzergrenadier Regiment 21, recalls savage street fighting, during which they 'gingerly tried doors which were often booby-trapped'. Slowly, inexorably, they tightened the ring around the bridge. Reaching the lower Rhine, 'we could see the bridge, and drew anti-tank fire'. They began to work their way along the Eusebius-Plein. Fleeting images remained imprinted on Trapp's memory:

'Throughout the night there was heavy fighting from house to house and sleeping was completely out of the question. Again and again I was positioned at different street corners with my sustained-fire [mounted on a tripod] heavy machine gun. We broke loopholes into the walls of houses to obtain good fields of fire, and to enable us to move from one side to the other.'

Rubble made it increasingly difficult to approach the British positions. It was either too hot to take cover in, or produced even more obstacles that had to be surmounted under fire.

'There were British wounded in our position. A young Englishman had been shot in the scrotum and was in great pain.'[3]

Wounded were immediately lifted out. Burning houses, meanwhile, panicked many civilians into breaking cover and rushing into the streets, only to be mistakenly cut down by both sides. Trapp recovered a number of these Dutch civilians, 'among them a badly wounded woman'. Adrenalin, with its attendant sudden exhaustion, was beginning to pick at their attention and awareness. They were being steadily ground down in a battle of attrition. This enemy was not going to be forced to surrender. It began to dawn upon the hard-fighting SS-troopers that this was going to be a long and wearisome slog.

At dawn Brinkmann's forces began their attack. Attempts were made first of all to infiltrate the British positions from the east. A number of different ruses were tried. Squads of SS-troopers would slip into buildings and then drive the British out. Prepared demolition charges were made up and tossed through windows as the precursor to an open assault. Not infrequently they were thrown back among the attackers. Next, a frantic infantry 'rush' would ensue to get into the building, often resulting in terrible casualties among the assaulting troops. Care was taken of the wounded where possible, but the nature of the fighting around the Arnhem road bridge was bitter and cruel. Quarter in these close range mêlées was neither anticipated nor given. A 21-year-old SS-Section Commander, Alfred Ringsdorf, summed it up:

'This was a harder battle than any I had fought in Russia. It was constant, close range, hand-to-hand fighting. The English were everywhere. The streets for the most part were narrow, sometimes not more than 15 feet wide, and we fired at each other from only yards away. We fought to gain inches, cleaning out one room after the other. It was absolute hell!'[4]

At the receiving end was Private James Sims, a 19-year-old mortar crewman serving in Frost's parachute battalion. His mortars were dug in on a small green island opposite Markt-Straad near the northern ramp of the bridge. From here he was able to witness the succession of savage and determined attacks mounted by the Kampfgruppe Brinkmann. Following the failure to infiltrate the British positions, a lorry attack developed, driving up Kade Strasse toward Sim's position and Frost's 2 PARA headquarters. The trucks' occupants were unaware that the houses on their right flank were occupied, and were riddled from end to end with small arms fire. Those who tried to escape were shot down before they could reach cover. Sims watched with sinking heart the progress of one of the survivors:

'One terribly wounded German soldier, shot through both legs, pulled himself hand over hand towards his own lines. We watched his slow and painful progress with horrified fascination, as he was the only creature moving among a carpet of the dead. He pulled himself across the road, and over the pavement, then he dragged his shattered body inch by inch up a grass-covered incline leading to the bridge road. Once he had cleared a slight parapet at the top of the incline he would be back in his own lines. He must have been in terrible pain but he conquered the

incline by sheer willpower. With a superhuman effort he heaved himself up to clear the final obstacle. A rifle barked out next to me and I watched in disbelief as the wounded German fell back, shot through the head. To me it was little short of murder, but to my companion, a Welshman, one of our best snipers, the German was a legitimate target. When I protested he looked at me as though I was simple.'[5]

An attack with SS-troopers hidden inside an ambulance, following the route taken by the lorried infantry, met a similar fate. Tumbling out, firing wildly from the hip with schmeissers, the charge was broken up, and annihilated virtually outside Frost's headquarters. 'Suppose they'll send a hearse next,' Sims heard a paratrooper remark.

Following a barrage of artillery and mortar fire, Brinkmann's reconnaissance battalion tried an armoured rush. Firing furiously, a column of light tanks, armoured cars and half-tracks clattered under the Arnhem bridge ramp which adjoined the eastern factory district. As they suddenly burst into Markt-Straad, the noise of their reverberating progress magnified by an echo effect as they passed beneath the tunnel of bridge supports, they were met by a withering concentration of fire. Two six-pounder British anti-tank guns sited in open streets brought the leading enemy tank to a flaming halt. German half-tracks, trying to negotiate the awesome conflagration that had slewed across their path under the bridge, were knocked out, one by one, as they attempted to squeeze by. Troopers baling out over the sides were cut down by fire. Sims observed the gruesome finale:

'Black smoke belched from the leading tank now well ablaze, but any movement from our positions still brought a stream of well-aimed machine gun fire from the turret guns. The paratroopers shouted to the SS man to come out, promising to save his life, for they were impressed by his fanatical courage. The only reply was a further burst of fire. As the flames got to him we could hear his screams of agony, muffled by the steel turret, but none the less disturbing for that. They seemed to go on for an awfully long time before this brave soldier died for Führer and Fatherland.'[6]

Attacks on the bridge by this stage were still not co-ordinated, or, if they were, liaison failed. Each was dealt with piece-meal by the British defenders. The warren of streets east and west of the fortified houses protecting the bridge prevented the Germans from levelling a combined tank and infantry punch to recover it. Only north and south offered the space for such an assault, but the time for such a *coup de main* attempt was over. Nevertheless, it was tried.

From the south . . .

SS-Captain Viktor Eberhard Graebner scanned the Arnhem road bridge, silhouetted now in the growing light of dawn through his binoculars. He had barely four hours left to live. Only conjecture and a piecing together of fragmentary reports can ever recreate these last few hours during which he condemned himself and much of his unit to death. Examining the flashes of gun fire which identified the British positions as being in houses around the northern ramp of the bridge, Graebner came to a decision. They would attack.

Graebner had volunteered to transfer from the Wehrmacht into the Waffen-SS. When the Hohenstaufen Division was initially formed at the beginning of 1943, he was the first Company Commander of

On the extreme right is the flamboyant SS-Captain Viktor Graebner, 'always the first to get stuck in!', as the Chief of Staff of the 9SS remembers. (Fuerbringer Collection)

the Reconnaissance Battalion, which later he would command in its entirety. Wilfred Schwarz, the chief of staff of the 9SS in Arnhem remarked that 'he was an impressive soldier, the right man for the job'. Like all armoured reconnaissance commanders ought to be, Graebner was a man of action. Dark, slightly built and slim, he was well liked and respected by his men. He had rapidly established a reputation in combat as always being well forward, and unafraid to expose himself when necessary in action. Schwarz, while not understanding his decision to attack the Arnhem bridge, admitted nevertheless 'that this was typical of Graebner – always the first to get stuck in!'[7] This remark provides the key to his subsequent actions.

Graebner had experienced a moment of personal triumph and pride when, a few hours previously, Harzer, his divisional commander, had hung the *Ritterkreuz* (the Knight's Cross) at his throat. Supporting the 277 Infantry Division in Normandy, he had personally led a number of armoured counter-attacks against a British breakthrough at Noyers Bocage. At dawn on 15 July 1944 a surprise attack led by him succeeded in overrunning an Allied penetration and saved a crisis. Major General Praun, the divisional commander, personally recommended Graebner for the honour. With the memory of this triumph still visible at his throat, the commander of Reconnaissance Battalion 9 made a similar combat appreciation of the problem of recovering the Arnhem bridge. Everybody knew the British 'stand to' at dawn, when they were most alert. Why not repeat the ploy so successfully used at Noyers Bocage and rush the position when they least expected it – namely after they had stood down? Perhaps the plan was meant to coincide with Brinkmann's advance against the bridge from the east, but there is no evidence to support this theory.

Surprise and shock were Graebner's only protection. It was a typical armoured commander's approach to an infantry problem. *Panzerleute* (armoured 'types') tended to disdain the resistance value of lightly-armed airborne infantry. Graebner had a mixture of 22 armoured vehicles at his disposal, armoured cars and half-tracks, some of which mounted 75mm guns. They represented the highest concentration of armoured vehicles in the 9SS. All, at the minimum, possessed a machine gun mount. Speed and the shock of concentrated firepower should be sufficient to get them through. At 0900, hoping against hope that these factors would protect them, the SS-troopers nervously mounted. Engines turned over, and were mercilessly gunned so that they should be warmed through;

they could not afford to stall at a vital moment. Wreathed in grey exhaust fumes, vehicles clattered into their ordained places in the attack column – and a column it would have to be. There was only a two-lane road, already strewn with the wreckage of earlier hapless victims. Before them lay a dash of 600 to 700 metres, up the ramp, across the 200-metre span, and down the ramp on the other side into Arnhem town centre. Armoured cars would lead. The cam of the road would give them protection until they crossed the summit in the middle of the bridge. Girders by then may also offer some cover. Armoured half-tracks would follow. Slightly underpowered, and fully laden with SS-troopers, they could not expect to reach more than 20 to 25mph – 30mph, if they were lucky, on the downhill stretch. A number of sandbagged lorries carrying some infantry would slowly follow up in the rear.

Engines revved up, waiting for the order to go. Vehicle commanders licking dry lips gazed anxiously at their commander, barely distinguishable in the gloom of clouds of exhaust. His fist jabbed the air twice – '*Marsch! Marsch!*' They were off.

Like a Grand Prix start, with exhausts roaring, vehicles lurched forward, drivers racing through gears, accelerating to the maximum speed as quickly as possible. Graebner, extrovert as ever, was near the front, directing operations from a converted British Humber armoured car, probably captured in Normandy. Soon the bridge began to vibrate at their approach, as, with tracks rattling and screeching, the column surged forward, dispersing as slower vehicles fell behind, racing for the high point in the centre of the bridge. Not a shot rang out. Graebner, thumping the edge of the crew compartment, completely exposed to the elements, urged them forward – '*Schnell! Schnell!*' As the wind snatched at camouflage smocks, SS-troopers huddled in the rear of the vulnerable open crew compartments of half-tracks winced in expectation of what was to come; they tried to contract their bodies into as small a target as possible.

The large 'Puma' armoured cars swept over the summit of the bridge, cannon and machine guns firing. Tracer arched majestically towards buildings on the north side crumpling and spewing brickwork, interspersed with sparking ricochets in all directions. Two more armoured cars tore, unscathed, straight down the ramp and into the town centre. British fire began to open up intermittently. Three more armoured cars were across. It looked as though they were going to get away with it, dodging expertly around the wreckage. A wheel exploded skywards, flying high into the air, and bounced in slow motion as one of the six wheeled vehicles hit the British mine 'necklace' strung across the road. As the slower under-powered half-tracks clattered over the summit of the bridge, they were met by a storm of concentrated fire. Machine guns, mortars and rifles opened up on both sides. Grenades were lobbed into vehicles as they sped by the houses bordering the ramp itself. Graebner must have been dismayed by the ferocity of this reaction. Resistance here was far in excess of what had been anticipated. The paratroopers, surprised that these armoured vehicles coming up from the south had turned out to be German rather than British, brought more mortar and some anti-tank fire to bear. Muffled crumps signalled the demise of the leading half-tracks as grenades thrown into open crew compartments wrought a terrible carnage in the confined space. Black smoke began to boil up into the air as burning fuel snaked across the road, quickly engulfing wounded and dead crews scattered around knocked-out vehicles. As one parachute officer fighting in the school opposite the north ramp stated, the half-tracks had 'no roof on them and so were dead meat'. Vehicles often came to a halt after both

driver and co-driver were killed. Graebner's attack began to disintegrate all around him. It is likely that he died in this moment of despair, because suddenly all direction and momentum went out of the attack. SS-Corporal Mauga, crouching low in his half-track, witnessed the initial set-back.

> 'Suddenly all hell broke loose ahead of us. All around my vehicle there were explosions and noise and I was right in the middle of this chaos.'[8]

Half-tracks following up, uncertain what to do, paused in the face of the awful conflagration spewing across the road in front of them. Vehicles came to a halt. For some ten minutes urgent consultations took place, command was re-established and some crew members changed. Two vehicles, their drivers taking their courage in their hands, surged forward. With all guns firing, they sped past the high buildings housing the school next to the ramp. One of the drivers was almost immediately hit. Losing nerve, he put the armoured personnel carrier into reverse, lurched backwards and rammed the following vehicle. The two became inextricably intertwined, their open crew compartments vulnerable to British fire from above, and the troopers within were massacred as they frantically tried to get out. As the vehicles burst into flames, smoke billowed across the road, cloaking the attempts of a third trying to squeeze by. This one was dealt with similarly. Confusion now reigned. Tracer converged on to the bridge as heavier British machine guns found the range, sparking and whining off the girders. SS-troopers desperately sought refuge from the slaughter amongst the nebulous cover afforded by the bridge superstructure.

Mauga remembers the dilemma: 'Some wanted to continue forward, others wanted to get back.' Graebner was driving a British armoured recce vehicle, probably to distinguish himself to his men, but he could not be found. By now, half-tracks that had reached the other side were nosing down the slopes of the ramp on the north-eastern side of the bridge. Any desperate measure was considered to avoid the intense defensive fire. One half-track careered out of control down the slope and crashed into the side of the school building; the soldiers within were cut down before they could escape.

So the carnage continued, almost until midday. Two vehicles, the drivers hit and out of control, crashed through the left barrier of the bridge parallel to Kade Strasse and plummeted to the street below in a shower of cascading burning fuel, wreckage, and screaming men. Pauses lasting thirty minutes or so occurred whilst SS-troopers, still under fire in half-tracks, waited for the funeral pyres ahead to abate sufficiently before attempting a further rush to break through. These sporadic forays, well anticipated, were met by a storm of concentrated and concentric fire. The situation worsened as artillery fire began to burst around the superstructure of the bridge, near-misses jetting up columns of spray from the river below. Realising their position was hopeless, and unable to defend themselves further, SS-troopers leapt over fire-raked balustrades into the lower Rhine, preferring an uncertain fate below to the certainty of death above. Slowly and sporadically the firing died down, until by midday it had virtually stopped. Of the 22 armoured vehicles that had participated in the assault, 12 flaming wrecks now totally blocked the road.

Graebner's gamble had proved to be a catastrophic failure, but he had very nearly pulled it off. The attack had caused genuine surprise, but the British had stopped it dead in its tracks. Surviving troopers from Reconnaissance Battalion 9 either fled or crawled back across the bridge to gain the safety of the southern bank. As they did so, a triumphant baying broke out in the houses along the northern ramp. It was the 2 PARA battalion war cry, '*Whoa Mahomet, Whoa Mahomet!*', to add to the humiliation.

At 9SS headquarters, radio contact with Graebner failed as the attack lost its momentum. It is quite possible that initial over-optimistic accounts may have resulted in the premature report of success sent to II SS Corps. Graebner's death within 24 hours of receiving one of the highest honours his nation could bestow was a tragedy for his unit. An enigmatic figure, he was well known and therefore sorely missed. SS-Corporal Mauga later found his commander's Humber armoured car, which was taken to Arnhem, 'but the commander had disappeared for good', he remarked. 'We could not recover him.' Neither also could they collect the other camouflaged and huddled forms lying by their vehicles where they had fallen. They were to remain there for another two days until the bridge could be finally taken.[9]

From the north . . .

Graebner's failure was not just distressing to those members of the Hohenstaufen's divisional staff who knew him, it was of paramount significance. As SS-Captain Schwarz, the divisional Chief-of-Staff, remarked: 'It had a big impact, you see, as we had lost an important part of our combat strength.'[10] The realisation began to dawn that this would be no easy task.

Rubble and debris were now beginning to hamper attempts to approach Frost's fortified houses. As Knaust's Kampfgruppe began to arrive and relieve the Battalion Euling, the focus of the battle for the bridge began to shift to the north. The green area bordered by the Eusebius Binnen and Buiten Singel offered manoeuvre room for

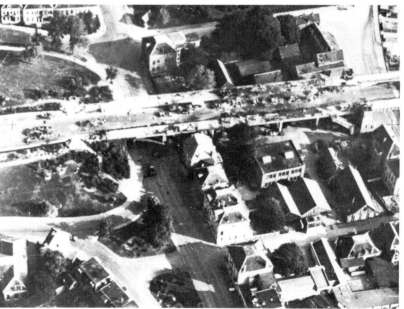

German assaults to recapture the Arnhem bridge between 17–21 September. The enlargement shows the scene on the northern ramp of the bridge taken by a PR Spitfire after Graebner's abortive attack on 18 September while fighting was still going on. Over 20 wrecked vehicles can be identified on this short stretch of road alone. (Imperial War Museum)

GERMAN ATTEMPTS TO RECAPTURE THE ARNHEM BRIDGE 17–20 SEPTEMBER 1944.
German attempts to recapture the Arnhem bridge between 17–18 September were characterised by confusion and badly co-ordinated piecemeal attacks. The first sustained effort began at dawn on 18 September with the Kampfgruppe Brinkmann's probes from the factory area to the east of the bridge. Graebner's abortive attack from the south was decimated on the northern ramp of the bridge (above/Imperial War Museum) and resulted in the destruction of

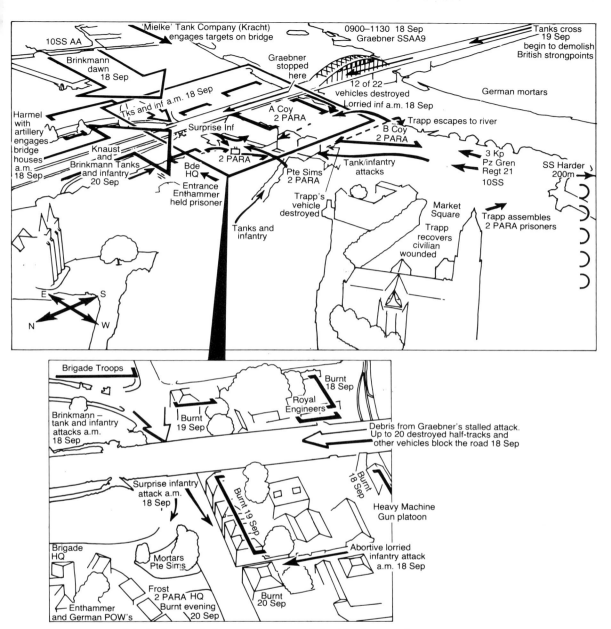

Map labels (top panel):

'Mielke' Tank Company (Kracht) engages targets on bridge

0900–1130 18 Sep
Graebner SSAA9

Tanks cross
19 Sep
begin to demolish
British strongpoints

10SS AA

Brinkmann
dawn
18 Sep

Graebner
stopped
here

12 of 22
vehicles destroyed
Lorried inf a.m. 18 Sep

German mortars

Tks and inf a.m. 18 Sep

A Coy
2 PARA

Trapp escapes to river

Harmel
with
artillery
engages
bridge
houses
a.m.
18 Sep

Surprise Inf

B Coy
2 PARA

3 Kp
Pz Gren
Regt 21
10SS

SS Harder
200m

Knaust
and
Brinkmann Tanks
and infantry
20 Sep

2 PARA

Bde
HQ

Pte Sims
2 PARA

Tank/infantry
attacks

Entrance
Enthammer
held prisoner

Tanks and
infantry

Trapp's
vehicle
destroyed

Market
Square

Trapp assembles
2 PARA prisoners

Trapp
recovers
civilian
wounded

E S
N W

Map labels (bottom panel):

Brigade Troops

Burnt
18 Sep

Royal
Engineers

Brinkmann –
tank and infantry
attacks a.m.
18 Sep

Burnt
19 Sep

Debris from Graebner's stalled attack.
Up to 20 destroyed half-tracks and
other vehicles block the road 18 Sep

Burnt
18 Sep

Surprise infantry
attack a.m.
18 Sep

Burnt 19 Sep

Heavy Machine
Gun platoon

Brigade
HQ

Mortars
Pte Sims

Abortive lorried
infantry attack
a.m. 18 Sep

Enthammer
and German POW's

Frost
2 PARA HQ
Burnt evening
20 Sep

Burnt
20 Sep

*most of the Hohenstaufen's available armour. Joined by the Kampfgruppe Knaust, heavier
attacks come in from the north-east during 18–19 September. Eventually pinned down by
superior numbers of infantry, Frost's battalion was reduced by artillery, and the concentrated
fire of the SPs and tanks who were able to roam virtually at will.*

tanks and infantry. A combined arms assault was now conceivable. Tanks would begin to arrive the following day.

They were already *en route*. Lance-Corporal Karl-Heinz Kracht, a 19-year-old tank loader, remembers entraining in Bielefeld on 17 September. Tank Company 'Mielke', to which he belonged (named after his Lieutenant Company Commander), formed part of the 6 Panzer Replacement Regiment 'Bielefeld'. When the landings occurred the unit was moved via Zevenaar to Elten, where they assembled with Knaust's 'Bochholt' trainee Panzer-grenadier battalion. Kracht described the tank crews, who were 'very young recruits and junior leaders who were about to face their first battle. As a young 19-year-old tank gunner and loader I was almost over-aged!'[11] This, Kracht explained, 'was the birth of the Kampfgruppe Knaust' which was primarily made up of raw recruits, 'many of whom were to "bite the dust" because of bad or insufficient training'. Kracht's account suggests that Knaust's Panzer-grenadiers may have arrived before the tanks, which did not arrive until 19 September. They were totally unprepared for what was to await them:

'When we moved out with our eight tanks, Mark IIIs and IVs, via Zeddam we were not told about the seriousness of the situation! All we had was the operation order! Hitler jargon! It equalled the horror experienced in our first contact with the enemy!'[12]

The young tank loader was also an amateur photographer, and still had his camera – an Agfa Karatt III – which had been given to him as a Christmas present in 1939. An enthusiast, he hoped it might be light enough to take pictures the following day.

Meanwhile, SS-Colonel Heinz Harmel arrived from Berlin in the early hours of 18 September, and resumed command of the

10SS Frundsberg Divisional Kampfgruppe. 'Firstly,' he relates, 'I went to Corps headquarters and was briefed on the situation.' He then received a further update from SS-Major Paetsch, who had been controlling the battle in his absence. From there he drove straight into the Arnhem town centre to see the situation for himself. House-to-house fighting was going on as he arrived. 'The divisional commander should always be seen by the boys to be forward,' he observed, 'a habit for which I was always berated by my superiors.'

Harmel witnessed the beginning of the drive from the north. 'Euling's battalion

Amidst the carnage of wrecked buildings near the bridge, a German soldier pulls at a cigar with evident relish during a pause in the battle. The realisation began to dawn that this would be no easy task. (Bundesarchiv)

was still partly there with Knaust's, unable to cross the bridge. His lead company, as well as Ziebrecht's armoured car company [1st Company 10SS Reconnaissance Battalion], were already totally locked into the fight and could not be extricated.' The rest of Euling's battalion had already left, taking detours until they found a clear route to Nijmegen.

Two 10cm artillery pieces had been unlimbered from tractors and sited in the green park area just north of the bridge. They were to be used in the direct fire role against Frost's fortified houses. A series of resounding crashes echoed around the buildings bordering the park area as they bombarded positions in houses and cellars. Harmel 'lay for a while between the guns,

directing them a little to the left or right – there! But, as much as I wanted to,' he said, 'I could not stay here for ever.'

Harmel received a dual task from General Bittrich, the corps commander, that very afternoon. He was to fight the bridge clear so that he could support the corps' *Schwerpunkt* in the south, which was also to be his responsibility. This made sense as all the Kampfgruppen at the bridge either came from the 10SS initially, or were under command. It therefore rationalised what had previously been a crude and somewhat confusing arrangement. Brinkmann came back under Harmel's command, and was ordered to co-ordinate the effort to recapture the bridge. The 9SS were to clear the remainder of Arnhem and defeat the British

Rubble and debris was now beginning to hamper attempts to approach Frost's fortified houses. (Bundesarchiv)

at Oosterbeek. Nevertheless, as Harmel recalls, this was not easy:

> 'It was actually difficult to direct the Kampfgruppe. I had to constantly drive my jeep between Arnhem and Nijmegen. My mission was to block the threat in the south long enough to enable the 9SS to settle with the British Division in Oosterbeek-Arnhem. This was the main task.'

Harmel recognised the hopelessness of Frost's situation. 'I could see it from my position, better than he.' He summoned a captured British Sergeant-Major. None of the POWs was unwounded, and this one was no exception, with his arm in a sling. 'Go to your commander,' Harmel explained, 'and tell him I have an all-round view which he does not have. I am in a far better spot to make a sensible appreciation. Tell him to surrender.' Off he went. Before long, back came the expected response: 'No surrender,' and, much as Harmel had anticipated, 'no Sergeant-Major!' [13]

Lieutenant Joseph Enthammer's fortunes still had not changed. He and his group of artillerymen were still prisoners. Early on Monday morning they were taken 800 metres from the terraced house where they had previously been held, to a stable. Wearing the uniform of Wehrmacht artillery, they were anxious not to be identified as V2 rocket troops. He recalled how

> '. . . on the way Dutch civilians spat and threw rotten fruit at us. Our sergeant captor fired over their heads and excused their conduct. This is something I will never forget.'

There were now up to 40 or 50 prisoners crowded into the stalls. On Tuesday morning they were taken to the building that housed brigade headquarters, near Frost's 2 PARA command post near the bridge. During the 15-minute journey,

> '. . . we were further interfered with by the Dutch population. It was an unpleasant surprise. They had been so friendly before. We were also aware now of the sounds of battle, rifle, hand-grenades and machine gun fire. Clouds of dust spiralled into the air, but we could see nothing directly. We were put into the basement of the building.' [14]

This appeared to be an improvement. It may even be safer.

CHAPTER XII

Schwerpunkt is South!

My mission was to block the threat in the south long enough to enable the 9SS to settle with the British Division in Oosterbeek-Arnhem. This was the main task.

SS-Colonel Harmel

Defending Nijmegen, 18–19 September . . .

SS-Colonel Heinz Harmel, commander of the Kampfgruppe Frundsberg, was under no illusions where his main task lay. Bittrich, his corps commander, had been absolutely clear: '*Schwerpunkt* is south!' A link-up between the Allied forces advancing from The Neerpelt bridgehead and paratroopers had to be denied at any cost. Harmel recalls 'every man in the division was aware of this task'.[1] At the very least he felt an Allied advance to the Waal river would be inevitable. He was not aware of the extent of their progress, only that much of his strength had been dissipated, and they were not even here yet.

> 'I was constantly required to send battle groups to counter the Allied thrust south of Nijmegen. This was a constant weakening factor. It was also a little sad, because Student's forces, continually obliged to establish new lines, were never able to give them any depth. Allied forces would burst through immediately. Thus we played a part in the defence of Son at Veghel and also at Overloon. Heinke's Kampfgruppe was separated from me for some two months, attached as he was to Ludwig Roestler's battle group.'[2]

Numerous Kampfgruppen were also committed to clearing Frost from the Arnhem bridge to ensure the reinforcement and resupply of the Nijmegen bridgehead. Somehow, substantial forces had to reach the city via an alternative route. An advance

SS-Colonel Heinz Harmel, the Commander of the 10SS Frundsberg, sheltering in a trench.

An aerial view of the two bridges at Nijmegen – (top) the railway bridge, and (bottom) the road bridge. (Imperial War Museum)

SS-Captain Leo Hermann Reinhold, tasked with co-ordinating defence measures in Nijmegen.

Kampfgruppe, commanded by SS-Captain Leo Hermann Reinhold, was ordered to advance on Nijmegen via Westerwoort and Duiven, in order to cross the lower Rhine at Pannerden. In the meantime Harmel wished personally to supervise his immediate and biggest headache – retaking the Arnhem bridge, which was fundamental to success in Nijmegen. He, therefore, remained on 19 September. Reinhold was to co-ordinate the inevitably slow build-up of the 10SS on the Waal until Harmel returned. Spearheading Reinhold's Kampfgruppe and under command was the Battalion Euling, recently transferred from the 9SS. Euling's lead company, snarled up in the battle for the Arnhem bridge, was only now being relieved, platoon by platoon, by the newly arrived Battalion Knaust. Harmel moved his headquarters from Velp to the river-crossing point at Pannerden, to control the forthcoming Waal battle.

By early morning on 18 September the 10SS Engineer Battalion began to set up and run the ferrying operation at Pannerden. Despite offering the quickest alternative route to Nijmegen, Harmel remembers:

> 'It cost time. Moreover, our engineers had to construct our own ferries because the Dutch civilian ferry was insufficient for our needs. We needed at least a 40-ton capacity. I had to telephone Wehrmacht [Army] engineers to get us across.'[3]

At Pannerden progress was painfully slow. Anything that could be found at the water's edge – rubber dinghies, small skiffs, barges – was pressed into service. Delays were caused by overflying Allied aircraft. Commanders strode frustratedly along the water's edge, hurrying dispersed and mixed-up groups across. The first Mark IV tanks trundled ponderously on to huge rafts, which were then manhandled across with ropes and poles. It was far from satisfactory; improvisation was the order of the day. At this rate it was estimated it would take two to three days to get all the armoured vehicles across. Would the time suffice? everyone asked.

The first troops across at Pannerden reached Nijmegen during the morning of 18 September. These were a company of 10SS Engineers, led by SS-2nd Lieutenant Baumgaertel. Arriving by bicycle and truck, they were set to work following a Corps directive to prepare both the massive road and rail bridges for demolition. The firing of the charges was to be done only under the express authority of Model's Army Group B headquarters. They also began to assist in strengthening the field fortifications at the south end of the bridge.

Around midday the Battalion Euling arrived. Its commander, 25-year-old SS-Captain Karl Heinz Euling, had managed to break clean from the fight on the Arnhem bridge. He had crossed the lower Rhine using the ferry at Huissen, and had then made good time via Elst to Nijmegen. His battalion numbered 100 men. He was met by Reinhold on the northern bank of the Waal, in the village of Lent, and a plan was quickly confirmed. Euling would immediately establish a bridgehead south of the Waal, securing the approaches to the main road bridge. Reinhold's forces were to provide the foot on the ground on the northern 'home' bank. Kampfgruppe Henke and some 10SS advance forces were already fighting a heavy contact in the southern suburbs of Nijmegen. Smoke could be seen curling skywards in the distance. Small arms and machine gun fire could just be discerned rising and falling on the wind, interspersed with the whine and crump of German artillery going into action. The race for this particular foothold was not yet over.

Earlier that morning, G Company of the 3rd Battalion 508 Regiment from the 82nd (US) Airborne Division, attempted an advance on the road bridge from the eastern and south-eastern fringe of the city. SS-Captain Schwappacher, commanding an artillery training regiment, had by now co-ordinated the 10SS artillery resources to support the German forces already occupying Nijmegen. Having walked the streets on a personal reconnaissance to seek out all the friendly force locations, he could now direct the fire of a heavy field battery on to suspected enemy concentrations. The front line still fringed the two traffic circles 1,000 metres south-east and south-west of both bridges. Firing, which had begun in the area of the Maria-Plein, became more pronounced as the American airborne company attacked along the Maria Franken Strasse heading toward the bridge. Schwappacher wrote in his post-action report that German infantry

'. . . were already streaming back to the rear, when the attack was brought to a halt with precise salvoes dropped among the leading enemy waves. Our own infantry, now reinforced from the rear and supported by further artillery fire, were able to force the enemy well back to the south. The northern traffic circles came back into our possession.'[4]

Euling's battalion had passed from fighting for one massive bridge in Arnhem to another in Nijmegen. As the leading armoured half-track company streamed across the open 700-metre span, roaring at full speed, accompanied by battalion headquarters, enemy mortar and artillery bursts spurted plumes of spray up and around the superstructure of the bridge iself. Clattering off into the Hunner Park on the other side, they quickly made contact with the Kampfgruppe Henke already occupying hastily prepared positions. Deciding the dash across the bridge was not worth the casualties, the remainder of the battalion arriving on bicycles were taken across the Waal in rubber dinghies during the afternoon.

Euling supplemented his 100-strong battalion by taking under command the Wehrmacht and Police reserves he found manning strongpoints jointly with his own advance elements. 'During the afternoon,' Schwappacher observed, spotting for his artillery, 'the initiative changed from the enemy back to our own forces.' In reality, American units had been pulled back to clear landing zones in preparation for a second lift of airborne reinforcements. Three attacks had been mounted against Nijmegen altogether since the landings, the largest only two companies strong. Each attack had become over-extended upon clashing with German

reinforcements arriving piecemeal to swell the city's defence force. Kampfgruppen from the Frundsberg were now arriving in some strength. Only a reinforced combined infantry-tank attack could succeed, now that the element of surprise was lost. Meanwhile, the Americans felt they could afford to wait for the ground link-up with Second British Army. All its other objectives had been taken. This one would follow, in its time.

Taking advantage of the lull in the battle, the Kampfgruppe Reinhold, consisting now of Euling's battalion, Henke's Kampfgruppe and Reinhold's own converted SS-tank-crew infantry, began to reorganise and improve the defences of Nijmegen.[5] Reinhold's group, having bypassed Arnhem to the east during the night of 17–18 September and waiting in Velp while a clear route was reconnoitred, moved via Westervoort-Duiven and Helhock down to the ferry at Pannerden, crossing during the early morning of the 18th. By the afternoon troops were feverishly digging in.

The focus for the defence now shifted to Euling covering the Hunner Park, whose location guarded the southern approaches to the Waal road bridge. Trenches and strongpoints were dug in along the southern end of the park, dominating all the roads converging on to the Kaiser Lodewijk, the last traffic circle exiting to the bridge. A battery of four SS Panzerjaeger Mark IV SPs trundled across the bridge, and these were incorporated within the Hunner Park defence system, dominating the same main avenues of approach and protected by dug-in infantry. 88mm flak guns were sited across the river on the north bank among the houses in Lent at the water's edge. Some had flanking shoots from below up on to the main span, while others covered frontally, straight down the main road, crossing the bridge itself. Euling's battalion headquarters was sited in the Haus Robert Janssen next to the foot bridge above the old town wall, immediately below the Valkhof. The 'Valkhof' or citadel was the highest point in Nijmegen, and indeed for many miles around. Historically significant, it dominated the approaches to both the rail and road bridges. Euling's headquarters was essentially a fortified keep, guarding the footbridge that led into the citadel, which, in turn, was to be fortified by the 10SS engineers. These, reinforced by a detachment from an SS Ersatz (Replacement) Regiment, were mostly experienced veterans, the majority of whom had fought on the Russian front. They were to be tenacious in defence.

Immediately to the west a mixture of SS and Henke's Kampfgruppe secured the southern approaches to the railway bridge, the focus of resistance here being positions dug in the Kronenburger Park.

Two traffic circles, the Kaiser Karel and Lodewijk-Plein, provided the 'outposts' to the German linked defence. 20mm cannon were placed at the access points of both bridges, able to fire across and mutually support each other. In the rear, on the home bank, Henke's forces covered the western flank in the area of the Fort Hof van Holland. Reinhold's battalion, steadily reinforced by the trickle of 10SS reinforcements being ferried across the canal at Pannerden, occupied the village of Lent.

SS-Captain Brandt, the 29-year-old commander of the Frundsberg's engineer battalion, remembers what was achieved during this lull. 'Mines were laid everywhere,' he wrote, 'but field fortifications were very much restricted by the terrain.' Demolitions were carried out with total military objectivity, regardless of the impact upon civilians. 'Even church towers had to be blown because they were pointers for enemy artillery fire stuck right in front of our noses.' Factory chimneys also came crashing down, once their usefulness as observation platforms had ceased.[6]

During the rest of the afternoon of the 18th, and the night of 19 September, German artillery fire harassed suspected enemy troop concentrations, or sought to duel with mortar positions south of Nijmegen. The line of outposts just beyond and inclusive of the traffic circles was reoccupied. Troops anxiously waited and watched. Some tanks, having crossed the Pannerden ferry, were despatched across the Waal bridge and incorporated into the defence line.

SS-Captain Schwappacher remembers that during the morning of the 19th 'peace reigned for the most part in the front line'. However, one of his SS-Sergeants, Hotop, spotted tanks later, gathering in the early evening. They appeared to be moving to the south-west of Nijmegen. This report raised a start at headquarters. What sort of tanks? II Fallschirmjaeger Corps had already reported sighting 15 armoured reconnaissance vehicles moving toward Nijmegen from a south-westerly direction, in a sighting passed on to Army Group B at 1445 hours.[7] Were they air-landed vehicles, or armour that had moved north-west from Eindhoven? It could not be determined. Sergeant Hotop could now see the vehicles clearly; an artillery observer, he brought down fire on the advancing infantry and tanks in the area of the railway line south-west of the town. The flash and then mushrooms of smoke were visible long before the audible crump, crump of shells reached his ears. As the smoke cleared, two tanks, tracks sheared, were unable to move. Hotop got a good look at them and saw that they were Shermans. As Harmel was later to recall:

'The first time the heavy tanks were set against us was an indication that the enemy armoured forces that had broken out of the Neerpelt bridgehead had now established contact with the 82nd (US) Airborne Divison.'[8]

Now they would have a fight on their hands; XXX Corps had arrived.

Slowing the advance. Jabs against the corridor 19–20 September. . .

What, in the meantime, was barring their progress to Nijmegen? 59 Infantry Division, commanded by Generalleutnant Poppe, continued its fragmented attacks against selected points of 101 (US) Division's corridor as and when he received reinforcements. Attrition, particularly the stalemate forced by the outnumbered Americans in the Son forest, was beginning to have a noticeable effect upon the quality of German resistance. Veteran paratroopers were fighting the German reservists to a standstill. Lacking the basic fundamentals, such as artillery support, and particularly ammunition, there was little more to be done with the resources at hand except maintain what pressure they could muster. LXXXVIII Corps, when exhorted to do more, advised Student that the logistic situation was tight, and that there were ammunition shortages; it was also pointed out that to fight a battle the troops must be adequately supplied. The Corps diary commented: 'Command has the tenacious will to achieve all that is possible, but one cannot hide the fact that a large proportion of the troops are showing signs of exhaustion, and a lowering of morale.' Student's response was that their mission – to hold their present position, and destroy the air-landed enemy troops – remained. In short – they were to get on with it.[9]

The troops were, however, beginning to crack under the strain. Kampfgruppe Chill (85 Infantry Division) reported difficulties, questioning the conduct of Fallschirmjaeger Battalion 'Stephan' fighting alongside von der Heydte's Fallschirmjaeger Regiment 6. Stephan's 5th Company had

reported an armoured breakthrough, in which the word 'surrender' had allegedly been overheard on the radio. In addition, 7th Company was overrun, 'leading to a part withdrawal of the battalion, without', as the Corps diary relates, 'the accompanying enemy infantry, mounted on lorries with the tanks, once being engaged'. Chill relieved Stephan of his command, transferring it to von der Heydte's Regiment. The hapless commanding officer was posted to rear-area bridge security duties.[10]

Despite the cost, German pressure was maintained. Resolve and the knowledge of British intentions were there, but sufficient forces to do anything about it were not. Inexorably the armoured spearheads ground onwards. 'Motorised movement on the road between Son and St Oedenrode towards the north' was reported during LXXXVIII Corps' evening situation report on 19 September.[11] Counter-measures to block this traffic had already been instituted by Student. Some of the reserve Fallschirmjaeger battalions that had been assembled in S'Hertogenbosch were now in position and began to interfere with traffic on 'Hell's Highway' between 18–20 September. Despite this, at around 1000 on the 18th the first British tanks began crossing the bridge at Grave, after having established contact with the 82nd Airborne Division 90 minutes before. Behind them, further delaying the Allied build-up, German units, having mobilised, attacked from the west.

Major Hans Jungwirth, previously attached to Student's 1st Fallschirmjaeger Army Headquarters, was sent to Hertogenbosch to co-ordinate attacks against the corridor between Oedenrode and Veghel. Four Fallschirmjaeger 'march' battalions and the Grenadier Regiment 1036 were ordered to block the highway. Jungwirth operated as a type of 'supremo', co-ordinating measures to obstruct the road as necessary. A veteran of Poland, France,

Fallschirmjaeger were sent forward mainly on foot to block 'Hell's Highway'. (Bundesarchiv)

Crete, Russia and Tunisia, he was supported by a cadre of similarly experienced troops, able to provide some backbone to these hastily raised formations. Pastor Willi Schiffer was serving in one of the battalions ordered on 18 September to cut 'Hell's Highway'. Coming down the railway line from Schijndel towards the station at Eerde, south-west of Veghel, Schiffer recalled how inexperience cost lives:

'The heavy weapons companies were held back, while the light infantry companies walked straight into the machine gun fire of the Americans who were hiding in the station. In a bitter man-to-man fight, the Americans were driven away and we went along the railway track. Supported by flak guns brought up from S'Hertogenbosch, we finally

collected enough troops to attack the railway bridge in front of Veghel, which we took in the afternoon.'[12]

General Student, forward at the front, recalled the hard-fought street battles that were conducted to clear the town:

'On one of these days I was able to observe a flak platoon attached from the *Reichsarbeitsdienst* [Pioneers], who fired with both of their 88mm guns at single American paratroopers sniping from high buildings, harassing our attack from the flanks.'[13]

Although relatively small-scale, these actions were bitterly fought. Willi Schiffer, at the point of victory in Veghel, discovered the futility of fighting with no clear direction:

'Shortly afterwards, to our complete consternation, we received orders to withdraw! What had happened? The battalion headquarters and headquarters company which had remained in Schijndel had been attacked by armoured cars, operating singly, from the direction of St Oedenrode, and they were afraid that an attack would now follow into our flank. Their fears were groundless, as it was several days before larger units could be brought forward by both sides, and the real battle began. But the very next day a regiment of our 59th Infantry Division had to retrace the path we had already taken, and was wiped out.'[14]

By the following day, the Allies had brought larger units forward. The failure of the Kampfgruppe Rink's attacks around Best was the outward manifestation of latent disintegration. At 1400 on 19 September the overstretched 59 Division units collapsed in the face of an attack supported by British tanks. Resistance around Best came to an end. Three days of bitter fighting ended in a rout – 300 dead and more than 1,400 prisoners taken. LXXXVIII Corps, fully recognising the significance of any pressure it could exert against the Allied corridor from the west, found itself powerless to do so. Indeed, the importance of this umbilical cord was underscored by the proportionally heavier counter-attacks it was meeting itself. It was felt, however, that unless more ammunition and fuel were made available, the thin security line holding the Aart bridgehead, through Lommel, Hapert to Best, and including 59 Division's area, could hardly be expected to hold. All the 75mm anti-tank and heavy field artillery ammunition had been fired off. Only a few light and heavy infantry field guns held one-quarter of their first line allocation. Despite this,

the order was to 'fight on'. LXXXVIII Corps' assessment of the situation on the evening of 19 September, while accepting the problems, was uncompromising:

'59 Infantry Division has been partly forced on to the defensive, and cannot now reach its ordered objective, Best. This is due in the first instance to a lack of artillery and the exhausted state of the troops. Only 5 batteries are ready for action and these with little ammunition. Despite this, the division still had the order, when the panzer brigade attack over Son to St Oedenrode made its presence felt, to attack again. The original objective "Son" remains.'[15]

59 Division was therefore *hors de combat*. It was due to support a planned thrust by Panzer Brigade 107, the only effective German formation within striking distance of the Allied columns pouring along the corridor toward Grave and Nijmegen. But where was the missing brigade?

The raids by Panzer Brigade 107, 19–20 September 1944 . . .

Major Freiherr von Maltzahn, the commander of Panzer Brigade 107, had been given a difficult task: attack across Son and take St Oedenrode, and thereby slice off the head of the British XXX Corps advance on Grave. Enemy forces were as yet an undetermined number of air-landed battalions, relatively easy meat for his mobile armoured formation. They had been rerouted from an original operational commitment on the eastern front, and this new task was eminently more preferable, but it could have its complications. Where was the promised assistance from 59 Division? Initial reconnaissance had not been encouraging. As always, the ground in southern Holland mitigated against von Maltzahn's need to concentrate the mass of his armour into a solid punch, sufficient to overwhelm his lightly armed opposition with one massive armoured blow. This was not to happen. Reluctant to commit his brigade to going recklessly into the unknown, von Maltzahn decided upon a reconnaissance in force. His chosen approach from the south-east towards Son was flat, but sandy and boggy; Eindhoven to his left was probably now occupied, and the axis of advance was further channelled by the line of the Wilhelmina canal itself, an obstacle forward and to the right. A small river tributary running due south from the canal, parallel to Eindhoven, restricted armoured movement even further. Weighing up his options, gazing through binoculars, von Maltzahn realised that his initial objective must be the small bridge 1,100 metres due east of the main canal bridge at Son. He would have to establish a foothold on the other side. Therefore, with infantry leading covered by tanks, the vanguard of Panzer Brigade 107 squeaked and rattled remorselessly toward its objective – the bridge at Son. A shock assault was an impractical proposition, but, by using the trees that screened their advance, a heavy 'raid' appearing ghost-like from nowhere might substitute. It very nearly paid off.

At 1715 one of the 'Panther' tanks in the leading group levelled its 75mm gun at the church tower and school. The optical triangle in the sight fitted above the tower, the centre line on the building itself, likely enemy observation posts. Having formed up in the *Molenheide* (heath) area, using the woods as protection, some 40 main battle tanks were spread around. Only a limited number, however, could spearhead the attack, alongside dismounted infantry from the attached Grenadier Regiment 1034. The attack came in from the south,

Panzer Brigade 107 squeaked and rattled remorselessly toward its objective. German tanks on the move in southern Holland. (Bundesarchiv)

and almost immediately threatened to over-run the recently erected British Bailey Bridge.

Looking through his TZF12 binocular sight, the Panther gunner made the final adjustments with his foot pedal: 'On . . . fire!' With a resounding crack the long 75mm barrel recoiled whilst, in the same instant, at short range, an eruption of flame and black smoke burst on the church tower. Seconds later the report of the impact and falling masonry could be heard. Other whip-like cracks from accompanying tanks signalled the opening salvoes of supporting fire. These, after a whoosh and explosion, also struck the schoolhouse. This was the first indication the Americans in Son had of the attack. General Taylor,

One of the Panthers almost reached the towpath on the canal before it was knocked out. The Bailey Bridge in Son, its objective, can be seen to the left.

commanding the 101 Division, emerged shocked and surprised from his headquarters in the schoolhouse. Enemy tanks! The threat he feared most had finally arrived. German infantry was now just discernible, moving in rushes across the flat fields toward the village, still screened by trees. A storm of 7·92mm machine gun fire began to flail buildings as the co-axial MG 34s of the Panther tanks attempted to fire them in. Rifles and BAR automatic weapons began intermittently to return fire. Tracer bounced off buildings in clouds of masonry dust and whirled in all directions, isolated sparks sometimes arcing lazily into the air.

Even without 59 Division's support from the other side of the canal, Major von Maltzahn's attack very nearly succeeded. Fighting continued even as dusk fell. A British truck from 'Q' Battery of 21 Anti-Tank Regiment, part of Guards Armoured Division's 'A' echelon, was struck by a shell as it attempted to cross the Bailey Bridge.[16] Explosions rent the air and lit up the surrounding scene as flames devoured the wreckage on the main span. German tanks continued to fire round after round into the buildings housing the American Division command post, but they were unable to get across the canal; this had deflected the assault, and now brought it to a halt. Elements of an American infantry glider battalion arrived and reinforced the besieged perimeter. With them was a 57mm anti-tank gun. One of the Panthers, which had almost reached the tow-path running up to the Bailey Bridge, was knocked out virtually with the first round. The shell penetrated the hull above the front road wheels and blasted off the bazooka plates around it. With its hydraulics shattered, the gun barrel dipped, pointing into the canal as if in salute to its own flaming reflection in the water. Darkness, and the length of this uncrossable waterway, had broken up the cohesion of the attack.

Bazooka fire suddenly clanged against another Panther, showering sparks and lighting up the night. It, too, began to burn violently, petrol and ammunition producing secondary bursting – tin-like reports that sent fresh bulbous clouds of oily black smoke into the night air. Separated from the tanks, infantry had been fought to a standstill, pinned down at the edge of the village. There was nothing for it but to disengage. With difficulty the tanks began to manœuvre back to the start point, in the direction of the Molenheide, south-east of the Bailey Bridge. Aided initially by the twilight glow of blazing vehicles, which could eventually be used as navigational reference points, von Malzahn's reconnaissance in force fell back, armour to the south, many of the grenadiers from Battalion 1034 moving towards the north.[17]

Despite the failure, the results had not been totally negative. Unfamiliar terrain, darkness and the arrival of unexpected enemy reinforcements had all conspired to prevent what had very nearly been a *coup de main* by the powerful raiding force. Von Malzahn might realistically conclude that he may well succeed if instructed to try again. Allied pressure dictated that, with 59 Division momentarily ineffective, something must be done to blunt the Allied progress if a front along the Waal was ever to be stabilised. The Americans listened with relief to the receding engine noises and the sounds of clattering and squeaking tracks rising and falling in the dark. They would be back but not here, they thought; somewhere else, not the same place.

Counting on this assumption, 107 Panzer Brigade emerged from the early morning mist the following day, 20 September. Few German units would have countenanced such a bold thrust, and in daylight, because

of the Allies' overwhelming air superiority. Von Malzahn, however, could count upon an abundance of air defence weapons. Besides the 37mm anti-air guns mounted on half-tracks in the tank companies, every infantry half-track had in addition one triple 15mm anti-air gun. In total, 250 guns and machine guns provided the sort of protection that enemy fighter bombers tended to respect. Generally the air space above this brigade was avoided.[18]

Hitting the same point achieved complete surprise. Despite the reinforcement of the night before, German tanks soon controlled the bridge again with fire. Again, just on the point of success, 10 British tanks appeared, belatedly responding to the SOS of the night before. This time four more German tanks were disabled, unable to close in on the village in any substantial force due to the channelling effect and the obstacle presented by the waterway.

Losing ever more casualties to an enemy markedly increasing in strength, von Maltzahn ordered his spearheads to fall back again. The crisis for the Allies had passed. Realising that only a co-ordinated tank-infantry attack on more suitable terrain would ever cross 'Hell's Highway', the commander of 107 Brigade pulled out. Two forays had cost him 10 per cent of his strength.[19] It was not easy for him to replace losses because the brigade's heavy workshop facilities had already been moved to the eastern front before his previous operation order had been rescinded. To cut the umbilical cord about to bring succour to the Allied airborne divisions to the north would involve a more fundamental regrouping of German resources. Panzer Brigade 107 was to play its part again within 48 hours. What was needed was not so much a series of raids, but a concerted attack, and this would take time. This was a commodity both sides would need if they were ever to achieve success.

147

CHAPTER XIII

The Impact on German Soil

Wesel women remember that they were never propositioned more imploringly by soldiers in transit, than during these days.

Local German historian, Wesel

Volunteers to defend the Reich . . .

PRIORITY SIGNAL FROM SUPREME COMMANDER WEST. COS NR 8197/44

The conflict in the West has spilled over into the German homeland in this latest attack. Commanders are therefore to be fanatical in the extreme. Every town, every village, every bunker is to be defended to the last drop of blood, and to the last round. All commanders, whatever their rank, are responsible for ensuring that this fanaticism is communicated to the troops and population, and is constantly raised. Whoever is indifferent or negligent is to be removed, and face the consequences of his actions. The determination of the soldiers is to be kept up with all means at your disposal.

ORAL TRANSMISSION OF THIS MESSAGE TO ALL OFFICERS AND TROOPS IS TO BE REPORTED TO SUPREME COMMAND WEST.[1]

Field Marshal von Runstedt's signal to all units received on 18 September was the first indication that land operations had now reached the western extremity of the Reich itself. MARKET-GARDEN was visibly to affect the lives of the German population on the northern lower Rhine and the western edge of the Ruhr. Transport aircraft had been spotted dropping paratroopers from Cleve and Emmerich on 17 September, and the result of all this air activity was soon to become very apparent. 82nd (US) Airborne Division had even succeeded in establishing itself on the Wyler Berg ridgeline, a part of which lay on German soil.

Much of the Reich had already been laid waste by the Allied air offensive. Land operations were a more unsettling development, and some of the impact had been felt already. Bridges in Holland, and in the anticipated areas of the Allied advance bordering Germany, had already been blown. The deputy commander of Wehrkreis VI issued a directive from his headquarters in Rheinburg on 17 September:

'Premature demolitions have caused logistical and resupply difficulties and communications problems for the troops. Railway facilities of any type in our own land may only be destroyed with the joint corresponding agreement of Reich railway officials *[Reichsbahn]*. Headquarters and soldiers are to be informed accordingly.'[2]

Conducting operations with any consideration for civilian requirements had not characterised Wehrmacht campaigns beyond the borders of the Reich to date. War had arrived with a vengeance. It now burst upon a number of small towns along the Rhine. During the evening hours of 17 September Field Marshal Model, comprehending the dimension of the crisis in and around Arnhem, took appropriate measures to stabilise the situation in Army Group B's area. All military personnel on leave in the *Bezirks* (counties) of Wesel, Dinslaken and Rees were recalled, assembled into *ad hoc* combat groups, and sent to the area of operations.

This order turned the towns of Emmerich and Wesel into a veritable hornet's nest. Unrest stirred in the soldiers' billets. Two companies of the naval air defence units, stationed in the barracks of the 7th and 43rd Regiments, moved off immediately to the combat zone. Wesel never again saw naval air defence units training; the remaining elements embarked for their return to the Naval School at Kiel. In Bielefeld, Panzer Replacement Regiment 6's tank driving school was wound up, and its obsolete tanks used for driver training entrained for Arnhem. Major Knaust's Panzer-grenadier Training Replacement Battalion clattered out of Bocholt bordering the Ruhr during the night of 17 September – destination, Arnhem.

An atmosphere of crisis and calamity reigned in the rear areas (in effect, along the West German border), 24 hours after the initial landings. Supreme Commander West's Chief-of-Staff decreed: 'Every soldier must – even in his accommodation or otherwise – have a weapon, ready for action and constantly to hand.' Also, 'in requisitioned or official barracks etc., anti-aircraft machine guns are to be set up and manned, so that low-flying surprise attacks can be immediately fought off'.[3]

Model's order did not only stir units in barracks. On the evening of the 17th, an order was received by the Military District Command, on the Willibrordiplatz in Wesel, to round up all soldiers on leave in the Rees and Dinslaken areas. Colonel Hellriegel, the senior post officer, was summoned from his accommodation in the soldiers' club-rooms (in a former pub, the 'Weselerhof', near the railway station), and told to carry this out. This easy-going Viennese officer was directed to get all soldiers to the combat zone. And so it started. Cars and motorcycles were assembled and sped off into the night to perform their repugnant duty. Soldiers on leave were traced to individual villages, knocked up, and pulled out of bed or from family celebrations. There were tears, desperate remonstrations and curses, but to no avail. All remembered the sad case of the soldier who was forced to say farewell, having arrived home on leave just two hours before. He had not been home for two years. Two days later he was killed near Arnhem.[4]

Soldiers' club-rooms in Wesel were kept empty during the last days of September. It did not take long before troops *en route* to leave destinations became canny. Once the panicky mood was detected, Wehrmacht registration points were avoided wherever possible. Sleeping in barns or in the company of helpful acquaintances was preferable to being marched to the front with an unknown unit. As one local historian comments: 'Wesel women remember that they were never propositioned more imploringly by soldiers in transit, than during these days.'[5] If it was necessary to stop in Wesel, soldiers would rather spend their time in civilian arms, ideally those of a woman, rather than in the claws of the Wehrmacht.

The new military situation made the war for the German civilian population of the northern lower Rhine ever-more apparent. Emmerich's inhabitants, looking down the Rhine, could now detect the muzzle flashes of numerous gun batteries sited between the oil refineries at Spyck and the Reichswald forest. In the distance the constant and forbidding crump and crack of gun fire could be discerned. Refugees from the Nijmegen area began to arrive at the Rhine ferry. Dirty, irritated and dishevelled, they carried only a few belongings. Some were wounded. It was a depressing scene, showing in a sinister way what could happen next.

Other military preparations were also in evidence. The home front was being mobilised. The Gauleiter of Essen, doubling as the Reich Defence Commissioner, was directed hastily to assemble a home guard. As they moved out, these hardly convincing replacement formations met the first casualty convoys from the front on the Elten road. As the home guard rode through Emmerich by train and truck, they witnessed the unsettling spectacle of wounded going the other way. Soldiers with blood-soaked bandages could be seen lying on thin layers of straw on a motley assortment of vehicles, ranging from ambulances to farm carts. It was not an auspicious beginning.

At the same time stragglers from the earlier retreat from Belgium were gathered on the Geist market square in Emmerich. They were about to be sent to the front again. Furtive glances and an air of resignation were the only outward signs of the gut-rending nervousness they must have felt. Amongst them were brown-uniformed SA – *Sturmabteilung* men – who had originally been despatched to the Netherlands to conscript foreign workers to labour on the West Wall, or Siegfried Line. Others were railway guards left over from the headlong flight from France. There were also a number of intimidated-looking signallers from the Wehrmacht's women auxiliaries. All were despatched to the front, apart from the *Blitzmaedel* – the 'lightning girls' named after the flash emblem they wore on their sleeves.

Scratch reinforcements . . .

Hastily-formed *ad hoc* formations suffered more casualties than regular units. Normally lacking both experience and capable commanders, they were thrown into battle, and had to look to neighbouring units for assistance or any expertise. Sergeant Emil Petersen was in command of a 35-man platoon of the *Reichsarbeitsdienst* – Reich army pioneers – waiting at Arnhem station for transportation back to Germany when the call to action came. Plucked off the platform on the first Sunday of the landings, his dismayed comrades found themselves incorporated into a combat group 250 strong. Nobody had any weapons, apart from Petersen and four others who had machine pistols. Weapons were issued at an SS barracks. Petersen commented cynically:

> 'The situation was laughable. First none of us liked fighting with the Waffen-SS. They had a reputation for being merciless. The arms they gave us were ancient carbines. To break open mine, I had to bang it against a table. The morale of my men was not exactly high when they saw these old weapons.'

Nevertheless, they were put into the fight near the Arnhem bridge. By first light their unit of 250 had shrunk, through death or wounds, to less than half the original size. 'It was nothing less than a massacre,' Petersen recalls.[6]

Competition for the available manpower was fierce, and units topped up their strengths by fair means or foul. It was not only the front in southern Holland that had to be stabilised. The West Wall was crumbling too. SS Panzer-grenadier Division 17's solution to the problem was that of all German units deployed in Reich border towns near the combat zone. A staff officer explains:

'Officers would stand at road crossings and shanghai every passing soldier who did not have a ready answer to an enquiry after his destination. In one instance I was directing traffic into the divisional area. The army men, not quite satisfied about the prospect of being impressed into an SS unit, circled the area until they hit another road, only to run into me at the road junction again. I redirected the men into the divisional area, rather amused at the merry-go-round. When anti-tank guns were needed, an officer with a few prime-movers at hand would set up shop at a road crossing and wait for passing guns, the crews of which were not quite certain about their destination or attachment. The horses would be unhitched, the crews piled into the waiting prime-movers, and the caravan then proceeded into the re-forming area . . .'[7]

From across the Reich reinforcements were summoned to swell the ranks of Student's First Fallschirmjaeger Army. Although a paper formation at the outset of MARKET-GARDEN, it was steadily gaining substance. Lothar Hinz, from the 6th Luftwaffe NCO School at Ramme aerodrome in Jutland, was despatched to southern Holland a few days after the landings. His unit was later renamed the 1st Battalion Fallschirmjaeger Regiment 22. Hinz's journey to the front was typical of those of the thousands summoned to fight this battle. He wrote about the move by train:

'Even while on board it appeared our area of operations had yet to be determined. The situation was not yet clear. As the decision approached our

transport took a number of peculiar detours.'

The train journey through Hamburg, Osnabrück, Munster, in and out of the Ruhr and across the Rhine, with interruptions, was to last four days.

'It was a memorable experience for us 18- to 19-year-olds. Most of us came from eastern Germany and had never seen a huge industrial works or even the Rhine before. The tall furnaces in Duisberg, working fully lit up despite the constant threat of air attack, were particularly impressive.'

They travelled on through the Ruhr. Between Duisberg and Dusseldorf they saw the 'Christmas lights' – air attacks – 'which in eastern Prussia until mid-1944 were familiar only through hearsay'. To the young and inexperienced, an air attack was as yet an unknown phenomenon. As they passed through Duisberg, they saw one. This made everyone feel 'as if we were in the combat zone at the front already'. They were not hit, but it had been a chastening event, sufficient to make many of Hinz's comrades 'feel uneasy' even at this early stage.

The train steamed across the Rhine bridge at Wesel in darkness and turned eastward, passing Bocholt and moving towards Borken. It was a full moon when suddenly they were attacked by two night fighter bombers. Bomb explosions caused the train to pull up, whereupon 'in a panic everybody leapt out of both sides of the railway embankment, and fled into the fields'. Hinz dashed through the pitch blackness to avoid the strafing runs of the fighters and 'ran full pelt into a wire fence', which, he remembered, 'practically strangled me'. Fire was returned at the aircraft but to no effect. The dead were collected and buried the following day in a cemetery belonging to one of the nearby local authorities. The others

Reinforcements are moved by train from the Reich. Lothar Hinz's train journey to Arnhem from Jutland lasted four days due to constant interruptions from air attacks. (Bundesarchiv)

reboarded the train but were strafed again by another lightning attack. This time Hinz ruined his best field tunic – when trying to get away he hung himself up on a barbed wire fence. This was all the more frustrating because 'we were ordered as usual to travel in our best uniforms; the rest of our kit would be delivered with the stores'.

At nightfall at the end of the fourth day the train began to approach Arnhem from the direction of Dieren-Doesberg. Hinz and his comrades became tense:

'Already from well out one could hear the sounds of battle from the direction of the town. This rose to a thunderous

roar the nearer we came. Large-calibre shells whined over our heads on their way. Many thought they must have come from naval ship batteries. But from where? From The Zuider-Zee?'

Although the intention had been to detrain at Arnhem, 'it didn't work, because we were fired at from several directions shortly after entering the station'. Shunting for all its worth, the train puffed out at high speed and travelled back towards Dieren. At Rheden the locomotive, starved of water, came to a halt. The entire battalion got off, formed a human chain, and used buckets, helmets and any other conceivable container to replenish the water from a nearby stream. Sometime later, after unloading in Dieren-Doesburg, the battalion was sited in a defensive position facing west. Nothing happened until after the battle for Arnhem was concluded. All they saw of it were twenty red-bereted paratroopers speeding by on the back of a lorry – prisoners driving eastwards.[8]

Lothar Hinz's series of unremarkable experiences illustrates the lot of the majority of German soldiers caught up in the MARKET-GARDEN battle. Common to all was a dearth of knowledge about the situation, often including where they were going. Despite this, whenever and wherever able, they fought, often with a tenacity that impressed their foes.

One of the greatest impacts the battle had upon the German homeland was the growing awareness, now overwhelmingly endorsed, of Allied air superiority. Indeed, the airlandings at Arnhem, Nijmegen and Eindhoven had changed the status of the lower Rhine communities, causing the area to become an active combat zone. The sounds of battle on the Wyl hill near Cleve, and in Arnhem, sounded very faint initially, but this was not so with the Allied air forces, who made themselves clearly felt. At the beginning of the war Reichsmarshall Hermann Goering had declared 'if ever an enemy plane flies over German soil, I shall henceforth be known by the name "Hermann Meier"'. The Luftwaffe supremo had been Hermann Meier for a long time already. 'Meier' lost even more credibility as the airborne armadas of 4,600 aircraft hove into sight. Strong formations of the 2nd Allied Tactical Airforce were committed to ensure air superiority over the areas of ground operations. Whatever desperate counter-measures were fielded by the Luftwaffe, a hint of bitterness replaced the previous irony of the term 'Meier'. Soldiers and population alike realised just how impotent the Luftwaffe had become. Largely grounded on airfields for lack of fuel, many aircraft were destroyed on the ground without a chance of fighting back. The citizens of Wesel witnessed a dog fight between a FW190 fighter squadron and the Allied armada as it encroached on the air space above the town. To onlookers it appeared as if the only result was a temporary disturbance of the enemy's flight path. Effective Luftwaffe sorties along the corridor were apparent only to the Allied side. As far as the Germans were concerned, 'Meier's' cause had long since been given up as lost.[9]

CHAPTER XIV

Arnhem. The Pendulum Swings Back

The enemy got new reinforcements. What would that mean for us?

SS Battalion Commander

The odds inverted. Second lift on Ginkel Heath . . .

Von Tettau's two-pronged attack on the landing zones west of Arnhem was making steady progress during the morning of 18 September. Success had been reported in the south, Renkum had been overrun by the SS NCO School 'Arnheim', and Heelsum penetrated. Despite heavy casualties, the inexperienced Naval Manning Battalion secured the Renkum brickworks by 1500. To the north, Helle's SS Wach Battalion 3 had crossed Ginkel heath and was engaging the British in the eastern forest line on the far side. The problem lay in the middle, opposite the British drop-zone 'X'. Here, the inexperienced Soesterberg Fliegerhorst Battalion was too weak to make any further progress. SS-Colonel Lippert, co-ordinating von Tettau's attacks on the ground, reinforced it with two companies from the SS NCO school. Tank Company 224 had arrived by now, and six old French Renault tanks were committed to spearhead this attack. These had been extracted from a group of eight that IISS Corps had brought with them from France.[1]

Lumbering through the woods bordering drop-zone 'X', and along the few tarmac roads from Renkum towards the landing-zones, the tanks fell easy prey to British anti-tank guns securing the few predictable approaches. 224 Company's tank crews were newly formed, unfamiliar with their equipment, and had no radio contact with the accompanying infantry. Necessity and practical difficulties, therefore, led to their piecemeal insertion. An NCO commanding a tank had to double both as gunner and commander, and was therefore not in a position to co-ordinate a combined tank-infantry assault. The bark and tell-tale 'clunk' of high-velocity armoured shot tearing through tank hulls confirmed the attack's failure, and swirling clouds of black smoke belching skyward provided vertical pointers indicating the extent of the stalled advance. All six tanks were quickly knocked out. Frantically attempting to bale out, crews were enveloped by a maelstrom of fire, as machine guns searched out their progress from British positions, and lashed into the accompanying SS-troopers now denuded of cover. Lippert deduced that this setback 'indicated that the British had deployed heavy weapons in the first 24 hours, and had had sufficient time to build up their landing-zone in peace and quiet, and had secured it in the west with heavy weapons'.[2] The attack petered out. Lippert gathered in his SS student company and platoon commanders from the NCO school, and decided upon a more daring surprise tactic.

This time a feint attack was mounted on the right, which included Lippert driving

Tank Company 224's Renault tanks fell easy prey to British anti-tank guns as they rolled along the few tarmac roads from Renkum towards the landing-zones. Here one has been knocked out on the Utrechtseweg near Koude Herberg. (Bundesarchiv)

wildly on to the drop-zone with his jeep, firing green verey flares. It worked. After 300 to 400 metres a storm of British fire followed his progress as all attention switched to this new and threatening development. With a loud 'Hurrah!', his companies stormed on to the landing-zone in the centre. Confusion broke out in the British positions and much ground was taken. Lippert remarked:

'The bluff was successful and enabled the landing-zone at this point to be cleared of enemy within an hour; but not without heavy losses on both

sides. Many British fled in an easterly direction toward Wolfheze and Oosterbeek, where later they were captured by other German units. Hundreds of gliders and many prisoners were taken in this action, including heavy weapons, ammunition and jeeps.'[3]

The assault continued on for a further 2 kilometres east of the landing-zone, until, reaching the western edge of Oosterbeek, it was brought to a halt by heavy British fire. Helle's Dutch SS Battalion on the Ginkel heath meanwhile began to swing south-east as part of the attempt to encircle the British landing-zones. They appeared to have the British in their grasp.

First British Airborne Division had dropped over 26 hours before with 8,000 men. This represented in essence six battalions of infantry. Three belonging to 1st Parachute Brigade, numbering some 2,400 men, were pushing into Arnhem. One battalion – Frost's 2 PARA – had reached and secured the Arnhem bridge. Three more – 1st Airlanding Brigade – were bitterly defending the drop-zones to keep them open for reinforcements. Nearly 2,800 divisional supporting troops were attached to or supporting both brigades. Within the same 26 hours the Germans had committed a six-battalion front west of Arnhem (Kampfgruppe von Tettau), with the promise of four more to come.[4] II SS Corps had assembled a force equivalent to eight battalions, and set these against Arnhem and the bridge from the east (the 9SS Hohenstaufen and elements of the 10SS Frundsberg Kampfgruppen). At 1500 hours on 18 September the odds, Germans against British, were broadly 14 to 6 fighting battalions, not including tanks, artillery and heavy infantry weapons. In short, the combat ratio was more than two against one, with an overwhelming preponderance of heavy equipments on the German side. The landings had been a shock to both sides. Overwhelmed by an immense technological and material Allied supremacy, the reeling Germans saw this reinforced by a massive air drop. Alternatively, the air-landed force, expecting to contest no more than a brigade, three days after landing was already fighting a heavily armoured force and was outnumbered two to one. Both sides were unaware of these figures and could only guess at them, but both within their individual situations felt moderately confident of success. This was until a familiar droning noise was detected coming in from the west. As the volume of sound

rose, it was matched by a corresponding sinking of German spirits. Having failed to break this airborne invasion in the first 24 hours, it appeared that the 'pendulum' of odds and success was about to swing back the other way.

'Achtung Fallschirmjaeger! . . .'

The only soldiers who had identified the dots growing in size emerging from the south-west were the British. From positions bordering the western edge of the forest overlooking Ginkel heath, soldiers from the King's Own Scottish Borderers (KOSB) were anxiously scanning the skies for any indication of approaching aircraft. They were late; and when they arrived a whole British parachute brigade would drop in the rear of Helle's Dutch-SS Battalion. That, when it happened, would signal their counter-attack.

Standing right in the middle of the flight path of the approaching aircraft streams was an anonymous *Propagandakompanie*, PK 'Berichter', a German war correspondent with a movie camera. Anticipating a victory, he was instead to film a catastrophe (although the finished product was to be edited for propaganda reasons).[5]

SS-Captain Helle's battalion was now fielding six companies. Four had already been committed along the forest line to the south and east of Ginkel heath. In reserve was a further infantry and heavy weapons company north of and in the vicinity of the Ede-Arnhem road. Despair turned their heads and eyes skyward as the aerial armada thundered in at low level. Vibrant with the sound of pulsating aircraft engines, the sky began to fill with blossoming, billowing parachutes. Panic gripped those in the forward companies already spread out in the advance, as they were counter-attacked from the ground in front, and by

'The only soldiers who had identified the dots growing in size emerging from the south-west were the British.'

masses of parachutists descending in their rear.

The cameraman dashes into the tree-line bordering Helle's headquarters, and films the breathtaking display of military muscle unfolding above him. Dakota transport aircraft approaching in victory 'V' formations of nine abreast fill his camera lens.[6] Finding the courage to remain still for a few seconds, he then runs to the protective company offered by lines of Dutch SS-troopers alongside, who are firing desperately and as fast as they can with all weapons into the skies above. Nearby a flak 'Vierling' quadruple 20mm anti-aircraft gun mounted on a half-track looses burst after burst of tracer and cannon into the air.

Around the vehicle groups of riflemen shoot, shoulders twitching back with the recoil of each round, and pause, glancing furtively at the spectacle as they operate bolt actions to eject empty cases and feed another round into the breech. Other SS-troopers are kneeling on the footpath in front of and in amongst the trees, balancing MG42s and captured British brens on empty upturned wooden ammunition boxes in a vain attempt to stabilise their weapons, and firing automatically in the anti-air role. Burst after burst rips into the air, as the firers become slightly obscured by a light mist of blue-grey, pungent-smelling cordite smoke. Some pause to adjust the boxes acting as pivots that slip and buckle under the recoil. Panning back

'Dakota transport aircraft approaching in victory "V" formations of nine abreast fill his camera lens.'

A flak 'Vierling' quadruple 20mm anti-aircraft gun mounted on a half-track surrounded by groups of riflemen loosed burst after burst of tracer and cannon in the air.

SS-troopers firing captured brens and their own spandau machine guns balance their weapons on upturned ammunition boxes in a vain attempt to stabilise them in the anti-air role.

Gliders steeply diving are engaged by small arms and cannon fire as they seek a place to land. Hit signatures can be clearly identified.

in the air, the camera records a change in scene. The swarms of transport aircraft have been replaced by tugs and flights of gliders. Camera shots of 20mm cannon, with excited gesticulating observers pointing skyward, alternate with views of gliders diving steeply from a horizontal flight path, having picked out a clear place to land. A crescendo of machine gun and cannon fire accompanies each one in, occasionally producing brief, wispy, smoke-like vapour trails behind, evidence that a burst has found its mark. The cameraman remains in the shadow of the trees. His lens records a troop-carrying aircraft hit on the way in. Aflame nose to tail, it slowly loses height, careering at a shallow angle above a peaceful scene of hay ricks, trees and barns. The crump-crump of flak is still discernible in

the distance on the soundtrack as, slowly and dreamily, the aircraft is panned down to its eventual contact with the ground. It bursts violently beyond the forest line bordering Ginkel heath. A flash and an inky bulbous column of smoke are seen a fraction of a second before the louder crack of the explosion, a note higher than the constant thumping flak.

Some paratroopers overshoot the dropzone and snag in the trees near Helle's headquarters. Their bodies are immediately scythed by machine gun fire. Corpses hang briefly from branches until they are cut down, or until they crash earthward as fire rips through the rigging lines snarled in the branches. Ginkel heath is a scene of utter pandemonium. Grass fires caused by tracer and intermittent mortar bursts begin to

Many paratroopers like this unfortunate sergeant were killed before they could reach the ground.

A sequence of three stills monitors the progress of one stricken transport, ablaze, exploding on impact with the ground beyond the drop-zone.

disorientate soldiers and hamper visibility. Paratroopers from the 10th Battalion the Parachute Regiment have to fight to reach their first rendezvous points. Helle's battalion is, however, finished.[7]

SS-Lieutenant Fernau, the most southerly of Helle's company commanders, was quickly captured. Helle himself had been sleeping on a table in the 'Zuid-Ginkel' restaurant, his adopted headquarters, when the aerial assault came in. Rudely awakened, he was now in a state of shock. He had only the presence of mind to order his reserve company commander Bronkhorst to defend a farm at Hindekamp immediately north of the restaurant, before he fled himself. SS-Lieutenant Hink and Bartsch, assailed on all sides by the landed paratroopers, attempted to form 'hedgehogs' in the mêlée, but were overrun and lost. Kuhne totally lost his nerve. Fleeing his scattered company, he ran northward, to be relieved of his command when he was found in hiding a few days later. Only the heavy weapons company commander Einenkel, a veteran, appears to have kept his head. Vainly trying to stave off the airborne onslaught in the concentrated fire of 20mm cannon and mortars, he eventually gave up, and conducted a fighting withdrawal to the north.

It was over. Brigadier Hackett's 4th Parachute Brigade landed three more battalions numbering a further 2,000 men in the rear of the enemy. Demoralised Dutch SS-troopers sought out the British now only to surrender. The northern prong of von Tettau's western advance had been snapped off in this sudden inversion of odds. Helle arrived back at Ede, whereupon he met the commander of Sicherheit's Regiment 42 who was supposed to have come to his aid earlier in the advance. He demanded to know why the Regimental Commander had not arrived sooner. The latter regarded Helle in silence for a moment before answering drily: 'Be glad you're still alive. A report that I received said you and your whole battalion were killed or captured.'[8]

SS-Colonel Lippert, totally preoccupied with the advance, now stalled before Oosterbeek, was not aware of events to his rear. 'Enemy aircraft and fighters flew over our positions in the afternoon, without' he observed, 'causing any damage.' Taking advantage of a pause in the fighting, Lippert decided to drive back to his command post on the other side of the landing-zone. As he re-crossed the drop-zone that they had overrun only a few hours previously, he noticed groups of gliders that had not been there before. Suddenly his vehicle was raked with small arms fire and his driver seriously wounded. Bandaging his companion's leg under cover he noticed 'swarms of British soldiers, groups from gliders that had landed again on the drop-zone during the interim period.' The enormity of what had happened began to dawn. Hailing and flagging down a 37mm gun mounted on a half-track, he instructed the crew to engage the group of gliders he had just discovered with tracer. They were set on fire. Assisted by a number of flak soldiers, 36 POWs were rounded up, and his own wounded driver recovered from his damaged vehicle. This, as Lippert realised, was a new and ominous development:

'It was now completely clear to me that new landings had taken place undisturbed in the areas recently cleared. There were no reserves that I could have left behind after clearing the drop-zones. My overall mission keeping up the pressure on Oosterbeek from the west had appeared more important.'

But it was not possible to contact von Tettau's headquarters, because there were no line or radio communications available.

Confusion reigned at von Tettau's headquarters. As the General recorded in his post-combat report, 'without doubt this new enemy airlanding had certain crisis dimensions'. But what they were was difficult to estimate, 'especially because the lack of communications assets meant that reports were mostly brought in by ADCs and reached the division only after long delays'.[9]

Lippert's interpretation at ground level was somewhat different. He declared: 'This was therefore how it was during the first days for battalions operating under von Tettau's command; all the units were operating independently of each other.' His situation was becoming increasingly tenuous. Regimental headquarters was manned only by lightly wounded officers and NCOs, or liaison representatives from units under command. Lippert himself had received a light leg wound. As he admitted, he had simply run out of resources. 'Not once was there even the possibility to transport the wounded and prisoners we had collected to the rear. Everything had already been committed to the front line.'[10]

Crouching under cover in that front line was SS-Officer-Cadet Rudolf Lindemann. His heavy weapons section, belonging to Lippert's NCO school, had been suitably impressed by the size of the landing, but they were young men, reckless, not over-imaginative, and 'therefore not too afraid'. Lindemann's mortar platoon was still not complete when the second lift arrived, still moving somewhere between Gorinchem on the Waal and Wageningen. In any event, the ensuing confusion following the landings meant 'we lost contact with the other platoons for half a day or so, before we regained full control again'. Since they were veterans they were not unduly worried, and realised that eventually it would all be sorted out.[11]

In time the situation was clarified. Von Tettau ordered the SS Battalion Eberwein,

advancing from Benekom toward the Ede-Arnhem railway, to get across the line and clear the forest to the north of it. The newly arrived Sicherheit's Regiment 'Knoche' was given Helle's original task of clearing the forest on the east side of Ginkel heath. This time, however, they were to approach from the north. It was not long before they were pinned down by fire. Lippert's regiment, over-extended now on the right due to Helle's failure, was ordered to secure its own northern left flank. By the evening of 19 September, the jump-off positions that had been achieved on the dawn of the previous day (according to the latest reports) could at least be held. Nothing further could be achieved that was positive until the arrival of fresh reinforcements – the remainder of the Regiment Knoche, and the battalion of the 'Hermann Goering' Training Regiment were already *en route* by bicycle from Katwijk an Zee.

The awesome reinforcement of 1st British Airborne Division had a sobering if not depressing impact upon the Germans, who up to this point may have felt that this particular threat had been nipped in the bud. SS-Captain Wilfried Schwarz, the 28-year-old Chief of Staff of the 9SS, had commented that 'the situation on the eighteenth was not rosy, but with the arrival of reinforcements, we began to think we might succeed'. But the parachute assault on Ginkel heath tempered this cautious optimism:

'The soldiers saw unceasing
reinforcements coming from the air,
they were naturally concerned. Could
our friends in the south hold out? Or
would the Americans succeed in
breaking through?'

Schwarz was constantly aware of the irony of the Hohenstaufen's predicament. It had originally been raised to forestall an Allied invasion in the West. He lamented:

'In Normandy after all the training of the previous year, because we had been sent to Russia, we were too late. In Arnhem we were too few! How were we to stop this elite airborne division?'[12]

SS-Captain Moeller, fighting in the western suburbs of Arnhem, echoed his sentiments:

'During the afternoon there were new airlandings in the Renkum Heath area, and we had to watch, unable to intervene, as wave on wave, thousands of parachutists descended 15 kilometres away from us. The enemy got new reinforcements. What would that mean for us?'[13]

The *Sperrlinie* blocking force Spindler . . .

Within 30 minutes during the afternoon of 18 September the strength ratio of the opposing forces changed substantially. 1st Airborne Division could now field nine consolidated full-strength airborne infantry battalions with their appropriate division 'slice' (attached supporting arms, artillery and anti-tank guns), against 14 German equivalent battalion groups.[14] The latter were *ad hoc* combat groups flung together by the pressure of events, but with armour and stronger artillery and mortar support. Local superiority for the British was feasible, given that the newly-landed British elements could be consolidated into a force sufficiently strong, and sufficiently balanced with supporting arms, to punch its way through to the bridge. But geography and an apparent paralysis of command were to bedevil the British effort.

Major-General Urquhart, the British division commander, was frustrated by poor communications, and, seeking information too far forward with one of 3

PARA's earlier attacks, was cut off by a German counter-attack in Arnhem's western suburbs. With him was his deputy commander, Lathbury. Brigadier Hicks, the commander of 1st Airlanding Brigade, next in the command order of seniority, faced a dilemma. Aware now of the strength and scope of the German counter-measures, he had to decide whether to compromise, form a strong perimeter in their present positions north of the Rhine, and await relief from XXX Corps coming up through the corridor, or whether to reinforce Frost's partial success at the bridge. He decided to adhere to the original MARKET plan, but in so doing he was obliged to change the pre-operation mission of some of his battalion commanders. Four battalions – 1 PARA, 3 PARA, the glider-borne 2nd South Staffordshire Battalion, and 11 PARA – were ordered to fight through to the bridge. This involved extracting 11 PARA from Hackett's newly-arrived 4th Parachute Brigade and exchanging it for 7 KOSB, already exhausted from defending the drop-zones. Hackett's original mission to secure the high ground north of Arnhem still applied.

The South Staffs began to move into Arnhem as part of their new mission to support the line of advance already being bitterly contested by 1 and 3 PARA. 11 PARA was to follow suit. The changes were not assisted by the problems now being experienced with unreliable radio communications. All these battalions had, moreover, until receiving this order, been operating well apart. Cohesion was inevitably lost as, with scant or no reconnaissance, four battalions were despatched towards a front only 200 metres wide where two battalions had already failed to break through. To the north, Brigadier Hackett's 4th Parachute Brigade was also to hit the right flank of the SS Kampfgruppe Spindler's *Sperrlinie*, or blocking line.

Spindler's *Sperrlinie* had, meanwhile,

thickened up. It stretched from the Ede-Arnhem road north of Arnhem, south along Dreyenseweg to the railway line and junction, and thence to the lower Rhine. Manning this line in the north were elements of Krafft's SS Training and Replacement Battalion, joined now by the Kampfgruppe 'Bruhns', a Wehrmacht battalion, and some of von Allworden's SS Panzerjaeger. Astride the marshalling yard and Utrechtseweg in the centre, and around the area of the museum was SS-Lieutenant Gropp's anti-aircraft Kampfgruppe and Moeller's SS Engineer Battalion. South of the road was Spindler's original artillery Kampfgruppe, reinforced now by a further combat team from SS Panzer-grenadier Regiments 19 and 20, who occupied positions down to the water's edge. On the other side of the lower Rhine, remnants of Graebner's SS Reconnaissance Battalion 9 occupied the brickworks. Behind and in depth, occupying a line running from the station due south to the river, was the newly-formed SS Kampfgruppe Harder. In essence, seven British battalions advancing down Utrechtseweg and against the Dreyenseweg were about to assault a line of seven to eight German battalions supported by armoured cars, half-tracks and self-propelled guns. Even at the point of the greatest British effort along the Utrechtstrasse, local superiority would not be achieved, because the paratroopers could only attack in battalion columns along two roads over a frontage of 200 metres. This funnel could be dominated by the combined fire of five different German Kampfgruppen working with armour.[15] Both sides were unaware of the true nature of their opposing dispositions. With an almost reckless abandon the British were to play out the tragedy of the 'Charge of the Light Brigade' in miniature. Their mission to reach the bridge was clear. Its execution, apart from advancing down a fire-swept urban valley, was not.

The charge of the parachute brigades . . .

British battalion commanders attempted to co-ordinate their joint thrusts toward the bridge as best they could. A maze of unreconnoitred streets and only a sketchy knowledge of enemy strengths and dispositions were to hamper the advance. The 2nd Battalion South Staffordshire Regiment was to assault along the Bovenover 'high road' (*Utrechtseweg*), followed closely by 11 PARA, taking the high ground past the Municipal Museum and then down to the Arnhem bridge. Parallel to this route, following the bend in the lower Rhine, was the 'low road' or *Onderlangs*. 1 PARA was to spearhead this flat route alongside the river and harbour, supported by the remnants of 3 PARA. Both of these battalions had already suffered considerable losses trying to fight through this bottleneck the night before. Indeed, none of the other battalions were aware that 3 PARA was even ready to mount yet another attack. Soldiers were, therefore, not fully briefed. When the assault started, delays were to be caused by paratroopers shooting at each other as the two axes diverged. All four battalions were attempting to force an urban 'valley of death'.

The houses on the high road were occupied on both sides by Moeller's SS Engineer Battalion. These were further overlooked by a group of houses beyond the marshalling yards northwards manned by Gropp's SS anti-aircraft gunners. The South Staffs and 11 PARA, confined to the streets if they wished to move in strength, were to be exposed to defilade and frontal fire once they were past the St Elizabeth's Hospital. There was no room for tactical manœuvre – it was punch through frontally, or fail. Similarly, the flat and exposed low road following the lower Rhine was dominated by 20mm and 37mm cannon set up in the brickworks immediately south of the

St. Elisabeth Hospital

THE ABORTIVE ATTEMPT TO RELIEVE FROST ON THE ARNHEM BRIDGE 19 SEPTEMBER 1944.

While Frost's 2 PARA fought for its life (right) on 19 September, First Parachute Brigade attempted to charge through an 'urban valley of death' in a vain attempt to reach it. Assailed on three sides by the concentric fire of Gropp's, Moeller's and Spindler's Kampfgruppen, as well as the remnants of the Hohenstaufen's Recce Battalion across the lower Rhine in the brickworks, the attack disintegrated. The arrival of Assault Gun Brigade 280 tipped the balance. The surviving British paratroopers streamed back to Oosterbeek as German forces regrouped for the subsequent advance. Frost was now totally isolated on the northern ramp of the Arnhem bridge. With the threat of enemy reinforcements removed, the Germans began to systematically batter the 2 PARA strongpoints into submission.

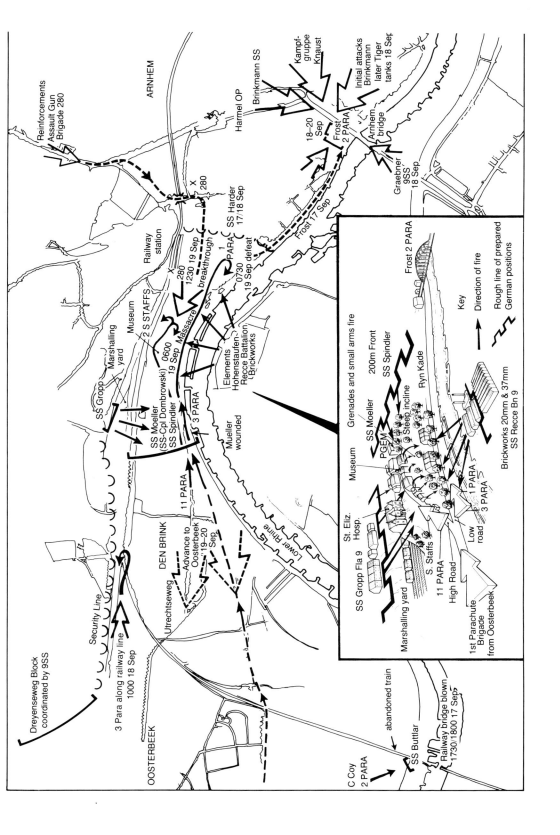

ARNHEM

Reinforcements
Assault Gun
Brigade 280

Harmel OP

Kampf-
gruppe
Knaust

Brinkmann SS

Initial attacks
Brinkmann
later Tiger
tanks 18 Sep

18–20
Sep

Frost
2 PARA

Arnhem
bridge

Graebner
9SS
18 Sep

X 280

SS Harder
17/18 Sep

Frost 17 Sep

Railway
station

X 280

1230 19 Sep
breakthrough

0730
1 PARA
19 Sep defeat

Museum

Museum

2 S STAFFS

0600
19 Sep Massacre

Elements
Hohenstaufen
Recce Battalion,
Brickworks

SS Gropp

Marshalling
yard

SS Moeller
(SS-Cpl Dombrowski)

SS Spindler

3 PARA

Mueller
wounded

11 PARA

Advance to
Oosterbeek
19–20
Sep.

DEN BRINK

Utrechtseweg

Lower Rhine

Key

Direction of fire

Rough line of prepared
German positions

Frost 2 PARA

200m Front

SS Spindler

Ryn Kade

SS Moeller

PGEM

Steep incline

Grenades and small arms fire

Museum

St. Eliz.
Hosp.

SS Gropp Fla 9

Marshalling yard

S. Staffs

11 PARA

High Road

1st Parachute
Brigade
from Oosterbeek

1 PARA

3 PARA

Low
road

Brickworks 20mm & 37mm
SS Recce Bn 9

Dreyenseweg Block
coordinated by 9SS

Security Line

3 Para along railway line
1000 18 Sep

OOSTERBEEK

C Coy
2 PARA

SS Buttlar

abandoned train

Railway bridge blown
1730/1800 17 Sep

Rhine. Furthermore, a steep-gradient embankment to the left, and the houses along *Onderlangs* all overlooking the axis of advance, were occupied by the Kampfgruppe Spindler.

Cloaked by darkness, and a sinister early-morning mist rising from the lower Rhine, the advance started at 0400 hours on 19 September. Denied the ability to flex their tactical muscle over a wider area, all depended upon the aggression and determination of the vanguard companies spearheading the columns. SS-Captain Hans Moeller recalled the initial contacts near the Rhine Pavilion: 'At 0400 the terrible noise of battle broke out on the left towards the Rhine, and left of us amongst Spindler's men.' Every sound in urban battle is magnified. Steel-shod boots scraped and clattered across the tarmac in the dark. Weapon reports were deafening and echoed around the streets in throbbing sound waves.

'There was rifle fire and machine guns rattled continuously. Muffled "dumpfs" signalled the barking of mortars, and the signatures of tank guns. These had to be ours? Flares rose steadily to our left, something like 400 to 500 metres away, where there was open ground down to the Rhine. The noise was increasing in intensity. We were all wide awake – when would they start in our sector?'[16]

Where joined, the battle was confused and chaotic. Its outcome was determined by whether or not junior leaders on both sides kept their heads. Manning a machine gun in a trench situated next to the Rhine itself, crouched 19-year-old SS-Corporal Paul Mueller. He commanded a grenadier section of the 9SS Panzer-grenadier Regiment 20, recently incorporated into the Kampfgruppe Spindler. Enveloped by the sudden fury of the 1 PARA attack, his group fought back savagely. 'At 0500 hours

sharp,' he remembers, 'the Tommies let loose all hell.' A cluster of hand-grenades lobbed around their positions preceded the attack. Machine guns and riflemen fired as fast as they could, but

'. . . the circumstances favoured our opponents. It was still so dark and foggy that you could only just make out the outline of a man walking upright from five metres away. Our line therefore was simply overrun, even though it cost our attackers heavy losses.'

Momentary panic gripped the defenders. 1 PARA, partially obscured by a protective shroud of mist and darkness, made good progress. In the eye of this storm, Mueller saw no practical alternative except to hold his ground. 'Shortly afterwards we heard both sustained-fire machine guns giving up their positions and withdrawing along the opposite road side ditch.' Disheartened by their inability to break up the momentum of the assault, the gunners continued to the rear, whispering urgently 'it's all useless anyhow, they'll simply overrun us'. Mueller could see no sense in that. Calling upon his riflemen to hold fast, he told them they were now the furthest friendly troops forward. 'They wanted to go back to the rear,' he remembered, because this was their first time in action. 'They had never heard the crack of a speeding bullet so close before.' Taking cover left and right of his machine gun, they awaited the second wave of the attack. Suddenly, seven to nine figures appeared out of the mist. A shouted challenge was rewarded by a hand-grenade that bounced and exploded in front of Mueller's trench. The enemy closed fast, and a terrifying hand-grenade duel developed in the subsequent hand-to-hand mêlée.

'Two bursts from my machine gun caused an explosion in the group of men. Its effect was devastating, only one of the Tommies remained standing, the rest were rolling and moaning in a heap on the ground.'

Slowly the lone surviving paratrooper advanced menacingly towards Mueller. On firing two more bursts, Mueller discovered his machine gun had run out of ammunition. He called frantically for a new belt, only to realise that his comrades had already fled. Unable to find his rifle, he picked up one of two 'egg' hand-grenades lying on the parapet of his trench. 'Tommy seemed to discover me,' he fearfully observed, and threw the first grenade. It was a dud. This Englishman was indestructible. There was a bang, and fire and dirt flew into his face as he detected the throwing movement from his opponent. 'I just had enough strength to throw my pulled grenade at the Tommy before I blacked out for a few moments.' Coming to after the explosion he could still see his assailant five metres in front of him. He remembers desperately trying to pull himself together otherwise he was going to die. 'You've got to get away fast now,' he thought, 'or Tommy is going to do you in completely.' He then felt a sharp pain, 'as if somebody was slashing a knife back and forth' on his upper arm. Blinded by the blood on his face, he groped around for the machine gun. It had been torn open at the breech. That was it; 'it was high time for me to get out of my hole,' he thought. As he vaulted out of the trench another hand-grenade exploded within it, peppering his back with small pieces of shrapnel. Bleeding profusely, he stumbled off into the night, pushing his now useless left arm into his belt for support, hastened by the crump of hand-grenades behind him.[17]

Dawn was now approaching, and with it the mist began to rise. As it did so the remnants of Graebner's SS Reconnaissance Battalion, positioned in the brickworks across the Rhine, were presented with an unbelievable target. Strung out in a column along the *Onderlangs* were 1 and 3 PARA, concerned only with exchanges of fire going on to their front by Moeller and to their left. 20 and 37mm cannon were able to lay on at short range over open sights with an uninterrupted traverse up and down the road. At 0600 the massacre began. Concentrated bursts of high-velocity shot flailed the ragged columns as they pushed on, unaware of the danger to their right flank. Bodies disintegrated and were dismembered by horizontal lines of tracer hammering across the river on a flat trajectory, exploding and splintering on the battered façades of houses beyond. The screams of the maimed were barely distinguishable above the crescendo of sound magnified by the surrounding buildings. Both battalions virtually ceased to exist. Spindler's men, occupying the houses and gardens bordering the high ground to the left overlooking the low road, grenaded and fired at anything that moved. Fire still continued from the front. Assailed from three sides, the attack collapsed in a withering concentration of weapons of all calibres. There was nowhere for the hapless paratroopers to turn, except to try and gain admittance to occupied houses on their left. Shelter had therefore to be fought for. At 0730 the advance elements of 1 PARA had reached the old harbour, barely 1,400 metres from the bridge. Sounds of battle were still apparent from that direction but they were finished. Behind, the column was in a shambles. Decimated desperate groups began now to flee or exfiltrate back to the start line. Most of the officers and NCOs were already dead or wounded. This was to be the nearest they would ever get to Frost; but 2 PARA, totally preoccupied with their own battle at the bridge, did not hear a thing.

Meanwhile, elements of Wehrmacht Assault Gun Brigade 280 began to clatter

Meanwhile, elements of Wehrmacht Assault Gun Brigade 280 began to clatter into Arnhem coming from the north.

into Arnhem, coming from the north. Consisting mainly of 'Sturmgeschutz III' SPs, mounting a 75mm gun, they were allocated to the Kampfgruppe Spindler. Spindler in turn employed them singly or in pairs to his various subsidiary Kampfgruppen, depending upon their needs. A start line was established at the head of Utrechtstrasse, as the armoured vehicles gathered in the vicinity of the railway station waiting for the command to move forward.

As it grew light SS-Captain Moeller's sector on the *Utrechtseweg* was subjected to the full fury of the paratrooper assault. The South Staffs, emerging from the protective cover of the St Elizabeth's Hospital and advancing on the museum on the high ground, were caught by flanking fire from SS-Lieutenant Gropp's Flak Kampfgruppe firing from the upper storeys of the houses across the marshalling yards. On the other side and front they were hit by Moeller's SS Engineers who, as the commander relates, 'fired without mercy. Panzerfaust projectiles literally tore a group of paratroopers apart. Flame-throwers belched flaming petroleum into the attacking enemy.' A self-propelled assault gun clattered into position by the museum supported by Moeller's two armoured half-tracks, and engaged the incoming assault frontally. It was a difficult battle to control at company and battalion level because whole platoons would disappear from sight defending just one house.

A self-propelled gun assisted Moeller's Kampfgruppe fighting by the Municipal Museum of the Utrechtseweg. (Bundesarchiv)

Commanders were literally on their own once this close-quarter fighting was joined. Moeller recalls the fight becoming

> '. . . a free-for-all. The streets were death zones. Dead and wounded could not be retrieved. Rubble was strewn everywhere. Fences and walls had been flattened by the assault gun, whose sharp gun reports spurted fire at the enemy.'

It did not all go Moeller's way, however. Frequently, 'damn well-aimed sniper fire' took its toll of his men. But the German fire was becoming increasingly effective as Moeller sought to combine all the weapons, including armoured vehicles, at their disposal. 'We had plenty of ammunition,' he claimed, 'and literally shot up attack after attack bravely launched by the enemy.' It could not last indefinitely, although at times he wondered despairingly whether it might.

> 'Wounded civilians, who had tried to save what there was to save, were screaming. But what did that matter! So many things had been destroyed, house and farm, property and livestock, all were consumed by flame, and a dark pungent smoke drifted through the streets of this once elegant residential area.'

By about 1000 hours the enemy's momentum was spent. 'His attack,' Moeller observed, 'became fragmented, spread out and uncertain.' It became apparent that the British 'were completely exhausted, their strength overtaxed, and their confidence shaken by excessively high losses'.[18]

Two hours earlier Major General Urquhart, the British divisional commander, released from confinement due to this determined but costly push towards the bridge, had realised that now they would never reach it. Even continued attacks by 4th Parachute Brigade would not be able to restore the situation. 11 PARA was therefore ordered to break off its assault behind the South Staffordshire Battalion and withdraw. A messenger was sent forward to warn the commanding officer of the South Staffordshires, but he did not get through. They had reached their furthest point of advance on the high road – the PGEM building just beyond the Municipal Museum. Their situation was desperate – only a few remaining PIAT light shoulder-fired anti-tank weapons were keeping the Sturmgeschutz III SPs of Assault Gun Brigade 280 at bay. At about 1230 they ran out of ammunition. Almost immediately the assault guns were launched down the road in the direction of the museum. The South Staffs had to scatter. Meanwhile, 11 PARA had formed up, oblivious to the threat to its rear, and had assembled for its withdrawal, apparently secure in the knowledge that they were covered. They were caught in the open with catastrophic results. It was soon over. For the rest of the afternoon of 19 September the survivors of the decimated British battalions fled or fought their way out in groups moving towards Oosterbeek.

Moeller reported that 'changeable fighting went on and on until it finally petered out at around noon'. All around lay the wreckage and the human flotsam of war marking this high tide of the paratrooper advance. SS-Corporal Wolfgang Dombrowski found himself asking the inevitable question on Utrechtseweg:

'What were we to do with our wounded? A red cross flag was produced and casualties approached slowly, step by step. To our astonishment fire ceased immediately. Stretcher bearers picked up the wounded, moved off, and the shooting started again. We couldn't understand this as we were used to conditions on the Eastern Front. These Paras were supposed to be hard men – we knew they were! – and yet we were allowed to pick up the wounded. The other side was then given the opportunity to do the same.'[19]

The *Sperrlinie* is forced in the north . . .

All along the Dreyenseweg, stretching north from the Ede-Arnhem road south to the bridge over the railway cutting at Oosterbeek railway station, the Germans lay in wait. This 1500-metre sector of Spindler's *Sperrlinie* was manned by the 9SS Panzerjaeger, von Allworden's Kampfgruppe, now commanded by the newly-arrived 'Bruhns' Wehrmacht Battle Group. Bruhns, a General-Staff Officer, had sited a number of *Sicherungen*, or defended outposts, west of his line. These were located in the wooded areas north-east and south-east of Johanna Hoeve, a collection of farm buildings also manned by a skeleton force. Giving forewarning of an enemy advance, these groups would then stay and fight until they had dispersed the approaching enemy and detected the main axis and direction of advance, before withdrawing and occupying reserve positions behind the main Dreyenseweg line itself. Hurriedly-dug shell scrapes and fox-holes camouflaged with freshly-cut branches afforded some protection. A variety of armoured vehicles thickened up the line. By the crossroads at the northern extremity of the road one of von Allworden's surviving Mark IV Panzerjaeger SPs was sited, supported by a towed anti-tank gun. An isolated hotel nearby was serving as an aid post and operating room for the wounded.[20] Some of Graebner's reconnaissance half-tracks and armoured cars appeared periodically, providing fire support on call. Some of the Hohenstaufen's SPs and armoured half-tracks moved as armoured pickets up and down the road, patrolling or acting as mobile fire support when required.

On the first day of the landings some indirect fire from mortars and artillery had harassed the drop-zones, largely unsuccessfully, because the line of trees effectively screened observation of the fall of shot. During that afternoon and most of the following day, desultory but occasionally heavy fighting took place as 3 PARA attempted to by-pass Krafft's SS Battalion already *in situ*. Only glimpses of Monday's air activity had been seen, as much of it had been shielded from view by the trees. Anti-aircraft gun activity, over-flights, rumour and word-of-mouth reports soon built up a picture of yet another substantial enemy aerial reinforcement. Probing attacks on the outposts were repelled again, and nobody was able to get any rest. Nerves were stretched taut. SS-Lance-Corporal Alfred Ziegler recalled:

> 'We were never absolutely certain where our men were and where the British were. We were so close once that I heard them transmitting Morse Code: "dit-dit-da-da-dit-dit". We ran. They had to be British soldiers sending because we didn't have any transmitters.'

A stalemate of sorts reigned. The initiative lay with the British, who appeared only to be able to mount company-size probes. These, nevertheless, caused considerable losses on both sides. Fighting raged again around the six-kilometre milestone on the Amsterdamsweg, the Arnhem-Ede road. Seven bodies still lay sprawled across the cycle path, where they had been ambushed by the SS Panzerjaeger 24 hours before. Pockets and equipment had now been rifled, and personal possessions and helmets were strewn around the corpses. Lifeless fingers now curled into the claws of *rigor mortis*. The bodies, grotesquely and untidily scattered on the pavement, had long since been stripped of anything of value. A bicycle, which had perhaps been briefly leaned against the milestone, had fallen with its wheels astride the marker which had been shattered by one of the 20mm high-velocity rounds that had scythed the group down. Ziegler remembered 'this photograph, which was later printed in all its reality in the newspapers, and even shown on the weekly newsreels'.[21] The war correspondent who took the picture, he recalled, 'had been with us for a few days, and was later killed in action in Oosterbeek'.[22]

The attacks continued on the *Sperrlinie*, but it held firm. Ziegler was a motor cycle despatch rider and was often instructed to carry wounded in his side-car. On one occasion he was told to pick up some British wounded in no man's land. His only indication of their whereabouts was to drive towards the smoke of their blazing vehicle. He picked up two survivors, one of whom spoke German. Worried, they asked him where they were going to be taken; Ziegler's response, in his heavily-accented southern German was 'to the hospital, and I hope I warrant the same treatment in a similar situation!' With such a dialect it is unlikely they understood him. Having dropped them off at the hotel dressing station on the northern end of the Dreyenseweg, 'I had to leap out of the window as soon as I was finished, because "Jabos" were attacking'. Cursing his misfortune, he reflected upon his dislike of war 'because nothing is impossible'. As he rode back to his unit he thought back on his personal contact with the enemy. 'I never knew if they survived,' he said after the war. 'One of them had a huge hole in his shoulder.' One of his grateful captives had offered his watch in recognition of his compassion, but he replied, somewhat testily, 'not for me, thank you. You hold on to it; I am not a thief'.[23]

During the early morning of 19 September, while it was still dark, the battle noises of the British pushing toward the Arnhem bridge could be heard, way over to their left in the suburbs of the town. Taut and nervous, the German soldiers crouching in positions along the Dreyenseweg waited expectantly. Their turn would inevitably come. First light almost always seemed to presage British activity.

When the assault came in at dawn the line was visibly shaken by its ferocity. Fourth Parachute Brigade, having moved to occupy the high ground north of Arnhem, had marched forward during the previous afternoon and night, and clashed with the *Sperrlinie* outposts. Now multiple company attacks came in along the woods running west to east both north and south of the Dreyenseweg, mounted by both 10 and 156 PARA. Although supported by some mortars and light artillery, they were assaulting a line numerically stronger and boasting greater fire power than their own.

Outlying German defended localities were overrun. 'These were determined British attacks,' Ziegler recalls. Standing next to his Kampfgruppe commander, Bruhns, the officer confided that 'if we do not get any reinforcements soon, we will have to withdraw when the next attack comes'. A prophetic statement, because Ziegler remembers the subsequent 'terrible' assault that came between the main road and the railway embankment:

'I was with Bruhns when the position first showed signs of cracking. In some places our men had to adopt isolated "hedgehog" positions with all-round defence, while some small groups of enemy managed to infiltrate through our lines. When Herr Bruhns heard about this I was directed to drive towards Arnhem and pick up reinforcements which were supposed to be on the way.'[24]

Who was there, where they were, and how many there were was not known. Eventually, riding around on his motorcycle, Ziegler found them in a forest outside Arnhem. They were a Waffen-SS company of self-propelled anti-aircraft guns mounted on half-tracks, commanded by a *Faehnrich* (an officer-cadet equivalent to sergeant), 'who was subsequently to lose all his vehicles in Oosterbeek'. In addition, a battalion of twin and quadruple 20mm AA guns, similarly mounted on half-tracks and led by a Major, also rolled up. With much shouting and gesticulating, the vehicles were immediately inserted into the line, occupying hastily-reconnoitred positions. Areas of fire were so tied up that nothing could move in the open, and attacking infantry would only be able to penetrate with difficulty through the wooded areas. They awaited the next assault.

As it came in, two leading company groups of 156 PARA were scythed down within a murderous interlocking network of 20mm cannon interspersed with tracer. This sudden crescendo of heavy-calibre fire was apparent even to the British parachute companies moving up to support in depth, as 20mm rounds exploded and ricocheted among top branches and from tree trunks. Empty shell cases clattered on to the metal floors of vehicles as the urgent shouting and fire orders of gun commanders grew louder with the British approach. Attacks petered out, mown down by this sudden increase in the concentration of fire. Exhausted survivors stumbled and exfiltrated back through

Awaiting the next assault on the Sperrlinie *on the Dreyenseweg.*

the trees, and began to dig in around the vicinity of the start line. None of the lightly armed airborne troops had reckoned upon resistance with this sort of firepower; moreover, it had been skilfully deployed. These were not line-of-communication troops; numerous seasoned SS-troopers had already been taken prisoner. Information concerning the push against the Arnhem road bridge had not been encouraging. Moreover, it was becoming increasingly apparent, even to private soldiers, that they were not going to break through at this point. What next?

The pendulum had swung back for the final time in Arnhem. Neither reinforcement nor resupply on the British side would influence the final outcome of the battle. SS-Lieutenant-Colonel Ludwig Spindler's *Sperrlinie*, or blocking line, had provided the focus for the defence of Arnhem. It was now to provide the start line for an inevitable advance upon Ooster-beek. A watershed had been reached, indiscernible to both sides. The British high tide had been reached, it could now only ebb, back towards Oosterbeek.

CHAPTER XV

Blasting the British out – The Arnhem Bridge

I did not see how anyone could live through this inferno. I felt truly sorry for the British.

SS-Grenadier

With artillery . . .

Lieutenant Joseph Enthammer had been moved into the house adjoining Frost's 2 PARA headquarters during the early morning of 19 September. The 19-year-old artillery officer, captured with his rear-guard unit, surveyed his new surroundings with some interest and relief, as they had been manhandled by Dutch civilians *en route*. He noticed:

'The house probably belonged to the Water Authority or Police or something. There were rows of files dealing with water levels and similar subjects aligned on wide shelves. I made a bed amongst the books on a shelf. Far preferable to the concrete floor. Others followed my example.'

The sounds of battle became increasingly more apparent. Shouts, small arms fire, the sudden rapid thumping of bren guns, and, more ominously, the distant crash of heavy shells and falling masonry could be heard. A British captain often called in to check on his captives and excused the lack of food and drink. Enthammer remembers him remarking that 'his soldiers had only what they had jumped with'. That, however, was scant compensation because 'dust and cordite burned our throats – we desperately

wanted to drink'. During this phase the artillery officer was kept active:

'As I could speak English I was directed to assist in steering German prisoners to the toilet, which was dug against a brick wall in the back garden. I was given a shovel to start it up, and, accompanied by three soldiers armed with sten guns, set off. Even as I lowered first my trousers and then my body to perform a natural function the barrels of their weapons followed me up and down. But for the seriousness of the situation, I could have found this amusing!'

Enthammer befriended the English corporal tasked with guarding them. Conversing freely, he discovered he was a student from London with a lively sense of humour. 'The Jerries have developed a new tank with a crew of 1,000,' he said. 'Impossible!' retorted Enthammer. 'Oh yes,' he replied. 'One man steers it, another commands it, the gunner fires it, and the other 997 push it!' Everyone, including the Allies, was aware of the lack of fuel in the German army. Nevertheless, the German officer remembers that the passage of time brought a change of mood as battle noises increased in intensity:

'The corporal admitted increasing unease and fears of a build-up of German reinforcements as their situation became increasingly hopeless.'[1]

The beleaguered British, their backs to the river, were being assailed by two Kampfgruppen – Knaust and Brinkmann – from three directions. 2 PARA's perimeter had shrunk from its original 18 houses to 10 by 19 September. SS Grenadiers were also digging in on the south bank, engaging the houses and bridge positions from across the river. They were further supported by artillery and a battery of Nebelwerfers. Outside the perimeter the Germans were coming to the same realisation as the corporal. The British position looked increasingly hopeless. SS-Captain Wilfried Schwarz, the divisional Chief-of-Staff of the 9SS, recalled that Graebner's failed assault on 18 September indicated that 'the situation was not rosy', but this changed; 'as reinforcements arrived, it dawned on us that we might succeed'. Confidence, following the futile and costly attacks of the first phase, was returning. 'Dozens of commanders reported to me at divisional headquarters,' he said, 'and these I parcelled out to the front.'[2] These forces were fed piecemeal to the two German Kampfgruppen now totally locked into the British perimeter, trying to wrest back control of the bridge approaches.

The failure of the abortive British attempt to reach Frost via the lower Rhine and the St Elizabeth's Hospital heralded a change in tactics. As infantry closed in from the west, tank guns began to appear in the east, covered by Panzer-grenadiers. From the north, heavy artillery was brought to bear on the front façades of the besieged houses. Strong points were slowly and systematically reduced to rubble. The focus of effort shifted to attacks down the wide boulevards from the north and north-east,

along the Eusebius Binnen and Buiten Singel, where tanks could at least operate in concert with infantry. Direct fire was brought to bear by the 88mm guns of a pair of 'Tiger' tanks which managed to nose their way through the wreckage of Graebner's attack from the southern bank. Two further 88mm flak guns were set up on either side of the southern approach to the bridge. These engaged houses with point-blank fire. The only way it appeared they were going to get the British out was, as SS-Section Commander Alfred Ringsdorf declared, 'to carry them out feet first'.[3] SS-Grenadier Private Horst Weber recalls the merciless barrage of fire brought to bear:

'Starting from the rooftops, buildings collapsed like dolls' houses. I did not see how anyone could live through this inferno. I felt truly sorry for the British.'[4]

Rudolf Trapp, a machine gunner, was still fighting with the 3rd Company Panzergrenadier Regiment 21 to the west of the road bridge. Taking cover in the Weerd–Jess Strasse, he observed the effect of artillery firing point blank directly down the Eusebius-Plein:

'An artillery piece was trundled into our street from the Battalion Knaust behind us. This was two or three days after the battle started. It was the biggest gun I've ever seen, and was manhandled up along the side of the Rhine.'

The initial problem, Trapp remembers, was to get it into action whilst under fire. 'I covered it by shooting up the British positions along the street with long protracted bursts from my machine gun.' He also caustically remarked this was 'the first time we saw the Wehrmacht [army as distinct from SS] in Arnhem'. Once in position against Major Crawley's part of the 2 PARA sector, the gun reduced a strongpoint to rubble. 'It fired seven to eight shots directly at it.' When the position was subsequently stormed, Trapp's men found 'the occupants, about a platoon strong, all dead lying in slit trenches and prepared positions'.[5]

With tanks . . .

Kampfgruppe Knaust's 'Tiger' tanks were an unpleasant surprise for the British. SS-Colonel Heinz Harmel, the commander of the Frundsberg, recalled:

> 'Knaust probably got his two Tigers directly from Model. This is how they could appear. Hitler would specifically direct sometimes that a unit was to be reinforced with Tigers because it was not sufficiently strong to carry out a task.'[6]

SS-Private Horst Weber saw them rumbling ponderously down the Groote Markt, pumping 'shell after shell into each house, one after the other'. The impact of the 88mm rounds at close quarters was devastating. He recalls a corner building where

> '. . . the roof fell in, the top two storeys began to crumble and then, like the skin peeling off a skeleton, the whole front wall fell into the street revealing each floor on which the British were scrambling like mad. Dust and debris soon made it impossible to see anything more. The din was awful, but even so above it all we could hear the wounded screaming.'[7]

It was the arrival of the armour, so unexpectedly and in sufficient quantity to tip the balance, that swayed the battle inexorably in favour of the Germans. Some tanks and assault guns had survived the Hohenstaufen's retreat from Normandy. They had been sufficient to halt the fierce but lightly armed parachute battalion assaults on Spindler's *Sperrlinie*, or blocking line. Reinforcement by Assault Gun Brigade 280 had forced the British airborne infantry off Utrechtseweg as they attempted to bludgeon their way to Frost on the bridge. It was no longer a close-quarter conflict – man against man as it had been during the suburban twilight of the night of 18–19 September. Dawn brought not only reinforcements to the Germans but a greater ability to use its overwhelming mobile and protected firepower. Around the perimeter defending the bridge, Frost's 2 PARA, immobilised now by the superior weight of infantry surrounding them, were systematically and deliberately blasted into submission by artillery and tank guns.

Lance-Corporal Karl-Heinz Kracht, the 19-year-old tank loader in the 'Mielke' panzer company, remembers his arrival on 19 September, heading for the northern approach to the Arnhem bridge:

> 'We drove speedily into the city, but it already appeared dead and empty. Only a few civilians tried to flee. We were forbidden to fire upon them even though there were probably quite a few underground agents in their ranks! Some of them fell victim to enemy fire, because the "Tommies" were not particularly scrupulous and fired at everything that moved.'

Kracht was a keen photographer, but, being the loader, 'had the darkest place at the tank commander's feet'. So, he remarked, 'I never really knew where we were going unless we stopped to occupy a position, and I had a chance to get off the tank to look around and take a few pictures.' As yet he had little opportunity. The column, a

Lance-Corporal Karl-Heinz Kracht photographed the arrival of his tanks on flat rail cars before disembarking for Arnhem. (Kabel-Kracht)

mixture of eight obsolete Mark III panzers and some of the newer more powerful Mark IVs, moved on. Information, he remembers, was scant; they 'knew that paratroopers had landed at Arnhem, but I did not know about the armada of glider aircraft outside the town'. Driving on, they began to notice the after-effects of recent fighting; there were 'destroyed vehicles and parts of bodies in bushes in the streets and on trees'. They were unused to such scenes, and tension mounted as they approached the city centre. Kracht admitted that 'we, the young "combatants" of the VI Bielefeld tank company, were quite shocked!' This was not what the inexperienced recruits had anticipated, and Kracht was no exception:

'Personally, I felt quite a bit of apprehension as our vehicles moved into Arnhem. I still had to overcome the shock at the destruction and the corpses lying by the roadside. Maybe we were to be the next victim of the British anti-tank guns? This feeling was amplified when the company lost its first tanks.'

The tanks began to approach the Arnhem road bridge from the east, using the houses on the bank road for cover. 'There were many Tommies hiding in the cellars!' remarked Kracht. 'They were winkled out by our accompanying Panzer-grenadiers.' About 22 prisoners were taken as the houses were cleared. Most, he noticed, were well equipped with 'A to C rations, cigarettes and rifles, etc'. They came 'in most cases quite peacefully. Poor blokes, they were rather tired and exhausted from

The tanks began to approach the Arnhem road bridge from the east, using the houses on the bank road for cover. Panzer crews and Panzer-grenadiers prepare for action. (Kabel-Kracht)

their continuous time in action.' He even managed to take a few photographs of a prisoner being taken, but this film was subsequently lost. Now the pace of action increased perceptibly as the tanks were put into action against the besieged houses covering the northern ramp. Kracht described the initial skirmishes:

'On Quay street we went into position behind a biscuit factory. Here we were ordered to provide fire support for the Panzer-grenadiers and to shoot at the houses and two steeples (around the market square and Eusebius church) which contained British artillery observation posts. We also fired at targets identified on the bridge, which was tenaciously defended by a large number of British.'

It was in this area that Kracht took out his treasured possession, an Agfa Karat III camera, and began to take photographs on the periphery of the action going on around him. One picture shows Panzer-grenadiers with shouldered weapons moving with a troop of panzer Mark III's in the area of the creamery. The superstructure of the Arnhem bridge can be made out through the background mist and smoke. Another

Mark III panzers and Panzer-grenadiers photographed by Kracht operating just north-east of the bridge, whose superstructure is just visible through the mist and smoke. (Kabel-Kracht)

frame reveals the emergency power station, surrounded now by battered houses, the original start point for Brinkmann's counter-attacks on the Monday morning. Whole walls of houses have been shot away by tank guns, exposing sagging floors still supporting furniture. Climbing a roof-top observation post, Kracht took a view of the damaged Eusebius church, surrounded by the gaunt and roofless shells of other houses torn open and exposed to the elements. At ground level again the camera captures a glimpse of the photographer's own panzer Mark III tank reversing into position behind the biscuit factory east of the bridge, its engine decks strewn with branches for camouflage. Crew members stand idly by, the tank's radio operator, Meuel, a youth of 17 years self-consciously grinning with his hands in his pockets. Behind the buildings forming the backdrop Frost's paratroopers are desperately playing out their last drama on the bridge.

Panzer company 'Mielke' had been incorporated into the Kampfgruppe 'Knaust'. Knaust was a leader of some charisma, and is mentioned by a number of German survivors who fought at Arnhem. Kracht commented that 'despite his wooden leg, Major Knaust was very agile and would not hesitate to present his person as a target for snipers and artillery in a

Whole walls of houses have been shot away by tank guns, exposing sagging floors still supporting furniture. (Kabel-Kracht)

Kracht's own tank reversing into cover. Meuel, his radio operator (hand in pockets), is in the foreground with other crew members. (Kabel-Kracht)

suicidal manner'. Both his men and the SS-Kampfgruppe Brinkmann kept up pressure in a steadily escalating battle of attrition to wrest back control of the bridge. Kracht on the mounting toll on both sides:

'As far as we were concerned, this shooting lasted for two days until nothing more stirred on the bridge. Panzer-grenadiers, also suffering most of the casualties, had to do the dirty work again. Even so we lost another tank. All around the bridgehead was a nightmare of buildings reduced to rubble, shot-up vehicles and guns, and corpses – of friend and foe alike.'

Constant fighting and casualties were beginning to have a psychological impact upon the attackers. Chivalry there was, and often the wounded were allowed to be evacuated, but this particular battle was at times in its ferocity more intense even than the siege of Oosterbeek that was yet to come. It produced a blood lust in the less stable, and engendered a cynicism in others, who began to view the carnage through a veil of hardened emotion. Kracht recalled the brutalising effect as initial 'apprehension slowly gave away to sarcasm and the will to survive'. He remembers hopelessly gazing skywards through it all:

'Viewing daily bombers formations heading for Germany gave rise to doubts about *Endsieg*, or final victory. It made everything appear absolutely useless.'[8]

And yet there was worse to come.

Do the 'Tommies' in! . . .

Collecting the wounded was increasingly becoming a problem. SS-Machine-Gunner Rudolf Trapp, fighting in the area of Lang Straat and the Eusebius-Plein, resigned himself to the fact: 'Because of my age and experience [19 years old], I got all the dirty jobs.' He described one such task:

'We were told to get some wounded or dead SS men out of the enemy field of fire. To achieve this we got an armoured half-track. Putting down covering fire with two machine guns on it, we would race down the street, open the rear door, pull our mates in, and fire away as we sped back to cover. All the time we would hope there would not be a stoppage on the machine guns because the British fired very accurately. In one case they shot a man in the heart straight through his military record book.'

The problem now was that very few armoured vehicles were actually capable of negotiating the rubble-strewn streets. Trapp claims he saw no tanks at all in his area, 'only the one half-track we had, which was only just able to get through narrow passages covered in wreckage'.

Trapp was ordered to use this vehicle to establish physical contact with Brinkmann's forces trying to break through from the opposite direction – the east – under the bridge ramp itself. Three of his unit made up the crew of the half-track. Nobody was enthusiastic because they knew a British anti-tank gun dominated the river-bank road they would have to use. Trapp recalls their misgivings:

'Bernd Schultze-Bernd was our driver, a farmer's son from Sendenhorst in Muensterland. He was one of the three old company veterans. During the orders group there were tears in his eyes. He told our company commander that this was not going to work. But an order is an order. To be on the safe side, the other two of us stuffed the pockets

Trapp and his companion swam in their underclothes through the murky waters between moored and sunken boats along Ryn-Kade until they reached their own troops. Kracht took this view of the same area from across the river. Note the Arnhem bridge in the background. (Kabel-Kracht)

of our smocks with hand-grenades and ammunition for the ·08 pistols. We raced past the crossroads and got hit on the left, near Bernd's driver seat. The vehicle came to a halt. Bernd was dead, a direct hit from the shell.'

Trapp and his companion baled out and took shelter in a ruined cellar. As the British attempted to close in on them they grenaded their way out of the tightening ring, and eventually made their way to the river bank. Abandoning their uniforms they swam in their underclothes through the murky water between moored boats repeatedly lashed by rifle and mortar fire. At last, seeing some SS men, they shouted: 'Trapp – 3rd Company – don't shoot!'

Their comrades, having interpreted their long absence as due to failure and death, were pleased to see them. Wounds were dressed and fresh clothes obtained by removing uniforms from their own dead comrades. There appeared to be no end to this torture. Even so, the 10SS men, hardened and cynical as they were to the death and destruction around them, were jolted by yet another loss. 'Vogel, our company commander,' Trapp mournfully recalled, 'was killed. The news of his death was passed on from man to man and we were depressed.' Vogel, married with children, had been a popular officer. He had served with the company in southern France the previous year, and had rejoined it after a period of absence with new replacements at

Deventer, just as the aerial armada had been spotted flying in. The men were incensed, Trapp included:

'Vogel was shot in the heart during close-quarter fighting. I didn't see it happen, but a medic was killed trying to reach him and this made the boys really angry!'

They vowed vengeance. Even so, the loss left them in a slough of despondency:

'The British even fired at unarmed medics; we were therefore determined to do the "Tommies" in! Everything was burning and the church was on fire too. The battle had been going on for days and nights already.'[9]

Lieutenant Joseph Enthammer, a prisoner now for over three days, sheltering in the cellar next to Frost's headquarters with sixty others, yearned for an end to the incessant fighting. He was developing a grudging admiration for the resolve of the British fighting around him. He also held them in some wary respect. 'We never admitted,' he said, 'despite questioning, that we were V2 troops – always artillery or transport.' The paratroopers were unlike any soldiers he had ever met. He noticed:

'The British soldiers were very close and informal with their officers. They were desperately tired. There was no saluting, they simply conversed normally. We would never have been allowed to conduct ourselves like that. These men we realised must be élite soldiers.'[10]

The end was inexorably approaching. The British would not be reinforced and both sides knew it. But still the stubborn resistance on the northern ramp was maintained. As long as it did so, German reinforcements could not be passed down the road to another beleaguered garrison – the 10SS holding on the Waal at Nijmegen.

CHAPTER XVI

Hold on the Waal

The biggest mistake historians make is to glorify and narrow-mindedly concern themselves with Arnhem and Oosterbeek. The Allies were stopped in the south just north of Nijmegen – that is why Arnhem turned out as it did.

Commander 10SS Panzer Division

The spectre from the Reichswald. II Fallschirmjaeger Corps attacks . . .

Arppe, a *Kriegsberichter* (war correspondent) attached to Student's 1st Fallschirmjaeger Army, stood on the Mook-Malden road just north-west of Gennep near a small hamlet called De Kroon. So far there had been nothing eventful to photograph. On the Reich border he had taken a number of scenes of German civilians – farmers, it transpired – digging anti-tank ditches near Gennep. Nearby some Fallschirmjaeger had been occupying defensive positions and preparing field defences; he took pictures of them as well.[1] It was the early morning of 20 September as the leading elements of the Kampfgruppe 'Hermann' swung into sight. This, at last, was material worth recording – German troops on the move again.

Arppe stepped into the road and began photographing, first the leading elements, and then the companies, bunched up together for a rapid road move. Up to 100 soldiers were soon visible, shoulders swinging, heads bobbing up and down, as platoons advanced in staggered anti-aircraft formation, using both sides of the road. In the photographs they are mainly teenagers, hot and perspiring, dressed in distinctive baggy Fallschirmjaeger smocks, wearing an

assortment of Wehrmacht and airborne helmets. Others wear the Luftwaffe field cap, or stride along bare-headed, long hair caught by the breeze. Stick grenades are stuffed in the front of belts ready for action, and full bandoliers of extra small arms ammunition hang like harnesses from the neck and across backs. Rifles are often carelessly slung over shoulders for ease of carriage or cradled in the crook of the arm. Helmets and mess tins suspended from belts clank noisily as they stride by. A few soldiers tap the road with crudely fashioned walking sticks as if on an afternoon hike. Panzerfausts perched on shoulders, however, belie the peacefulness of the scene. Faces turn and smile easily at the camera. These troops have yet to be committed to battle. A considerable number viewed through the lens will be dead or maimed before evening. Few will eventually survive the war.

For many in the column, it has already been a long march, starting as far back as Wahn in Cologne. Their boots are dry, dusty and worn. After being transported by electric train to Kranenberg they have had to walk the rest of the way. Tired and grimy, the men march by the neatly fenced prosperous houses in De Kroon, tidily fringed with cultivated shrubs. Veterans are easily identifiable by the stubble on their faces which the youngsters are incapable of growing. One teenager, barely 17 years old,

'Up to a hundred soldiers were soon visible, shoulders swinging, heads bobbing up and down.' The Kampfgruppe 'Hermann' advancing on Mook seven kilometres away during the early morning of 20 September. (Bundesarchiv)

Wearing the distinctive baggy Fallschirmjaeger smock, a youngster pushes a wheelbarrow with the company 'box', followed by veterans loaded with ammunition. A Feldwebel monitors the progress of the column from a bicycle. (Bundesarchiv)

pushes a wheelbarrow with the company box. Smiling encouragement, a few experienced NCOs ride up and down the column on bicycles checking their charges. More of the wily *alte Hasen* (literally 'old hares' or 'old salts'), smile confidently as they march by. Older and more self-assured, they have cannily loaded their possessions into commandeered wheelbarrows. These primitive all-wooden constructions are stacked high with machine guns, radios and, more importantly, blankets. Looking smug they grin impishly at the camera, with hands thrust into pockets bulging with food. Having mastered the immediate problem of marching with all this heavy equipment, they are pleased with themselves – for now.

Orders are passed down and the column halts. Arppe follows the soldiers off the road and into recently harvested corn fields, where they settle in amongst high undergrowth that provides some protection from detection by enemy aircraft. The veterans, caps off, immediately relax; not so the new boys, who, less assured, glance nervously around and at the camera. Company echelon begins to pass apples over the barbed wire garden fence, doubtless foraged from the orchard beyond. Soldiers gather around noisily, weapons clanking on mess tins and metal gas mask containers in their haste to receive something from this hand-out. There follows a welcome break, with a few jokes, and a chance to chat. They

'Soldiers gather around noisily, weapons clanking on mess tins and metal gas mask containers in their haste to receive something from this handout.' (Bundesarchiv)

188

bite into apples that are late season, slightly cidery, grimacing at a refreshing and familiar taste.[2]

Not too long and they would be in action. There had been the inevitable delays *en route*. In Tegelen nails, glass and barbed wire had been placed on roads disabling some Wehrmacht vehicles. Hostages had been seized as reprisal. In Venlo signals cables had been cut. It all contributed to a depressing picture. Within another five kilometres they could expect their first contacts with the enemy.

Artillery fire could be heard bursting in the distance as the battery, in support for their attack, and flak began registering on targets on the east side on the Gennep-Mook road. Some of Captain Goebel's group in the ranks were a little more nervous. Only 36 hours before they had been flung out of Mook by the American paratroopers. That little contest had cost six dead and five more wounded. Goebel's men were hungry. There had been no medics or doctors to treat his wounded, and his men had been without food for three days. Two Dutch civilians had reported that enemy entrenchments stretched for 1,000 metres south of Mook. They had few illusions about what was going to happen.[3]

These Fallschirmjaeger had been put into the line to reinforce 406 Division. They were all that was left of the 3rd and 5th Fallschirmjaeger divisions belonging to II Corps. Training and refurbishment under way at Wahn near Cologne had been prematurely halted by the airborne landings. It was hoped they would reverse the débâcle suffered by 406 Division two days before. Model, hearing of the initial failure, insisted these new arrivals be launched immediately against the American screen protecting Nijmegen. But the commanders of both Corps Feldt and II Fallschirmjaeger Corps argued prudence, at least until more substantial forces were assembled. These were those forces.

Field Marshal Model's plan was to hold on the Waal with forces already *in situ*, and buy time for an eventual reinforcement and counter-offensive by the 10SS Panzer Division. Spoiling attacks from out of the east and the Reichswald forest were part of the conception to distract the XXX Corps' pressure on Nijmegen. The assault by the forces co-ordinated by the Corps Feldt – 406 Division, elements of Wehrkreis VI and II Fallschirmjaeger Corps – were to impose this vital delay. Three attack prongs were to lance the American defences, composed of three Kampfgruppen named after their respective commanders.

Major Karl-Heinz Becker was to lead a conglomeration of remnants from three regiments: 5, 8 and 9 of the former 3rd Fallschirmjaeger Division. Kampfgruppe 'Becker' included the division's reconnaissance, anti-tank, anti-aircraft and engineer units. It was a divisional cadre reformed as a weak regiment. The survivors from the badly mauled division were mainly the service and supply soldiers, supplemented by recently drafted and largely untrained recruits. Captain Freiherr von Fuerstenberg provided further substance in the form of a number of guns mounted on armoured half-tracks. This was further supported by a small flak battle group of one 88mm gun and two 20mm cannon, and an attached infantry battalion, 'Isphording'. Becker could muster in excess of 800 men spread over three battalion-sized groups. The mission was to advance in a north-westerly direction, storm the American positions around Wyler and reach the Maas-Waal canal. Thereafter, they were to clear the east bank of the Waal as far as the Neerbosch bridge.

Kampfgruppe 'Greschick', commanded by a Major, was a three-battalion organisation with 400–500 recently conscripted infantrymen. Fire support was provided by two combat teams, one with six and the other with eight 20mm cannon. Its task was to envelop Groesbeek from two sides, penetrate to the Maas-Waal canal, and link in with 'Becker' during the east bank consolidation phase.

Kampfgruppe 'Hermann' was led by a Lieutenant-Colonel and based upon survivors formed from the 5th Fallschirmjaeger Division. It was reinforced by Goebel's battle group which had already been bloodied in the previous attempt to take Mook. A flak combat team of one 88mm and three 20mm guns provided direct support, supplemented by a battery from Fallschirmjaeger Artillery Regiment 6. This weak regimental force was to try the

already proven and favourable attack route to Nijmegen via Malden, Hatteit and Hees. The objective was to secure the southern bank of the Waal between the Pontveen road bridge and the Maas-Waal Canal.[4]

'H' hour for this three-directional attack was to be 0630 hours on 20 September. By this stage the Americans were beginning to feel complacent. Earlier fears of an armoured threat coming from the direction of the Reichswald had not materialised. German attacks so far had not been sustained, or were so dispersed and uncoordinated that they were easily beaten off. 505 Parachute Infantry Regiment, patrolling the Reichswald after landing, found 'towers . . . empty, woods and tank obstacles – too

'H' hour for the attack by the three Kampfgruppen was to be 0630 hours on 20 September. (Bundesarchiv)

thick'. The division G2 (Intelligence) estimated the enemy had 'probably two battalions of mixed line-of-communication troops' available. There was every likelihood of continuing piecemeal attacks from the forest, 'in increasing strength'. Dutch civilians on 18 September 'continue to report massing of German troops in the Reichswald Forest'.[5] By 20 September, however, General Gavin, the commander of 82nd Airborne Division, was more intent on channelling resources into an assault boat crossing of the Waal to secure the Nijmegen bridge in concert with ground attacks. It was not until 1100 on the same day that it was realised that the persistent squalls of 88mm, Nebelwerfer and mortar fire preceding the continued advance of the three Kampfgruppen was going to detract from this aim.

The assault, co-ordinated from General Feldt's headquarters in Cleve, was delayed in starting. At 0925 the picture was still unclear. The first attack waves met little opposition. Greschick's Kampfgruppe in the centre reported good progress one kilometre after crossing the start line, but nothing was heard from the other two battle groups. What was going on?[6]

Villages in the objective area were often defended by only one or two American airborne platoons. This was the inevitable result of having to disperse forces over wide frontages; the 505 Parachute Infantry Regiment had a front of two miles. As a consequence, assaulting German combat teams attained a marked local superiority in numbers. Becker's initial thrust in the north against Wyler was, however, broken up by artillery fire, where, by 1100, the battle was in full swing. Scattered Fallschirmjaeger groups were pinned to the ground amidst flashing and crackling mushrooms of black smoke. Wyler was penetrated following a hasty reorganisation, and two platoons of the 508 US Infantry pushed out. It was, however, a hollow victory because a high

feature – the Teufelsberg, occupied by the Americans – dominated any further westward advance. Flak batteries, including a Fallschirmjaeger flak detachment in direct support, and other German artillery batteries west of Cleve pounded the feature, but to no avail. Renewed attacks on the high ground north and north-west of Wyler failed. High tide, at least in this sector, had been reached by 1600.

Kampfgruppe Greschick's central thrust reached the edge of Groesbeek, and even managed a tenuous foothold on the outskirts. The crackle of small arms fire mixed with cries and screams, and the thump of hand-grenades rose to a crescendo and then died. Here also at 1600 some progress was reported.

Once again it was the Kampfgruppe Hermann – like that of Goebel some 36 hours before – pushing up from the south, that was to cause the greatest concern to the defenders. Hermann reported the capture of both Riedhorst and Mook after heavy fighting at 1410; by 1600 he was on a line between Knapheide and Mook. He was only 1,500 to 2,000 metres from the Heumen bridge, which at that moment was carrying the British ground advance across the Maas-Waal canal on its way northward to Nijmegen. Hermann was therefore within a few thousand metres of achieving his operational aim. Bitterly contested, Mook had been battered into ruins. But it was not to be. An American counter-attack during the late afternoon, supported by six British tanks from the Guards Armoured Brigade, prised Mook from Hermann's grasp. The German effort finally collapsed. That evening Hermann's Kampfgruppe retired under pressure to Riedhorst, using darkness as cover.

Corps Feldt tried to sway the balance by feeding additional reinforcements into the line during the late afternoon and early evening. Three more weak battalion groups, each about 300 men strong, were involved:

Major Molzer's assault pioneer battalion, a Fallschirmjaeger battalion commanded by Lieutenant-Colonel Budde, and another Kampfgruppe led by Captain Lewin. But the three Kampfgruppen were approaching their furthest points of advance; all piece-meal reinforcements could achieve was the consolidation of some gains.

Major Becker, supported by other units from 406 Division, pressed further attacks home and finally broke into Beek. By early evening a battalion-size Fallschirmjaeger wedge had penetrated the village. Fighting was savage as street obstacles were overrun in a grim costly assault, supported by Captain Fuerstenberg's armoured half-track guns firing at point-blank range. Beek became the critical point in the American defence chain when two platoons of parachute infantry were pushed up the hill to the Berg en Dal hotel. The attack, ebbing and flowing, was only barely contained by the Americans. General Gavin, remarking on the closeness of the contest, was to recall: 'If the Germans had had the wit to move even several hundred yards to the right, they could have walked into the outskirts of Nijmegen almost unmolested.'[7] But Becker's Kampfgruppe had locked itself on to this strongpoint, intent on the kill. It had little to do with wit, and more to do with stamina and attrition. Counter-attacks were stalled in mid-stream by opposing attacks launched at the same time. Shortly before midnight, Fallschirmjaeger night attacks surrounded yet another group of American paratroopers, but they did not have the strength to turn in and destroy them.

General Scherbening's 406 Division reported to Corps Feldt at 2125 hours that Wyler and Riedhorst had been taken during the course of the day, but bitter resistance was still being encountered at Mook and Groesbeek. Disturbing news was, however, beginning to filter through concerning the day's events in Nijmegen. Fighting was to continue through the night and into 21 September on the Kampfgruppen axis, but it was becoming increasingly apparent that something serious had happened in the city. General Feldt personally took over command at his headquarters in Cleve. His spoiling attack had failed. Higher command signalled that he should hold on to the objectives already secured. All this was of little consequence now because the day's events in Nijmegen had negated all their efforts so far – they had been too little, and too late.[8]

Hold on the Waal! The defence of Nijmegen by the Frundsberg . . .

In Nijmegen, the arrival of British armour had raised the intensity and scale of the fighting. Extensive fires had broken out, marking the progress of the XXX Corps advance. Combined Sherman and infantry attacks during the early night hours of 20 September had been halted by accurate artillery fire around the traffic circle south of the Hunner park. SS-Captain Krueger of 21 Battery had personally directed the fire. At 0130 two Shermans remained with sheared tracks after the attack had been repelled. During the course of the morning three more combined arms attacks were concentrated upon the gradually shrinking 10SS perimeter defending the southern bank of the Waal. Supported by tanks and infantry of the Grenadier Guards, Vander-voort's 2nd (US) Battalion of the 505 Para-chute Infantry Regiment fought their way through intense street fighting toward the Waal bridges. D Company was bogged down with a tank column in the area of the Kronenburger park near the railway bridge, while E and F Companies were locked into the SS Battalion Euling around the Canisiussingel, the Valkhof and the Kaiser Lodewijkplein traffic circle south of

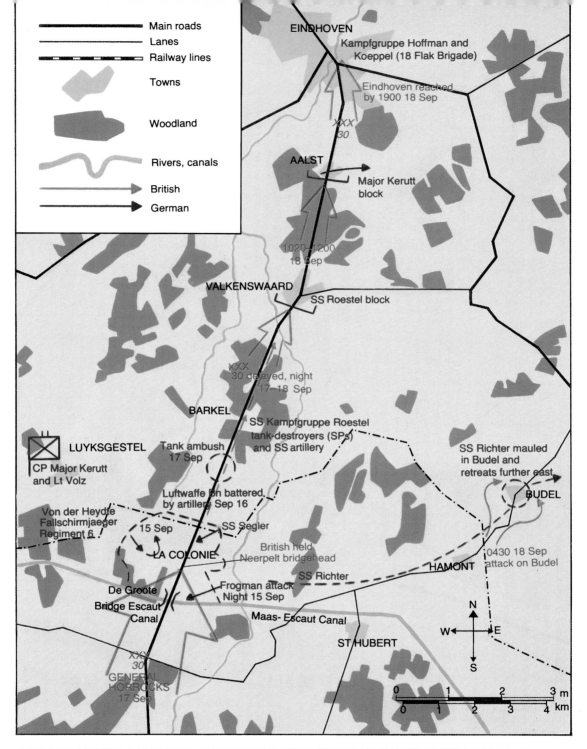

BREAKING THROUGH THE NEERPELT BRIDGEHEAD TO EINDHOVEN 17–18 SEPTEMBER 1944.

After breaking through the defensive crust established by the Regiment von Hoffman, the way to Eindhoven was virtually open. Tank ambushes and temporary blocking actions delayed 30 Corps advance south of Valkenswaard and Aalst until Eindhoven was reached by 1900 hours on 18 September.

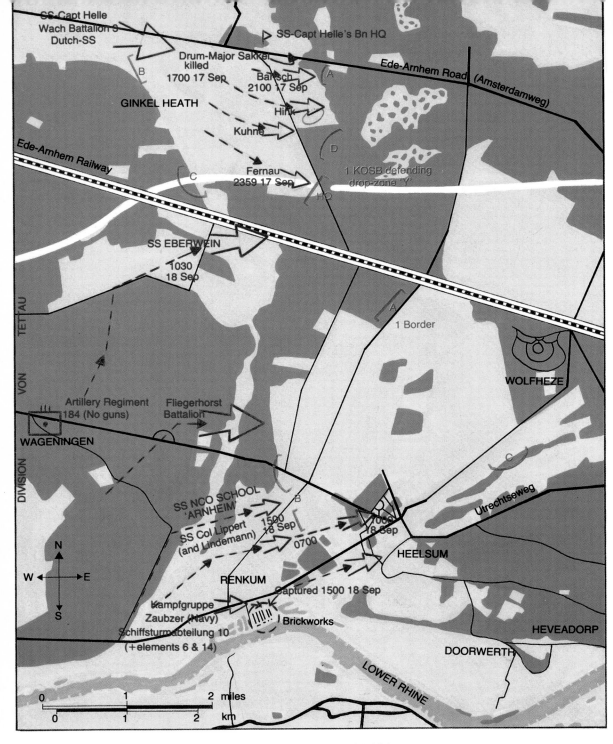

SS-Capt Helle
Wach Battalion 3
Dutch-SS

B

SS-Capt Helle's Bn HQ

Drum-Major Sakkel
killed
1700 17 Sep

Batsch
2100 17 Sep

(A)

Ede-Arnhem Road (Amsterdamweg)

GINKEL HEATH

Hink

Kuhne

(D)

Ede-Arnhem Railway

Fernau
2359 17 Sep

C

1 KOSB defending
drop-zone 'Y'

HQ

SS EBERWEIN

1030
18 Sep

TETTAU

A

1 Border

VON

WOLFHEZE

Artillery Regiment
184 (No guns)

Fliegerhorst
Battalion

DIVISION

WAGENINGEN

C

Utrechtseweg

SS NCO SCHOOL
'ARNHEIM'

B

SS Col Lippert
(and Lindemann)

1500
18 Sep

0700

1000
18 Sep

N

HEELSUM

W ← → E

RENKUM

S

Captured 1500 18 Sep

Kampfgruppe
Zaubzer (Navy)

HEVEADORP

Brickworks

Schiffsturmabteilung 10
(+elements 6 & 14)

DOORWERTH

LOWER RHINE

0   1   2 miles

0   1   2 km

THE FORMATION OF THE KAMPFGRUPPE VON TETTAU.

During the night of 17–18 September the hastily formed Kampfgruppen of the 'Division' von Tettau began to form up in their holding areas on the eastern edge of the Wageningen forest. Six battalions spread across an eight-kilometre front began to advance towards Oosterbeek from the west at dawn on 18 September. The contested advance was to average two kilometres per day until the formation of the Oosterbeek pocket.

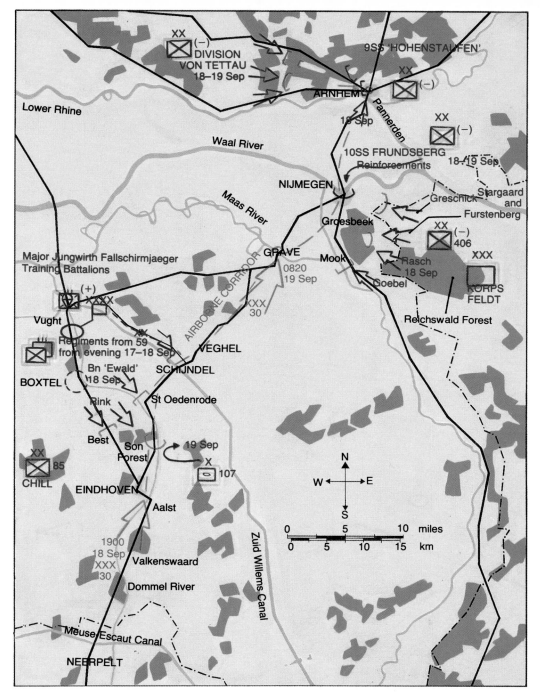

THE SITUATION WITHIN THE AIRBORNE CORRIDOR 18–19 SEPTEMBER 1944.
Guards Armoured Division has reached Grave by 0820 hours 19 September. Units up to two
regiments strong have arrived on the western edge of the corridor from 59 Division. These,
with Fallschirmjaeger training battalions from S'Hertogenbosch, begin to apply pressure on
the 101 (US) Division sector between Eindhoven and Grave. 82 (US) Division begins to face
the first attacks by Kampfgruppen from 406 Division (Corps 'Feldt') pushing from the east
across the Groesbeek heights and from the Reichswald toward Nijmegen. As they do so the
10SS begins to reinforce the Nijmegen garrison. First British Airborne Division remains
isolated in the north between a pincer movement mounted from the west by the Division von
Tettau and the 9SS in the east.

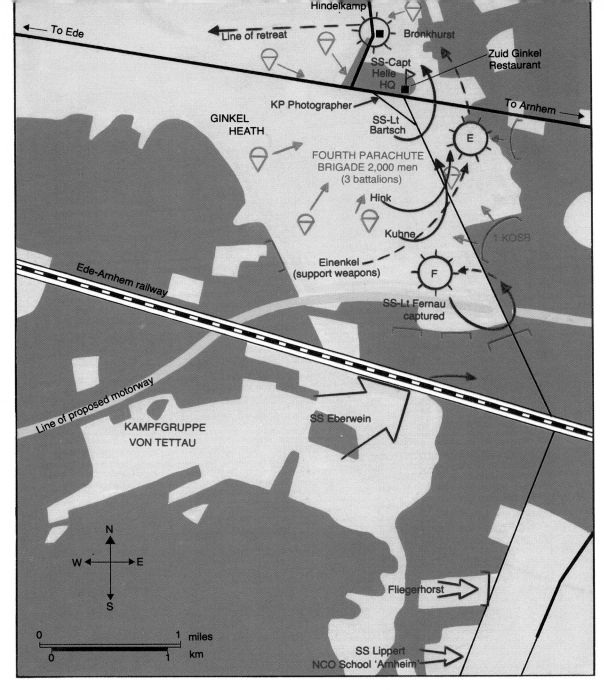

To Ede

Line of retreat

Hindelkamp

Bronkhurst

Zuid Ginkel
Restaurant

SS-Capt
Helle
HQ

To Arnhem

KP Photographer

SS-Lt
Bartsch

GINKEL
HEATH

FOURTH PARACHUTE
BRIGADE 2,000 men
(3 battalions)

E

Hink

Kuhne

1 KOSB

Einenkel
(support weapons)

F

SS-Lt Fernau
captured

Ede-Arnhem railway

Line of proposed motorway

KAMPFGRUPPE
VON TETTAU

SS Eberwein

N

W ← → E

S

Fliegerhorst

0   1 miles
0   1 km

SS Lippert
NCO School 'Arnheim'

THE ARRIVAL OF THE SECOND LIFT ON GINKEL HEATH.

*The German westward advance had been going to plan when suddenly Hackett's Fourth
Parachute Brigade landed on Ginkel heath, 1500 18 September. SS-Captain Helle's Dutch-SS
battalion, already committed to clearing the eastern treeline opposite the landing-zone, was
overrun. Most companies fled, formed temporary 'hedgehogs' or were captured. Only
Einenkel, Helle's support weapons company commander, retained sufficient composure to
cover the retreat. Although reformed after this débâcle the battalion was subsequently
disbanded when it continued to perform ineptly during the fighting for Oosterbeek. The
general advance of the Kampfgruppe von Tettau was resumed the following day. (Map based
on Dutch interrogation of Helle's officers)*

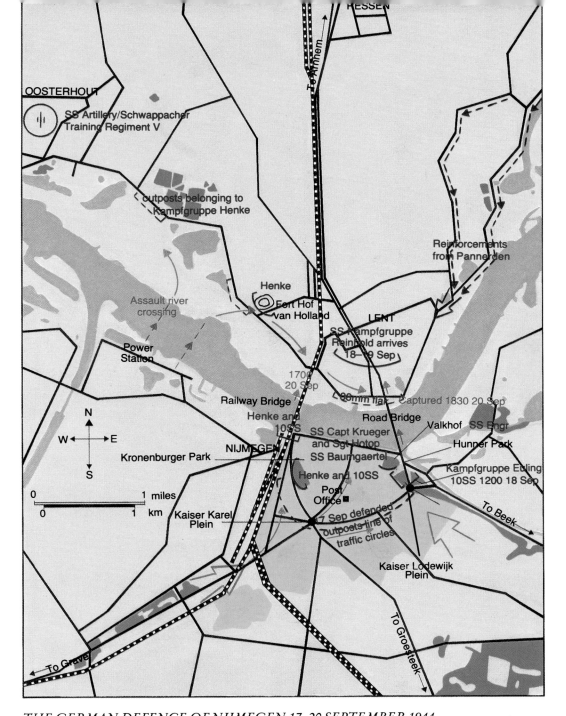

THE GERMAN DEFENCE OF NIJMEGEN 17–20 SEPTEMBER 1944.

The Kampfgruppe Henke initially established a line of defensive outposts based on the two traffic circles south of the railway and road bridges on 17 September. The 10SS Kampfgruppe Reinhold arrived the following day and established a triangular defence with Euling on the road bridge, Henke and other units defending the approaches to the railway bridge, and his own Kampfgruppe on the home bank in the village of Lent. A surprise assault river crossing by the (US) 3/504 combined with a tank assault on the road bridge on 20 September unhinged the defence. The Waal had been secured by 1900 on the same day. There was nothing further barring the road to Arnhem 17 kilometres to the north.

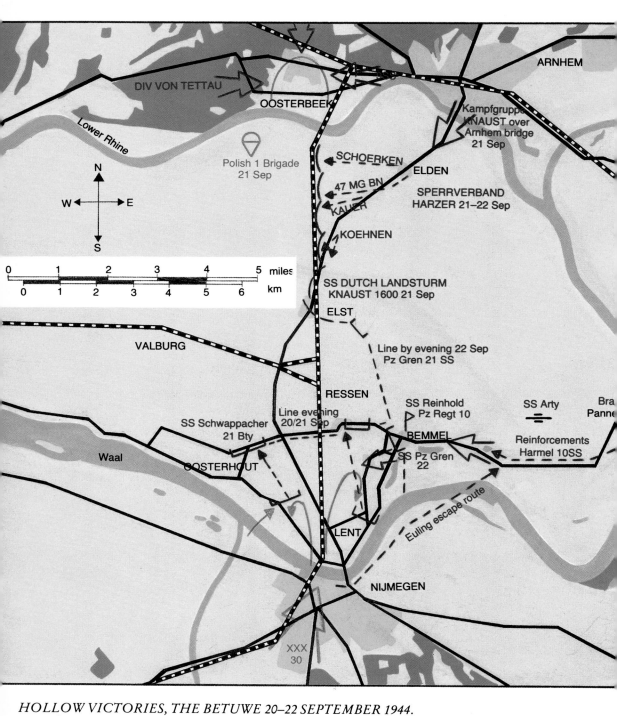

HOLLOW VICTORIES, THE BETUWE 20–22 SEPTEMBER 1944.
Any advantage accruing from the Allied capture of the Nijmegen bridges during the evening of 20 September was cancelled out by the fall of the Arnhem bridge to the Germans the following day. An opportunity was missed during the night of 20–21 September to relieve Arnhem. The Poles landed at Driel the next afternoon but were countered by the formation and deployment of the 'Sperrverband' Harzer, which linked with the Kampfgruppe Knaust holding Elst. Allied reinforcements were now effectively blocked from reaching Arnhem in any strength, in time to relieve the Oosterbeek pocket.

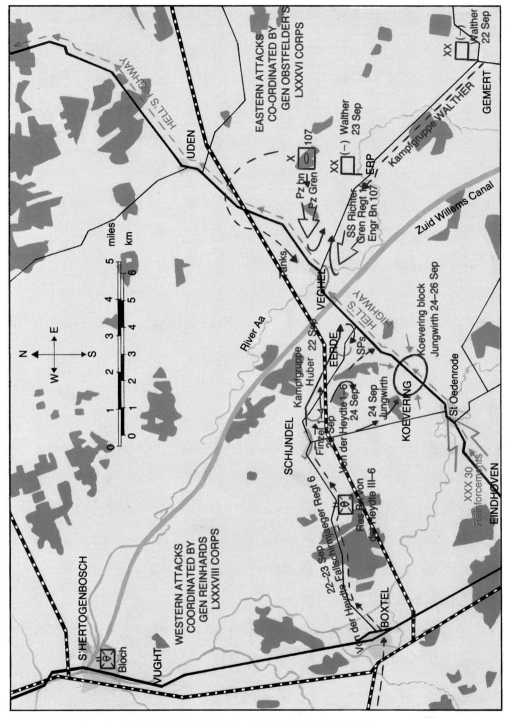

ATTEMPTS TO CUT 'HELL'S HIGHWAY' 22–26 SEPTEMBER 1944.
The first attacks by the Kampfgruppen Huber and Walther on 22 September were simultaneous, cut the corridor, but were uncoordinated and failed. Von der Heydte's Fallschirmjaeger Regiment 6 was fought to a standstill west of Eerde on 23 September. The final cut was achieved by the Battalion Jungwirth at Koevering, blocking the corridor between 24–26 September. Walther had already withdrawn the day before, suffering losses of 25 per cent of his infantry and 20 per cent of tanks. 'Hell's Highway' was never decisively cut again.

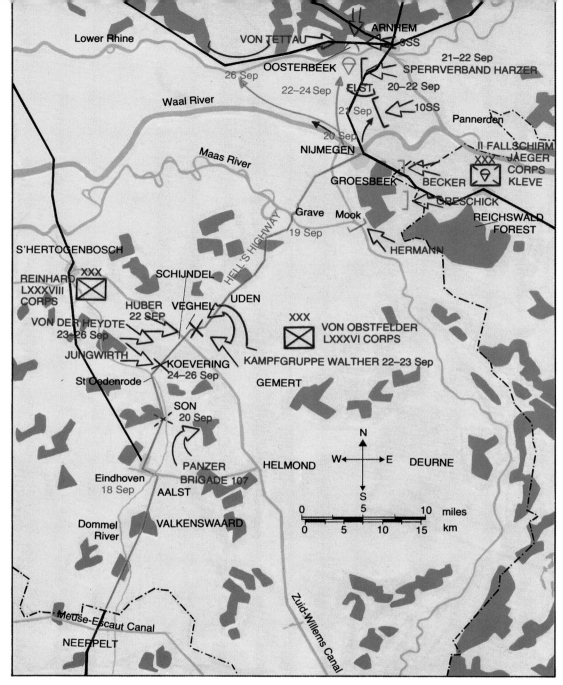

THE SITUATION ON 'HELL'S HIGHWAY' BETWEEN 20–26 SEPTEMBER 1944.
Panzer Brigade 107 is driven from Son after temporarily interfering with traffic. General
Meindl's II Fallschirmjaeger Corps launches spoiling attacks on the 82 (US) Airborne Division
screen S.E. of Nijmegen but fails to influence the Allied capture of the Nijmegen bridges.
Uncoordinated attacks from both sides of the corridor: the Kampfgruppe Huber (22 Sep), the
Kampfgruppe Walther (22–23 Sep) and von der Heydte's Fallschirmjaeger Regiment 6, block
the road at Veghel for 36 hours. The Kampfgruppe Jungwirth is able effectively to block the
corridor for the third time at Koevering between 24–26 September. Although the vanguard of
43 Division has reached the Poles at Driel, it is already too late. First British Airborne Division
were ordered to exfiltrate across the lower Rhine during the night of 25–26 September.

the road bridge. Spiralling smoke and dust was making observation increasingly difficult for both sides.

The 10SS bridgehead had shrunk to an area one kilometre wide by 300 metres deep. Its left boundary was approximately 100 metres east of the road bridge, stretching to the right boundary on the railway bridge. Euling's 10SS Kampfgruppe held the area of the road bridge and Hunner park, with the Kampfgruppe Henke and other 10SS elements holding the railway bridge and the Kronenburger park immediately south of it. Providing depth to the south bank positions were two weak 10SS engineer companies commanded by SS-2/ Lieutenant Werner Baumgaertel, holding a bastion position in the Valkhof, a 'keep' separating both bridges. All these units were co-ordinated by and under the overall control of the SS-Kampfgruppe 'Reinhold', which was dug in on the north bank of the river in Lent, thus completing a defensive triangle.

Crucial to the overall defence of Nijmegen was the retention of the road bridge. This responsibility was given to SS-Captain Karl-Heinz Euling whose battle group, some 100 strong, was reinforced by four assault guns and elements of the Kampfgruppe Henke 'whose combat quality', Euling remarked, 'was poor'.[9] Euling's forces controlled all the roads leading north through the city towards the road bridge, which converged on the Kaiser Lodewijk traffic circle. The area was dominated by his own observation post in the Belvedere tower which overlooked both bridges and Baumgaertel's engineers in the Valkhof. His headquarters was situated in the Haus Robert Jannssen. Thus far, all attacks had broken on his positions dug in on the southern extremity of Hunner park. During the course of the fighting between 19–20 September, step by step covered withdrawals were conducted in contact with the enemy to a more defensible perimeter.

Euling commented, 'after the failure of General Field Marshal Model's promise of "Tiger" tanks to materialise, I was forced under strong enemy pressure to withdraw to the line 1 and 1b'.[10] This amounted to the loss of part of the Hunner park, but still enabled the main bridge approach roads to be dominated by fire.

Communications within Reinhold's bridgehead command were becoming tenuous. Despatch riders between himself and Euling had to run a gauntlet of long-range enemy machine gun fire from the west, which would lazily pan along the bridge's superstructure each time a dash was attempted. Observation alone was not sufficient to indicate what was going on. Only personal contact at all command levels could maintain any control and co-ordination amid the turmoil of street fighting. Throughout it all, often shrouded in smoke, but tantalisingly intact, beckoned the massive superstructure of the Nijmegen bridge. It was a mirage galvanising both sides to greater efforts – but just out of reach.

SS-Colonel Heinz Harmel, the commander of the Frundsberg, suspected he was fighting a losing battle. He felt the Waal would have been more defensible if the Germans had fought from the home bank. Endorsing this view after the war, he remarked:

'Model said don't blow the bridge because I need it for a counter-stroke. By that he meant a counter-attack at the higher operational level. Bittrich [the Corps Commander] and I believed it should be blown straight away. We realised we would never mobilise sufficient forces for an offensive on that scale. It was a question of cutting one's coat according to one's cloth. Model's shirt was always too short, it never reached!'[11]

Nevertheless, for the time being the Frundsberg held on to their increasingly tenuous grip on the bridges.

Both the American 82nd and British Guards Armoured Division were aware they were up against a substantial number of seasoned SS troops, and not the forecast line-of-communication soldiers. The G2 of the 82nd Division estimated that about 500 top-quality SS soldiers held the road bridge alone, supported by an 88mm gun on the traffic circle, and four 47mm and a further 37mm with mortars in the Hunner park. There was no shortage of artillery supporting them from across the Waal.[12] German resistance was also tinged with fanatical courage. SS-Captain Schwappacher narrates the example of SS-Gunner Albrecht from the 21st Battery of his regiment in his post-combat report. Albrecht had been acting as a radio operator for his SS-Sergeant observer Hotop during an infantry counter-attack. When his radio set had been smashed by machine gun fire, he fought on as an infantry 'tank-buster', knocking out a British Sherman tank by dropping a grenade down an open turret.[13]

Arnhem still lay a long 17 kilometres away to the north – as the Allies were well aware. Moreover, the first foreboding details of setbacks in 1st British Airborne Division's area were starting to emerge. XXX Corps and the Americans pushed on tenaciously, but it was not only fanatical courage barring the way. For the first time in this battle the enemy seemed to have prodigious quantities of artillery ammunition and the artillery resources to match.

Harmel described the potential that his commander of artillery SS-Lieutenant-Colonel Zonnenstahl had at his disposal. Not the usual 'three battalions of artillery with three batteries in each, but this time four batteries, and not of four guns as normal, but six'. This situation stemmed from the booty recovered on the abandoned train in Arras the month before.[14]

SS-Captain Schwappacher, whose Training and Artillery Regiment V was supporting battle groups in the west of Nijmegen, endorsed this view of their effectiveness:

'Whenever the enemy was ready to advance on the bridge we hit him with the full impact of an artillery barrage, which immediately halted the attacks, whereupon our infantry, reinforced, were able to maintain their positions.'

Forward artillery observers 'brought down fire', he maintained, 'to within 100 metres of our own positions'. Thereby overcoming 'critical moments' which were 'witnessed daily, indeed, almost hourly by the infantry'. This did much to sustain confidence and morale.[15] It may well have been a factor slowing the rate of the Allied advance towards Arnhem. Harmel further described the simple but effective system employed:

'The area west of Arnhem and up to the Waal was covered by an imaginary belt or *Sperrfeurlinie* [artillery blocking line] drawn on the map. We had only to give a number from that strip and the whole weight of a regiment's artillery would descend on the ground, in that grid square, after only a short reaction time. SS-Lieutenant-Colonel Zonnenstahl's map shows us he was able to cover a frontage of 20 kilometres.[16] The commander of Artillery OB West was so impressed with this solution that he visited our command post to see it in action for himself, so that the method could be passed on to other units. Prisoner of war interrogation reports suggest this lightning reaction demoralised the enemy.'[17]

A combination of all these factors enabled the line on the Waal, tenuous though it was, to be held. At 1530 on 20 September

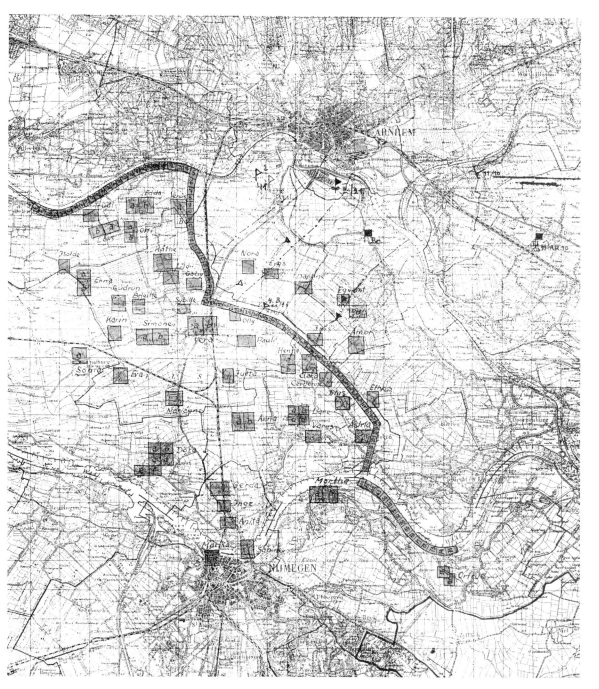

SS-Lieutenant-Colonel Zonnenstahl's actual map used to co-ordinate the 10SS artillery blocking line covering the envisaged Allied approach to Nijmegen and Arnhem. Fire boxes were given a code name: 'Anna', 'Jutta', 'Kathe', which could be further subdivided 'a', 'b', 'c', and 'd'. The blocking line itself was numbered by squares 1 to 75. Upon receipt of a code word, number – or both – artillery fire could immediately be concentrated upon the area requested by ground commanders. The method was to prove devastatingly simple. (Harmel)

SS-Lieutenant Richter reported to Army Group B from IISS Corps that 'the enemy was pressing with strong infantry and tank forces on both Nijmegen bridges'.[18] Model was still determined to use the bridge as a springboard for a future counter-offensive. To this end he directed 'additional forces and all available anti-tank weapons' were to be sent south from Arnhem.[19] This should have occurred during the night to be ready for the joint assault by 406 Division and II Fallschirmjaeger Corps on 20 September. The best that could be achieved, however, was the removal of some of the 82nd Airborne's infantry from the assaults against Euling – no more.

At 1500 an intensive bombardment by 40 Sherman tanks and 100 artillery barrels and aircraft focused German attention to a sector well to the west of the railway bridge, opposite the power station. Twenty-six canvas and wooden constructed assault boats were launched into the fast-flowing river; they contained the leading wave of Major Julian A. Cook's 3rd Battalion of the 504 (US) Parachute Infantry Regiment. The men within paddled frantically to reach the opposite bank. The Germans, observing from the northern bank, were taken completely by surprise.

'There was nothing left available to form a defence line . . .'

Even at worst case the Germans would have considered an attack here improbable. Artillery fire had given no real indication, because it had not been matched by activity on the south bank. Indeed, Cook's attacking troops had not received their boats until after the supporting fire programme had started. Reinhold, co-ordinating the defence plan, had considered the attacks against Euling and the main road bridge to

be the greatest threat. Consequently there were few troops opposite the landing sites: some Fallschirmjaeger from Henke's headquarters staff, a few *Reichsarbeitsdienst* (pioneers), and the flak battery 'Beck' with its command post. The nearest infantry were a few artillerymen from SS-Captain Schwappacher's training regiment behind the high dyke road south of the village of Oosterhout, left of the proposed landing site. Schwappacher suspected they had been seen the night before by the enemy because they were subjected to 'harassing fire and white light', and the enemy 'kept their distance' during the attack.

Nevertheless, the Americans faced an imposing task. The German-occupied railway bridge dominated their approach to the right. Fortunately, it was often shrouded in smoke. Upon crossing the river, running at a swift eight to ten miles an hour, there was 600 metres of flat terrain to cover, completely overlooked by a high dyke road, thought to be occupied.

Schwappacher wrote in his after-action report:

> 'After the enemy was successful in piercing the bridgeheads on the railway and road bridges, at about 1500 he launched an assault boat operation from the electric power station [one kilometre north-west of Nijmegen] against the north bank of the Waal. The enemy reached the north side in regimental strength.'[20]

The Germans could only react with the outposts they had *in situ*, and what SS forces could be mustered from Lent. Schwappacher was presented with a dilemma. His heavy battery was totally committed to engaging possible enemy forming-up points in the city across the river. 'Every individual gun,' he claims 'was zeroed on a particular block.' All that was left was his 19th battery, which was now turned on to the entry and exit points for the assault boats labouring across the water.

Once the assault boats – now detected – reached the deep water of the main channel, they were seized by the strong current. The paratroopers within, unfamiliar with their craft, lost direction; buffeted by the current, boats whirled crazily around until some semblance of order to the assault was restored. Any hope of maintaining unit cohesion on the far bank was quickly dispelled. Enemy fire began to build up, rifle and machine guns at first, leading gradually to mortar bursts. Artillery shells, too, began to fall, lashing and flailing the water with shrapnel. Bullets and shell fragments tore through the thin canvas skins of the assault boats. 20mm cannon, wheeled into position, slashed great rents in their hulls as they found the range, chopping and clawing remorselessly towards occupants thrown into the river. Before long a fierce response to this daring incursion had been thrown together. Some boats began to sink amid huge geysers spurting from the water. Schwappacher, grimly observing through binoculars, later reported:

'The battery was able with directed fire (250 rounds were allocated) to lay concentrated barrages, and harassing fire for one and a half hours, causing considerable enemy casualties during the crossing. Several assault boats were destroyed. The precise number cannot be given.'[21]

Incredibly, almost half the boats reached the north bank, the survivors returning to pick up the second and subsequent waves. American paratroopers spilled ashore, exhausted, dizzy from the gyrations, some vomiting with the fear and tension of the frightening experience that they had just barely survived. Devoid of unit organisation, and incensed, they closed with their tormentors.

Many of the German defenders were 15-year-old teenagers, or 60-year-old previous exemptions from service. They were totally unprepared to meet these enraged paratrooper veterans rushing at them. Having engaged in a slaughter while holding the upper hand, the outposts were now mercilessly extinguished, with no quarter asked or given. 20mm cannon could not, even at maximum depression, cover both the river and the beach close in. They were overwhelmed. As the Germans ran out of ammunition, small groups dashed to the rear for more. Having fallen back, the survivors were ordered to counter-attack; 'unfortunately', as Schwappacher observed, 'I never ever saw these troops again'.

Desperate attempts were made to restore the rapidly disintegrating situation on the north bank. A quick-reaction platoon, commanded by SS-Lieutenant Bransch, was summoned from Valburg six kilometres away, where it had been standing by to apprehend any further surprise parachute landings. Schwappacher's battery positions went into all-round defence, reinforced by another platoon. Meanwhile, the remaining motorcycle despatch riders and staff from the artillery regimental headquarters were sent out under SS-Lieutenant Buettner to defend the dyke road south of Oosterhout. Schwappacher, monitoring the American advance, saw that it

'. . . divided when it reached the north bank. The majority of the forces attacked toward Oosterhout and further along the Waal to the north-west. The second element attempted to penetrate Lent from the west.'

What was there to do now? The situation was critical. Schwappacher was running out of resources. His flak battery commanders under command to engage ground targets in Nijmegen had pulled out.

'When this critical situation developed, nobody was left available. My fifteen motorcyclists were lying alone on the dyke road, trying to keep an ever-increasing number of enemy pinned down with rifle fire and one machine gun. As there was nothing left to form a defensive line, I decided to adopt all-round defence positions with the staff and 21 battery.'[22]

One of Henke's outposts, manning the Fort Hof van Holland behind the dyke road beyond the landing area, was overwhelmed shortly after 1700. Schwappacher, having adopted his 'hedgehog' stance by 1800, began to send fighting patrols and deception attacks against the enemy who had now occupied the Waal dyke road. The artillery gun crews were not, however, allowed to leave their guns to man trenches. Fire support was still being provided by 21 battery for the beleaguered 10SS engineers, cut off, and fighting desperately to retain possession of the Valkhof in Nijmegen across the river. SS-Captain Krueger, the battery commander, was still directing fire from within. With his radio smashed, enemy positions were indicated with a verey pistol. By 1930 Schwappacher lost all contact with him.

At about the same time enemy tanks were noticed on the main span of the Nijmegen bridge, driving for Lent. A breakthrough had occurred.

'I now gave the order on my own responsibility to blow . . .'

At about 1700 infantry and tank probes were mounted once again against the Waal bridges in an attempt to secure both ends, in concert with the assault boat crossing of the river. Coming in from the east along the Ubergsche way, it found the Kampfgruppe Euling in difficulties. Most of the assault guns guarding the traffic circle south of Hunner park had been overcome in close combat. Houses in the area were either totally destroyed or burning fiercely. Tanks could barely negotiate the scattered rubble. Intense heat from burning buildings scorched faces and made breathing difficult, while smoke and dust obscured everything. Pressing for a *coup de main*, a troop of four Shermans, extracted from a squadron whose second-in-command was Captain Peter Carrington of the Grenadier Guards, was ordered to rush the road bridge. Only the easterly feeder roads were still open to tanks. The crews regarded it as a suicide mission. Soldiers from the 1st Company 10SS Engineers had already shot the tracks off a number of Shermans with panzerfausts which had tried. They now stood abandoned on the southern approaches to the bridge. The situation was totally fluid. Both sides were sure of each other's intention, but commanders were unable to discern what progress had actually been made. Harmel, the 10SS Commander, having now arrived, summed up the dilemma:

'The British probably did not know what lay ahead in the smoke anyway. This smoke worked very successfully for us, for it always seemed to hang over the two bridges, and cloaked much movement.'

Confusion and artillery fire were to be the main factors instrumental in securing the objective. Why the bridge was not blown as Sergeant Robinson's lead tank nosed on to the Arnhemsche Weg, enclosed by the bridge's massive superstructure, has never been satisfactorily resolved. Quite probably artillery fire may have cut much of the wiring or dispersed demolition charges without initiating them. Many of the German soldiers hanging in harnesses from the bridge's superstructure as the tanks crossed

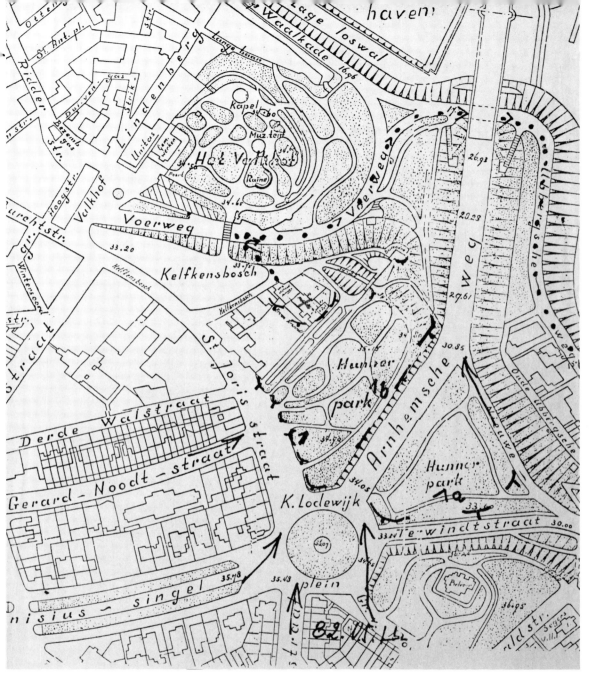

SS-Captain Karl-Heinz Euling's sketch map of the Kampfgruppe Euling's defence of the Nijmegen bridge, 18–20 Sep 44. The Arnhemsche Weg leads on to the southern ramp of the bridge. SS-2/Lieutenant Baumgaertel held the Valkhof citadel north of the Voerweg with a company of 10SS engineers. SS-Captain Krueger's bunker was dug in on the Valkhof. The positions marked at 1 and 1a were held on 18 September, falling back under pressure to 1b by 19–20 September. Arrows indicate the direction of Allied attacks. Euling's HQ was situated in the Haus Janssen, marked with an 'X' by the author. The dotted line indicates Euling's escape route under the bridge during the evening of 20 Sep. (Schneider)

over were not snipers, as often assessed, but more likely engineers trying to remedy the damage identified by the bridge demolition guard commander. As the tanks crossed, these hapless pioneers fell victim to the crew's machine guns spraying their approach route; many tumbled down from the girders into the road or plummeted into the river Waal below. Harmel later felt:

> 'It is doubtful whether any snipers would have remained in the metal work of the bridge. Nobody could have survived in that maelstrom of artillery fire. In any case the bridge was always shrouded in smoke.'

They would, therefore, have had a reasonable albeit risky chance of completing the necessary critical repairs under fire. In the event the tanks got through. Well spread out, they duelled with flak guns ahead, and those firing up from the water's edge on the shoreline. However, by then, the tremendous impact of the Allied counter battery fire had successfully negated much of the tanks' effectiveness. Harmel was later to declare:

> 'Artillery fire was decisive. Because of this the flak crews were dead, or had fled. That is why the tanks managed to get across!'[23]

A similar view to that seen by SS-Colonel Harmel as the bridge fell. Confusion reigns, Nijmegen is shrouded in smoke, and there are reports of Allied tanks on the bridge. What had happened? The view from the north bank.

Meanwhile, having witnessed the successful river assault, many of the German defenders in the west of Nijmegen tried to make their escape over the railway bridge. Small groups of American paratroopers, however, from 'H' and 'I' Companies of Cook's 3rd Battalion, were already at the northern end. Quickly setting up BAR machine guns they began to rake the fleeing columns with fire. Although outnumbering this small outpost, the Germans were intent on flight alone. The last of SS-Captain Krueger's forward artillery observation parties to get out made their escape at this time. Schwappacher recalled:

'Following a direct hit on their radio equipment, SS-Sergeant Hotop retreated with his forward observation party after joining with the SS Company Runge. Hotly pursued by the enemy, they escaped over the railway bridge into the south-west part of Lent. The main OP site occupied by the battery commander SS-Captain Krueger was now totally cut off, and found itself in hand-to-hand combat against enemy forces.'[24]

Later 267 German bodies were recovered from the railway bridge after the retreat.[25] At about 1930 hours SS-Gunner Albrecht knocked out a Sherman tank with his panzerfaust on the south-west edge of Lent, but to no avail; even more tanks were thundering across the Nijmegen road bridge.

Harmel drove into Lent to get a better picture of what was going on. He feared the worst, but could not understand how the daring *coup* against the bridge could possibly have succeeded. Standing on the roof of a bunker, surveying the scene through binoculars, he pondered events. Communications with Euling had gone. The only development that was certain was the stark reality of what he saw before him – enemy tanks on the bridge. Only one course of action remained, as he later recalled:

'I now gave the order, on my own responsibility, to blow the road bridge, over which further tanks continued to advance. It failed to go up – probably because the initiation cable had been cut by artillery fire.'[26]

It was all over. Still cut off in the Nijmegen citadel, SS-Captain Karl-Heinz Euling came to a decision:

'As the first enemy tank was finally able to pass over the road bridge during the evening of 20 September, the railway bridge had already fallen. I decided to escape impending captivity with the rest of my battalion – about 60 men were left.'[27]

The only avenue of escape lay under the enemy-occupied Nijmegen road bridge itself.

CHAPTER XVII

Putting the Lid on the Box

The situation started to stabilise once the Oosterbeek ring was closed and the bridge retaken.

Chief of Staff, 9SS Panzer Division

The pocket forms.
Division von Tettau . . .

During the afternoon of 19 September it became apparent, after the failure to pierce the Kampfgruppe Spindler's *Sperrlinie* on the Dreyenseweg, that the position of Brigadier Hackett's 4th Parachute Brigade had become untenable. Its remnants were ordered to reorganise and begin withdrawing towards the Wolfheze level crossing and tunnel beneath, prior to retreating south across the obstacle of the Ede-Arnhem railway line. Later that night Major-General Urquhart, the commander of 1st British Airborne Division, ordered their withdrawal into a perimeter around Oosterbeek. Attempts to reach Frost at the bridge were abandoned. Establishing a perimeter north of the lower Rhine at Oosterbeek, he assessed, might salvage some positive gain from the original MARKET-GARDEN plan if XXX Corps could arrive in time.

German advances during the afternoon of 19 September were placing the 4 PARA Brigade plan in jeopardy. There was pressure from the east as the 9SS Kampfgruppe Spindler began its advance, pushing out of the western suburbs of Arnhem toward Oosterbeek, capitalising on 1 PARA Brigade's collapsed attempt to reach the bridge. To the west of Arnhem, the Kampfgruppe von Tettau, having now stabilised the situation since the rout of Helle's Dutch-SS Surveillance Battalion during

Hackett's landings, was advancing on all fronts. Three battle groups, numbering in total six to seven battalions, were advancing in a three-pronged move. In the north was the Regiment 'Knoche' with three tanks, advancing east along the Ede-Arnhem road. Its task was to clear Ginkel heath and the forests north west of Wolfheze. To the south SS-Colonel Lippert's regiment, built around the SS-NCO School 'Arnheim', was clearing Heelsum and the forests north of it. The wedge in the centre was the SS Battalion 'Eberwein' pushing down the line of the Ede-Arnhem railway, and protecting the flanks of the other two battle groups north and south. Eberwein's objective was Wolfheze, of crucial significance to 4 PARA Brigade because this was the only point where the British could get their motorised transport across the railway cutting. By mid-afternoon his lead elements were bearing down on the complex of forest roads and tracks on the station and level crossing approaches.[1]

SS-Captain Sepp Krafft's Training and Replacement Battalion 16, which had distinguished itself resisting the initial landings, had, upon retreating northwards, been reorganised in the area of Deelen airfield. Incorporated into Spindler's 9SS Kampfgruppe, it was formed into a subsidiary battle group in its own right, reinforced by 642 Marine Regiment, 1 Marine Cadre Regiment, and 10 Company from 3 Police Regiment. Krafft's 2nd Company was attached

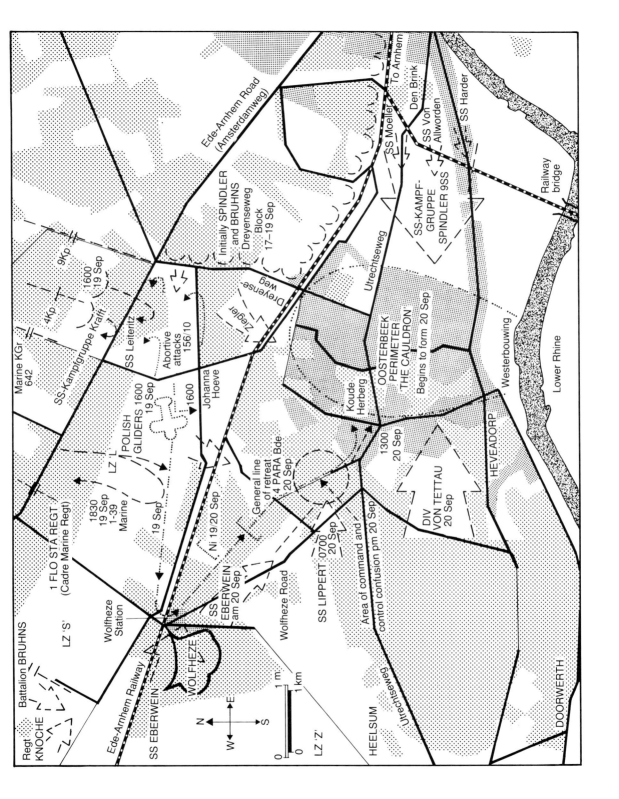

203

By mid-afternoon of 19 September the SS-Kampfgruppe 'Eberwein' was approaching the crucial railway level crossing at Wolfheze, the only point where the withdrawing British vehicles could cross the railway cutting.

to the Kampfgruppe Moeller. This expanded battle group began now to advance southwards, tasked initially to secure the line of the Ede-Arnhem road, and then to exploit beyond to the railway. Advancing on its left flank was the Kampfgruppe 'Bruhns'. Steadily and irresistibly the Germans were attempting to put the lid on a box from the north that now enclosed 1st

British Airborne Division from both the east and west, with its back to the lower Rhine in the south.

Shortly after Krafft's southerly advance began, specks were seen in the air to the south-west and the tell-tale and now familiar drone of two- and four-engined transport aircraft began to fill the air. At 1600 the Polish glider-borne elements of 1st Polish

(Preceding page) THE FORMATION OF THE OOSTERBEEK PERIMETER 19-20 SEPTEMBER 1944.
Fourth Parachute Brigade (Hackett) fails to pierce the Dreyenseweg block and retreats via the Wolfheze level crossing into the perimeter. The disastrous Polish glider landing descends on its line of retreat and adds to the confusion. German units close in from three directions, but owing to command and control difficulties fail to discern or cut off Hackett's line of retreat. By mid-afternoon 20 September the 'lid' has been put on the box, enclosing the Oosterbeek perimeter. The siege has begun.

The aftermath of the Polish glider landing. 'We had never expected things to be so bad, so very bad.' Remaining gliders were torched by the Germans.

Brigade began to swoop down on drop-zone 'L' between the Ede-Arnhem road and railway. They landed astride retreating units from 10 PARA, and between Krafft's advancing SS Battle Group and covering troops from Hackett's 4th Brigade headquarters. At the same time the Luftwaffe put in a rare appearance. The landing was a catastrophe as Marek Swieciki, a Polish war correspondent and witness to the scene, relates. Messerschmidt 109 fighters tore into the hapless transports and gliders as they landed:

'It grew hot and terrible in the air. Several gliders caught fire and, rolling over from wing to wing, dived in a mad flight to the ground. Several others landed helplessly with shattered undercarriages. Even from some distance we could see the torn walls and hanging rudders. One of the gliders broke up in the air like a child's toy, and a jeep, an anti-tank gun and people flew out of it. We had never expected things to be so bad, so very bad.'[2]

Confusion was total. Krafft could hardly believe his luck. '4 and 9 Company' he reported, 'therefore cross the [Ede-Arnhem] road and inflict considerable losses again on the British.' Krafft's men were well rehearsed on the procedure: all infantry weapons were directed against the gliders; 'a standing order' because they are 'a larger and slower target'. The results, as Sepp Krafft subsequently reported, were predictable:

Krafft's men advance across the glider landing-zone. He reported 'it has been found on examination that nearly every shot gets home . . . blood stains inside showed that the enemy had suffered quite appreciable casualties in the air.'

'It has been found on examination that nearly every shot gets home. The gliders were holed by countless hits and the blood-stains inside show that the enemy has suffered quite appreciable casualties in the air.'[3]

Von Tettau recorded the result with grim satisfaction:

'Another enemy airlanding took place in the area south-west and north of Wolfheze. This time directly within range of our attack forces, resulting in a catastrophic failure of the landing enemy forces.'[4]

The unfortunate Poles, shocked by the savage reception on landing, fired at friend and foe alike. Retreating, the 10th Parachute Battalion returned fire as did some brigade defence units. Krafft's forces exuberantly pushed southwards, attempting to capitalise on the débâcle. Mistakes were not, however, totally one-sided. The Germans themselves were experiencing difficulties in co-ordinating their advance on the pocket from three directions. Eberwein's SS Battalion had already reached Wolfheze by 1600, where it, too, received the Luftwaffe's attention. As von Tettau laconically reported: 'Approximately 50 German fighters attacked Wolfheze, unfortunately, however, our own reconnaissance was already there.'[5]

Krafft's battalion similarly overreached itself. The 9th Company, commanded by SS-Lieutenant Leiteritz, having crossed the road and the Polish landing site, was suddenly hit by a series of counter-attacks on both flanks, as the British 4 Brigade defence platoon meted out an appropriate response to a reckless advance. Leiteritz was killed – 'a hero's death,' Krafft observes – having had 'some very bad luck with his tactics, the company suffering heavy casualties in consequence'. Krafft was obliged to retreat as he states in his post-combat report:

'This is the only success Battalion Krafft has as the salient across the road is withdrawn due to concentric counter-attacks on both its flanks.'[6]

Alfred Ziegler, the young despatch rider belonging to the 9SS Panzerjaeger attached to the Kampgruppe Bruhns, now operating on Krafft's right flank, wistfully regarded the same dangerous scene. Being veterans, they had decided to hold back. 'I remember all those black and white cattle,' he said 'just north of the railway line' after the attack to the south had begun. 'All that meat and milk! But my friends said it was too dangerous to go and get them. In any case they had all "bought it" by the time we reached the railway line.'[7]

4 Brigade's fighting withdrawal was conducted so aggressively that neither Krafft nor von Tettau appreciated the significance of what was happening. As they followed the retreat, the Germans simply believed they were overrunning fresh positions. For the British the situation was critical. Major General Urquhart, the commander of 1st British Airborne Division, decided on the night of 19–20 September to withdraw Hackett's brigade and bring it into the Oosterbeek perimeter. During the subsequent daylight hours of 20 September the brigade fought a series of tenacious rearguard actions through the woods and forests, from Wolfheze to Bilderberg near the north-west suburb of Oosterbeek. The Germans, meanwhile, placed their main effort into an advance from north to south by the two battle groups Krafft and Bruhns. Eberwein's SS Battalion, having secured Wolfheze, was ordered to push on south-eastwards toward the Wageningen–Arnhem road. Meanwhile, Lippert's regiment still advanced eastwards along this same road, seeking all the time to gain contact with Eberwein. Co-ordination was never successfully achieved, because fierce retaliatory attacks from the British 4 Brigade columns caught on the march often threw the Germans off-balance.

As 4th Parachute Brigade retreated, the perimeter constricted, resulting in further checks to the German advance, as the Kampfgruppe von Tettau reorganised and consolidated. Eberwein's SS Battalion completed the mopping-up of the Wolfheze station area, capturing 100 prisoners. Early on the morning of 20 September, Krafft discovered that the enemy had already given him the slip and had retreated south across the railway, 'so that,' as he reported 'the Battle Group has only small pockets of enemy in the woodlands to mop up in the new attack at 0600.'[8] As the ring closed clashes resulted, with units of 4 PARA Brigade frantically trying to clear an impending trap. Still the Germans were unaware that these companies were at last on the run and barely able to maintain cohesion. Krafft found himself unexpectedly heavily engaged again at 0830, despite the fact that 'units of the Division von Tettau had leap-frogged past us'. It did not seem like a retreat to him. Krafft's interpretation of the fierce response was that 'the enemy threatened to break out of the pocket to the north'. His response was equally energetic:

'All previous orders are rescinded and the two Marine Regiments are ordered

German infantry attempting to close with the retreating British 4th Parachute Brigade in the woods north-west of Oosterbeek.

in to close the gap. The enemy put up a spirited defence, especially the snipers in the trees, so that the Marines cannot advance any further.'

Krafft was totally hoodwinked, as he expansively and self-importantly continues in his report, reflecting his concern and urgency at the time:

'The enemy now increases pressure on our right flank neighbour, threatening to break through to the east.

'It becomes necessary to withdraw one of the Marine Regiments and send it into the attack at the threatened point together with 4 Company.'[9]

Krafft, like so many other commanders in history, fell victim to the fog of war. Quite simply, both sides were unaware of what their opponent was really trying to achieve. Despite the fact that some units had actually penetrated the 4th Brigade column, the Germans could not see the opportunity that presented itself, and this is revealed by von Tettau's appreciation of the situation himself. By mid-afternoon elements of 4 Brigade headquarters were actually cut off in a depression, besieged by infantry and tanks. Eberwein's SS Battalion, moving south-east towards the Wageningen-Arnhem road, was making good progress. By 1300 he had reached the road at Koude Herberg and took 578 prisoners. But von Tettau had made a decision, as revealed in his report:

'Here the attack had to be stopped
because both neighbours were far
behind and there were not enough
forces to secure the flanks.'

Von Tettau, accompanying Eberwein at the
time, totally misread the situation. Instead
of administering a *coup de grâce*, the unit
was halted. The General congratulated
himself on having 'personally influenced a
quick establishment of contact and thus
averted a threat to the great success of the
battalion'.[10] The prize, if he had continued,
would have been even greater. Alternatively, the British were hardly aware they
had experienced any luck. 4th Parachute
Brigade had been badly mauled. By the end
of the day the Germans had assembled 800
POWs, 20 mortars, 18 jeeps, 15 anti-tank
guns and 44 motorcycles.[11]

It was a disaster. More to the point, the
'leap-frogging' reported by Krafft beyond
his positions by the Division von Tettau
had meant that the lid had been finally
closed on a box containing the remnants of
the 1st British Airborne Division. As SS-
Captain Wilfried Schwarz, the Chief of
Staff of the 9SS Hohenstaufen, described it:

'The situation started to stabilise once
the Oosterbeek ring was closed and
the bridge retaken.'[12]

Rapid movements and advances now came
to a halt as both sides took up siege positions.

Improvisation . . .

The achievement by the Division von Tettau
had in fact been considerable. Bearing in
mind the *ad hoc* nature of his forces and the
speed with which his Kampfgruppe had
been assembled, it is hardly surprising that
the advance – slow, dogged and unspectac-
ular – was unable to exploit the opportunit-
ies offered by the 4th Brigade's fighting

withdrawal. SS-Colonel Lippert's damaging
condemnation of von Tettau's performance
as a commander was the opinion of a
professional, denigrating what was essentially a scratch-built formation. He described its failings:

'Co-operation with von Tettau's staff
was a catastrophe. It was, according to
my information, thrown together, and
was non-functional, at least during the
first few days. It was unable to
produce weapons, ammunition,
support weapons, radio
communications, rations, transport,
military police, doctors, medics,
ambulances and many other things
besides. How far Lieutenant-General
von Tettau was responsible is not for
me to judge. Units were required in all
respects to provide for themselves.
The NCO school, normally based in
barracks, was not at all equipped to
conduct such tasks, and this was also
the case for all units subsequently
attached. Rations had to be purloined
from the Dutch population, and
luckily the soldiers were able to get
near to some dropped food supply
containers from the British.'[13]

Improvisation, once again, proved to be the
key to the German success. Much of their
resupply was gathered up after costly British air-resupply sorties. As Krafft relates:

'Increased fighter-plane activity
always indicated a new drop over a
particular sector, and because we had
captured ground signs and white flare
ammunition, we succeeded in
deceiving the enemy to drop supplies
in our lines, which he usually did.'[14]

SS-Officer-Cadet Rudolf Lindemann, serving in a mortar section in Lippert's NCO
School 'Arnheim' Regiment, remembers:

'We watched the supply drops every afternoon, when they were expected at about 1600. Having found the key to signal the aircraft using panels, we would start setting these out at about 1600 hours every afternoon. The aircraft always dropped on to the signs. We always had sufficient supplies – the British did not get anything.'

It was not only the Germans who were obliged to improvise. Lindermann recounts the experience of a 32-year-old soldier captured from his platoon, who was witness to a conversation in the German POW cage in the tennis court of the Hartenstein Hotel in Oosterbeek. The British Major in charge, watching the usual resupply run at 1600, remarked dryly to the senior German POW (a Captain in the Waffen SS), that both sides ought to exchange weapons, 'as the opposing forces were in any case fighting with each other's captured equipment, weapons and ammunition'.[15]

Lippert's regiment was not, however, totally dependent upon captured supplies. Its commander solved his logistic dilemma in a typically resourceful manner. Von Tettau was distrusted within the unit as an 'SS hater',[16] but when, on the evening of 19 September, SS-General Hans Albin Rauter (the C in C of the SS and German police in occupied Holland), visited, seeking up-to-date operational information, Lippert took the opportunity to present his logistic difficulties. Rauter, although not holding a military command, 'promised to help as far as he was able'. Civilian cars began to appear, bringing up weapons, ammunition and rations, and transporting his wounded to field hospitals. POWs were also taken off the regiment's hands. 'Rauter,' Lippert states, 'visited me daily to get information and help produce what was needed and what was possible.' This assistance, which lasted until the end of the battle, was the decisive factor in maintaining his regiment's operational capability.[17]

Locked now into static positions, the fighting took on an even more desperate nature. Labelled the *Hexenkessel* – the 'witches' cauldron' – the investment and reduction of the Oosterbeek pocket now began. Trapped within were the remnants of 1st British Airborne Division, whom the Germans had no intention of allowing to escape. Success or failure for both sides was dependent upon the events now unravelling in and beyond Nijmegen. Would XXX Corps, spearheading the Allied ground advance, push through in time?

The formation of the pocket, and the threat now of a possible British breakthrough by ground forces from Nijmegen and the south, had an impact upon the nature of the fighting. German battle groups paused to regroup, and operations became increasingly deadlocked. Lindemann remarked that 'the fighting became harder in the last phase. We were static in defence positions in light woods with bushes and clearings.'[18] At the moment of success, however, an ominous new development occurred. Lindemann and his comrades initially gave it little thought, merely observing that:

'We then came under artillery fire. At first we thought it was our own gunners firing from the other side of the perimeter. So we fired verey pistols to stop it.'[19]

Strangely enough, SS despatch rider Alfred Ziegler, north of the pocket with the Kampfgruppe Bruhns, experienced the same phenomenon. He remembers 'we always believed our artillery was dropping short'. So did other German soldiers in positions around the airborne perimeter. It came as a sobering realisation to learn that it was British artillery – firing from Nijmegen.[20]

CHAPTER XVIII
Hollow Victories

It was ironic really. At the same time we lost the Nijmegen bridge, we were just about over the Arnhem bridge.

Commander, 10SS Panzer Division

Mopping up and breaking out. Nijmegen, night 20–21 September . . .

At 2015 SS-Lieutenant Richter signalled Army Group B from the IISS Corps headquarters, giving an up-to-date situation report:

'. . . The area east of the road bridge has been smoked off, and about evening time the northern end of the railway bridge has been reached. Heavy artillery fire on the north bank of the bridge. At 1830 both the railway bridge and north bank are in enemy hands.

'Enemy Intention: The enemy is attempting with all means at his disposal to seize the bridges in Nijmegen and Arnhem as quickly as is possible.'[1]

Richter reported again at 1100 the following day that 'until now something like 45 enemy tanks have crossed the bridge moving north'. Model's reaction was predicable but already negated by the speed of events. His Chief of Staff notified General Bittrich, the commander of IISS Corps: 'We must hold, and, if necessary, blow up the road bridge at Nijmegen.' Bittrich, receiving the message at 2330 on the night of 20 September,

replied that the word had come too late. Nothing at all had been heard from the Nijmegen garrison for two hours. General Bittrich could only assume, therefore, that the German units there had been destroyed.[2]

In Nijmegen fearsome hand-to-hand fighting was still continuing within isolated pockets of resistance inside the former German perimeter. Many attempted to escape over the still intact bridges. SS-Gunner Albrecht fled with an escaped Fallschirmjaeger and an officer, Lieutenant Schulz, who they had picked up from an abandoned command post. As they moved across the road bridge, scenes of savage fighting were evident; other sights were more disturbing. SS-Captain Schwappacher later wrote:

'Shameful mutilations had been committed against the wounded lying on the road bridge. Stab wounds to the head, throat and heart were seen by Lieutenant Schultz and Albrecht. These were recorded on paper and passed on to the next higher authority.'[3]

Survivors of the Hermann Goering Division Company 'Runge' submitted similar reports. Lieutenant-Colonel Fullriede, after interviewing survivors, commented upon their experiences in his diary:

*General Bittrich, the Commander of IISS Corps, reported at 2330
hours 20 September that 'nothing [had] been heard from the Nijmegen
garrison for two hours' and that he could 'only assume the German
units had been destroyed'. Allied units begin to cross the Nijmegen
bridge.* (Imperial War Museum)

'The Americans behaved as they always do, throwing our wounded from the bridge into the Waal, and shooting the few prisoners among the army reservists.'[4]

Fighting was intense, with little quarter expected or forthcoming. Fanatical resistance still continued around the command post of the commander of 21 Battery, SS-Captain Krueger, cut off in the Valkhof citadel in SS 2/Lieutenant Baumgaertel's sector. Baumgaertel survived this battle and received the German Cross in Gold for his exploits, only to be killed later in Stettin.[5]

Krueger frantically rallied all the resources at his disposal, flinging the escaping or shell-shocked infantrymen, from every branch of the Wehrmacht, who came his way, into the trenches that led to his first-aid bunker. Bloody hand-to-hand fighting raged around the position until 2030, causing considerable losses to the enemy. At about 1800 Krueger was wounded in the back by a Tommy-gun burst; despite being wounded again later, he fought on, continuing to direct his battery's fire from across the river with a verey pistol. Eventually a tank round exploded in the trench injuring him severely in the upper thigh – his third wound. He was finally carried out of action on a stretcher, into the first-aid bunker. Only twelve men and NCOs now remained. These were eventually driven out of the trenches with phosphorus grenades and overwhelmed in a close-quarter struggle. Survivors were to report the eventual outcome:

'Led by an American officer overseeing with a sub-machine gun, they were stood up against a wall. At that moment SS-Corporal Kochler and SS-Lance-Corporal Burgstaller overpowered three Americans, and managed to break through to the survivors of the Battalion Euling. Nobody in the observation post had known of their existence until then. As they fled, Burgstaller saw how two other SS-Corporals, Lindenthaler and Beissmann, and a Fallschirmjaeger were shot down by the Americans. One can only assume the other six prisoners were also shot. Further witnesses reported the happenings which occurred in the bunker one hour later. The lights were still shining as shots were heard. It is likely the enemy massacred the six to seven severely wounded left inside, including SS-Captain Krueger, together with two medical orderlies. The light, according to precise estimates, was doused at the same time.'[6]

SS-Captain Karl-Heinz Euling's situation was similarly hopeless. Once he saw the German forces streaming rearwards over both bridges, he reorganised his defences. Outlying outposts had now all been over-run. He relocated the last 60 survivors of the 1st Battalion Panzer-grenadier Regiment 22 around his command post in the Haus Robert Janssen. With enemy tanks and vehicles now roaring across the Nijmegen road bridge 250 metres to the east, he and his men realised they were surrounded. A Sherman tank rolled up to the front door and fired. Concussion picked up dust and debris and whirled it around into a choking cloud as the first round screeched through the house. Churning on one track for another shot, the tank was suddenly disabled by a panzerfaust. Having now indi-cated their whereabouts, the command post attracted heavy enemy fire. Another tank fired three rounds point-blank into the communication trench leading from the front door. One shot picked up the company commander of 8 Company and threw him with the door and part of the wall through the house. He survived.

Shortages in ammunition were temporarily resolved by breaking down machine gun belts and redistributing the rounds as rifle ammunition. Only single rounds were fired; and eighteen hits were claimed.

By 2230 the house was fully ablaze. The wounded were dragged out into the back. Despite the critical situation, Euling retained his normal composure, which relaxed his men, and was fully confident in his ability to take the appropriate decision. This was to break out, as Euling recalled, 'under the Waal road bridge and infiltrate eastwards, until finally over the Waal at Haalderen, to reach our own unit lines'. Euling felt he would succeed because, as he remembered, 'the enemy was concentrating on getting strong forces over the road bridge as quickly as possible'.[7]

Believing that everyone had perished in the blazing building, the enemy did not bother to observe the command post any longer. In single file, the battalion commander leading, Euling and the survivors of his battalion began to slip away, using the rippling shadow effect of the flames to cloak their movement. The column quickly crossed a small street – Kelfensbasch – and scrambled down the embankment to the right of the small footbridge adjoining the Kelfensbasch to the Valkhof. From there they followed a communication ditch that wound its way along the old high wall of the Valkhof 'Medieval keep'. Soon a small pathway – the Voerweg – took them to the river bank. An open bunker bathed this pathway in light. The column continued, hardly daring to glance at the smoking and reading Englishmen within.

SS-Captain Karl-Heinz Euling was awarded the Knight's Cross for the exploits of his 'ghost' battalion, which successfully fought its way out of Nijmegen, escaping underneath the road bridge whilst Allied tanks were crossing toward Arnhem. (Fuerbringer Collection)

Suddenly a machine gun post was starkly silhouetted in the blood-red sky produced by the burning buildings. Euling, at the head of the group, immediately flung himself into a barbed wire obstacle alongside, followed by the others. Skin and clothes were torn by the cruel barbs, but the machine gun, firing bursts into moving shadows, struck nobody. Disentangling themselves, the group managed to scale a high palisade fence and dropped down on the other side on to the river bank. So far, so good.

Banking upon the Allied distraction of getting forces rapidly across the road bridge, the column followed the Ubbergsehe Weg, which led under the ramp of the massive bridge itself. Above, the roar and clatter of armoured forces could be clearly heard as further columns trundled across the bridge to Lent. Most of the columns of marching infantry encountered were fortunately always moving to their left. All at once, however, on turning a corner, they came across a group of 30 to 40 loudly talking and smoking English soldiers. Both sides fled in opposite directions, but Euling decided to stop the panic and bluff his way. Brazenly and openly, the SS column continued marching. Any contact with counter-marching columns was greeted with a loud 'Halt!', whereupon the SS-Captain waved his own men through.

Before long the column reached the Het Meer, a subsidiary feeder canal from the Waal. It had to be crossed. A number of soldiers searched for a skiff in a boat-house, while others sought a crossing further along. They accidently bumped into a British patrol, and a savage hand-to-hand mêlée ensued. No shooting could be allowed, at any cost, without jeopardising the whole escape attempt. Eventually, bodies splashed into the waters of the canal. They were through, but two SS soldiers were missing.

This particular odyssey had a happy ending. A crossing point was discovered over the canal, and subsequently the surviving members of the Kampfgruppe and a group of Fallschirmjaeger commanded by a Major Alhorn crossed the Waal at Haalderen and reached their own lines. SS-Captain Euling was awarded the Knight's Cross shortly after for the exploits of his 'ghost' battalion.[8]

By 2200 on 20 September in Oosterhout, immediately north-west of the Waal assault boat-crossing site, SS-Captain Schwappacher's remaining 21st Battery and his regimental headquarters were desperately holding a 'hedgehog' outpost against the rising tide of Allied reinforcements. Still holding positions in all-round defence, the battery continued to harass Nijmegen and the dyke road south of Oosterhout with fire. Five houses on the eastern side of the village were set ablaze to compensate for a lack of illumination shells and to prevent surprise attacks. 'At about midnight,' Schwappacher reports, 'a radio message was sent to General von Tettau, that the positions in Oosterhout would be held to the last living man.'[9]

After a short fire fight conducted on its southern perimeter, Allied tanks broke into Lent and eliminated the last resistance by remnants of the 1st Company 10SS Engineer Battalion, and the flotsam of reservists and others from the now dispersed Kampfgruppe Henke. Harmel, the commander of the Frundsberg, left Lent dismayed. Despite all his efforts, both bridges were still standing. Allied tanks were now mixed in amongst the fleeing German survivors of the Nijmegen garrison. All appeared lost.

Closely monitoring the advance, and seeking solutions to the unsolvable, Harmel noticed that the Allies were 'moving more cautiously, hindered by their own smoke; delays were slowing the advance'.[10] He drove on to Bemmel, where the command post of the Kampfgruppe Reinhold – coordinating the defence of Nijmegen – was now located. There may yet be a chance to salvage something from this catastrophe.

To Schwappacher's relief in Oosterhout, 'the enemy remained quiet all night'. After the war, Harmel was to be more explicit: 'The English drank too much tea . . !', in contrast to the feverish activity that was to characterise German attempts to formulate counter-measures that night. Both sides were exhausted. Nevertheless, as Harmel later remarked:

'The four panzers who crossed the bridge made a mistake when they stayed in Lent. If they had carried on their advance, it would have been all over for us.'[11]

Ironically it was nearly all over for another beleaguered garrison defending another bridge 17 kilometres to the north. The Second Battalion the Parachute Regiment, defending the Arnhem bridge, was in its death throes.

'Just about over the Arnhem bridge.' Night 20–21 September. . .

Frost's battalion was still fighting its nightmarish battle around the northern ramp of the Arnhem bridge as the first Shermans of the Guards Armoured Division skirmished their way across the Waal during the early evening of 20 September. A truce was agreed to remove some of the wounded. Rudolf Trapp, with the remnants of 3 Company Panzer-grenadier Regiment 21 of the 10SS, had penetrated the position to the houses around the justice courts and provincial government offices. They were immediately west of Frost's and Brigade headquarters. SS Corporal Trapp realised that

'. . .the British had POWs in the cellars of the houses they were occupying. These started to cry out: "Cease fire! The Tommies are giving up!" German soldiers then appeared carrying a white flag, none of them were wearing helmets. "Give us some weapons so we can fight," they said. They had suffered, not having received any proper food and drink for days. We told them to quieten down and go back. There was no funny business.'[12]

Among those captives in the cellars were Lieutenant Joseph Enthammer and his 'V2 rocket soldiers'. Enthammer also described the scene:

> 'By about 2100 on Wednesday 20 September the building, which now contained about one hundred British soldiers, was surrounded by the SS. A one-and-a-half to two-hour truce was declared to pick up the wounded. As we cleared up, we threw bodies of both English and German dead from the upper storey into the street below. Later, the SS told us that the response to surrender terms had been "English officers do not give up".'[13]

Trapp's men took the seriously wounded, 'and those British who also had their nerves shot to pieces'. The latter 'had the shakes!', he said; 'biscuits and chocolate were offered to them.' Enthammer remembers that 'Frost was then seriously wounded,' leaving 'some 40 to 60 men who were to surrender shortly after.' During the truce every opportunity was taken by the Germans, as Trapp remembers, to look over the positions they would eventually have to storm. There were further surprises for them when

> '. . . during the truce I walked with a companion through the British positions right up to the bridge. There we saw the results of Graebner's attack.'

It was typical of what had happened ever since the beginning of the fighting. 'We only ever knew,' Trapp commented, 'what was going on in our area.' Before them, bathed in a sinister red, shimmering glow reflected from blazing buildings, were

> '. . . vehicles shot to pieces and dead bodies lying everywhere. We were surprised . . . because we had not known about it. At that moment we had to return to our positions.'

Trapp was totally objective about the whole experience. 'The truce was good for us, we improved our positions, reconnoitred the enemies and moved a little nearer.'[14] The next step would be to close in for the kill.

In the meantime the remainder of Panzergrenadier Regiment 21 arrived and was placed under the Kampfgruppe Brinkmann's command. Knaust's Kampfgruppe was warned off to begin reorganising and regrouping for a different mission: to block the breakthrough of the Frundsberg's defences in Nijmegen. Brinkmann was tasked to administer the *coup de grâce*. In the morning *Konigstiger* – 'King Tiger' – heavy tanks would arrive to help finish off the job. Until this occurred, the grip on Frost's perimeter was maintained and more pressure applied.

Exhaustion was taking its toll of attackers and defenders alike. Lance-Corporal Karl-Heinz Kracht's 'Mielke' tank company was still operating on the periphery of the perimeter. Rubble piled high in the streets was reducing the effectiveness of the Mark III panzers. The strain, he recalled, was beginning to tell:

> 'We never got out of our clothes. Hygiene was miserable. There was hardly any time for sleeping! Many actions were carried out under cover of darkness, together with grenadiers, because a tank alone is helpless in street fighting. The British were still lurking in strategic locations along the street to Oosterbeek, along which we drove. During lulls in the battle, three of our crew would be dozing in their seats, while the other two kept watch. Conditions were similar for the grenadiers, except they could utilise the available deserted houses.'[15]

The plight of Lieutenant Joseph Enthammer and his fellow captives became increasingly

By about 1100 on 21 September it was almost over. Many of the prisoners were wounded.

desperate as the SS ring closed in. He described how

'. . . eventually after the truce we were taken to the building to our rear. Again we hid in a cellar with a bren gun carrier parked outside the entrance, which offered some protection from the wild shoot-out that took place between the two buildings. We sang the *Deutschlandlied* – the national anthem – hoping that the encircling SS would realise that we were German POWs in there.'[16]

It was just about all over. Brinkmann's Kampfgruppe, reinforced with 'King Tiger' tanks and 88mm flak guns, reduced the last strongpoints into a dust and smoke-shrouded submission. At 1100 on 21 September SS-Lieutenant Richter at IISS Corps headquarters passed on the news of the previous night's successes to Army Group B:

'Sometime in the evening about 200 of the bridge's defenders surrendered. Precise numbers to follow. Wounded prisoners were taken, among them the backbone of the defence, the 34-year-old Colonel Frost as well as the G4 officer of 1st British Airborne Division.'[17]

As this report was given, Brinkmann's Kampfgruppe began finally to remove the debris of Graebner's failed attack from the bridge. Surviving British groups had attempted a break-out the previous night. Resistance was not totally suppressed, fighting was to continue haphazardly until mopping-up operations were finally complete on 23 September,[18] but at least no hostile fire could reach the Arnhem road bridge.

Enthammer was wounded in the leg by a grenade during the final clearance of his cellar. Liberation, he recalls, brought mixed feelings:

'The SS wanted us to fight with them, incorporated for further operations once freed. But on the backs of our paybooks was the stamp that we "the undermentioned by order of Adolf Hitler" should not be employed elsewhere but immediately returned to our unit concerned with *Kriegsentscheidenden Waffen* – decisive weapons – able to influence the outcome of the war. Whatever our rank we were to be sent back. We were lucky, therefore, not to be recruited into the ranks of the SS!'

They were indeed fortunate. The 'V2' label they had sought to hide whilst with the British could now offer some benefit. Enthammer continued:

> 'We were taken to a high-ranking SS officer who was genuinely pleased after suffering such heavy casualties to recover some live Germans as reward for all their labours. Having fought on all fronts before, he had never encountered such a hard yet fair foe.'

The point was rammed home by the charnel house surrounding them. The artillery officer now noticed 'the crew of the anti-tank gun that had been sited outside our building – they had both been decapitated'. With some relief and not a little anticipation they awaited the transport that would ferry them onward to their original destination in the Reich.

> 'We spent the night in an empty house. There was naturally no electricity or water. We heard a little shooting, but not much, as the last groups of Englishmen still resisting were cleared out'.[19]

This battle, despite the care taken for the wounded, had been a brutal contest of attrition. Quarter was not forthcoming in the frenzy of some of the close hand-to-hand fighting for possession of vital strongpoints. Combat stress was at times evident, reflected in paradoxical scenes as prisoners were taken at the end. The SS had no illusions about their captives – having fought with them for four days, they regarded them as exceedingly dangerous. They had even less consideration for Dutch Resistance fighters whom they considered 'terrorist bandits', to be treated accordingly. Private Sims of 2 PARA remembers, on being captured, that:

> '. . . the Germans came along our line and pulled out a young Dutchman who was with us. He was a member of the Resistance and had fought right through with the British, getting both arms badly burned when he tried to pick up a phosphorus bomb which had landed in our positions. He was forced to his knees and shot through the back of the neck. The lifeless body slumped to the ground, the heavily-bandaged hands sprawled out in front like two grotesque paddles. The German officer who did this said to us: "That is how we deal with traitors in the Third Reich." Stunned, we lay on the cold pavement and waited.'

Sims also witnessed the shooting of a paratrooper who resisted when his wallet was taken. The young German executioner 'looked through the wallet and, finding nothing of military importance, carefully replaced it on the dead body'. Approaching Sims, he frisked him for weapons and remarked in a matter-of-fact voice that he would join his comrade if any items of military value were later found on him. 'This,' Sims remembers, 'was all said in a quiet, even tone as if it was the usual routine stuff, which, if anything, added to its menace.'[20]

Tension ran high. Lieutenant James Flavell, a platoon commander in B Company 2 PARA, felt the guards 'were jittery', and that security was 'heavy'. The Germans, he suspected, 'were frightened of us'.[21] Guards were taking no chances – nerves and battle fatigue often caused them to over-react at the slightest provocation. POWs in Flavell's lorry were shot and killed by German soldiers during one incident along with their hapless SS guard. Many trucks carrying POWs had SS personnel armed with schmeissers standing on the running boards as well as in the back.

Both sides appeared relieved it was all

Both sides appeared relieved that it was all over. The British were totally exhausted.

over. SS-Private Rudolf Trapp was now appointed escort to 2 PARA prisoners:

'At midday on the Thursday we took the POWs along Rynkade to the old gate at the entrance to the church market place. The prisoners were bloody and bandaged, pockets bulging with medical and other supplies. Our enemy had been well equipped. We took them north through the town and then west to another church where they were handed over.'

En route they would have passed Knaust's column forming up, reinforced and ready to move across the bridge to Elst. Sims remembers a similar scene, later that night, probably on the Jans Binnen Singel:

'The road we turned into had trees down each side and under these, parked nose-to-tail, were never-ending lines of German Mark IV tanks. In the dusk it was a truly impressive sight. Seeing my wonder, a young enemy soldier remarked, "Yes, Tommy, these were for you in the morning if you had not surrendered." Several of the German tank men called out to us, "Well fought Tommy," "Good fight, eh Tommy?". They seemed to regard war in much the same way as the British regarded football.'[22]

219

SS-Corporal Rudolf Trapp could not help comparing himself to his captives: 'We looked exactly as filthy and bloody as the British.' It had been an appalling experience for both sides. Here the British are led away.

Trapp, marching along as prisoner escort, could not help comparing his own situation with theirs, because 'we looked exactly as filthy and bloody as the British'.[23] Both sides, reacting to the uninterrupted violence and ferocity of the previous four days, began mentally to take stock. Trapp pondered on the situation:

'The company commander and our second in command, a senior SS-Corporal, had been killed. At the start we had been about 50 strong. Casualties were difficult to estimate because of the insertion of piecemeal reinforcements, and the fact that other soldiers had collected our dead. There were a lot of huddled forms clothed in SS camouflage smocks lying about in the streets.'

The Arnhem bridge had been fought free.

CHAPTER XIX
The Missed Opportunity

Why did they not drive on to Elst instead of staying in Lent? At this instant there were no German armoured forces available to block Elst.

Commander, 10SS Panzer Division

Plugging the gap.
Betuwe, 'the Island' . . .

Karl-Heinz Kracht, the young tank gunner moving with Knaust's armoured column, used a golden opportunity to take photographs as his Mark III panzer, grinding through its gears, began its ascent to the high point of the Arnhem road bridge. His lens began to take objective stock of all around him. Silhouetted against the sky ahead was the majestic span of the bridge's superstructure. To the left and right, burnt-out vehicles had been bulldozed or towed to the side of the road, the debris of Graebner's failed attack. As they passed the rudimentary barrier erected by Frost's men, they observed curious SS soldiers sifting through the tangled wreckage. On the main span the wind, whistling through the girders, brought some of the stench of burning from the battle now raging in the west towards Oosterbeek. Kracht took a shot of the ruined church by the market place, whose towers were now burnt out. With the 50mm tank barrel pointing down the road toward Elden he took another picture of the southern ramp of the bridge. This showed the built-up area where Graebner had formed up and rushed to the high point of the bridge before coming under fire from the north bank. There was no wreckage here. This had been a blind spot. Coming towards Kracht's vehicle was a simple horse-drawn cart, carrying refugees back

toward the wasted city centre. The focus of German activity appeared now to be moving south towards Nijmegen. Many of these villagers wanted to be spared the horrors that had already engulfed the citizens of Arnhem. In the far distance, separated from the tanks, were marching columns of infantry. Kracht later wrote:

> 'We were well aware of the significance of the bridge because we had been informed of the pincer movement planned by the British and American forces, and of the attack to the north of the Ruhr area. We crossed the bridge towards Nijmegen on the day when it was evacuated, or a day later. I can't remember exactly.'[1]

SS-Colonel Heinz Harmel, the commander of the Frundsberg does remember, and with some alacrity. Knaust's Kampfgruppe, 'reinforced with 8 "Panther" and assault guns, crossed the Arnhem bridge shortly after midday [21 September]; he was ordered by the 10SS to quickly occupy Elst.'[2] Harmel had spent an anxious night. Knaust's arrival offered a degree of relief to a problem that had appeared for the moment insoluble.

Harmel wondered, even after the war, why the tanks that had rushed the Nijmegen bridge with such *élan* had not continued further. The Allies had certainly missed an opportunity. They might possibly have

A remarkable sequence of photographs: Karl-Heinz Kracht's panzer Mark III turns the final corner before approaching the Arnhem bridge. Grim evidence of the intensity of the fighting lies all around . . . (Kabel-Kracht)

. . . Ahead, silhouetted in the sky, is the Arnhem bridge. Kracht photographed curious SS soldiers sifting through the wreckage of Graebner's abortive attack . . . (Kabel-Kracht)

. . . A view behind the church from the high point of the Arnhem bridge . . . (Kabel-Kracht)

. . . His tank gun barrel moves across to the southern bank. Refugees are returning to Arnhem. The focus of German activity is moving south to Nijmegen. (Kabel-Kracht)

pushed a battle group into Arnhem itself. 'Why did they not drive on to Elst instead of staying in Lent?' he asked; 'at this instant there were no German armoured forces available to block Elst.'[3] It was a lost chance:

> 'It gave us time to get Knaust down there. It was ironic really, at the same time we lost the Nijmegen bridge, we were just about over the Arnhem bridge. The Allied infantry were too late supporting their tanks.'[4]

The capitulation of the bridges, so hard fought and costly, was to prove a hollow victory for both sides. Frost's obstinate resistance was instrumental in forcing IISS Corps to depend upon the Pannerden ferry to get its reinforcements to the Waal. In the event the 10SS were unable to reinforce sufficiently quickly to reverse the outcome at Nijmegen. Likewise, the Allies were unable to capitalise on their seizure of the Waal bridges.

Crucial in tipping the scales for both engagements was the ferrying operation conducted by the Frundsberg at Pannerden. SS-Captain Brandt, the 10SS Engineer Battalion Commander, achieved much in difficult circumstances. Badly battered in Normandy, his force was weak in both manpower and equipment. After sending his only motorised *ad hoc* company to Nijmegen under SS-2/Lieutenant Baumgaertel to assist in its defence, he was left with a hastily reorganised company under SS-Lieutenant Munski to assist around Pannerden. Brandt recalls that 'much work had to be done at the ferry sites as we only had map references indicating the location of existing sites'.[5] Throughout the operation he remembers they were harassed by Allied 'Jabo' attacks and artillery fire. Utilising rafts and commandeered motor boats the ferrying operation painstakingly transported units that had by-passed Arnhem across the lower Rhine and canal. By the evening of 18 September Baumgaertel's engineers and the Kampfgruppe Reinhold had crossed. During the night the depleted 10SS Panzer Regiment was ferried over, so that by 19 September four assault guns had reached Nijmegen, and a further 16 Mark IV panzers and SPs were available for operations on the north bank of the Waal. The process continued during daylight hours when the Kampfgruppe 'Hartung' – a Wehrmacht reservist battalion – and one and a half battalions from the SS-Panzergrenadier Regiment 22, also got across. Included among these were both forward command posts of the 10SS and IISS Corps. Progress was slow, marred by inadequate transport and repeated air attacks. Units after assembly were faced with a 15-kilometre march to Nijmegen, much of it across exposed dyke roads. Consequently, few were available for effective operations until late on 20 September. When the Nijmegen bridge was captured, the one and a half battalions of Panzer-grenadier Regiment 22 and the tanks were either in the process of re-forming after the river crossing, or still laboriously on the move in well-dispersed formations to avoid attracting air attacks.

The only forces on the 'Island', or Betuwe, able to oppose a breakthrough were the survivors of Graebner's Reconnaissance Battalion 9. This decimated group was deployed with one weak company on picket duty on the southern bank of the lower Rhine, opposite Arnhem's western suburbs and the bridge, and the remnants of another in Elst. As the first Sherman tanks, scattering escapees from the Nijmegen garrison, surged into Lent, the road ahead was open. All that stood in the way of XXX Corps and Arnhem during much of the night of 20–21 September were a few security pickets.

Improvisation . . .

Arriving at Reinhold's command post in Bemmel during the evening of 20 September, Harmel frantically tried to retrieve the situation. Those parts of Panzer-grenadier Regiment 22 and the tanks that had already crossed the ferry were ordered to counter-attack immediately from the east. But these elements of the reconstituted Kampfgruppe Reinhold lacked heavy weapons. Only one light battery of field howitzers had been brought across the ferry so far, and they were positioned east of Flieren. The counter-attack, therefore, lacked punch. By darkness a rudimentary line had been established one kilometre north of Lent, and this gradually thickened into linked outposts as more units, including the Kampfgruppe 'Hartung', became available to Reinhold. By first light German blocking positions occupied the crossroads one kilometre south-west of Ressen, south of the village itself and south of Bemmel down to the Waal river.[6]

Bittrich, the IISS Corps Commander, instructed Harmel to counter-attack at first light on 21 September to forestall and spoil the anticipated Allied thrust on Elst, and thence to Arnhem. 'All the forces available from Pannerden,' ordered the General, 'are to be collected and attack the eastern flank of the enemy vanguards, overwhelm them, and throw the enemy back over the Waal river.'[7]

SS-Captain Schwappacher's 21 Artillery Battery, his regimental headquarters, and other collected units, were still holding on to the 'hedgehog' position around Oosterhout. Apart from imposing a degree of caution upon any projected Allied thrust to Arnhem, they provided an anchor to the right of the thin screen raised by the Kampfgruppe Reinhold to cover the approach to Arnhem. Early on 21 September, Knaust arrived for a preliminary reconnaissance and was briefed on the Oosterhout situation by Schwappacher. New battery positions were established south of Elst. Many of Schwappacher's personnel, gun crews and radio operators, currently manning trenches as infantry, were needed there. At 1200 the SS Artillery and Training Regiment V finally thinned out as more of Knaust's Kampfgruppe arrived. Flight was still in the minds of the soldiers. Schwappacher mentions three Wehrmacht batteries originally located north-east of Oosterhout which, 'despite appeals from me to hold their positions during the critical situation the day before, had already withdrawn their positions further back to the north-west'. The atmosphere of unease and alarm prevailing since the bridges' loss remained.

Harmel's punch against the eastern flank of the breakthrough was eventually assembled and mounted. Thinly spread over a four-kilometre front, a force of about three battalions, divided into three to four Kampfgruppen, supported by 16 Mark IV tanks, advanced westwards. Artillery resources were sparse: a light battery east of Flieren, and two more from the 10SS Artillery Regiment firing from the east bank of the Pannerden canal. These were desperate measures. SS Panzer-grenadier Regiment 21's one and a half battalions could not be included, because they were delayed by the ferry crossing, and had only got as far as Haalderen, one and a half kilometres west of Bemmel. It was all that could be scraped together in the time allowed by General Bittrich. Even ferrying operations were interrupted to assist in the attack SS-Captain Brandt at Pannerden recalls:

'*Ja* – and then there was a breakthrough somewhere, and we were taken out. Even during actual loading operations I had to take part in the defence of a wooded area with my headquarters company, and any other soldiers that could be found around, supported also by six tanks.'[8]

These scant resources were flung against an ever-growing enemy lodgement. This, with the impact of Allied artillery, conspired to water down the decisive blow that Bittrich sought. His appreciation was, as ever, correct, but his means simply did not match the task. All that was achieved was a westward adjustment of the line, which did have the effect of imposing a cautionary check on any thoughts of an Allied dash to Arnhem.

It is quite possible that the Allies might have been able to feed a battle group into Arnhem, before the road was finally blocked again. During the first night of 20–21 September there were only security pickets reinforced by one or two outposts in position. This situation continued until Knaust finally arrived in force during the afternoon of the 21st. For five hours between 1900 and midnight on the 20th the road was clear. Nothing of substance could close it effectively until Knaust began to drive south after midday on the 21st. It was truly a missed opportunity. Frost's forces were overwhelmed just as the window of opportunity closed again.

By 1600 Knaust's Kampfgruppe had reached Elst. He proceeded to block the road effectively with the armoured forces at his disposal. Liaison was established with the advancing flanking movement from the east. By the evening of 21 September the German line ran from the southern edge of Elst, held by the Kampfgruppe Knaust, via Aam north of Ressen, fortified by Hartung's reservists. It continued over the western edge of Bemmel, defended by the few tanks of the 10SS Panzer Regiment, then south to the Waal, manned by Panzer-grenadier 22. A firm line was at last emerging, able to block or, in the worst case, threaten any further Allied advance northwards to Arnhem. It was an amazing achievement. Harmel summed up the driving factor: 'It was astounding to see what could be achieved by improvisation.'[9]

Allied superiority on the 'Island' meant very little in these low-lying polder marshes, criss-crossed with water-filled ditches and waterways. Cover was also sparse. There were only a few orchards and the villages. Harmel was able to exploit his few tanks covering the exposed and slightly raised dyke roads that traversed this terrain. 'This had an impact,' he remembers; 'the terrain between Nijmegen and Arnhem was the worst possible for tanks – for both sides.'[10]

'Improvisation' for the German soldier meant march and counter-march in an atmosphere of emergency and alarm. Soldiers in the line appeared aware only of the basic situation: there were British paratroopers in Arnhem, and Americans coming up through Nijmegen trying to link up with them. Enemy airborne soldiers in the rear always unsettled the veterans. Their recollections of this period are confused and uncertain; a few village names can be remembered, but little else other than the frantic nature of the activity characterising these operations. A breakthrough somewhere else always meant yet another town or village to be by-passed in order to reach their objective, often by night and with little or no warning. Scant knowledge of the overall situation generated unease.

Kampfgruppe Reinhold's reconstituted units achieved little more than an advance in column, until they were ordered to consolidate and dig in on the line they had reached. Few units, apart from the tanks and grenadiers providing the vanguards, even made contact with the enemy. Allied artillery tended to dictate the speed and extent of progress.

The typical experience of the *Landser* (Wehrmacht equivalent to 'Tommies') and SS was for the most part unremarkable. Most had been delayed on the outskirts of Arnhem, aware that fighting was going on in the suburbs, but unable to gain an unimpeded passage to Nijmegen. This was resolved by forced marches through the night followed by further interminable delays around the Pannerden ferry sites. After crossing there were more tiring marches on exposed dyke roads, frequently harassed by 'Jabos' as daylight approached. Exhausted, they were required to change direction again, fan out, and advance in attack formation upon new objectives over boggy ground. Having clambered across water-filled ditches toward an enemy whose location was unknown, the order to stop and dig in was a relief. If the situation stabilised sufficiently, they might engender some form of front routine – and get some sleep.

Lance-Corporal Karl-Heinz Kracht's panzer Mark III, part of the Kampfgruppe 'Knaust', clattered southwards towards Elst. Nobody knew what lay ahead; they were watchful, nervous and expectant. The Arnhem experience had left them jittery.

'There was only one citizen left in Rijnwik a suburb north-east of the Arnhem bridge. He fired his pistol from the house, behind us, at the Grenadiers.'

The response was immediate.

'He was killed by a sub-machine gun burst. It was sheer nonsense! Otherwise, all the buildings and the butcher's shop were empty.'[11]

Suddenly, contact was made with the leading elements of 1st Guards Armoured Division, whom Kracht assumed to be Americans:

'The encounter we had with the Americans and Shermans on a railway embankment in Elst was quite characteristic in a way. Some German-speaking joker shouted "Don't shoot, we're Germans" as the first tanks appeared. And then they cut loose with everything they had. This cost us two of our tanks and quite a number of our grenadiers!'

This skirmish encapsulates the situation as it was occurring all along the irregular line being established in the Betuwe during 21 September. Kracht continued:

'Confusion reigned, with friend and foe not only in front, but also on the flanks and in the rear. A front line was not discernible, and I believe that some people fired on their own troops. Through a miracle our vehicle escaped destruction in the mêlée. Along with two other tanks, we were sent to Zeddam for refitting with reserves.'[12]

The Germans were beginning to feel that the front in the south was at last beginning to stabilise. But at 1700 hours the roar of aeroplanes could be distinguished approaching from the south – louder and louder. Squadrons of Spitfires appeared out of the clouds. Circling German positions in the Driel area they swept down and engaged identified emplacements with a murderous strafing fire. Machine gun fire was returned, and flak artillery began to bark out, attempting to register on these new targets. A new tumultuous roar of aircraft, stronger than before, pervaded the scene. Dakotas now followed up behind the Spitfires. The roar changed pitch as aircraft reduced speed, flying low. Below the first Dakota one parachute, then another, and then a third opened up – the 1st Polish Parachute Brigade was jumping. As far as the Germans were concerned this scene, repeated again and again until countless black shapes filled the sky, was a harbinger of doom. It was more reinforcements. Fighting paused momentarily in Oosterbeek as every gun barrel swung to meet the new threat of another airborne attack.

CHAPTER XX

The Witches' Cauldron

The Red Devils still fought back and battled for every room and every house, for every piece of ground or garden, no matter how small it was – like cornered tigers.

SS Battalion Commander

The German build-up around Arnhem

From 18 September Field Marshal Model had been appearing daily at SS-Lieutenant Colonel Harzer's CP located in the Heselbergherweg secondary school about two kilometres north of the Arnhem bridge. From here he attempted to organise counter-measures. It was difficult to co-ordinate the offensive thrusts of Harzer's 9SS Division Kampfgruppe in the east with that of von Tettau in the west, because there were no radios. The moves of both Kampfgruppen were regulated by telephone from IISS Corps direct to the 9SS or, in the case of von Tettau, via the Supreme Wehrmacht Commander Netherlands. Paradoxically, the British who did have radios found them virtually inoperable, screened as they were by the forests around Arnhem, and due to other factors. By contrast, the Germans were able to exploit an effective telephone network still operating in Holland despite the fighting, even in Arnhem itself. The Dutch resistance was never able to convince the wary British that it could be used.

Model's presence did much to facilitate the rapid build-up of German forces around Arnhem which quickly contained the Oosterbeek pocket. In order to speed up the passage of reinforcements and logistic support, Model approved a direct command interface between Harzer's 9SS divisional headquarters and Army Group B. This paid immediate dividends. Army High Command was able to move relief columns direct from Germany within a very much shorter time. Coastal machine gun battalions 37 and 41 were immediately despatched to the Arnhem area. Ammunition could, furthermore, be delivered direct to artillery fire positions, air defence batteries and heavy infantry weapons rather than through the normal logistic chain. Speed of response was matched with effectiveness. When Harzer complained that his grenadiers were suffering unacceptably high casualties storming buildings without flame-throwers, Model immediately had a quantity brought forward from nearby storage sites. Pionier-Lehr Battalion 9, an assault-pioneer school from Glogau in the Reich, was specially equipped for street fighting and air-landed at Deelen airfield north of Arnhem. Junkers JU52 transport aircraft began the shuttle operation on the night of 21 September and continued the following evening. Model often visited battalion command posts at the front, putting his personal stamp on the battle and urging his commanders to clear the pocket as quickly as possible. Many of these reserves were to arrive at a propitious time.

On 19 September Lieutenant Colonel von Swoboda's flak brigade arrived. It consisted of five battalion-size detachments of 88m flak, but also included 20mm and 37mm cannon and some 105mm heavy

*On 19 September Lieutenant-Colonel von Swoboda's flak brigade
arrived and began to set up around the landing-zones.*

artillery. Three of these detachments were attached to the Hohenstaufen. These had been static formations hastily redeployed from the Ruhr industrial basin, unsuited for mobile operations. The guns, despite their bizarre appearance – towed by tractors and gas-fuelled lorries – represented the beginnings of an effective air-defence umbrella that was steadily developed around Arnhem and the drop-zones. In order to unify the command and control of these air-defence assets, all flak in the Arnhem area was placed under the control of Swoboda's brigade headquarters.

Supplementing this organisation was the 'Reich' Jagdflieger (Fighter) Division 1 of the Luftwaffe, recently released by Wehr-macht Headquarters West for operations in the Arnhem-Nijmegen area. The FLIVO (or airforce liaison officer) reported to Harzer's headquarters and began directing the air effort. Three hundred fighters from the division soon made their presence felt periodically over Arnhem. Both the disastrous landing of the Poles' glider-borne equipment and the retreat of Hackett's 4th Parachute Brigade into the Oosterbeek perimeter were harassed by the German Luftwaffe. The division was eventually to claim 40 transport aircraft and 112 gliders to its credit. Of 431 British transport aircraft and gliders flying from England on 19 September, about half were obliged to abort over the Channel because of poor weather. The remainder encountered Swoboda's flak or strong fighter forces. Of these 100 bombers and 63 Dakota transport aircraft, 13 were shot down and at least 97 damaged.[1] Whatever the accuracy of the claims, German soldiers gazed skyward in astonishment, proclaiming 'the Luftwaffe is back!' Fighter squadrons were tasked from as far afield as Dortmund, Werl, Paderborn, Guetersloh, Stoermede, Achmer, Lippspringe and Plantluenne inside the Reich, to interdict the Allied airforce air-landed troops, and support offensive operations against the pocket.[2]

Using the newly-established Luftwaffe communications system, 9SS headquarters were now able to talk with 1st Jagdflieger Division and direct wing commanders in the air. Possession of 'fortress Dunkirk' now bestowed a particular advantage. Far behind Allied lines, it had remained in German hands and was able to report all over-flying aerial transports by radio direct to Army Group B. Incoming waves that had been detected could be expected within the hour over Arnhem. On arrival they faced a forewarned flak belt or flew into the teeth of 'scrambled' German fighter opposition.

No doubt the appearance of the Luftwaffe made a positive impact upon German troop morale in those sectors where they were seen. But, despite valiant efforts, they never escaped the thinly veiled sarcasm of the majority of front soldiers. Rudolf Trapp, fighting with the 10SS in Arnhem, remarked:

'We even got visitors in our rubble positions. These were German pilots who drew sketches and wanted to drop bombs on the British positions. But we never saw or heard anything of them again.'[3]

On 20 September the 9SS were offered Artillery Regiment 191 by Army Group B.

There was, however, a complication. The regiment reconstituting in the Zutphen area was ready for action in terms of guns and crews, but had no towing vehicles. Harzer's divisional Kampfgruppe gladly agreed to arrange transport, improvising from its own skeletal resources. Battery after battery was slowly deployed to positions around Arnhem using the few vehicles still left under divisional control. As in the case of the air defence brigade, 191 Regiment headquarters was designated the coordinating agency for all heavy weapons, including flak, in the Hohenstaufen's sector. It was ordered to cover the landing-zones, harass or engage point targets within the cauldron with concentrated fire missions, as well as provide protective and counterbattery fire. On the following day the SS Mortar Group 'Nickmann' joined the new artillery command labelled 'ARKO 191'. This was the II and III batteries of SS Mortar Detachment 102, consisting of two groups of six 32cm 'Nebelwerfer' (multi-barrelled, electronically-operated) mortar launchers each,[4] which had been operating in the Arnhem area since 17 September. All artillery was now subordinate to one agency, tasked with reducing the pocket.

As the German situation around Arnhem stabilised, so too did the various staffs and headquarters supporting the overall effort. The scale of the fighting now obliged the Germans to consider evacuating the civilian population, a measure promulgated by Army Group B on 20 September. SS-Lieutenant-Colonel Harzer, directed to execute the order, informed the mayor he was to clear the city in four-day sections moving from south to north. So far as the occupation forces were concerned, they had little compunction: civilians were a drain on resupply, they got in the way, and were suspected – often correctly – of offering support and succour to the Allied forces. But the measure was more easily ordered then enacted. Only the police, fire-

Kracht photographed the SS-Mortar Group 'Nickmann' in action near Elst. (Kabel-Kracht)

men, air-raid rescue agencies, hospital staffs and non-transportable sick and wounded were allowed to stay. Understandably, the Dutch resented the measure. Many of the inhabitants simply moved to Velp, a reaction silently tolerated by Harzer, who had more pressing problems at hand.

Resupply of rations was not an immediate problem for the Germans. Sufficient rations had been in Arnhem prior to the Allied landings. Distribution, particularly in the early days, was the main problem. Alfred Ziegler, the SS despatch rider fighting with the Kampfgruppe Bruhns, remembers 'Wednesday the 20th as being memorable because it was the first time we got a hot meal, delivered to a house north of the [Ede-Arnhem] railway cutting'.[5] It

was paradoxically the Allies who solved the distribution problem.

On the first day of the landings the Hohenstaufen captured a British officer in possession of ground-marking instructions for aviation sight panels, including the use of smoke and flares to indicate drop-zones. Harzer's divisional IC (intelligence officer), SS-Captain Schleffler translated the directions, which enabled the 9SS to mark and designate drop-zones for enemy supplies behind their own lines. From 18 September onwards the RAF began dropping weapons, ammunition and medical supplies to the Germans. There was no water or electrical power in Arnhem, so water was requested from England and promptly delivered. It is estimated that of some 390 tons of supplies delivered on 19 September, for example, 369 tons landed within German lines.[6] What this meant to the British is revealed in a live BBC commentary, recorded by war correspondent Stanley Maxted in the pocket on 20 September:

'Yesterday and this morning our supplies came and were dropped in the wrong place. The enemy got them, but now these planes have come over and they've dropped them right dead over us.

'Everybody is cheering and clapping and they just can't give vent to their feelings about what a wonderful sight this is. All those bundles and parachuted packages and ammunition are coming down here all around us through the trees, bouncing on the ground; the men are running out to get them, and you have no idea what this means to see this ammunition and this food coming down where the men can get it. They're such fighters, if they can only get the stuff to fight with. But it's a wonderful sight – it's a shame when they can't get the stuff to fight with. You can hear the kind of flak that those planes are flying through, it's absolutely like . . . [noise of flak] . . . hail up there. These enemy guns all round us are just simply hammering at those planes, but so far I haven't seen anything, I haven't seen any of them hit, but the bundles are coming down, the parachutes are coming down . . . [noise of planes and flak] . . .'[7]

The British and the Americans were to lose 144 transport aircraft between 17 and 25 September.[8]

Herbert Kessler, a young NCO serving with the 'Hermann Goering' Training Regiment, wrote about 'the discovery tours' that soldiers went on by day, to feed themselves from the proceeds of these parachutes:

Herbert Kessler serving with the 'Hermann Goering' Training Regiment.

'The soldiers went on "separate rations" and were no longer required to rely on their field kitchens. The best and finest tinned food that you only dared dream of – cigarettes and chocolate to go with it of course – all these treasures fell from the sky.'[9]

German force levels had now surpassed the strength ratio required to begin eradicating the Oosterbeek pocket. On 20 September Field Marshal Model placed the Kampfgruppe von Tettau under command of Bittrich's IISS Panzer Corps headquarters. All forces in the west, including von Tettau's, were tasked to achieve unified joint attacks along the whole of the encircled perimeter. These concentric attacks Bittrich ordered were to commence on 21 September. The British were to be attacked from the west,

Soldiers went on 'discovery tours' picking up the 'treasures' that fell from the sky from British resupply missions, including 'the best and finest tinned food that you only dream of'.

north, and east, before they could be relieved or resupplied.

From the west: von Tettau . . .

Reinforcements alerted since the beginning of the airlandings were still arriving on the western side of the perimeter and immediately committed to battle. Those arriving from northern Holland and the Utrecht area were generally attached to the Kampfgruppe von Tettau. Soldiers were confused by constant march and counter-march instruc-tions caused by reports of scores of fresh airborne landings. Most were untrained and apprehensive about their reception on meeting the enemy. Lieutenant Martin, whose platoon from Fliegerhorst Battalion 3 had observed the first awesome fly-past of the aerial armada near Tilburg on 17 September, recorded the furious pace of events in his diary account of subsequent days:

'20 September. We leave for De Bilde near Utrecht. Ration truck ran over mine and was destroyed. Raining. Bottle of cognac with sergeants Reuter and Westenese.

'21 September. Marching order at 1100. Everybody very nervous. Travelling through Zeist, Doorn, Amerengen, Rhenen and Grebbe arriving at 1400. Division reserve; dug in. March order at 2000. "Immediately go to the front", west of Arnhem. Went into position at night. Very dark.'[10]

Herbert Kessler, the 19-year-old NCO from the 'Worrowski' Battalion of the Hermann Goering Training Regiment, had spent the night of 19–20 September, between sleeping and guard duty, along the same route – the Ede-Arnhem road – that Lieutenant Martin's unit was to use to reach the outskirts of Arnhem. Kessler's company had bicycled from Katwijk an Zee on the North Sea coast above Rotterdam. 'Rumour had it,' he recalls 'that they were earmarked to become a reserve for countering further parachute landings.' On 20 September they had their first tenuous brushes with the enemy near the Ginkel heath:

'After a strafing run by low-flying aircraft, orders came to clear a patch of woods where it was suspected enemy paratrooper stragglers were located. Nothing was found except for the dead of the first few days of fighting; clear evidence of the grim events that had taken place.'

Herbert Kessler's company had bicycled from Katwijk an Zee on the North Sea coast above Rotterdam to Oosterbeek. Reinforcements approach Arnhem.

There was still no positive contact with the enemy. At nightfall the company remounted its bicycles and continued along the Ede-Arnhem road until reaching Wolfheze. They spent the night in the park 'which', as Kessler remarked, 'had been the hub of their airborne operations'.[11]

General von Tettau's westward advance towards Arnhem had assisted in 'closing the lid' on the box enclosing the Oosterbeek perimeter. He now paused to reorganise for simultaneous attacks planned by Harzer's 9SS from the north-east and east on 21 September. Von Tettau had also been tasked by the High Command Netherlands to safeguard his rear areas against further enemy parachute attacks, and any further developments resulting from the Allied breakthrough at Nijmegen. To achieve this, a line was to be occupied stretching from the canal position between Ochten east of Kesteren, to the lower Rhine south of Grebbe to Heveadorp.[12] Fliegerhorst Battalion 2, commanded by Major Liebsch, and the 10th Schiffssturmabteilung were withdrawn from SS-Colonel Lippert's right flank and fed into the new line. The Regiment 'Knoche' was formed from various disparate units, including the 4th Flak Abteilung of Regiment 668 to guard against further possible enemy airlandings in the rear. In effect, von Tettau moved his less experienced units into depth as reserve, saving more effective forces for the concentric attacks planned against the cauldron on 21 September.

The 'front' facing the British in the west consisted now from right to left of the 'Worrowski' Battalion of the Hermann Goering, and the SS battalions 'Shulz', 'Eberwein' and 'Helle' belonging to Lippert's Regiment 'Unteroffizierschule Arnheim'. SS-Captain Krafft's battalion was to wait and assemble as division reserve in the Wolfheze area. 'H' hour was to be 0800 hours for all units surrounding the British pocket.[13]

This neat paper solution expounded by von Tettau in his post-combat report did not entirely mirror events in the line. Lieutenant Martin graphically described the situation as he saw it in his diary the next day:

'22 September. Cold and foggy. The three majors are in the command post. We're dug in towards the Rhine. Combat team Marhmas [not legible] in Heveadorp. Snipers working at night. Heavy rain. No idea of the situation. No mail. Very cold.'[14]

There was no precise 'front'. Only soldiers at its very edge were in any position to transcribe any information on to higher formation maps. Consequently, when Herbert Kessler's Hermann Goering Battalion began its assault, its soldiers were unaware of the objective or indeed even where the enemy was. Not surprisingly, this was to have catastrophic results. Martin wrote in his diary:

'The order to move on came at first light. The battalion was to be committed to battle during the day. Nobody knew the exact situation. They drove on without reconnaissance in front, led by the company commander's car. There could be no talk of a clear front line trace due to the peculiarities of the fighting. Enemy stragglers were scattered all over the area and fought doggedly to honour their reputation as an elite unit.'

The company bicycled past the Hotel Wolfheze and along the road Krafft's battalion had defended on the first day. They turned south on a minor road that led towards Heveadorp. After crossing the Oosterbeeksche Weg, Kessler recalls they later . . .

'. . . turned off the road to the right on to a forest trail, where they halted, packed closely together. So far as they could see there was no trace of the enemy. But this was to change rather soon. The soldiers were sitting on their bicycles without a care in the world when they were surprised by a murderous machine gun fire from the flank. Some of them did not have enough time to take cover somewhere on the ground. On the left of the trail there was a strip of bushes and brushwood. At its edge stood the Westerbouwing Inn, where the enemy had obviously established an OP in its lookout tower. From here the British had observed the approach of the German unit, sited their machine guns, and opened fire. After the initial shock was overcome, the inevitable order came, "company attack!".'[15]

The high ground at Westerbouwing was held by a platoon of B Company 1st Bn Border Regt glider infantry. Tactically it was vital ground, as it totally dominated the 1st British Airborne Division perimeter and the Heveadorp ferry, whose loss was significantly to affect the chances of reinforcement from across the lower Rhine. Much of this importance has, however, been attributed by historians, wise after the event. Major General Urquhart, the division's commander, had been trapped on ground not of his own choosing and was powerless to react. In any case, the significance of the feature had not been appreciated by the British. Likewise, the Germans, as Kessler's account suggests, were not necessarily aiming to capture it either; they had simply stumbled upon British forces securing the inn. They too were to overlook the hill's immense tactical worth. Von Tettau was totally preoccupied with the more immediate task of clearing the western side of the Oosterbeek perimeter. Few of his head-

quarters staff would have been tactically astute enough to appreciate the significance of this windfall. Lieutenant Colonel Fullriede was as scathing as SS-Colonel Lippert in his opinion of von Tettau's headquarters, whose staff 'could be likened to a club for old gentlemen'.[16]

His subordinates in the Hermann Goering Regiment, meanwhile, pressed home their attack. Kessler, pinned down, saw that:

'. . . the heavy weapons platoon had placed its sustained-fire machine guns into positions and returned fire. Soon the soldiers, overcoming their surprise completely now, began to attack. They got into the underbrush and opened machine gun fire, just to hear the reassuring sound of their own weapons.'

Eventually, some sections fought their way through the trees and broke into the inn buildings, capturing the British inside. Victory brought little satisfaction, only high casualties and the sobering realisation of what lay ahead. Kessler, watching prisoners file past, felt apprehensive:

'Even a cursory glance at the first enemy soldiers revealed that these indeed belonged to a select unit. The lads were as tall as trees, well fed and well equipped.'[17]

His regimental commander, Lieutenant Colonel Fullriede, caustically commented upon his unit's contribution to the assault: He wrote:

'In the attack on Westerbouwing the Worrowski battalion lost all its officers except a lieutenant, and half its other ranks. These casualties were due to a certain Colonel Schramm who was in command of this operation and had forbidden the use of heavy weapons because he was afraid his own men would be hit. The idiot preferred to let hundreds of them die.'[18]

Colonel Schramm was relieved of his command at Fullriede's insistence three days later.

The remainder of the attacks mounted by the Kampfgruppe von Tettau made little progress that day. SS-Colonel Lippert reported by mid-morning that he was 'making only very slow progress against heavy enemy resistance', and soon after that only 'some 800 metres of ground has been gained against strong enemy resistance'. Lippert also revealed that 'especially heavy losses are reported for the battalion Hermann Goering'.[19] Herbert Kessler chronicled the further disintegration of his company after the Westerbouwing débâcle:

'After a brief reorganisation the company continued the attack towards the town of Oosterbeek. It was difficult to spot the enemy in the forest fighting. Tree-top snipers caused considerable losses, enemy automatic weapons which frequently moved could only be silenced with difficulty and sometimes with numerous casualties. At noon, the company was completely scattered and pulled back while a neighbouring unit continued the attack on Oosterbeek. The remnants of the company were only a small group, with their missing comrades dead, wounded, or scattered as stragglers.'[20]

There was simply a limit to what could be expected of untrained soldiers; and the complications and exigencies of the attack often surpassed their limited skills and experience. Fullriede commented again the same day about an Army High Command feeding in untrained troops, determined to salvage the situation cost what it may. 'Despite OKW's intervention, I returned about 1600 recruits back to Germany. To send them into battle would simply have been infanticide.'[21]

Fullriede's assessment was probably correct. On the other side of the perimeter, Harzer's furiously attacking veterans in the 9SS were making even less progress. Von Tettau was informed by the High Command Netherlands:

'The 9SS Panzer Division has only gained 200 metres of ground against strong enemy resistance.'[22]

From north-east and east: the 9SS . . .

Following the collapse of 1 PARA Brigade's attempt to reach Frost at the bridge, the SS Kampfgruppe Spindler had gone on to the offensive. But by the afternoon of 20 September, despite tenacious fighting, it had only been able to move forward towards Oosterbeek by a few blocks. Some of the delay was caused by the assimilation of fresh, but largely untrained replacements. SS-Captain Moeller was still spearheading the advance along the Utrechtseweg when his reinforcements arrived:

'On 20 September, the engineer battalion received the promised replacements from the *Reichsarbeitsdienst* [pioneers], the Navy and Luftwaffe. The replacements had no combat experience whatsoever and were totally inexperienced in street fighting. Nevertheless we were glad to have them. These men were rather sceptical and reluctant at the beginning, which was hardly surprising. But when they were put in the right place they helped

'The 9SS Panzer Division has only gained 200 metres of ground against strong enemy resistance'. Moellers' Kampfgruppe pinned down on the Utrechtseweg. (Bundesarchiv)

us a lot; and in time they integrated completely, becoming good and reliable comrades.'[23]

At this point SS-Lieutenant Colonel Walther Harzer, the commander of the Hohenstaufen, decided to review his tactics in order to improve progress. During the night of 20–21 September the various 9SS Kampfgruppen were ordered to regroup to include small penetration groups of assault-pioneers (*Sturmpionieren*), and attack in echeloned units one after the other on a selected but reduced sector. The aim was to form narrow but deep penetration points in the British front. Assault guns and armoured half-tracks mounting heavy weapons

trundled up to forward staging areas in the half-light of dawn, to assist in shooting a way through for these 'roll-over' assaults. Constant attacks were to concentrate on a small front, with reserves standing by in echelon to follow through immediately on success. *Schwerpunkt*, or the main focus of effort, was to remain in the Kampfgruppe Spindler's sector. Spearheads were tempered by the inclusion of the three SP batteries belonging to Assault Gun Brigade 280. The brigade, which had only just refitted in Denmark, was briefly under 15th Army command before being despatched to Arnhem where it had swung the balance in the German favour on 19 September. Its commander, Major Kurt Kuehne (subsequently awarded the Knight's Cross for his unit's contribution), had penny-packaged his batteries of three Sturmgeschutz III each to the Kampfgruppen Spindler, Harder and von Allworden. Kuehne's third battery commander, Sergeant Josef Mathes, had already been killed on the first day's fighting.[24] The brigade included its own integral heavily-armed infantry. Each battery had eight light machine guns and seven panzerfaust.[25] Many of its personnel were still lacking in combat experience.

This regrouping of resources achieved some deep penetrations but at considerable cost. Pockets containing trapped enemy troops are referred to as *Der Kessel* – the cauldron – in German military parlance. This particular battle was embellished with a more meaningful term by German soldiers, who referred to their situation as *Der Hexenkessel* – the witches' cauldron. This was very much the picture described by SS-Captain Moeller as his assault-pioneers battled along the Utrechtseweg. They were now engaged in:

'. . . bitter isolated and hand-to-hand fighting, as my men fought their way from room to room, from the ground floor up, from garden to garden and from tree to tree. One tank and one armoured half-track were knocked out by anti-tank fire. Schmatz and the second company had kicked off their attack at the same time to cover the right flank of third company. He attacked the surprised paratroopers from the rear with flame-throwers which enabled SS-Lieutenant Linker to catch his breath and retain and consolidate the new position. The Red Devils still fought back and battled for every room and every house, for every piece of ground or garden, no matter how small it was – like cornered tigers.'[26]

They only achieved a penetration of a few hundred metres. The problems of assimilating the new recruits now became apparent during these hard-fought actions. SS-Corporal Wolfgang Dombrowski, fighting in the second company, records how the assault gun was lost:

'A Sturmgeschutz III was attached to my section. It had a motley crew, there was a Wehrmacht NCO in charge, a Luftwaffe man – probably the loader – and two other army men. We were making really good progress with this until we eventually came under fire from infantry supported by an anti-tank gun. The crew, which had been virtually thrown together for this action, panicked when the vehicle was hit. Even though the damage was only superficial the gun abruptly reversed into a side street where the crew baled out over the rear and fled. Only the NCO remained with us – somewhat disgusted!'

But their troubles were far from over. Darting across the street, dodging and weaving as they ran, came a group of British paratroopers, racing straight for the abandoned vehicle.

'The enemy took it over. We heard them test the engine, and it started. Presently the gun traversed up and down; but they could not drive it in order to lock the tracks and move the gun left or right. "My God!" exclaimed the startled gun commander. The barrel was however still fortunately pointing at the house occupied by the British. We were getting very nervous about all this. Although we were engaged by the machine gun on board, the British were not able to get the main armament working. Eventually the engine was turned off and they came out. It was left standing there, a constant and potential threat to both sides!'[27]

By late afternoon on 21 September three distinct thrust lines had emerged locked into the eastern side of the cauldron. The SS Kampfgruppe Spindler, which included Moeller, was driving along and north-east of Utrechtseweg. Covering the ground left to the lower Rhine were the two SS Kampfgruppen Von Allworden and Harder. Whole streets and some blocks had been taken. But the battle, now more or less static, had become one of attrition, steadily increasing in intensity as both sides doggedly fought over the same ground. SS-Captain Moeller remembers how horrors could be interspersed with lighter moments, as when an occasional 'bottle of whisky lowered on a string' was exchanged in a deadlocked position between the floors of a jointly occupied house, with 'my engineers sending up chocolates in return'. But one could never afford to be complacent:

'There was fairness – but this could not conceal the fact that the battle continued with unabated ferocity. Many a man who regarded these gestures with blind faith was found dead with a hole in his head. What had happened to them? Well – street fighting! Other men ventured too close to a window instead of remaining in the middle of the room and observing from there. An invisible enemy sniper punished this carelessness with a well-aimed round. SS-Corporal Tornow, a brave and circumspect leader of his men, died in this way, paying a dear price for one moment's inattention. It was incomprehensible to us all these vagaries of fate, the many faces of war, its unpredictability.'[28]

While the Kampfgruppe Spindler attempted to enlarge the penetrations achieved in the east, to the north and north-east of them was the Kampfgruppe Bruhns, mopping up the gliders that had overshot between landing-zone 'S' and the Polish glider site at 'L'. Alfred Ziegler, a despatch rider from the SS Panzerjaeger 9 with Bruhns, remembers their costly and laborious progress:

'Our unit was pulled out of line to get some sleep because we were earmarked to fight from house to house with "panzerfaust" anti-tank rocket launchers in Oosterbeek the next day. However, our strength had dwindled to a small bunch of 50 to 60 men.'

This had been from an original complement of 120. Eventually they broke into a small house north of the Ede-Arnhem railway cutting. 'It was a fine building,' Ziegler recalled. Gazing out of the window, scanning the ground over which they would advance, he:

'. . . noticed shell bursts landing in a distinctive pattern before us, registering on the railway cutting. I mentioned this to our lieutenant, who said "Don't let your imagination run away with you! They're strays." Well they weren't. He was wounded later and I got him out in my motorcycle combination. We managed to get over the obstacle by crossing the cutting in rushes, one section at a time.'

Once across, they still made only slow progress against stiffening enemy resistance.

'I dug a hole near the bridge over the railway line, pulled my motorcycle over the top of it for protection against overhead shrapnel and fell asleep at the bottom of it'.

As in the east, once the line of houses at the northern edge of Oosterbeek was reached, the advance deteriorated into a savage battle of attrition. Ziegler recalled the continuation of the attack into the afternoon of 21 September:

'Our small unit was engaged in house-to-house fighting throughout the day and paid a terrible toll. In the evening there were only 21 unwounded men left, absolutely leaderless.

'Herr Bruhns told me to go and look for Von Allworden and tell him that if he did not withdraw his few surviving men left in the line, there would be none of the original tank destroyer crews left.'[29]

And then the Poles landed.

CHAPTER XXI

The Crisis

This was all we needed – enemy in our rear!

SS-Corporal

Another front – Betuwe, 21–22 September

Only one possibility remained for the Allies to save the Red Devils at Arnhem. By 1400 on 21 September cloud above airfields in England cleared sufficiently to enable the parachutists of 1st Polish Parachute Brigade to take to the air. Under the new plan, the Poles were to drop close to the village of Driel near the southern terminus of the Heveadorp ferry. During the night it was hoped to cross the river by ferry in order to strengthen the British perimeter on the north bank until XXX Corps might break through.

Unfortunately, weather over the Continent had not cleared. Over the Netherlands they were awaited by the forewarned Luftwaffe and flak. Squadrons of Jagdgeschwader 26, under Lieutenant Colonel Priller, and aircraft of Jagdgeschwaders 2 and 11 attacked the transport aircraft and claimed victims mainly after they had dropped. Of 100 planes only 53 dropped their loads. Those who jumped included the brigade commander, Major General S. Sosabowski, and the equivalent of two weak battalions, about 750 men.

The effect on the Germans was electric. 'This was all we needed,' exclaimed SS-Corporal Rudolf Trapp, witnessing the spectacle on the western outskirts of Arnhem – 'enemy in our rear!' His men immediately swung into action:

'When we saw fresh paratroopers landing we lined up along the Rhine's edge and shot for all we were worth. I set up my machine gun and fired long protracted bursts because there is so little time before they all get to the ground. This was a shock – a second front! We thought they would likely head for the bridge and try to cross the river, so we stood under the trees and fired up into the air.'[1]

Elements of the Kampfgruppe Knaust and the Hohenstaufen's Reconnaissance Battalion were on the road near Elden, and soon their light air defence guns, machine guns and riflemen joined in the mêlée. The landings were a total surprise. As a consequence, much of the shooting was wild. Artillery Regiment 191 and the SS Werfergruppe Nickmann very quickly began to drop whole salvoes on to the drop-zone. Some paratroopers were hit in the air before their canopies had even reached the ground. But, despite the storm of fire that rose up to meet them, Polish casualties on landing were found to be light. After overcoming minor opposition on the drop-zone, General Sosabowski made the disheartening discovery that a short while earlier the Germans had dislodged the British from the north end of the ferry site – part of the Hermann Goering attack – and the ferry boat had been sunk. There seemed little immediate prospect of reaching and reinforcing the airborne perimeter.

The Germans, unaware of all this, feared the worst. SS-Colonel Lippert, in his command post on the north bank, had still to hear confirmation of the Hermann Goering Battalion's progress. He declared:

'This was, so far as achieving my mission went, one of the most critical situations that ever arose. Driel lay only a few kilometres south of the Heveadorp – Rhine ferry, not yet in our possession. It appeared to indicate the likelihood that the Poles would be over the ferry as quickly as they were able to assist the surrounded Englishmen in the pocket.'[2]

But the threat was even more significant than that. The implication was not simply that the Poles would force a passage of the Rhine, but that they might make a quick dash to the north-east and cut off the 10SS from the recently recaptured Arnhem road bridge. The Frundsberg was fully committed to pushing south across the Betuwe back to Nijmegen. The Polish landing resurrected familiar fears among the SS-troopers. Nobody felt safe with enemy paratroopers in their rear. Should the southern end of the Arnhem bridge be taken, the whole unpleasant business may start again. It had taken a massive three-day effort to fight the Arnhem bridge clear to reopen an important line of communication. History could not be allowed to repeat itself.

The scale of the German reaction provides some measure of the importance attached to this latest twist in the crisis. The Hohenstaufen was directed to employ all available reserves against this new enemy. Its commander, SS-Lieutenant Colonel Walther Harzer, commented with some relief that 'neither the capture of the Arnhem bridge nor the formation of the powerful reserves by the Kampfgruppe 9SS Panzer Division had happened a day or even an hour, too soon, as was to be proved in the early afternoon of 21 September.'[3] All his reserves that had been formed from arriving 'stand-by' units were committed against this new threat.

A *Sperrverband* or blocking formation was therefore formed south of the lower Rhine, in the Betuwe: the 'Sperrverband Harzer'. This improvised force demonstrated again the German ability consistently and effectively to plug gaps in the line as they appeared, whatever the scale of the overall crisis. It consisted of five battalions: 'Schoerken', a naval battle group, 'Koehnen', from Marine Kampfgruppe 642, the Luftwaffe battalion 'Kauer', Coastal Machine Gun Battalion 47, and the III Dutch-SS 'Landsturm Niederland' battalion. In all there were 14 infantry companies numbering some 2,461 men, rising to 17 companies by 24 September. Artillery support was also forthcoming. A detachment each from Artillery Regiment 191 and the Flak Brigade Swoboda were ordered to occupy positions at Elden. Their tasks were to engage the Poles immediately, support the Sperrverband and keep the Elden to Elst southerly road open to the 10SS. The detachments numbered 15 to 16 88mm flak guns, eight 20mm cannon and additional 37mm flak. Despite the fact that the Poles were unable to reinforce the British immediately, their impact on operations was greater than that ascribed by some official histories. They drew off a considerable number of troops and resources which would otherwise have been included in the concentrated attacks planned for 22 September. They had prolonged the survival of 1st British Airborne Division.[4]

Harzer moved swiftly during the night of 21–22 September to establish the new *Sperrverband*. Coastal Machine Gun Battalion 47 spearheaded the attack against the planned objective: the Arnhem-Nijmegen railway-line embankment. This was reached amazingly quickly without any enemy resistance. Meanwhile, the Poles had concentrated upon occupying Driel and began to prepare it for all-round defence. From north to south a German line gradually began to take shape following the north-south course of the railway embankment facing Driel. From top to bottom it consisted of the battalions Schoerken, Machine Gun Battalion 47, Kauer, Koehnen, with finally the Dutch SS Landsturm battalion linking up with the Kampfgruppe Knaust and the 10SS north of Elst.

Bittrich, the IISS Corps commander, was convinced that the Polish objective was to cut off and isolate the Frundsberg. He therefore ordered the Kampfgruppen Knaust and Brinkmann, based in Elst as a contingency reserve following the recapture of the Arnhem bridge, to begin redeploying in order to attack the Poles in Driel. Adjustments were made to the boundary lines of the two SS divisions, to rationalise and co-ordinate the measures now required to defeat this latest threat. Velden became inclusive to the 9SS and Elst was placed under control of the 10SS. All elements of the Kampfgruppe Hohenstaufen operating south of the lower Rhine were incorporated into the 'Sperrverband Harzer'. Command was further streamlined by Army Group B who offered an uncommitted regimental headquarters under Colonel Gerhard to command the blocking force. Gerhard's command post became effective during the night of 21–22 September after it established itself on the north-east edge of Elden. 'ARKO 191' still co-ordinated the artillery effort but worked closely with the new headquarters.

All these measures enacted by the staffs to stabilise the crisis should not detract from the reality of the situation on the ground. Improvisations can only be made to work by the Herculean efforts of troops actually enacting them. The soldiers forming the backbone of the Sperrverband Harzer were untrained Navy, Luftwaffe, newly-joined Wehrmacht and Dutch-German nationals recently conscripted into the SS. This made the achievement all the more remarkable. Soldiers were fed haphazardly into the new line to plug gaps or replace casualties. Feldwebel Erich Hensel's experience was typical of most.

Hensel, a 23-year-old *Nachrichten* (signals) sergeant had barely escaped the Allied advance in Normandy, crossing the Scheldt with the fleeing 15th Army. His divisional signals unit had just departed Student's 1st Fallschirmjaeger headquarters in Vught when the first landings started. 'We did not see the landings but certainly heard of them,' he remembered, but they merely 'added to the impetus to get back to Germany.' Dependent upon rumour and hearsay for information, the thirty-odd signallers became concerned. There was generally a lack of knowledge about the overall situation and 'we were worried we might be surrounded'.

They had hoped to escape the impending action because they 'thought the war was as good as over'. But not for them; they were apprehended and re-routed by military police seeking out stragglers. '*Es geht wieder los!* Here we go again!' they realised. There was fearful anticipation of the coming battle. Hensel admits he was 'very frightened that he may yet be killed,' after all they had endured 'so late in the war'. On the way to the front they became caught up in the myriad units belonging to II Fallschirmjaeger Corps marching via Cleve to the front. 'English "Jabos" *en route* were terrible,' Hensel related, but there was no mistaking the inevitability of what was to come. To an eastern front and Normandy veteran it was depressingly all too familiar: 'We could only march at night due to the air threat.' Progress was therefore slow, although 'poor weather at least enabled us to move'. As they neared the front, tensions increased. Hensel confided:

'The main fear is always going into action. In other words, on the way to the combat zone, rather than after fighting has started. All that we knew was that new landings of English paras had taken place in this area, and my God we were on our way there!'

They were put into the line immediately south of Arnhem and the lower Rhine. Hensel's signals platoon was required to occupy a section of the 10SS front thinned out by casualties. This was not an onerous mission because, although not a National Socialist, Hensel held the Waffen SS in some respect as soldiers. An SS battle group had rescued him from an isolated pocket and certain Soviet captivity on the eastern front at Zhitomir in 1942. His view was admiring:

'I have never seen better soldiers than the SS. They were volunteers and well disciplined. The officers were particularly hard and showed no quarter for any minor lapses in battle discipline. Despite heavy losses they still maintained their morale and fought well.'

There was some folklore attached to the SS, believed in part by the Wehrmacht. Hensel had been told tales of the SS *Hitler Jugend* in Normandy. Here, fanatical teenage soldiers had remained on the backs of tanks raked by naval gun fire, unflinchingly maintaining positions, despite the cost, because of a perverted sense of regimental pride.

Small arms ammunition was distributed by the Frundsberg, and they occupied positions 'by the railway bridge on the southern side of the Rhine facing the newly arrived paratroopers'. Hensel was placed in charge of the heavy machine gun section. Mortars were manned by the SS because the signallers were not trained to use them.

'Typically, nobody was aware of the true situation. It was simply "enemy to your front and dig in".' (Bundesarchiv)

Typically, nobody was aware of the true situation. It was simply, 'enemy to your front and dig in'. The first shocking realisation of what was going on came after ten to twelve POWs appeared in their sector. Hensel commented:

'The first prisoners I saw wore British uniforms – but with a start we noticed they were not British, but Russians! No, not Russians – Poles!'

A steady trickle of reinforcements arrived. 'Any unit that was in reasonable shape, that is,' Hensel explained, 'still integrated as a whole, was immediately stuck in against the Poles.' They were dug in behind the railway embankment with one of the few woods to their front. Conditions were miserable. A low water table meant that brackish water immediately bubbled up into their trenches as they dug down. The best that could be achieved were shallow scrapes. The weather was generally poor, with fog most mornings. Rations were British, passed on by the SS, but by the time they reached the signallers, they were minus the cigarettes and chocolate. On most days life was fairly uneventful. Casualties were light and mainly from artillery fire, although two machine gunners were shot and wounded by Polish snipers. Hensel's men felt in contrast that they 'were inflicting heavy casualties on the enemy, who were often well pinned down by our machine guns.'[5]

Tanks were of limited value in this swampy terrain. Karl-Heinz Kracht's 'Mielke' tank company, reduced now to three surviving tanks, was occupying an orchard assembly area between Elst and Elden. All that was left to do waiting in reserve was to improve creature comforts, taking advantage of their static location.

'We dug a pit there two metres long by two metres wide and drove the tank over it, thus giving ourselves a roof and some protection above from artillery fire. This pit was cushioned with straw and rags and offered room enough for three men to sleep.'

Food re-supply was becoming a serious problem for this part of the front, 'especially,' Kracht recorded, 'as fighter-bombers fired at everything that moved.' The tank loader fondly recalled that previously, when based in Zevenaar, they had been supplied with soup, coffee and bread from their logistic train:

'But that stopped altogether when we were near Elden and Elst. We had to "requisition" things – that is, we went

looking for food in houses, and to farms for chickens, pigs, butter and bread. As emergency rations we had only crispbread and four-fruit jam, which we were absolutely fed up with. Every now and then we had some chocolate.'[6]

Like Hensel, the tank crews were totally reliant upon verbal reports for any knowledge of the situation. Soldiers privy to only incomplete information shared the unease felt by their officers. On the railway embankment, Hensel's Nachrichten troops listened to their new SS comrades talking about their predicament:

'The SS reported heavy battles to the south in Nijmegen. They constantly feared they might be cut off with the river on their right flank if the heavy American forces at Nijmegen broke through.'[7]

It was felt the battle might go either way.

Time is short . . .

SS-Colonel Heinz Harmel, the Commander of the 10SS, was totally preoccupied with containing the XXX Corps advance northwards into the Betuwe beyond Nijmegen, when he received 'the surprising report of enemy parachute landings next to Driel'. He was immediately ordered by IISS Panzer Corps headquarters 'to employ the leading elements of the newly arrived Battalion "Knaust" in Elst against this new threat without delay'.[8] Allied pressure building up from the south could not be ignored because it intensified at the same time to coincide with the Polish landings. Knaust's battalion was obliged to counterattack through Elst and clear out the enemy spearheads, which it proceeded to do. The momentum of the assault petered out south of the village. Lack of cover forced a retreat back to the buildings at its edge where the Kampfgruppe went over to the defensive. SS-Corporal Rudolf Trapp's 3rd Company Panzer-grenadier Regiment 21 took part in the action:

'After the surrender [on the Arnhem bridge] on Thursday we were immediately sent towards Nijmegen across the Arnhem bridge. Our objective was Elst. Some of us travelled by lorry, but for most of the way we were on foot. We were fired at by the Poles *en route*. I prepared a trench for my heavy machine gun in the new position.'

Fighting was hard, and, as ever, confusing. Many veterans today are unable to pinpoint their movements with accuracy during this hectic period. Trapp, after his many narrow escapes in Arnhem, finally became a casualty:

'In Elst I was wounded by small arms fire in the knee. An armoured half-track took me back. On board there was also a major of the Wehrmacht. When I moaned he showed me his wooden leg and told me to cheer up. Later in the hospital in Rees I dis-covered that this was Major Knaust.'

Major Knaust photographed by Karl-Heinz Kracht in Elst. (Kabel-Kracht)

Knaust, he remembered, had 'moved pain-fully on his wooden leg', and had been obliged in Elst 'to command the battle from a half-track'. Trapp remembers him over all the intervening years as 'a very good officer' who had taken the trouble, despite all the obvious operational pressures, to take an interest in the wound of a simple front soldier.[9]

The Kampfgruppe Brinkmann, consisting primarily of the remnants of the Frunds-berg's Reconnaissance Battalion 10, newly released from the Arnhem bridge, was attached by Bittrich's corps order to the Sperrverband Harzer. Brinkmann was instructed to advance via Elden and engage the newly-landed enemy forces in Driel during the night of 22–23 September. The terrain was devoid of cover and provided difficult 'going' for armoured vehicles. Sergeant Erich Hensel on the Arnhem-Nijmegen railway embankment declared it was 'an amazing achievement' that any side managed to get tanks into the area at all. Brinkmann's half-tracks and armoured cars had to disperse and reform in echeloned columns along the several small tracks running immediately north of Elst before commencing their attack.[10]

As they approached the village in darkness they were suddenly subjected to a flank attack from the direction of Valburg. This heralded the arrival of a previously undetected British unit: the 43rd Wessex Division. Unbeknown to the Germans, these were only the lead elements. After a short fire fight a reconnaissance troop, commanded by SS-Sergeant Stocke from Brinkmann's 2nd Company, captured an English armoured car – a radio communications vehicle. The crewmen, possibly from 5 Dorsets, were taken prisoner, but the real prize was the vehicle, with its radio still intact, which was recovered back to the railway embankment. It was left in no man's land where, untouched by Allied fighter bombers, it enabled the British signals net to be monitored by the Germans over the next few days.[11] Brinkmann's forces felt that they were unable to contain this new threat although it was only the vanguard of 43 Division. They retreated under cover of darkness in a south-easterly direction, until reaching and establishing new positions along the Arnhem-Elst railway embankment.

The crisis had worsened. German intelligence quickly spotted the character of this new threat – the 43rd Wessex was an infantry division.[12] With the limitations imposed by terrain, infantry could prove to be more effective than tanks. German fire had thus far prevented the Poles from crossing the river in any appreciable strength. Nickmann's SS-Werfer batteries in particular were effectively straddling the river banks and Polish positions. All were aware of the potential significance of the new arrivals. Field Marshal Model urged the rapid elimination of the encircled British. He knew that General Urquhart could not resist for

much longer. The cauldron had to be overwhelmed before the infantry elements of XXX Corps could effectively reinforce it. Moreover, the Poles had to be prevented from interfering any further. They had drawn so many reserves from the forces poised to invest the cauldron that the impact of attacks programmed for 22 September was reduced. Time was short, and victory was almost within their grasp. It all depended on how quickly XXX Corps could move forward, and how effectively German counter-measures directed against the corridor could slow them down. The race was on!

Bellowing engines punctuated by shouted commands signalled the beginning of the loading process. Forty-five factory-new 68-ton Porsche 'Tiger' II B tanks were carefully coaxed and swivelled from loading ramps on to the flat rail cars. Even in Ohrdruf in the Reich, eyes anxiously scanned the skies for signs of enemy air interference. Chains rattled through retaining rings and wedges were hammered home as crews secured their valuable charges for the rail journey to the front. By midnight the steam locomotive, cascading steam and blowing sparks into the air, had puffed vigorously out of the siding on to the main line. Crews made themselves comfortable as best they could in the few personnel carriages made available. It would be a long journey. Heeresgruppe B had been notified at midnight on 21 September that its valuable reinforcements had departed. Schwere Panzer Abteilung – Heavy Tank Battalion – 506 was supposed to arrive in the Arnhem area by the early morning of 24 September. Mounting an 88mm gun, they were the most powerful tanks in the west, and were vulnerable only to the heaviest of calibres. They were bound for Oosterbeek and Elst.

CHAPTER XXII
Cutting the Corridor

The Chief of Staff asked the Chief of Staff 15th Army General Hoffmann whether the operation ought to still go ahead. The Chief of Staff's response was 'if the Field Marshal has ordered the attack then it should still happen'.

LXXXVIII Corps Diary

Objective Veghel . . .

There was still hope among the Allies as daylight arrived on 22 September that the British 43rd Infantry Division might yet break through at Ressen north of Nijmegen, relieve the British paratroopers, and bring overall success to operation MARKET-GARDEN. This was, however, dependent upon events in the airborne corridor. General Taylor, still holding 'indian territory' with the 101 (US) Airborne Division south of Grave, faced a major task keeping 'Hell's Highway' open because of the slow progress of the VIII and XII British Corps attacks coming up on either flank of the corridor. The former was still south-east of Eindhoven, the latter was stalled south and south-west of Best. Report after report from Dutch civilian sources spoke of large-scale movements of German columns against the narrow corridor from both east and west. At a time when XXX Corps needed all its resources to reach the Oosterbeek pocket, severance of this umbilical cord could prove disastrous. General Taylor did not have the strength to maintain a static defence line along his 15-mile length of responsibility. His only recourse was to keep the Germans surprised and off balance with limited offensive thrusts of his own. Until now he had been generally successful. The Germans, having appreciated his dilemma, regrouped

forces of sufficient weight to produce the conclusive impact on operations they now desired.

Field Marshal Model issued his orders on 21 September. While Bittrich's IISS Panzer Corps and General Meindl's II Fallschirmjaeger Corps stepped up operations against the British at Arnhem and the Americans at Nijmegen, General Student's First Fallschirmjaeger Army was to sever the Allied corridor further south. LXXXVIII Corps diary succinctly records the Army Group's intention:

'Field Marshal Model has ordered that the enemy columns marching on Nijmegen are to be attacked at the Veghel bottleneck on 22 September from the west and east. This is to be by a panzer brigade from Heeresgruppe B from the east and through a battle group of the 59th Division from the west, consisting of two battalions strongly supported by artillery and tank-destroyers.'[1]

General Reinhard's LXXXVIII Corps would mount the attack from the west using General Poppe's 59 Division and other hastily assembled reinforcements. The panzer brigade operation from the east was to be mounted by a headquarters new to the fighting, the LXXXVI Corps under General der Infanterie Hans von Obstfelder. He had arrived on 18 September to assume control of the Division Erdmann and 176 Division, enabling General Student to give his undivided attention to his units more actively involved in containing the Allied salient on the western side of the corridor.

The heaviest attack this time was to come from the east. Obstfelder was to employ the now regrouped and reinforced Kampfgruppe 'Walther' that had originally been cut in two by the XXX Corps breakthrough in the Neerpelt bridgehead. Colonel Walther received his orders at LXXXVI Corps command post in the Hillenraed-Swamen castle near Roermond during the afternoon of 21 September. His mission was to cut the Eindhoven-Grave road at Veghel, seize the town, and destroy the bridge across the Zuid Wilhelms Vaart canal. He was to prevent the passage of reinforcements along this road, and re-establish contact with German forces operating on the other side of the corridor, who would be mounting a joint attack from west of the town.[2]

The new Kampfgruppe Walther was to control Major von Maltzahn's Panzer Brigade 107, a small contingent from the 10SS Panzer Division – the Kampfgruppe 'Richter'[3] – an artillery battalion (105mm and 150mm) from the Regiment 180 and the 1st Battalion of Grenadier Regiment 16 – a 'replacement' battalion – also from 180 Division, and a heavy flak battery. The other units of Walther's group would rejoin him as soon as they were relieved in the line, that is, two reinforced infantry battalions and an SS artillery battery. These included the 1st Battalion Fallschirmjaeger Regiment 21, and the SS Tank-Destroyer Battalion 10, commanded by SS Captain Roestel, who were picking up replacement assault guns and crews in Gemert. Colonel Walther commanded an imposing force. Von Malzahn's panzer brigade was still at 90 per cent strength, despite its losses in action against the 101 Division at Son 48 hours before. The infantry, however, lacked combat experience and the artillery was short of ammunition.

'H' hour for the attack was to be early on 22 September. Walther voiced his concern at the short time available to march his units to their forward assembly areas and conduct a reconnaissance of the attack terrain and forming-up points. General von Obstfelder overruled all objections; the situation demanded that the Kampfgruppe Walther attack as soon as was humanly possible. Contrary to all expectations, the marching units arrived on time. Although the bulk of his original units were not relieved in the line until 23 September, the new assault formations were already arriving in the vicinity of this newly established command post in Gemert during the early morning hours of 22 September. Major Freiherr von Maltzahn, commanding Panzer Brigade 107, reconnoitred the forming-up places and secured the road bridge across their first water obstacle, the Aa river in Erp. Security screens were posted to cover the Uden flank. Undetected by the enemy, the strongest force yet assembled to strike the corridor from the east awaited the signal to advance.

Meanwhile, in the west a regimental combat team from the 59th Division, shored up with replacements after its initial disastrous commitment at Best, lay waiting in its forming-up points. Commanded by Major Huber, this Kampfgruppe included three infantry battalions, a battalion of 105mm howitzers, a battery of 20mm anti-aircraft guns, seven anti-tank guns and four 'Jagdpanther' from the 1st company of Tank-Destroyer Battalion 559 attached from the Kampfgruppe Chill. Huber's right flank was loosely covered by the Kampfgruppe Zedlitz on the Wilhelmina canal around Oirschot, and the Fallschirmjaeger Battalion 'Bloch' held S'Hertogenbosch to his rear.[4] The axis of attack for the Kampfgruppe Huber was from Schijndel through

Von der Heydte's Fallschirmjaeger Regiment 6 faces a march of more than 60 kilometres in two days, before arriving late, footsore and weary at the attack start line. (Bundesarchiv)

the villages of Wijbosch and Eerde to Veghel.

What all this meant for the troops on the ground is graphically illustrated by the example of Von der Heydte's Fallschirmjaeger Regiment 6, tasked to support Huber's attack from the Boxtel area. As German troops awaited the signal to attack in their jumping-off points on 22 September, Von der Heydte's Falschirmjaeger were still strung out on the line of march between Tilburg and Boxtel. Theirs was an exhausting experience, typical of the lot of German soldiers marched and counter-marched to plug gaps caused by constant Allied breakthroughs. After its mauling in Normandy, the regiment had been recon-stituted and reinserted in southern Holland at the beginning of September where it had been continually in action ever since. Brushed aside by the Allied breakout on the Neerpelt bridgehead on 17 September, they were on the move again. Von der Heydte records that

'. . . . during the night of possibly the 21–22 September the Regiment marched to the Poppel area and continued to move all the way to the designated forming-up place during the following night.'[5]

This had involved a 33-kilometre night march, followed immediately by a further leg of just over 30 kilometres. Each soldier carried his weapon, ammunition and rations of up to 30 or 40 pounds, perhaps in addition manhandling heavy support weapons. Only a limited number of vehicles and bicycles were available. Bone-weary, von der Heydte's teenage soldiers stumbled doggedly through the night and following day with the adrenalin of the anticipated fighting providing the nervous energy to keep them going. Getting from their forming-up point to the objective would involve a further 10 kilometres of fighting across country, which in reality, because of the need to move tactically and manœuvre in the face of the enemy, would add a further third of the distance. Von der Heydte's Fallschirmjaeger would not be in time for 'H' hour; they would not arrive for a further 24 hours. When they did, they would be tired out before they even crossed the start line.

From east and west.
The blow falls,
22 September . . .

On the other side of the corridor, 22 September dawned with low grey clouds and a gently swirling ground mist. The Kampfgruppe Walther began to gather in its attachments and shake out into attack formation in the steadily growing half-light. Gradually the line of the attack axis, the Gemert-Erp road, and the dark mass of the village of Erp beyond became discernible. To the left of the road was the infantry from Grenadier Regiment 16 – huddled forms, barely distinguishable, dispersed in their assault groups. Grey spectre-like outlines of Armoured Engineer Company 107's half-tracks floated motionless on the mist behind the infantry. Shortly before 0500 there was activity as three Sturmgeschutz III SP guns noisily slipped and slid their way across the wet meadows,

seeking out the SS Kampfgruppe Richter positioned with the canal and river Aa on its left flank. Ten minutes later six 'Panther' tanks from Brigade 107, belching exhaust in the half-light, moved to the rear of SS-Captain Richter's infantry. They were accompanied by a hastily formed infantry company of logistic personnel formed from stragglers led by SS-Lieutenant Hoefer. The deep-bellied growl of tank engines ticking over gave the waiting infantry concealed in the long wet grass a little more confidence to face the future.

Richter's Kampfgruppe was to assault with two companies forward supported by the Panther (Panzer Mark V) tank company. In depth was a weak 3rd Company, only one platoon strong, which was to accompany the three SPs who would advance along the line of the canal. Behind them were a further two sections of assault pioneers, commanded by an SS-Sergeant, which constituted the force reserve. To the rear was the armoured engineer company, whose job it was to move up in its half-tracks at the appropriate moment and prepare the Veghel bridge for demolition. The two lead SS companies were to 'fire and manœuvre' covering each other through Erp and beyond on to the St Oedenrode-Grave road. They would then protect the Engineers until their task was complete, while the reserve company provided security along the canal bank.

On the right of the Erp-Gemert road, Walther had concentrated the bulk of von Maltzahn's Panzer Brigade 107, the panzer and panzer-grenadier battalion. The ground on this side was slightly higher and dryer, and therefore easier going for tanks. These revved up and clattered into position, locking squeaking tracks and churning up the meadow as they lined up. Shrouded by exhaust fumes and mist, the squat shapes waited menacingly dinosaur-like in the early morning fog.

Commanders intently scanned the terrain

Commanders intently scanned the forward terrain with binoculars.
Fields of observation were poor. A typical view of the ground in the
vicinity of the corridor as viewed from the German front line.
(Bundesarchiv)

forward with binoculars. There was some concern. Fields of observation were poor but at least this had enabled the force to assemble undetected. It was far from ideal tank country – meadows on both sides of the road were water-logged – but this was the only opportunity presented thus far to cut the vital Allied route with an armoured force. On the left, Richter's Adjutant, the 23-year-old SS-Lieutenant Heinz Damaske, shared his commander's view of the approaching task. As he remembered:

'The terrain was unfavourable, 700 to 800 metres of practically no cover over meadowland, then thick scrub with the occasional tree which reached to something like a half-kilometre to the St Oedenrode-Veghel road.'[6]

Nevertheless, at 0545 von Maltzahn, the tank brigade commander, visited Richter, followed shortly after by Colonel Walther to tie up the final details. The attack would commence at 0900.

General Taylor, the commander of the 101 (US) Airborne Division, had already engaged the bulk of Colonel Johnson's 501 Parachute Infantry Regiment to a limited offensive action near Schijndel. They would soon come into contact with the Kampf-gruppe Huber. This left one battalion of the 501 in defensive positions in Veghel. There was nothing in Uden, seven kilometres north-west of Veghel, which was shortly to be brushed by the right fringe of Walther's attack. Concerned now at recent sightings of German tanks between Gemert and Erp, adding to the previous unease stemming from Dutch Resistance reports, Taylor decided to despatch additional forces to Uden and Veghel. One battalion immediately set off by truck, another on foot. Colonel Sink's 506 Parachute Infantry Regiment was ordered to send troops to Uden as they were relieved by British troops at Eindhoven and Son. About 150 men hastily clambered aboard trucks for the northward journey; they should arrive by 1100. The only other Allied force in Veghel at that moment, apart from columns moving through, was the XXX Corps Nijmegen anti-aircraft group. They had parked up in the early morning in order to allow 69 Brigade Group to pass through a priority move. There was urgent activity as they took up defensive positions and began to deploy guns in both the anti-air and field role.[7]

At 0900 German commanders in the Kampfgruppe Walther stared intently at watch faces as the final seconds ticked off 'H' hour. Fists jabbed skyward in the tugging motion that signified 'advance'. Slowly, reluctantly, the infantry got to their feet and walked steadily forward. Stomachs tightened with fear – this was it! Tanks and half-tracks to the right of the road roared off at speed to achieve their first tactical bounds. On the left the advance progressed at infantry pace. Artillery began bursting on the initial objectives.

SS-Captain Damaske, moving with the Kampfgruppe Richter, noted with relief

Artillery began bursting on the initial objectives. Ammunition was short. (Bundesarchiv)

that the 'enemy had obviously not noticed the forming-up point'. The advance gathered momentum. 'On both sides of the road,' Damaske reported, 'we quickly made progress against only weak resistance.' Erp was rapidly overrun, and Colonel Walther quickly moved his command post into the village to control the assault upon Veghel. Uden and the outskirts of Veghel had been reached by 1100. Colonel Sink's contingent from the 506th Regiment arrived minutes before the first skirmishing outside Uden. The Germans, however, had eyes only for Veghel. Its unmistakable church spire was already proving to be an excellent artillery aiming point.

Virtually unopposed on the right of the road, the Panther and Panzer-grenadier battalions cut 'Hell's Highway' between Veghel and Uden. In Veghel Lieutenant-Colonel Ballard's Second Battalion 501 Regiment warded off the first German blow in a stint of furious fighting from fox holes and houses along the Erp road. They observed the armoured part of the column side-stepping to the north and Uden. Upon cutting the route, the tanks turned left and attempted to drive down the main road to Veghel itself.

On the other side of the corridor the Kampfgruppe 'Huber' from 59 Division was also engaged in its simultaneous attack. Because the Americans had taken Schijndel the night before, Huber had had to alter his plan of attack. Diverting an infantry battalion to act as a screen against Schijndel, he had advanced with the remainder of his force along back roads and tracks to Eerde. One of the Jagdpanther tank-destroyers from 559 Company destroyed two British armoured cars in a skirmish, as the Kampfgruppe penetrated the village at about 1100.[8] This was the first real indication road traffic in the corridor had of an impending attack from this direction. By about 1400 Major Huber's tank-destroyers and artillery began to bring down fire upon the bridge over the Wilhelms canal at Veghel.

At that moment Colonel Sink's truck-borne element of the American 506 Parachute Infantry Regiment arrived from the south, driving for Uden. They were supported by a squadron of British tanks. Discouraged, Huber's Kampfgruppe recoiled from the roadside. The British tanks left one troop behind and went on to Veghel.

Walther's Kampfgruppe was now in difficulties; the tanks were too far ahead of the infantry, who were struggling to keep up. SS-Lieutenant Damaske recalled how

'. . . the English then fired a protective barrage out of all available barrels, including smoke, particularly in Richter's sector. At the same time, the attack along the main road stalled against formidable [enemy] tank units.'[9]

Despite this, Richter's Kampfgruppe had at least reached the scrub area near the road. Concurrently, a battalion of the US 327 Glider Infantry Regiment, commanded by Lieutenant-Colonel Ray C. Allen and backed up by a 57mm motorised anti-tank platoon, arrived breathless in the middle of the mêlée. They were directed to defend in the north, near the railway bridge over the Aa river.[10]

The German attack now began to run out of steam. Bearing down on the north-east corner of Veghel was the lead Panther company. Its first tank was struck by the opening 57mm shot from the Americans. Slewing to a halt, the Panther burst into flames, belching rolling columns of greasy black smoke into the sky. Faced with what they could not realise was a makeshift defence, the other German tanks backed away.

Physically separated by the corridor, the simultaneous attacks by Walther and Huber could not be effectively co-ordinated.

Unable to speak to each other by radio or telephone, both Kampfgruppen were unaware of the progress or indeed presence of the other. Huber reasoned that if he could not reach Veghel he might at least cut 'Hell's Highway'. This he did by quickly rallying his men again and side-slipping to the south. Advance elements were actually crossing the main road again when American reinforcements – this time the remaining battalions of the 327 Glider Infantry Regiment – reappeared. The glidermen quickly drove the Germans back.

Meanwhile, Colonel Johnson's two American battalions of the 501 Regiment at Schijndel had been moved southwards in an attempt to assist the defenders of Veghel. As they advanced they caught up with the rear echelons of the Kampfgruppe Huber. Pandemonium broke out. One German soldier Karl Max Wietzorek, a Normandy Fallschirmjaeger veteran, was visibly moved by the hopelessness of their situation. He despairingly recalled their plight:

'If only I could describe it properly, the close combat in the Dutch woods! I wish I had the chance to go back to this country, Holland and tell what happened there . . . at the hydrochloric acid factory by the canal road – a fight against parachute troops on the ground and snipers in tree-tops. That night the former General der Flieger Student himself took part in the German counter-attack. We came up against hard, bitter opposition and our desperate attempt at attack was brought to a halt. It was raining and many of our men slipped and slithered down the wet slope into the canal where they drowned. Then the Americans let the hydrochloric acid into the trenches, which were partly filled with water. This acid caused terrible injuries on the bodies of the soldiers; few survived this ordeal.'[11]

One American battalion was directed to occupy each of the villages of Wijbosch and Eerde, forming the western segment of an Allied defensive ring round Veghel. In the process the Kampfgruppe Huber's infantry battalions were cut off. Only a few stragglers managed to escape.

Richter's Kampfgruppe also faced a crisis. SS-Lieutenant Damaske recalled his commander's dilemma. 'He changed his attack plan,' he remembers, 'which he now felt to be totally impractical.' Unable to enter Veghel, denied them by a storm of fire, Richter directed

'. . . that fire now be opened from the flank against the [Allied] armoured forces moving on the Veghel road. The canal bridge was taken under fire by the "Sturmgeschutz" assault guns from the line we had reached.'

Fortunately for the Americans, the canal bridge was protected by a moat of swampy ground produced by the river Aa. Damaske observed that:

'Further progress through this marshy terrain was not possible. Morever, the engineers and Panzer-grenadiers came under well-aimed rifle fire delivered by the American paratroopers and were not able to take a further step forward.'

More Allied tank forces entered Veghel in the afternoon. Although losses within the Kampfgruppe Walther had been heavy, they had effectively blocked the corridor with fire. But they would not be able to hold their tenuous positions indefinitely. Ammunition was running short. Damaske described the difficult predicament of the SS-Kampfgruppe Richter in the following way:

'This attack also broke apart under the heaviest artillery fire we had

SS-Lieutenant Damaske reported that 'the canal bridge' on the Veghel road 'was taken under fire by the Sturmgeschutz assault guns from the line we had reached'. SP's in the attack. (Bundesarchiv)

experienced since Eterville and Hill 112 in northern France, a superiority of material we could not match. Even during darkness and long after the attack had come to a halt our positions were hammered without pause by artillery which had no regard for ammunition expenditure rates. While this was going on, the infantry in the first company who had been set in defence were reduced to getting a few belts of machine gun ammunition passed on from the panzer crews, in order to carry on fighting.'

It was hopeless. The commanding officers of Panzer Battalion 107 and its sister Panzer-grenadier Battalion, and that of Grenadier Regiment 16 were all killed in action. The spearhead assault units were leaderless. Damaske remembers Richter's group had already lost two dead, and fifteen wounded. The tank company commander's Panther had been knocked out, and he and his crew had perished within. SS-Lieutenant Hoefer, the commander of the company of stragglers raised shortly before the attack, had been riding on the same tank and was also killed. 'The situation,' Damaske reported, 'is confused. The armoured Engineer Company has broken

Virtually all the officers commanding the spearhead elements were killed in action. Casualties were heavy. A field dressing station in action. (Bundesarchiv)

off the action and some of its half-tracks are driving eastwards; they could not be pressured into remaining any longer.'[12]

So far as the troops on the ground were concerned it was finished. Most of their commanders had perished. But still that night orders were given and further reconnaissance information passed on to continue the attack the following day. Nobody felt confident about its outcome.

Maintaining the pressure.
23 September . . .

On the western side of the corridor Lieutenant-Colonel von der Heydte's

Fallschirmjaeger Regiment 6 was to pick up the gauntlet now dropped by the virtually annihilated Kampfgruppe Huber. His exhausted soldiers had arrived too late to meet the attack deadline of the day before. Companies began arriving in the forming-up place east of Boxtel. Von der Heydte's knowledge of the situation was sketchy: American paratroopers had given up Schijndel and had established a blocking position either side of Eerde.

Fallschirmjaeger Regiment 6 was directed to attack the American positions south of the Veghel bridge again, this time advancing from Boxtel astride the Boxtel-Coch railway line. The aim was to seize the Veghel bridge, and cut off the Americans in Nijmegen from those in Eindhoven.

Von der Heydte was later to confide that 'he went about the execution of the task given to [his] regiment with little hope of success'. Already critical of the tasks given to his men by High Command, this particular situation seemed to promise no less a débâcle than that already endured in the Neerpelt bridgehead. As far as the Regimental Commander was concerned, 'the training and combat experience of the troops were inadequate to meet the requirements of such an attack'. His troops were 'physically fatigued because of two long night marches and would really have required some rest before any attack'. The chain of command was illogical, in that he was tactically controlled by 85 Division – the Kampfgruppe Chill – but logistically supplied by Poppe's 59 Division. Moreover, his regiment had been required to give up a battalion to 245 Division, and in its place had received Finzel's 1st Battalion of Fallschirmjaeger Regiment 2 – a unit whose capabilities he considered unimpressive:

'A battalion whose combat-
effectiveness was even lower than that
of the Regiment and whose
commanders were very bad. It also left
a lot to be desired as far as discipline
was concerned, and was apt to take
liberties, to go looting and commit
offences against the civilian
population.'[13]

Von der Heydte's comments were those of an uncompromising professional who had already fought campaigns in France, Crete, Tunisia, Russia and Normandy. There were some veterans in Finzel's battalion. But Germany, already bled white by casualties, could no longer call upon the quality of manpower that had served her so well in the past. The attack had to go ahead immediately to ensure co-ordination with the anticipated armoured attack by Walther on the other side of the corridor. As soon as Fallschirmjaeger Regiment 6 arrived in Boxtel, companies were to be launched straight into the attack following a hasty form-up. 'H' hour was to be 0700.

On the other side of the corridor there was still no contact with the Kampfgruppe Walther, and, therefore, no chance of co-operation. A night attack on Veghel failed, 'with painful losses', according to Major Schacht Walther's Chief of Staff. There were worries concerning their open right flank. A successful continuation of the attack on the next day, 23 September, was dependent upon the arrival of the original force, delayed in another sector – the Fallschirmjaeger Battalion Kerutt, Segler's SS battalion and Roestel's SS tank-destroyers.

Dawn brought with it better weather and Allied air attacks. Panzer Brigade 107 downed a number of aircraft. Attacks alternated with counter-attacks in front of the bitterly contested village of Veghel, supported by strong artillery strikes from both sides, but no decisive change in the situation was achieved. The advance parties of the missing battalions turned up at 1200, but main bodies could not be expected to arrive until later in the afternoon. Any further major attack against Veghel would have to wait until then.

With assaults temporarily suspended in the east, the impetus swung again to the western side of the corridor. Unsynchronised with the Kampfgruppe Walther's effort, von der Heydte's regiment was reluctantly obliged to pursue a solo attack with little or no hope of assistance. The wearisome march had taken its toll. Companies began arriving in the forming-up place east of Boxtel separated by long intervals. Time was required to reassert control before the hasty attack could begin. With no opportunity for anything other than a hasty visual reconnaissance, battalions were shepherded forward. Well aware of the likely reception, the Fallschirmjaeger resolutely advanced.

It was not long before they were in

difficulties. The 1st Battalion to the right of the Boxtel-Coch railway line quickly cleared some ragged scrub before emerging into an open plain which, von der Heydte observed, 'hardly offered any cover'. Finzel's battalion was, however, stumbling through 'bush-covered terrain where observation was very limited'. By about 1200 the right-hand battalion was stalled by tightening American resistance along a wood line south-east of Schijndel. Having made good progress across the plain, they were ahead of Finzel's supporting battalion. Small arms fire popped and snapped, echoing eerily through the woods. The vicious crack and thump of returning fire unnerved the Fallschirmjaeger, as they attempted in ragged lines to rush through small clearings to reach the shelter of trees beyond, supported by noisy rapid-firing spandau machine guns. Shouts and screams, punctuated by the metallic crump of hand-grenades, signified the storming of isolated American positions. These signatures were the only means, aside from shouted snippets of information, by which hard-pressed commanders could monitor progress. As prisoners were brought back, von der Heydte realised he was up against '101 Airborne troops':

'Heavy weapons made hardly any appearance at all on the Allied side during the course of this defensive battle; quite the opposite. The defence seemed to rely, at least according to impressions gained by the Fallschirmjaeger, mainly upon small arms fire directed from excellently camouflaged pockets of resistance.'

Von der Heydte, located with the forward right-hand battalion, realised that 'the attack was hopelessly stalled, and that it would be impossible to seize and retain Eerde, much less the Veghel bridge, with the forces already committed'. Finzel's battalion on the left, having been totally disorientated by the thick scrub on its side of the railway line, 'got lost and strayed into the sector of the right-hand battalion'. Assailed further by Americans on its flank as it turned, 'it also got stalled just to the west of Eerde'. The situation was hopeless. Von der Heydte, doubting from the start that he would reach his objective, decided enough was enough. 'The losses among the attackers' he declared, 'were considerable.' Once again it was demonstrated that poorly trained and hastily inserted reserves were no match for the veteran American paratroopers in close-quarter fighting over difficult terrain. Commanders now attempted to unravel the confusion. Finzel's battalion regrouped and was moved back into its original sector. Von der Heydte stopped the attack and ordered his men to dig in along the line they had reached.[14]

The commander of Fallschirmjaeger Regiment 6 was reacting to realities which his higher command had yet to grasp. Colonel Walther's armoured punch, even with surprise and local superiority, had failed to cut the corridor decisively for anything more than 36 hours. Huber's Kampfgruppe had been cut to pieces; only the tank-destroyers got back. At midday General Reinhard, the commander of LXXXVIII Corps, discussed the Veghel situation with Generals Chill and Poppe at 59 Division's headquarters. The thrust had quite obviously failed. Reinhard enquired (according to his unit diary) 'whether the operation could still be carried out'. No real discussion was required for the response, so further direction was requested from Fifteenth Army. The war diary reveals:

'The Chief of Staff asked the Chief of Staff 15th Army General Hoffmann whether the operation ought to still go ahead. The Chief of Staff's response was "if the Field Marshal has ordered the attack then it should still happen".'[15]

'Lying in ditches by the roadside were scores of drivers and infantry soldiers anxiously scanning the huge clouds of black bulbous smoke rising in the skies above Veghel. (Imperial War Museum)

It was wishful thinking. Lieutenant-Colonel von der Heydte had already correctly deduced the key deficiency. He was later to write:

'During the attack by Parachute Regiment 6 there was nothing to be noticed of the allegedly simultaneous attack at the Veghel bridge by German units coming from the Maas. No sound of battle nor any appreciable relief could be detected. As this armoured attack was launched from another army's sector – from that of the Fallschirmjaeger Army – there was no way of establishing contact with the attacking armoured troops; the Regiment was never told if this attack had been launched at all and what its results were.'[16]

. . . Time was running out. 43 Infantry Division took 48 hours to negotiate 40 miles of 'Hell's Highway'. Medics tend the wounded. Still no progress. (Imperial War Museum)

It appeared that lives had been ungenerously squandered. But south of Veghel Allied trucks waited, parked nose to tail, jammed by the deadlock to the north. Lying in ditches by the roadside were scores of drivers and infantry soldiers, anxiously scanning the huge clouds of black bulbous smoke rising in the skies above Veghel. Detonations and the sounds of battle could be clearly heard. Trucks loaded with American paratroopers and jeep-borne anti-tank crews wove in and out of the myriad of parked vehicles driving towards the sound of gun fire ahead. There was an infectious feeling of crisis in the air. The corridor was cut. Infantry were needed well forward if they were ever to relieve the British paratroopers trapped at Oosterbeek. It took 43 Infantry Division 48 hours to negotiate 40 miles of 'Hell's Highway'.

Time was running out for both sides.

CHAPTER XXIII

The Investment of Oosterbeek

The pause to hand over wounded really emphasised what a nonsense war is.

SS-Corporal

The siege, 22–24 September . . .

'The 22nd September began with brilliant sunshine. The surrounding terrain offered a bleak view with the debris of battle, dead soldiers and damaged equipment scattered around.'[1]

This was the view observed by Herbert Kessler from the parapet of his trench. He was a young NCO in the 'Worrowski' Battalion of the Hermann Goering Regiment. It was a scene familiar now on all sides of the cauldron. The British, their backs to the lower Rhine, had been invested from three directions. To the west the Kampfgruppe von Tettau occupied a line from the gasworks through Sonnenberg, and Ommershof through to KP87 on the Ede-Arnhem railway line.[2] Pressing down from the north was the Kampfgruppe Bruhns, a Wehrmacht Battalion 'Junghan', and elements of the SS-Kampfgruppe Krafft, now fighting in houses south of the railway line. To the east was the Kampfgruppe 9SS Hohenstaufen who had reached a north–south line in the area of the Oosterbeek crossroads next to the Vreewijk and Schoonard hotels. Field Marshal Model had until now regarded the Arnhem–Oosterbeek battle as a 'side-show'. The British division had clearly overreached itself, was surrounded, and would be reduced in time. Its importance paled into insignificance compared to the crisis in the south, heightened by the fall of Nijmegen and the Allied advance beyond the Waal, and exacerbated by Model's inability to cut the airborne corridor effectively for an appreciable length of time. The Polish landings had come as a shock for those battling to reduce the Oosterbeek perimeter, and would clearly delay its collapse. Bittrich's corps order to SS-Lieutenant Colonel Harzer succinctly stated the objectives and problems he wanted resolved on 22 September:

'The 9SS Panzer Division Kampfgruppe is immediately to mount concentric attacks against the remainder of First British Airborne Division, and annihilate them as soon as possible.

'The Sperrverband Harzer is to operate offensively from its blocking positions, and above all prevent a link-up with those elements of First British Airborne Division north of the river. It is particularly important that the remaining British forces north of the river Rhine are quickly destroyed, and the enemy bridgehead there cleared.'[3]

The attacks began at 0900 hours. SS-Colonel Lippert directed the assaults from his regimental headquarters in the West. Helle's Dutch SS battalion began advancing

'The surrounding terrain offered a bleak view with the debris of battle, dead soldiers and damaged equipment scattered around.'

left and forward of the Kourde Herberg crossroads; the SS Battalions 'Shulz' and 'Eberwein' attacked in the centre, along and south of the Wageningen-Oosterbeek road. Worrowski's Hermann Goering Battalion moved along the right, parallel to the lower Rhine. *Schwerpunkt* was to be provided by Eberwein, who was tasked to shift in a south-easterly direction and cut through to the river. But he made 'only slow progress', as the unit diary relates, 'in the close forest terrain, and against dogged enemy resistance'.[4] Helle's Dutch SS battalion 'suffered very high losses'. Having now stretched everybody's patience with its incompetent performance, it was disbanded on SS-General Rauter's orders and its survivors integrated within Eberwein's bat-

talion. SS-Colonel Lippert laconically commented: 'The commander Helle was not a field officer of any experience, and had little idea of his own situation, never mind that of the enemy. I had therefore to relieve him of his command.'[5] By dusk all attacks had stalled.

It was reported, by contrast, that the 9SS, also attempting to reach the gasworks from the opposite side of the pocket, was 'making good progress'.[6] Any progress could be graced with such a term in the bitter street fighting now raging around the perimeter. Four Kampfgruppen were assaulting from the east. SS-Lieutenant-Colonel Spindler's group was immediately to the right of Utrechtseweg, upon which Moeller's SS Engineer Battalion 9 was still battling. Left of them, and attempting to clear the houses down to the lower Rhine block by block, was the SS-Kampfgruppe von Allworden. Moving along the river side itself towards the Oosterbeek-Laag church was the SS-Kampfgruppe Harder. The day's attack objective was the Hotel Hartenstein, whose true significance as the headquarters of 1st British Airborne Division had yet to be realised. Little progress was in reality being achieved. SS-Corporal Wolfgang Dombrowski, fighting with Moeller on Utrechtseweg, said:

'Our front line stabilised at the crossroads [by the two dressing stations]. We remained lying on this line virtually until the end of the battle. The focus of pressure moved both to our left and right, but never with us again.'

Pressure was none the less maintained until darkness. Soldiers felt a turning point was approaching. Harzer's battle tactics now became apparent. By day he ordered ceaseless attacks, while by night heavy weapons shelled the pocket. Eventually, he felt he could batter the British into submission. Dombrowski sensed some progress:

'We achieved much success with our mortars. Most prisoners claimed the "whump-whump-whump" of the "moaning minnies" [Nebelwerfers] was their most frightening experience. Many of them emerged from cellars with their nerves shot to pieces.'[7]

By the evening of the 22nd Harzer assessed that the pocket had been reduced to an area of two square kilometres.

During the night movement was detected on both banks of the river as the Poles attempted to ferry reinforcements into the perimeter. Lippert reported an incursion by the gasworks which was 'repulsed by the

SS-Corporal Dombrowski reported upon the effect that Nebelwerfer fire had upon prisoners: 'Many of them emerged from cellars with their nerves shot to pieces.'

fire of our heavy weapons'. Ominously, at 1730, the first sightings of enemy vehicles in the Driel area were passed on, adding to the incentive to get the job done as quickly as possible. Flares and heavy machine gun fire signalled activity observed from the 9SS sector. Nickmann's SS-Werfer-Gruppe quickly straddled both banks, sinking some Polish dinghies in the process.[8]

The task for 23 September remained the same. Bittrich summoned General von Tettau to Harzer's command post where he confirmed his order for 'an all-out attack along the whole front on the 23rd at 0800 hours'.[9] But the situation the following day simply mirrored the stalemate of the preceding days. Von Tettau commented that 'the enemy had established a strongpoint type of defence in the numerous villas and parks of Oosterbeek. Each of these pockets of resistance had to be stormed and taken out in close-fought actions.' There was a

SS-Junker Rolf Lindemann reported: 'I saw a lot of prisoners. We were taking whole companies, almost complete with their officers and NCOs'.

price to be paid, because 'for units with little training, this method of fighting leads to high losses and is time-consuming'. Little could be achieved, the General summarised 'apart from slowly wearing down the enemy'. Prisoners taken numbered 145, including 10 officers, but 'no major progress was made on that day'.[10] Although there was nothing dramatic to report, the strain was beginning to tell upon the hard-pressed British forces. SS-Junker Rolf Lindemann, fighting with the battalion 'Oelkers' (with Eberwein), saw a slightly different picture at soldier level:

'I saw a lot of prisoners. We were taking whole companies, almost complete with their officers and NCOs. After they had surrendered these men were always surprised to see so few Germans, claiming that if they had been aware of the true situation, they would have fought on!'[11]

The break in the weather on 23 September brought with it a degree of assistance for the Red Devils. Typhoons of the 2nd Allied Tactical Air Force and P47s of the Eighth Air Force struck German positions all along the airborne corridor leading up to, and particularly around, the Oosterbeek perimeter. Wincing beneath this aerial onslaught were Lieutenant Martin's Luftwaffe infantry from Fliegerhorst Battalion 3, who were moving into positions near the lower Rhine. He recorded in his diary:

'23 September. Day begins with attack by low-flying airplanes. One killed and six wounded. Being hit by mortar and heavy machine gun fire. Battalion arrives 1720. Hundreds of enemy planes drop coloured parachutes. First really heavy aerial attack begins. Six planes knocked down. AA gun jams and drops out. Heavy machine gun is out. One killed and three wounded. We'll move into positions on the river bank tonight. Factory across the river has been hit and is burning. Slept in the "Jaghuis". Very restless.'[12]

The Luftwaffe also appeared. Captain Willi Weber of 213 Nachrichten (Signals) Regiment, who had distinguished himself on the first day of the landings by attacking landing-zone 'S' with a scratch-built force of signallers, was running the FLIVO-Luftwaffe forward air control net – in Harzer's command post on 23 September. At about 0800 he took two fighter 'Gruppen' from Jagdgeschwader (fighter squadrons) 2 and 26, led by a Captain Eder, under control. Using his call sign, 'Teerose II', he directed Eder – Aster-Anton – to attack the Poles immediately south of the lower Rhine. A record of the subsequent sortie was kept in the radio log. It began with Weber directing Eder on to the correct target:

'You are attacking Elst. Elst is blue [i.e. friendly]. Attack Driel. Between Driel and the lower Rhine, two small ponds – Hullo Victor?'

Captain Eder redirected his attacking aircraft, speaking through his intercom to the pilots of II Jagdgeschwader 26:

'We are to attack Driel, between Driel and the lower Rhine – two small ponds.'

After the strafing run was complete, Eder's squadron was set upon by Allied aircraft. Weber, seeing the threat, radioed:

'Teerose to Aster-Anton – a new target to attack. Swarms of bandits over the Zuider-Zee.'

Eder relayed the warning to all his aircraft:

'New target. Swarms of aircraft over the Zuider-Zee.'

At this point one of Jagdgeschwader 26's pilots – 'Aster 53' – declared to his leader that he had 'a mechanical problem'. Eder's response, somewhat sarcastic, produced whoops from those listening and anxious for the support on the ground:

'You've filled your trousers! Ram them and then climb out. After that then you can say you've got a mechanical problem.'[13]

Some of Harzer's staff in the command post may have been appreciative of the Luftwaffe's efforts but the majority of the German front-line soldiers were not. SS-Corporal Dombrowski made no distinctions for either side: 'As soon as we heard an aircraft, everyone would immediately dive into a ditch.'

Harzer's SS forces pressed remorselessly from the east, but only achieved 'small gains' on 23 September. Spindler's battle group was ordered to shift its *Schwerpunkt* leftwards toward the lower Rhine to cut the beleaguered British off from the river, and break through and establish contact with von Tettau's forces along the river bank on the other side of the pocket. Moeller's SS-Kampfgruppe to the right of him, enjoying a comparative lull, grimaced at the lot of their unfortunate comrades. SS-Captain Moeller remembers that:

'. . . outside, further to the left, the battle raged on unabated, especially near the banks of the Rhine. The noise of battle carried all the way to us. There were gun reports and impacts; when they were further away they sounded dull, but very often they were damn close, leaving the broken windows vibrating. The hectic clatter of machine guns and the roar of hand-grenades gave testimony to the bitter fighting, as German battle groups tried to cut off the enemy from the banks of the Rhine.'[14]

At 1345 on 23 September, von Tettau's headquarters received reports of 'enemy armoured reconnaissance vehicles on the southern bank of the lower Rhine at the Wageningen ferry'. In addition, 'motorised enemy reconnaissance' was observed, 'on the dyke road south of the lower Rhine between Driel and Lakemond'.[15] It could only be assumed that these forces were from Nijmegen. XXX Corps had, therefore, at least achieved a ground link-up with the Poles. What were the implications?

Von Tettau had already secured his rear areas as a precaution against a possible breakthrough from Nijmegen. Along the line of the Waal and 'canal sector', newly arrived reinforcements, suitable for defence only in practical terms, were fed into the line. Lieutenant-Colonel Haenisch control-led a battle group consisting of Fliegerhorst Battalion 2 under Major Liebsch, and Coastal Fortress Battalion 1409 from a newly established command post in Lien-den. The Regiment 'Knoche', previously tasked to secure the rear areas against further airborne attacks, was moved into potential blocking and security positions

along the lower Rhine. His Kampfgruppe consisted now of Sicherungs Regiment 26, Fortress Machine Gun Battalion 30, and Merkens' Fliegerhorst Battalion 3 – in which Lieutenant Martin was serving – and all the scattered air-defence platoons now operating in the area. Martin's men were exhausted. They had been marched and counter-marched constantly under enemy pressure, with seemingly no clear directive on where to go. Casualties as a result were not being properly looked after. He wrote:

'24 September. Planes attack at 0900. We have to move into position on the Rhine by day by order of General Tettau – without consideration for the wounded. Major Merkens inspects positions. Planes attack reserve positions. Our anti-tank gun is supposed to sink boats on the opposite side of the river. Captain Schaarschmidt is sick.'[16]

During the previous evening a brigade from the British 43rd Infantry Division had fought into the outskirts of Elst, while another brigade had established itself in the Driel area. Another 150 Polish para-troopers crossed into the cauldron. But the Germans still continued to dominate the northern bank. Without reinforcements the Oosterbeek perimeter must collapse.

Chivalry – and what to do with the wounded?

The battle of Arnhem has often been refer-red to as a chivalrous engagement. Intensive street fighting is, however, rarely con-ducted in such a manner. Evidence suggests that excesses were committed in the heat of battle by both sides. Throughout the bitter fighting that characterised MARKET-GARDEN, Allied soldiers became increas-ingly incensed at the conduct of a foe who fought so tenaciously when his cause was so clearly lost. SS-Corporal Wolfgang Dombrowski echoed the opinion of his comrades in the Hohenstaufen and Frundsberg divisions:

'These divisions were superbly trained. We had constantly fought in rear-guards since Hill 112 in Caen. After a brief pause we were stuck into the battle of Arnhem – again unprepared. We wanted this battle over as quickly as possible so that we could get back to Germany. The bottom line was, should we be unsuccesful, the Allies would be on German soil. We fought bitterly to resist this.'[17]

The storming of Nijmegen had been hard fought. Little mercy was shown or expected from those conducting a last-ditch defence. SS-Lieutenant Richter complained to Army Group B on 22 and 23 September that German wounded had been murdered 'in a bestial fashion' by American soldiers, 'probably the 82nd Airborne Division', with pistols and knives, and that 'Dutch women had taken part, with some of the wounded being thrown into the Waal river'.[18] Whether substantiated or not, the reports were believed and would inevitably have an impact upon the character of subsequent fighting.

Any Dutch assistance rendered the Allies was matched by the calculated brutality of the occupying German authorities. Dutch resistance fighters captured fighting openly as volunteer irregulars, wearing orange armbands, alongside Allied regular forces, were executed out of hand. This happened when the Arnhem bridge was retaken from Frost, and on occasions in Oosterbeek. SS-Captain Krafft, the commander of SS-Panzer-grenadier Depot and Reserve Battalion 16, had no illusions about whose side the civilians were on. His post-combat report observed that:

'. . . a further difficulty for us is the attitude of the civilian population. They will surely side with the enemy and will be particularly dangerous on the appearance of the enemy in the battalion's rear. As a matter of fact we did have some trouble with Dutch terrorists about two to three hundred metres from the battalion's original defence position. They were suitably dealt with!'[19]

Even after the battle, Lieutenant-Colonel Fritz Fullriede of the Hermann Goering Training Regiment took part in the punitive sacking of the Dutch village of Putten, after a number of German soldiers had been killed by partisans. Eight civilians were indiscriminately shot and the village razed to the ground. All the women and children were evacuated and the male population transported as forced labour to the Reich.[20]

In any case, the SS units fighting in Oosterbeek were hardened to excesses. Six months earlier at Tarnopol in Russia 34 soldiers from the 9SS captured in a Soviet counter-attack were found bound and gruesomely mutilated by their Soviet captors after the position was retaken. Why should Oosterbeek be any different? Wolfgang Dombrowski remembers:

'The battle for Arnhem was something completely new for us. We were used to dealing with Russian "human wave" attacks where there was no regard for human life. Hand-to-hand fighting was normally required to stop the fourth or fifth wave because we had run out of ammunition. The Americans had been our main opponents in Normandy. Their aircraft had often shot up medical columns. We had fought against the Poles at Falaise and they had been brutal. The British were an unknown quantity.'[21]

But it appeared that the British were different. Lieutenant Joseph Enthammer, who had been held captive near the Arnhem bridge, claimed:

'We had no hatred for the English, nor the French nor Americans – but we certainly did for the Russians. That was not only my view, but also that of many other German soldiers.'[22]

Despite the furious fighting, a sense of genuine respect did slowly appear to develop. SS-Junker Rolf Lindemann, fighting with Lippert's Kampfgruppe on the west side of the perimeter, believed 'there was no hatred or "enemy" feeling on our side'. Before this he had fought near Leningrad in Russia:

'There it was absolutely different. Even medics with or without weapons and hospitals were fired at. We hated the Russians, and the French because we had always been at war with them. But not the British.'

Of all the European nations, it appeared the only country with some similarities of race and custom, and a degree of kindred spirit, were the British. 'Nobody,' Lindemann emphasised, 'felt they were an enemy to the British, and I think it was the same on their side.' It was certainly unlike anything they had experienced in Russia. Lindemann told of a time where:

'. . . one of our ambulances which had got lost was stopped by British troops. The driver thought his number was up! A British officer enquired "would he be so kind as to take a seriously wounded British officer to hospital?" The British even put the driver on the correct route and rewarded him with a gold watch for his trouble!'[23]

With the introduction of the Poles into the cauldron, the nature of the fighting changed perceptibly again. SS-Captain Moeller, fighting on the Utrechtseweg, noticed that the previous restraint accorded to allow the recovery of wounded and dead 'was to change rather drastically on 23 September when a Polish unit was committed to the fighting opposite Steinhart, my first company'. SS-Corporal Dombrowski, in the same unit, bitingly remarked:

'As far as the Poles were concerned you could forget fairness. I remember the case of a wounded *Reichsarbeitsdienst* man, a machine gunner from a labour battalion, unable to fire. We waved a white flag and two stretcher bearers went forward to pick him up. Immediately they were fired upon, and they disappeared ashen-faced into a house. "What's the matter with them!" they shrieked. "Have they lost their nerve! It was all right to pick them up until now." The Poles continued sniping at the wounded man and kept the medics at bay until he was dead. He had fallen behind a wall, and with the Poles firing at us through the loopholes of their house, he couldn't be reached.'

Fighting continued, devoid of compassion. 'You didn't take any chances with the Poles,' Dombrowski confided.

'The approach was made with boots wrapped in rags to deaden the noise. Once the house was surrounded hand-grenades would go in from all sides until they had had enough.'[24]

The conduct of the Poles should be seen in the context of what their homeland had been subjected to by the German occupation. As Moeller commented, 'That was the grimace of the East. The distorted mask of hatred and sheer violence which would never be willing to display fairness!'

Chivalry aside, the few available dressing stations in Oosterbeek were now overflowing with seriously wounded British and German soldiers. Those situated inside the British perimeter lacked medicines and water. All the rooms in the Hotel Schoonard were completely full with casualties. Unofficial truces produced pauses in the fighting which enabled even more broken bodies to be collected, until corridors and hallways were overflowing too. On 22 September, SS-Lieutenant Colonel Harzer, at last moved by the appalling plight of the wounded, ordered his senior divisional doctor SS-Captain Dr Egon Skalka to discuss the issue with his opposite British number Colonel Warrack. They were to investigate the possibility of delivering some of the paratrooper wounded into German care. As the pocket progressively shrank, it became impossible to avoid hitting the dressing stations. An artillery shell struck the Hotel Tafelberg in Oosterbeek, causing further casualties among the wounded awaiting attention. Colonel Warrack, meanwhile, thanked the Germans for their offer and conferred with his divisional commander.

Selected truces were announced for certain periods in particular sectors to allow for the recovery of the wounded. Rolf Lindemann, the SS-Junker with Lippert's Regiment on the west side of the perimeter, recalls:

'Information was simply given to cease firing at 1200 and carry on at 1300. Both sides respected this. You could even go for a walk during this period and nobody would disturb you.'[25]

Although the St Elizabeth's Hospital now lay behind German lines, it was still run by

SS-Captain Dr Egon Skalka, senior doctor in the 9SS Hohenstaufen, negotiated the evacuation of the British wounded. He later spent two years in a British POW camp. (Fuerbringer Collection)

its British staff, watched over by German guards. Dr Skalka resupplied it with medicines and supplies, and provided any further support which was requested. Blood plasma, dropped by the RAF resupply aircraft, ironically at terrible cost, was also passed on to the British wounded in the hospital.

SS-Corporal Paul Mueller was a 19-year-old section commander in the Kampfgruppe Spindler, severely wounded by a hand-grenade in the bloody fighting alongside the Rhine as 1 PARA had attempted to reach Frost at the bridge. His experience was typical of many German wounded. First of all he had to make his own way back to the nearest aid post under fire from the British:

> 'While I was running I really felt all my injuries. My left arm hurt so much with every pace that I stuck it under my belt and held it in place with my other hand to keep it from dangling around. Warm blood was running into my ears and mouth and also down my body into my boots.'

He had to find the command post. Upon reaching it he fainted from loss of blood. From here a medical orderly picked him up in a commandeered Dutch civilian car. He 'managed to squeeze inside,' he said, with another severely wounded section commander. Negotiating the rubble and debris, the car eventually reached the aid post, which was a small shop whose front display window had been blown in. 'There, everything started to spin again.' One of the medics caught him and placed him in a chair. 'He wanted to cut off my field jacket, which I tried to prevent, because I told him all my papers were in there.' Mueller's concern was not as trivial as it appeared. Without them he might either be suspected of desertion or, equally serious, be redrafted into a strange unit where he would be an outsider. 'But then,' he recalls, 'I passed out for good.'[26]

Lieutenant Joseph Enthammer, who had been held captive by Frost's men near the bridge for four days, was all too aware of the problem. After being rescued by the SS, he remained with his unit, despite a grenade leg wound, until they reached Emmerich. By then, however, the wound had become so seriously infected that he was transferred to a hospital train which took him to Limburg an der Lahn. He was a reluctant patient:

> 'I did not want to remain in the hospital and exercised my right as walking wounded to get out after

treatment. Otherwise I would have been sent to a *Feldersatz* or Field Replacement battalion, and I wanted to stay with my unit.'

But until he could achieve this release, he was surrounded by strangers. Whilst awaiting further care, two British POWs were brought in, one of whom was the paratrooper corporal who had looked after him in the Arnhem cellar. This was the ultimate irony; surrounded by his own countrymen who were nevertheless strangers, the delighted officer remembers:

> 'We greeted each other with pleasure, overjoyed that the other had survived the hell of that place. The *Oberstabsartz* [senior doctor] was far from impressed and rounded on me for my conduct. When I explained the circumstances that had led to our special relationship he relented and excused himself. I wrote down the corporal's name and address but lost it later in the war. I would still like to meet him again.'[27]

When SS-Corporal Paul Mueller woke up he was in Apeldoorn hospital. 'I was lying on a mattress placed on the floor of a long hallway,' he recalled, 'with countless other wounded soldiers.' He had been asleep for eight days. Sitting in front of him on a chair was a wounded section commander who came from his same platoon, who 'did not recognise me when I spoke to him. He only knew me by my voice when I told him my name. I must have looked terrible with all the blood.'

Mueller was still in a twilight world of shock and pain. Over a week had passed by and he still had not been operated upon. 'In the meantime,' he noticed, 'a comrade next to me had died of an abdominal wound.' He passed out again, and woke up this time in a church among many other wounded, lying at last on wooden beds. 'The blood-soaked clothes which I was still wearing were beginning to stink.' When finally he was carried through a park to an operating room, it transpired that the surgeon who had been working non-stop for 24 hours had left to get some rest. Eventually, another came and operated on him. Mueller, like all German wounded, was fearfully aware that field doctors tended to believe that it was only worth while in human terms to administer blood and plasma to seriously injured soldiers because they were less likely to return to active service. All Mueller could remember before passing out was the doctor's caustic comment to a nurse that 'this chap is drinking up all our ether'. After the operation he remained in a hallway marooned with all the other hopeless cases until, thankfully, he was moved to a general ward containing the other wounded. Survival was, for the first time, a possibility.

The next step was transference to a hospital train. 'I had a nice place by the window,' he remembers. At 2000 hours the train pulled out under the protective cover of darkness; he was going home to Germany. Soon, however, he 'was awakened unpleasantly by some jerking and jolting'. The train had been derailed 'and our coach had an awful list'. Wounded patients were painstakingly transferred from the derailed coaches and spread in the corridors of those remaining. A new locomotive began shunting them rearwards. This, too, was blown up, 'probably by mines', and this was not all:

'Simultaneously our train came under a hail of bullets. Since ours was a red cross train, there were no weapons inside, and we were all helpless.'

Two flat rail cars mounting anti-aircraft guns puffed up with another locomotive and beat off the partisans. But, as Mueller recalled, 'we were in a real mouse-trap'. There were destroyed rails to both their front and rear. Their discomfort continued:

'There was beautiful sunshine throughout the day, and enemy fighter bombers dived down on our train countless times. It was by no means a pleasant feeling. Our medics came through the coaches and told us, especially the lightly wounded, not to leave the train under any circumstances, as the pilots may get a false impression and attack the train after all. The pilots were more decent than the partisans, and they flew off again every time without firing.'

It took until 30 September to get across the Rhine. The following day the train divided and transported Mueller to a field hospital in southern Germany, thirteen days from the time he had first staggered into his company aid post.[28]

Back in the Oosterbeek perimeter further negotiations, this time cleared by Bittrich the IISS Corps commander, led to the declaration of a two-hour cease-fire to come into effect at 1500 hours on 24 September. During this period, up to 1,200 wounded British POWs were taken out of the pocket and transported to German hospitals. It was not easy to confine the fighting to areas outside the truce, because, as SS-Corporal Dombrowki saw, 'the truce was only valid within this corridor; fighting still carried on around it'. The irony of the situation was not lost on the SS Engineers, Dombrowski remarked:

'The pause to hand over the wounded really emphasises what a nonsense war is. We all checked our watches and it became quiet, the British paras came out. Words were exchanged and a few cigarettes thrown across. We had plenty to offer as many of their supplies had landed in our lines. I looked at them and they looked at us and I thought we have never seen each other before, had nothing against them, nor they against us. But then it will start up again.'

A final pull on a cigarette, a whimsical look at the other side, then a fresh outbreak of firing would drive the last reluctant groups into cover. SS-Captain Moeller, witnessing the same scene, found that:

'. . . it was deeply moving for all concerned to see how a seemingly endless column of wounded was taken through the Utrechtseweg by shuttle to the St Elizabeth's Hospital which was located on the edge of Arnhem, as well as to other smaller dressing stations and field hospitals. Thus the wounded and mangled people could receive qualified treatment . . . A Dutchman asked me, "Why do you wage war? Is it really necessary?".'[29]

A rhetorical question because, as Dombrowski observed,

'. . . ten minutes before the end of the truce everybody would disappear. Then, depending on the situation, it would slowly start up – or more suddenly as a German attack went in.'[30]

Tanks and flame-throwers . . .

Clanking and thumping, the rail flat cars came to a final squeaking halt in the railway siding in Zevenar and Elten during the night of 23–24 September. Climbing over dimly-lit hulls, panzer crews began removing foliage and camouflage netting. Following a harsh whirr, Porsche engines burst into

throaty, smoky life. The complicated task of unloading the 60-ton steel Tiger IIs across ramps began and continued throughout the night hours; whirring chains clattered through rings and wedges were knocked loose. Schwere Abteilung 506, the heavy Tiger tank battalion, had arrived. By early morning on 24 September Major Lange's 45 Panzer Mark VI 'King Tigers' were marshalled into columns, and noisily and jerkily set off towards their various forming-up points. Two companies – 30 tanks in all – were despatched to the 10SS in the Elst area, where they leaguered up in a small wood three kilometres north of Elten. The remaining 'Hummel' heavy assault company of 15 Tiger IIs was sent to the 9SS in Oosterbeek. Harzer, aware of the limitations imposed by the railway line and forests north of the pocket, attached them to the Kampfgruppe Spindler operating against the east side of the perimeter.

Tanks had proved to be of decisive value in halting the British attempts to relieve Frost at the bridge. They were less successful, however, in the advance through Oosterbeek. Von Tettau had already identified the underlying problem in his divisional order two days before. He angrily announced that:

'In the fighting over the last few days no less than six tanks have been knocked out due to misemployment by junior commanders, and a lack of accompanying infantry.'[31]

Panzer Company 224 was thereupon taken directly under divisional command; its surviving three tanks were attached to the most experienced troops in the Kampfgruppe – Lippert's SS Regiment – and 'held back only for special tasks'. All six of the destroyed tanks had been knocked out on a single day: two to anti-tank guns, two by mines, one severely damaged, and one other was simply missing. Lieutenant May, the company commander, was directed to explain his losses personally to von Tettau.[32] Lack of experience was the fundamental problem. Units had been flung into action never having worked together before, and the problems of infantry-tank co-operation were not being rectified. Similar mistakes were being sorted out on the eastern side of the perimeter between the 9SS and SP guns of Sturmgeschutz Brigade 280. The problem was further compounded by a shortage of radios.

Von Tettau sought to instill the combined infantry-tank teamwork required to crack this tough nut. Tanks, he said, 'were now only to operate with the battalions Schulz and Eberwein'. These two SS battalions contained the only veterans under command. Special tank protection squads were to be formed and armed with automatic Schmeisser machine pistols. Tanks were no longer to operate singly, but together in platoons accompanied by directly supporting infantry. Artillery forward observation teams were to be attached to these mixed companies 'to immediately identify and annihilate enemy anti-tank guns'. SP assault guns ought also to be used to protect their own tanks against this threat. Von Tettau was lecturing on the need to overcome enemy strongpoints by employing a mix of combined arms. 'Above all else,' he emphasised, 'success depends upon rapidly identifying enemy anti-tank weapons,' and then 'allocating tanks and heavy weapons to neutralise that particular point so that they may be overcome.'[33]

Similar problems were experienced in the 9SS sector. Darkness now attracted artillery fire inside the perimeter, while on the outside assault guns eerily clattered about in the darkness, changing position. They prowled like beasts of prey just beyond the perimeter. Brigade 280 was also paying the inevitable price for an insufficient regard for infantry protection and guidance. SPs, having trundled around by night in strange sectors forgoing liasion with their infantry colleagues, tended to occupy exposed positions in blissful ignorance, until they were picked off at first light by excellently camouflaged and sited British anti-tank guns. After 21 September, however, regrouping and reorganisations produced effectively balanced street-fighting teams which had a greater impact upon progress.

This progress was slow and losses were high. By 24 September Panzer Company 224 had lost all its eight converted French Renault tanks, Brigade 280 had three or four Sturmgeschutz III SPs destroyed, and the Herman Goering Regiment had at least two Panthers knocked out. Karl-Heinz Kracht's 'Mielke' tank company from Bielefeld lost three of eight tanks in Arnhem and a further two around Elst. Frost's battalion had claimed six tanks destroyed and a Tiger damaged around the Arnhem bridge. Losses are difficult to quantify because of the piecemeal and unrecorded committal of tank platoons sent into the fighting as they became available. Up to 50 per cent of those employed – more on the western side of the perimeter – had been lost up to this point.[34]

Lieutenant Hummel's 'King Tigers' began to make their presence felt at daybreak on 24 September. Protected by infantry, their 88mm guns began spectacularly to demolish British strongpoints. Although they produced a considerable psychological impact on the British side, they were far less effective than envisaged. These 68-ton steel colossi could barely negotiate the narrow winding streets of Oosterbeek. Tracks simply ripped off the top layer of cobblestones and sank beneath the level of the road. Turrets, restricted by the long 88mm gun, could hardly revolve. German expectancy turned to dismay as the first exploded in front of the elementary school at the bottom of Weverstraat, shrapnel scything across and scarring the entire front of the school building. This was not meant to

An SP gun knocked out on Benedendorpsweg in Oosterbeek. Up to 50 per cent of the German armour deployed up to 24 September was destroyed.

happen. The crew frantically baled out as the entire hull burst into a fiery violent conflagration. A mortar round had struck an air vent on the petrol tank.[35] Although virtually impregnable, the 'mobile bunkers' could be immobilised by PIAT anti-tank rounds, or gammon bombs cutting tracks or affixed to vital points by reckless but more nimble British paratroopers. Their effectiveness once again was dependent upon the quality of the accompanying infantry. Even in Elst, where they were attached to the 10SS, there were considerable problems – it was found the small canal bridges collapsed under their weight.

The investment of Oosterbeek was taking on a medieval character. Artillery fire tore into the once prosperous middle-class suburb. Special street-fighting teams had been

An assault gun changes position on Weverstraat near the Oosterbeek church. A dead British paratrooper lies in the foreground.

formed to scale strongpoints. Tank guns fulfilled the role of battering rams, breaking strongpoint walls, followed up by assault pioneers now armed with flame-throwers. Whatever the courage of the defender, few could withstand the pyschological horror and shock of attack by flame. Indeed, there was no effective antidote or physical defence to such an attack, apart from stalking and killing the flame-thrower operator. It was a decisive close-quarter weapon, so violent in its effect that operators, if captured, rarely survived surrender. The British had used it to reduce resistance on the Arnhem bridge. Now the roles had been reversed. Pionier Lehr Battalion 9 from Glogau had been flown into Deelen airport during the nights of 21 and 22 September. Flame-thrower teams were employed in concert with tanks and infantry against the stubborn British strongpoints. Gerald Lamarque, a platoon sergeant with the British 21 Independent (Pathfinder) Company fighting in the northern part of the perimeter against von Allworden's SS Panzerjaeger, has described the devastating impact of such an attack:

'A great ball of fire filled the whole of his vision, blotting out the houses and the sky and everything around him. He felt heat such as he had experienced only once before, when he had stood well back at the opening of a furnace. He felt his breath catch and dry in his lungs; he was flat on the bedroom floor, his hands clawing at the floorboards, his mouth open and his throat choking.

'. . . The torn-down curtains were burning where they had been flung in one corner of the room, and two armchairs were smouldering,

occasional flames darting like spiders across their brocade. The walls were seared, and the paint on the windowsill swelled and popped in soft bubbles. The two men were by the wall on the left.

'. . . What he had known of Roy Fraser was gone. Where his fair fastidious face had been was something beyond horror. It was impossible for Gorman to take in and appreciate what had been done to the other man. He simply looked at the smouldering smock, at the shrivelled veil round the neck, and at the hand, twisted and crooked like a chicken's claw, which groped and jerked on the chest.

'. . . The long broken succession of sobs had stopped, and out of the lipless cavity came a word repeated over and over again. "Please . . . please . . . please".'[36]

IISS Corps directed that the attack on the pocket for 25 September was to be an east–west thrust by the SS Kampfgruppe Harzer toward Hemelscheberg, to be met by a reciprocal attack by the SS-Battalion Oelkers from the west side 'with strong assault force operations to force contact' between the two. Local deception attacks supported by heavy fire were to come in from the north. 'H' hour was to be 0715. Von Tettau was even discussing the possible employment of 'Goliath' remote-controlled tanks with the commander of Panzer Company 224.[37] These caterpiller-tracked mines were packed with explosives and designed to be detonated inside enemy positions. The British, it was felt, could not take much more of this.

CHAPTER XXIV

The Final Cut: Koevering

The mission: first the railway bridge, then the road bridge remains.

Commander 15th Army

Prelude: the corridor, 23-24 September . . .

Blessed by genuinely favourable weather for the first time since 17 September, Allied airborne reinforcements began on 23 September to catch up on schedules. Even as fighting continued around Veghel, the 101 (US) Airborne Division final glider serials arrived. The division, joined also by its seaborne tail, was now complete. At around the same time General Gavin at Nijmegen received his 325th Glider Infantry Regiment, and the remainder of Sosobowski's (1st Battalion) of the Polish Brigade also flew in.

Depressing reports of further Allied reinforcements began to flow into various German higher command headquarters. The Kampfgruppe Walther observed additional airborne drops made between Vokel and Erp, and south of the Veghel-Erp road even as General Student was visiting their units in Gemert. Captain Scipa from 59 Division telephoned LXXXVIII Corps at 1725 and said that 120 gliders had descended in the Liempde area. At 2055 he confirmed his original report claiming that anti-aircraft fire had shot down two transports and eight gliders, with 25 prisoners taken. 'The mass of the aircraft' he advised 'appear to be east of a line between the Son heath and St Oedenrode.'[1] General Reinhard's response was immediate. He issued a Corps order stating that:

'Divisions are to implement draconian measures and be merciless in their quest to provide reserves again, even so-called stragglers are to be reformed in this role, under tight control.'

Colonels Boehmer and Dewald were immediately appointed the Kampfgruppe commanders of Tilberg and S'Hertogenbosch threatened by the latest developments, and tasked to enact the necessary counter-measures.

Field Marshal Model was becoming increasingly pessimistic with regard to the overall situation. 'The situation of Army Group B's northern wing' he reported on 24 September 'has continued to deteriorate.' All that they had achieved in one week's bitter fighting was 'merely to delay the enemy in achieving his strategic objective'. The renewed airlandings of the previous day, he felt, were 'bound to result in highly critical developments'. What was required was 'minimum reinforcements' of one infantry and one panzer division, a panzer brigade, two assault gun brigades, more infantry replacements and greater supplies of artillery ammunition.[2] He knew he would not get them.

The Germans were convinced the new landings were designed to alleviate their own pressure on Veghel. The Kampfgruppe Walther was simultaneously attacked by Allied armour along the Uden-Vokel-Boekel road, and south of Uden. Panzer Brigade 107 took the blow in its right flank.

But only a shell of German defenders still remained on 'Hell's Highway'. Despite the arrival of Colonel Walther's delayed SS-Battalions Segler and Roestel, the situation was past stabilising. The attack on Veghel was called off. By 1900 hours the Kampfgruppe Walther had retired just east of Gemert between Beek and Boekel. Its commander was becoming increasingly concerned by the subsidiary advance by the British VIII Corps to his rear. The corridor was now clear. As soon as tanks and bulldozers could nudge damaged vehicles aside, Allied traffic rolled once again on 'Hell's Highway'. By midnight on 23 September XXX Corps traffic was again passing over the Grave bridge. The corridor had been closed for 36 hours.

Field Marshal Model, recognising the limitations of the German response, decided to reorganise his command to produce a simpler and more effective arrangement. He drew an imaginary line along the western boundary of the Allied airborne corridor. All forces to the west of this line came under General von Zangen's 15th Army. Armed Forces Commander Netherlands and Wehrkreis VI were thereby relieved of their unorthodox tactical responsibilities. Student's First Fallschirmjaeger Army was assigned Bittrich's IISS Panzer Corps (including the division von Tettau), General Meindl's II Fallschirmjaeger Corps, von Obstfelder's LXXXVI Corps and the Corps Feldt. Student was now directed to execute the main effort against the Allied corridor with these forces. The problem, as ever, was where to find the manpower and tanks amongst these depleted formations to cut the corridor again.

They were not to come from the Kampfgruppe Walther, whose headquarters on 24 September in Bakel Post Office received some alarming news. Around midday the German exchange in Helmond Post Office reported that the Dutch postmaster in Deurne wished to talk to his colleague in Bakel. Colonel Walther's adjutant, who spoke fluent Dutch, answered the telephone, pretending to be a Dutch post official. His 'colleague' in Deurne asked him about the situation, information which the Germans knew was generally passed on to the Dutch resistance. He said his house was occupied by a British command post. This was disturbing news. Major Gerhard Schacht, Walther's Chief of Staff (who spoke English with an American accent), asked to speak to an American officer. Explaining he was 'Lieutenant Gordon' cut off from his parent unit, the 101 Division, he asked his British 'friend' for instructions. He was told when to expect a British armoured assault upon his headquarters in Bakel and 'expressed the hope that he would soon be able to shake hands with his American comrade'.

Regrettably, 'Lieutenant Gordon' was not able to report on the Bakel situation, because he was hiding in the cellar and could not speak Dutch. Becoming suspicious, the British officer challenged 'Gordon' to spell his name using the army phonetic alphabet. Understandably, he had problems with this, at which point the British officer in Deurne cursed and hung up.

Not to be outdone, the British staff in Deurne tried the same ruse. 'Hauptmann Schulz' of the 3rd Pionier Battalion telephoned Bakel and said he had seized Deurne in a counter-attack and requested Walther's support. A funny conversation ensued as, with the intent clear from the outset, the caller was gently teased. The information was as valuable as it was alarming. Colonel Walther was able to establish a security line screening Deurne in time to repulse the enemy's first offensive probes.[3]

Walther's Kampfgruppe was now in a vulnerable position, threatened by XXX Corps to the west in the corridor and by the British VIII Corps to his rear in Deurne.

LXXXVI Corps ordered him to disengage that night, a process that was completed by dawn on 25 September. He was required to thicken up a German blocking position in the Venlo area between Boxmeer and Oploo. Walther's headquarters moved to Venray. His departure essentially removed the German threat from the eastern side of the corridor south of Nijmegen. Losses had been considerable – up to 25 per cent of the Kampfgruppe infantry and 20 per cent – of its armour had been squandered during the abortive attacks on Veghel. The troops were exhausted.

Objective Veghel – again; 24 September . . .

As Colonel Walther's armoured force with accompanying infantry laboriously wound its way toward Venlo, ever-watchful for 'Jabos', the focus of activity on 24 September now switched to the west of the corridor. In the wake of the reorganisations enacted by Model the previous day, a renewal of the attack by Lieutenant-Colonel von der Heydte near Veghel was to be made under the auspices of 15th Army rather than Student's First Fallschirmjaeger Army. With supreme irony the German High Command was to launch an attack with scratch-built forces to secure an objective that a reinforced panzer brigade had taken 36 hours only to neutralise. All that was left were remnants of the Kampfgruppe Huber, together with the surviving Jagdpanther from the First Company of Tank-Destroyer Battalion 559. 59 Division provided an *ad hoc* group: the Battalion 'Jungwirth', consisting of a mixture of Fallschirmjaeger, stragglers and the 'baggage tail' of soldiers from Fusilier Regiment 1035. Chill's 85 Division provided Fallschirmjaeger Regiment 6, which also included Finzel's 1st Battalion Fallschirmjaeger Regiment 2 and elements from the

Fallschirmjaeger Battalion 'Bloch' which had been taken from the defence of S'Hertogenbosch. This 'Kampfgruppe' numbered four weak battalions and some tank-destroyers. It represented the visible manifestation of General Reinhard's desperate trawl for reserves the evening before. Paradoxically, it was to achieve more than the reinforced panzer brigade thrust that had preceded it.

Much of the success later achieved by this raiding force was to be historically attributed by the Allies to chance.[4] Its commitment, however, was pioneered by extensive and detailed German reconnaissance conducted by the battalion Jungwirth which had already infiltrated Schijndel by 1350, and continued throughout the afternoon and evening of 23 September. Captain Scipa of 59 Division telephoned the results through to LXXXVIII Corps at 1915. The railway running east to Veghel was free of enemy. Eerde was occupied, but further east reconnaissance revealed only weak defences north of it, while the area northeast and east of Schijndel was clear. Confirmation followed at 2025: 'no enemy reported in recce from Schijndel to Dinther in the north-east.' The nearest enemy positions south of Schijndel appeared to be two and a half kilometres north of St Oedenrode. Gaps and weak spots had been identified.[5]

General Reinhard tied up the final details with General Chill who had established his command post in Schijndel at 0800 on the 24th. The objective was set: the Kampfgruppe was to capture the rail and road bridges at Veghel. 'H' hour was to be in 60 minutes' time. Final orders were given to the artillery after a confirmatory look at the ground from the Weibosch Church tower. Von der Heydte's command post in Hermalen did not receive Reinhard's confirmatory visit until three hours after 'H' hour.

Shortly before 1000, Fallschirmjaeger Regiment 6 struck the American positions in Eerde, supported by the Jagdpanthers. It was defended by Kinnard's 1st (US) Battalion of 501 Regiment. A line of outposts established in the sand dunes outside the town was quickly overrun. Shellfire began to burst around the windmill covering the direction of advance, and mortar bursts began to straddle the western streets of the town. Nine tanks from the British 44th Royal Armoured Tank Battalion were summoned to assist the hard-pressed Americans in Eerde. German tank rounds had already begun to strike the church steeple as the first troop of Shermans began to jockey for fire positions. An 88mm shell smashed into the turret of the first and set the crew compartment on fire. Foolishly, the second tank sought cover behind the flaming wreck of the first. Another 88mm screeched through this Sherman, setting off a secondary explosion that blew the hull apart. Only the commander of the first tank survived. Within minutes the third tank of the troop was enveloped by artillery fire and also burst into flames. Further Shermans moving up were reluctant to enter the sand dune area. American infantry counterattacked and before long a savage hand-to-hand mêlée developed. Von der Heydte's inexperienced infantry were once again

'Within minutes the third tank of the troop was enveloped by artillery fire and also burst into flames.' A view from the German lines of one of the corridor battles in southern Holland. An Allied armoured vehicle has been hit and is wreathed in smoke. (Bundesarchiv)

'*On the main road Allied drivers frantically baled out of trucks as the SP began machine-gunning and shelling the highway.*' *An Allied convoy crippled on 'Hell's Highway'. The corridor was cut again.* (Imperial War Museum)

fought to a standstill by the veteran US paratroopers in the 'battle for the dunes' outside Eerde.[6]

Bellowing and squeaking along the subsidiary dirt tracks heading down to the objective – 'Hell's Highway' – a Jagdpanther of Battalion 559 pursued a British tank patrol that had been sent up from the main XXX Corps axis to investigate the noises of battle. On the main road Allied drivers frantically baled out of trucks as the SP began machine gunning and shelling the highway. Ammunition vehicles disintegrated into flaming, spitting pyres as drivers scurried for cover, throwing themselves into roadside ditches. A troop of three British tanks churning down the main road to deal with this formidable new threat were brewed up one after the other.

Within minutes, huge writhing palls of black oily smoke were boiling up into the sky. Traffic to the south jerked to a halt as this awesome spectacle of destruction began to blot out the skies before them. Vulnerable, trucks began to jam up nose to tail, and confusion reigned as two companies of the 502 Parachute Infantry Regiment, moving up from the south, tried to wind their way through the congested traffic. The corridor was cut again.[7]

Only two Jagdpanther had as yet reached the road. General Chill reported von der Heydte's progress at 1500. There had been 'penetrations south of Eerde, and they were 700 metres from the railway bridge, and had reached the northern edge of the canal.' But 'there was strong enemy resistance in Eerde', where his forces were locked into the western edge. So far, the corridor had only been cut by fire.[8]

The Koevering raid, 24-26 September . . .

While the Americans were locked into von der Heydte's Regiment in the sand dunes outside Eerde, and the Jagdpanther of 559 Battalion continued to prowl near the highway, the Battalion Jungwirth was on the move. Major Hans Jungwirth, a seasoned campaigner, had already taken part in the earlier Fallschirmjaeger attacks from S'Hertogenbosch against Veghel and Dinther on 18 September. He was now to reap the benefit of his extensive patrolling. Advancing down the secondary south-easterly road from Schijndel, his force avoided any contacts with the Americans.

As dusk approached, his men neared the small hamlet of Koevering astride 'Hell's Highway', a little more than one-third of the distance from St Oedenrode to Veghel. Before the gratified eyes of the approaching Germans lay columns of motionless vehicles, bumper to bumper, keeping a wary distance from the lurking SP guns reported ahead, whose presence was confirmed by the distant sounds of battle and fresh pillars of smoke rising into the air. At about 1900 the destruction began, as the raiding Fallschirmjaeger poured heavy automatic and panzerfaust fire into the lines of serried vehicles. The mayhem continued throughout the night, punctuated by fire-balls and explosions as conflagrations lit up the low clouds and fields around.

The two companies of the American 502 Parachute Infantry Regiment arrived and managed to keep Jungwirth's men out of

'At about 1900 the destruction began as the raiding Fallschirmjaeger poured heavy automatic and panzerfaust fire into the lines of serried vehicles.' An ammunition lorry cascading incendiaries explodes on 'Hell's Highway'. (Imperial War Museum)

Major Jungwirth reported 'approximately 50 vehicles destroyed'. Here a number of Humber British scout cars have been knocked out by German anti-tank fire. (Bundesarchiv)

the village, but the damage had been done. Scarcely more than 24 hours after the Allies had reopened the main road between Veghel and Uden, the Germans were astride it again at Koevering. By daybreak Major Jungwirth reported that 'approximately 50 vehicles [were] destroyed, and until now 8 officers and 32 NCOs and men had been captured and assembled at the (59) Division command post'.[9] Throughout the night American airborne and British artillery had pounded the penetration point in an attempt to prevent reinforcements getting in. But as soon as von der Heydte received news of Jungwirth's success, his battalion 'was immediately reinforced by elements of Fallschirmjaeger Regiment 6'. Steps were taken by the Allies to clear the incursion, but the Germans still enjoyed an element of local surprise at the penetration point. Von der Heydte described how:

'. . . a number of British officers, who drove on the road unaware of what was going on, were taken prisoner as also a number of vehicles, including two undamaged and operational British tanks, were captured.'[10]

Allied counter-attacks began to come in: 506 regiment from the north-east, supported by nine tanks, and from St Oedenrode in the opposite direction a reinforced battalion from the 502 Parachute Infantry Regiment, and a further regiment from the British 50th Infantry Division. One battery from the 907th American Glider Field Artillery battalion laid its guns in direct fire only 400 yards from the German positions. Nevertheless, the German defence remained firm throughout 25 September. Stymied by this resistance, wider sweeps were employed by the Allies in an attempt

Lieutenant-Colonel von der Heydte reported 'a number of vehicles, including two undamaged and operational British tanks were captured'. Fallschirmjaeger picking over the booty. (Bundesarchiv)

to envelop the position. By nightfall the penetration point had been enclosed on three sides. But Jungwirth's infantry still held grimly on to a small segment of the highway.

XXX Corps was paying the price for committing its entire offensive force along one road to reach the besieged airborne divisions. Operationally controlling its forces snarled up in such a narrow corridor was proving difficult. The gamble had rested on the assumption that the Germans were too spent to fight. 50th Infantry Division was unable to negotiate the congested roads south of the German block and get into action until after midday on 25

September. It would require more than artillery to clear the penetration, because pockets of enemy and 101 Airborne Division had become so thoroughly mixed it could not be safely or decisively employed. Mutual recognition in such close terrain was difficult. British M10 tank-destroyers were removed forward of 50th Infantry Division positions, 'to prevent any mistakes', after it was reported German SP guns were roaming its area.[11]

Jungwirth's position, was, however, becoming increasingly untenable. The Chief of Staff 59 Division telephoned Corps at 1055 and reported that the Koevering Kampfgruppe:

'. . . has been cut off from its rearward communications by the enemy north of Koevering.

'The right flank of our left neighbour is now at least two kilometres behind. Division requests action soonest from our left neighbour to restore the link with Koevering.'[12]

The nearest troops to Jungwirth were von der Heydte's Fallschirmjaeger Regiment 6. He had provided all the assistance he could. As dusk fell he could do no more than listen to the distant sounds of battle, and monitor events. Three more enemy tanks were reported knocked out by Jungwirth. But the future was plain for all to see. General Reinhard telephoned his superior General von Zangen and updated him on the progress of the Veghel attack. It underscored once again the gulf between the situation map and reality. The Corps diary records the outcome of the conversation:

'The Army Commander grants permission to the Corps Commander to order the Kampfgruppe Huber [Jungwirth's force] to retire to the wooded area to the north-west if it does not appear possible to hold Koevering. But this is not to happen until a blocking position has first been established. The mission, first the railway bridge, and then the road bridge, remains.'[13]

But the conditions assumed in the staff appreciation bore no relation to conditions on the ground. There was nothing left; the barrel of resources had been scraped clean.

Reinhard came to the reluctant conclusion that Jungwirth's position was indeed untenable. General Poppe, the Commander of 59 Division, telephoned almost immediately after and declared that 'without the introduction of fresh forces – two companies – contact with the surrounded

Kampfgruppe in Koevering will not be recoverable'. General Chill from 85 Division conformed that 'he likewise had no forces at hand available'.[14] Reinhard ordered the abandonment of the position, and a fighting withdrawal to the north-west. Facing his superior the following day, Reinhard accounted for his decision, and forcefully pointed out:

'. . . the terrible combat capability of our own troops, which in the case of Luftwaffe units were simply recruits under questionable commanders. He remarked that one could hardly expect to take the road bridge at Veghel with these.'

Von Zangen knew all this, he merely reiterated and 'emphasised the position was to be held'. MARKET-GARDEN was mincing up all the half-trained German reserves in north-west Holland. Reserves, and in particular armour, were stripped away from quieter areas in order to invest the corridor. A sergeant serving in 712 Infantry Division described the situation for those who were left behind (in this instance, west of Antwerp):

'25 September 1944. We march about 45 kilometres. Everybody is dead tired.

'26 September 1944. There is not a dry thread on us. The battalion slummocks along the road.

'27 September 1944. The men are done. They are all old chaps. Unnecessary marching and counter-marching is making them discontented. We have now been two days without food. Three companies attacked Hees. Only a few stragglers came back . . . Poor Germany. Everybody is under the impression that he is selling his life cheaply.'[15]

Having established a blocking position to the north-west, Jungwirth's battalion began to exfiltrate from its salient during the night of 25–26 September. This was no easy task and was conducted under pressure of enemy attacks. H. Sitter's sketchy notes reveal the situation in part of Finzel's battalion area, from Fallschirmjaeger Regiment 2:

'Dusk. Order to break out. A march of a few kilometres, then enemy contacts towards dawn. We lie up with Captain Ortmann and a Sergeant, name unknown, in a farm house. Enemy artillery is pounding us, then come the tanks. Next to us is an anti-tank gun with a truck full of ammunition which does not fire a single shot. Apparently, a broken firing pin. Tanks are shooting us up in direct lay. Opposite us is supposed to be a unit called "Black Watch" or something like it. Rumour has it that it is manned with convicts etc.'[16]

Units extracted with difficulty to the north-west. Heavy weapons were towed out by the surviving Jagdpanthers. Most of the exfiltrating troops reached the nominated assembly area on the railway cross south of Schinjdel between 0800 and 1000 hours.[17] Others under pressure from the pursuing Allies did not make it. Sitter saw that:

'. . . tanks have rolled over our positions and are returning now. We do not have any anti-tank weapons, not even hand-grenades. Our position is under fire again. I hear the sergeant screaming, shot in his leg, then I don't remember anything.'

He was wounded. As in the case of many veterans he could not remember the precise date, only 'the day I was wounded'. The advancing Allies were uncompromising in their treatment of the defeated, and Sitter's company was disintegrating. His company commander, however, paused:

'Captain Ortmann gives me first aid, no more medics there. Later he sends me to the rear with a Red Cross on my back. Didn't get far before fired at by a machine gun, drop into a brook, can't remember anything until I wake up in the aid station. Ortmann is with me and takes care of me until I am in the hospital train. That was outside Utrecht. This train is attacked several times by "Jabos" before we get back to Germany.'[18]

The battalion Jungwirth manned the penetration long enough this time to mine the main road extensively. It was not open to traffic again until 1400 on 26 September when the mines and debris had been cleared. The removal of this obstacle marked the stabilisation of 101 Airborne Division's front. Despite various attempts, the Germans were never to succeed in cutting the road again. The best that could now be achieved was harassment through artillery fire. But traffic had been congested for more than two days, and, more importantly, infantry units bound to relieve the Oosterbeek perimeter had been taken out of the line of march. Delays had been considerable; however, it transpired that the fate of the beleaguered British in Oosterbeek had already been decided before 26 September.

CHAPTER XXV

The End

It stopped all of a sudden – the silence appeared treacherous to all and almost 'hurt'.
Was it all over?

SS Battalion Commander

The decision . . .

The British, it seemed, still refused to give up the idea of establishing a bridgehead across the lower Rhine at Oosterbeek. During the night of 24 September two companies of the Dorsetshire Regiment, the vanguard of 43 Infantry Division, managed to paddle over the river. Problems with insufficient boats, a strong current, and harassing fire from the Germans meant that the Poles were unable to support them. Four hundred Dorsets were across by first light, but they failed to assemble in cohesive units on the north bank. This continued inability to positively reinforce the perimeter brought with it a growing awareness that MARKET-GARDEN may have passed the point of saving. Subsequent events confirmed this suspicion.

IISS Corps was notified at 0515 by von Tettau through Supreme Commander Netherlands that 'the enemy has crossed the Rhine at Kasteel Doorwerth and Heveadorp after heavy artillery fire'. 'Counter-measures' it was stated 'have been initiated.' By 0610 it was established that the enemy 'had only crossed at the Driel Ferry in approximately battalion strength and penetrated Schiffsturmabteilung 10 – the naval battalion's sector'. The response was immediate. Lieutenant-Colonel Shennen's 1st Battalion of Sicherungs Regiment 26 launched a counter-attack from the Renkum area via Noorberg. Knoche's Regi-

ment, responsible for rear area security by the drop-zones, was reinforced by two companies of Fliegerhorst Battalion 1 and also moved into the assault. An SS company 'Moll' reinforced Fliegerhorst Battalion 3, which was securing the start line. The incursion was cleared. Von Tettau reported with grim satisfaction that 'the enemy has high losses. 140 are taken prisoner, including nine officers and the battalion commander, a colonel.' Only 75 of the 400 Dorsets who crossed over made it back to the south bank.

A watershed had been reached. Both sides realised that time had run out. The prisoners were identified as 43 Infantry Division, who 'had moved by foot march from Nijmegen'.[1] XXX Corps was now arriving in strength. Field Marshal Model again ordered the pocket cleared before it was too late. At 0930 General Horrocks, the Commander of XXX Corps, agreed with General Browning, the Commander of 1st Airborne Corps, that they had shot their bolt. The survivors of the 1st British Airborne Division were to be withdrawn from the north bank that night.

Deadlock

Fresh German units were still arriving in Oosterbeek. Individual infantry companies and flak units were being constantly added to the German order of battle. A Propaganda PK Kriegsberichter team arrived and began filming sequences for the *Deutsche-Wochenschau* (the German equivalent of Pathe News), for showing as news in cinemas in the Reich. Filming from a high vantage point in an occupied house, the cameraman stood behind a German machine gunner firing a captured British bren gun across the battered roof-tops of Oosterbeek.

He is firing through a shattered glass pane, and bursting strike marks can be discerned around one of the opposite house windows. In the background is the constant thump and rumble of artillery. Tiles stripped from roof-tops by air-burst artillery shells and machine gun fire have piled up in the gutters, or are strewn across gardens. Only the skeletal outline of wooden beading

Street fighting in Oosterbeek as reported by the German Wochenschau, *equivalent of 'Pathe-News'. A German machine gunner fires a captured British bren gun through a shattered window pane.*

Strike marks burst around the windows opposite.

'Soldiers move wearily by in pairs through devastated gardens, unshaven, rifles at the trail.'

'A lone soldier runs into view.'

remains. The progress of an infantry assault group is monitored from this upstairs window. Soldiers stroll wearily by in pairs through devastated gardens, unshaven, rifles at the trail. There is a pause and a lone soldier runs into view, two stick grenades at his belt, clutching a Schmeisser machine pistol, intent only on locating the source of fire so audible on the soundtrack. A 20mm cannon engages another house at point-blank range, tracer scything the tops off decorative conifers sheltering a once prosperous-looking bungalow. All around German soldiers are climbing and stumbling over ornamental metal railings, trying to get into an advantageous position for an attack through beautifully laid-out suburban gardens. It is safe for the cameramen to shoot. They are merely recording a mopping-up action. Triumph exudes from the screen and its fast-talking commentator. Victory is in their grasp . . .

The film, however, belies the reality of what was actually happening. SS-Corporal Dombrowski, still fighting along the Utrechtseweg on the eastern side of the perimeter, remarked 'our nerves had been shot to pieces after nine days of this'. There appeared to be no end in sight. Surely the British could not take any more of this! SS-Captain Moeller was depressed by the constant 'ferocity of the fighting' still raging that same day:

'We saw how countless wounded were dragged into the hotels, we watched when unnumbered dead were laid down in the hotel garden. And then came more wounded. It was sheer carnage! There were also fresh losses in the 1st Company. This 25 September surpassed everything there had been before in Oosterbeek. Fighting grew fiercer and fiercer, man against man with bayonets and knives, and smoke grenades and smoke pots to blind the enemy's view.'[2]

On the west side of the perimeter the trenchant SS-Colonel Lippert had finally been relieved of command by von Tettau, who was not prepared, despite the experience of his veteran commander, to put up with his outspokenness. Although Lippert could see the hopelessness of the British position, he considered his own to be not much better. His forward advance had ground to a halt under bitter opposition and occupied a line that stretched now from the gasworks on the Rhine via the Oosterbeek villas up to the Renkum-Oosterbeek road to where it linked in with the 9SS.

'Units had dug in or established themselves in houses. The enemy was where shooting could be heard. It became a battle from street to street, house to house, man against man. We no longer ordered large territorial gains to be taken in the face of a foe who defended himself so bitterly, because the end was in sight.'[3]

But how to break the deadlock? Even Field Marshall Model had been made to realise by Harzer that quickly annihilating an elite British division with so many disparate Wehrmacht units would be no easy matter. In order to save German lives, Model agreed to the employment of more artillery to batter the British into submission.[4] The ARKO commanding Artillery Regiment 191 was directed to train all the available heavy weapons within range on to the steadily-shrinking perimeter, now less than two kilometres square. Some 110 artillery pieces, not even including the heavy Werfer Abteilung, ranging in calibre from 12mm through 75mm field and 88mm flak and 105mm field guns, began systematically to rake the perimeter from top to bottom. Harzer soberly recorded:

'This systematic grind began to break the morale of the paratroopers, who had already now been in action non-stop for eight days. Many soldiers came over to our lines, and the numbers of prisoners rose.'[5]

Counter-battery fire by XXX Corps attempted to relieve some of the pressure on the cauldron, but this had only a limited effect.

Inexperienced reinforcements that had been used to supplement the depleted German attacking battalions were now causing some concern. Casualty rates were becoming excessive. SS-Captain Krafft, after lending one of his companies to another of von Tettau's units, complained in his report on 25 September that:

One hundred and ten artillery pieces including 88mm flak guns began systematically to rake the perimeter from top to bottom.

'. . . the concentrated British forces fight desperately and ferociously for every house and every position. The attack has little success because our troops have little experience in house and wood clearing.'[6]

Major Geoffrey Powell, a British company commander in 156 PARA fighting in the north-east corner of the perimeter, remembers an occasion when a full German company group, obviously unaware of his company's presence, actually formed up for an attack within range of his positions. They were totally oblivious of the potential impact fully-automatic fire could have upon their densely-packed ranks. The inevitable consequence was 'very satisfying' for the British troops.[7] Herbert Kessler of the Hermann Goering Regiment described a similar action, whereby German companies, often attached to neighbouring units in other parts of the perimeter, paid a similar price for recklessly continuing abortive advances without any extensive prior knowledge of the ground or situation. One company from Kessler's unit was tasked for an operation

'. . . to the east, towards the freight train station. There were some rows of houses which the enemy was still clinging to. During their further advance they put together an assault force to seize these houses. Using all the cover and concealment available, the assault force advanced. Not a shot was fired. But before they could cross the street, the enemy opened up such a volume of fire from the occupied houses that the operation collapsed. The assault force leader, a sergeant, was instantly killed, other casualties both killed and wounded compelled the assault force to withdraw.'[8]

SS-Junker Rudolf Lindemann, fighting in Oelker's battalion on the west side of the perimeter, was frank in his condemnation of inexperienced 'other outfits' which proved to be 'no unit at all'. They had 'no idea of fighting, as was also the case of the navy, Reichsarbeitsdienst and Luftwaffe'. Lindemann was briefly attached to Schiffsturmabteilung 10 as a liaison NCO and adviser, but was unable to influence events. 'During the final attacks on the pocket, the navy unit on our right simply got lost on the way,' he remembered. 'I was sent as an envoy to tell them what to do. When I reached them they were all lying closely packed together on the ground, terribly exposed to artillery fire.'[9]

Harzer decided on 25 September to regroup all the forces on the eastern side of the perimeter. 'It was no longer a case of forming large battle groups,' he explained, 'but forming units of veterans for the decisive attacks.'[10] Spindler's Kampfgruppe reorganised so that it was left only with elements from Panzer-grenadier Regiments 19 and 20, part of Panzer Artillery Regiment 9 and the Hohenstaufen's flak group. The combat teams thereby created were mixed with sections of assault pioneers from Moeller's 9SS and the 'Glogau' Lehr engineer battalions. 'King Tiger' tank platoons from the 'Hummel' company of Heavy Tank Battalion 506 were splintered on to these. From north to east Harzer fielded the following order of battle: to the right was the battle group 'Krafft', left of him the Wehrmacht Panzer-grenadier Battalion 'Bruhns', and finally stretching down

to the river the SS Kampfgruppe Spindler divided into its component parts: 'Moeller', 'Spindler', 'Von Allworden' and 'Harder'. On the opposite side of the perimeter von Tettau's forces were grouped from the river right to left with the 'Worrowski' Battalion of the Hermann Goering, and the SS Battalions 'Schulz' and 'Eberwein', who linked into the 9SS. All the other remaining quick-reaction 'alarm' units were taken out of the line and assembled as reserves in Elden or Velp, east of Arnhem.

During the afternoon of 25 September the most effective assault yet mounted on the cauldron pierced the British perimeter on the eastern side. Von Allworden's Kampfgruppe, supported by Harder battling against 'Lonsdale Force' alongside the river, suddenly broke into the encircled division's artillery positions. Moeller recalls:

'The Division then reinforced the left wing. The battle groups Allworden and Harder in particular were reinforced by a newly moved up armoured force . . . which was to cut off the enemy from the river by an attack with their Tiger tanks between Utrechtseweg and the road along the bank of the Rhine.'[11]

One British battery of 1 Airlanding Regiment was overrun. The attack was finally brought to a halt a mere 600 metres from the opposite edge of the perimeter, and about 500 metres from the Hotel Hartenstein. Its momentum could not be maintained. It was finally broken by British medium artillery fire brought down inside the perimeter itself, and the attacks petered out. Moeller commented wearily that 'the more pressure we exerted from all sides on the encircled enemy, the fiercer his resistance grew'.

Johanna Hoeve

Ommershof

The White House

Koude Herberg X roads

Oosterbeek Laag Church

The Gas Works

Heveadorp Ferry

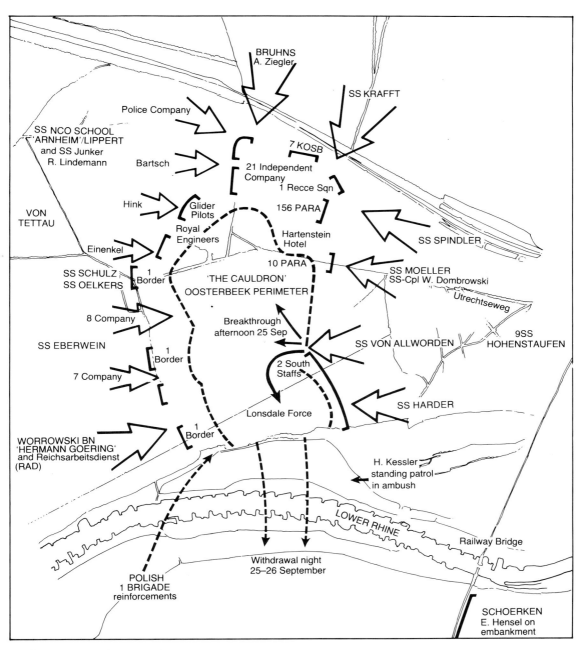

BRUHNS
A. Ziegler

SS KRAFFT

Police Company

SS NCO SCHOOL
'ARNHEIM'/LIPPERT
and SS Junker
R. Lindemann

7 KOSB

Bartsch

21 Independent
Company

1 Recce Sqn

VON
TETTAU

Hink

Glider
Pilots

156 PARA

Royal
Engineers

Hartenstein
Hotel

SS SPINDLER

Einenkel

10 PARA

SS SCHULZ
SS OELKERS

1
Border

SS MOELLER
SS-Cpl W. Dombrowski

'THE CAULDRON'
OOSTERBEEK PERIMETER

Utrechtseweg

8 Company

Breakthrough
afternoon 25 Sep

9SS
HOHENSTAUFEN

SS EBERWEIN

1
Border

SS VON ALLWORDEN

7 Company

2 South
Staffs

Lonsdale Force

SS HARDER

WORROWSKI BN
'HERMANN GOERING'
and Reichsarbeitsdienst
(RAD)

1
Border

H. Kessler
standing patrol
in ambush

LOWER RHINE

Railway Bridge

Withdrawal night
25–26 September

POLISH
1 BRIGADE
reinforcements

SCHOERKEN
E. Hensel on
embankment

THE REDUCTION OF THE OOSTERBEEK PERIMETER 21–26 SEPTEMBER 1944.
A savage battle of attrition reduced the Oosterbeek perimeter to the dotted line shown above
by 26 September, less than two kilometres square. 110 German guns of all calibres were
directed to reduce the pocket assailed by heavy tanks, SPs and infantry from three sides: von
Tettau to the west, the 9SS in the east, and a northern group consisting of the Wehrmacht
battalion Bruhns and SS Krafft. Despite some Polish reinforcements, the British were forced to
evacuate the pocket during the night of 25–26 September.

The silent evacuation . . .

One incident that particularly impressed veteran Panzer-grenadiers of the Hohenstaufen Division was the unconfirmed tale of two British paratroopers who, out of ammunition, attacked a section of SS armed only with knives. Although they were unsuccessful, it was obvious that one of them had intended to draw fire whilst the other closed in. True or not, the story was believed. The enemy was commanding respect. SS-Captain Krafft assessed the battle potential of these troops who 'were about 25 years of age on the average, and the best type mentally and physically'. His post-combat report stated that 'they were well trained, particularly for independent fighting and of good combat value'. They fought savagely:

'Unconfirmed reports have stated that in some cases British soldiers have dressed in SS uniforms and fought as free snipers, and that they also have deceived Germans by shouting in German "Don't shoot," and then opening fire at the last moment.'

Casualties told the same story; they were up against an impressive foe. Moeller's veteran assault pioneer companies had now been reduced to an effective strength of 30 to 40 men each. Krafft appreciated that 'the enemy was very skilled in house fighting and had a great advantage over our troops, who, it must be remembered, were not all of our best type'. The British NCOs and officers made 'an outstanding impression' on Krafft, who wrote 'all positive things said about the troops apply even more so to the NCOs' who were led by officers who 'were the finest of the whole British Army'.[12] Having committed themselves to such a heavy human and material investment in a pocket that had cost so many lives to reinforce and resupply, the Germans

were convinced that the British would never abandon it. They would therefore fight to the finish, or at any moment try to break out. SS-Colonel Lippert confided that:

'. . . my greatest concern was a breakout attempt by the despairing British and Poles to the west, in order to use the Heveadorp ferry to reach the Poles there. There must have been a plan for this because patrols were always being despatched in this direction.'[13]

The British withdrawal, however, began on the night of 25 September. At 2145, with a dark overcast sky, strong winds and driving rain, the Red Devils, boots wrapped in rags to muffle the sound of their progress, began to run the gauntlet of German patrols to the banks of the lower Rhine. The ferrying operation began at 2200 with 14 assault boats and smaller craft. The steady exfiltration continued throughout the night.

An examination of contemporary German documents, war diaries and eye-witness accounts reveals that the Germans were totally surprised by the silent evacuation. Like the British before them, who only belatedly took the decision, the Germans had not appreciated that MARKET-GARDEN had passed the point of saving. It was a defeat. Steeped in the blood and emotion of overwhelming the pocket, the Germans could not see it was all over. Clues there were, but they remained unrecognised. Krafft, for example, wrote in his later report: 'Towards the end of the fighting, many gave themselves up because of hunger and other privations, including breakdown of morale.' But the British, having already resisted beyond the norms of human endurance, still fought on. Defying normal military logic, their actions could not be objectively assessed.

There was nothing to suggest to the Germans that an evacuation was taking place. At 2100 XXX Corps artillery began to initiate the covering barrage. Lieutenant Martin, entrenched near the evacuation point with Fliegerhorst Battalion 3, noticed nothing untoward. He wrote in his diary on 25 September: 'Was at river at night. Received uninterrupted fire from 2100–0800. No casualties. Captured five prisoners.' Even on the following day he was still unaware of the significance of the events of the preceding night: '26 September. Conference at CP. Two wounded by mortar fire. Captain Schaarschmidt relieved.'[14]

Von Tettau's forces on the western side of the perimeter were completely duped. The General was in the process of relocating his command post and missed the significance of all reports: 'The enemy's resistance' von Tettau wrote 'seems to slacken, caused by the high losses and the dogged assault force operations.' Verbal instructions were given for the attacks on the 26th to 'continue assault force operations'. Von Tettau's inexperienced naval unit Schiffsturmabteilung 10 detected the movement of boats on the river, but misinterpreted their importance:

> 'In the sector of the Regiment Knoche on the lower Rhine front the enemy made renewed crossing attempts from opposite the 10SS St A which were mostly repelled by concentrated fire.
>
> 'Only individual boats managed to cross and infiltrate. The crews were eliminated or captured during the course of the morning.'[15]

Artillery salvoes bracketed the evacuation craft, and caused casualties both on the river bank and in the water. Nevertheless, the evacuation continued in the driving rain. Herbert Kessler formed part of a German standing patrol lying in wait along the river bank in the Hermann Goering Regiment's sector. He recalls:

> 'The position was located in the Rosande-Polder in the immediate vicinity of the lower Rhine. At nightfall, elements of two sections moved out to occupy the prescribed position. Once they were in place they lay motionless in the wet grass, paying attention to every movement in the vicinity, when figures appeared nearby. They knew that theirs was the only outpost in this sector, therefore these figures could only be enemy. Further considerations proved futile because a wild fire fight ensued rapidly at short range. There were casualties on both sides. The outpost obviously had the better nerves because the enemy pulled back. Quiet had scarcely returned when a figure rose in front of the positions, calling repeatedly "Don't shoot!". A closer look revealed that this figure was a British Flight-Lieutenant who had bailed out and lost contact with friendly units. One man escorted him back to the company command post.'[16]

Clashes with British paratroopers infiltrating to the river bank were interpreted as either patrols or break-out attempts. This provided a logical explanation for the large number of British prisoners taken. SS-Colonel Lippert was more concerned with what might come across the river towards them, rather than what was retiring in the other direction, because 'the Poles on my right flank on the southern bank of the Rhine were ever more threatening'. Lippert always felt:

> 'It remained a puzzle why the Polish Brigade did not come over the Rhine and attack the battle group in our rear. The north bank of the Rhine from Heelsum to Wageningen was only occupied by Territorial Army

soldiers. A crossing in this sector would have been a walk-over.'

On the other side of the Rhine, Sergeant Erich Hensel on the railway bridge was not aware of any significant troop movements that night. 'Oosterbeek was burning', and, as usual, one could hear 'the heavy sounds of battle. There was obviously a bitter fight going on there.'[17]

As indeed there was. Covering fire from the XXX Corps artillery barrage was straddling German positions around the perimeter. SS-Captain Moeller remembers the lurid scenes during that last night:

'After nightfall the artillery bombardment intensified; reports and impacts followed, almost without let-up. The earth was trembling and a curtain of fire and dirt of hitherto unknown dimensions rose over and between our positions. We ducked down and sought shelter, but still we remained exposed to the blind raging of the shells. Houses burned brightly and collapsed; tree-tops splintered; and the new impacts dealt death and destruction. Terrified civilians ran for their lives – sought cover – wept and cried, others took heart but resignedly took cover where they found it, and find it they did – with us in the hospital area around both hotels, within or behind our "demarcation line", which like a miracle remained unscathed . . .

'But all around us, to our left and right and also further west towards Heelsum the bombardment continued. The detonation of the shells mingled with the cries for help of the wounded who were lying out there in the driving rain or among the rubble of collapsing houses.

'. . . and so it went on throughout the night without let up!'[18]

SS-Lieutenant-Colonel Harzer suggests that by midnight the enemy's intention had become apparent: 'Loud engine noises were reported from the south bank of the Rhine.' But whatever his personal suspicions, the majority of German forces deployed near the river felt these were simply more reinforcements coming across, and only brought artillery to bear. Harzer's unit memorandum written after the battle confirms he was still unsure, because he interpreted a heavy clash in front of the SS-Kampfgruppe Harder by the river bank as a break-out attempt. 'At about midnight' he writes 'the British even attacked the forward line of the battle group Harder left of Spindler.'[19]

Ferrying continued until 0550 hours on 26 September. German artillery fire had by then become so intense and accurate with the arrival of daylight that further crossings had to be abandoned. Left stranded on the north bank were 300 British personnel. On the other side of the river guides led the weary evacuated British soldiers to a reception point south of Driel, where friendly hands plied them with rum, hot food and tea. The survivors included 1,741 officers and men of the 1st Airborne Division, 422 British glider pilots, 160 men of the 1st Polish Parachute Brigade and 75 of the Dorsetshire Regiment – a total of 2,398. These were all that remained of approximately 9,000 men who had fought on the north bank.

And still the Germans were not completely aware of what had transpired. Herbert Kessler, still concealed in the Rosande-Polder, remembers:

'The soldiers breathed a sigh of relief when dawn broke, the signal to pull back to the rest position. The outpost took the same route to the river bank a few more times, but had no more direct contact with the enemy.'[20]

After first light German assault troops began to press home further attacks. The advance continues through devastated Oosterbeek.

The end

After first light German assault groups began to press home further attacks. At 0930 von Tettau was informed by IISS Corps that 'the enemy made another attempt to break out to the east in the early morning hours but was repulsed'. The Germans did not realise that the large number of prisoners taken – 170 during this operation – were the unfortunates who had been left on the river bank and picked up by the Kampfgruppe Harder's initial advance.

At 1025 the first successes were being announced. Eberwein's SS Battalion had at last cleared the houses north of the Arnhem-Wageningen road, and was thrusting toward the Hotel Hartenstein to estab-lish contact with the advancing elements of the 9SS. Oelker's SS Battalion and the Kampfgruppe Bruhns continued the concentric advance. Small British rear-guards put up spirited resistance. SS-Officer Cadet Rudolf Lindemann finally reached the Hotel Hartenstein. 'It was not a real attack,' he recalls, because 'the paras had gone already. We found only weapons and dead people.' It slowly began to dawn on the Germans what might have happened. Lindemann described how 'we went up to the tennis courts, and then the action was over for us', an anti-climax.[21]

Alfred Ziegler, the SS despatch rider advancing southwards with the Kampfgruppe Bruhns, arrived at a similar conclusion. 'On the last night,' he said 'the paras

Small British rear-guards put up spirited resistance and are here grenaded into submission.

SS-Junker Rudolf Lindemann reported when they reached the trenches around the Hartenstein hotel that 'the paras had gone already. We found only weapons and dead people.' (Bundesarchiv)

must have been withdrawing. There were break-out attempts and patrols attacked us. These withdrew and finally gave up in the morning.'[22]

By 1200 Eberwein and Oelker's SS Battalions had wheeled to the south and finally established contact with the Hermann Goering Battalion and the 9SS advancing from the east side of the perimeter. SS-Captain Hans Moeller, his head still ringing from the impact of the XXX Corps covering artillery barrage of the night before, realised:

'But then – it stopped all of a sudden – the silence appeared treacherous to all and almost "hurt". Was it all over? Would it start again?'[23]

He now appreciated the significance of the artillery hammering his men had experienced the night before. 'The Red Devils had withdrawn and disappeared during the night behind this curtain of dirt and destruction.' By 1400 it was over. The Germans, having fought so hard for 10 days, could hardly believe their good fortune. The encirclement battle was at last finished.

Alfred Ziegler remembers 'on the last morning there was no noise at all from the pocket'. 'Come on,' said his commander Bruhns, 'we might as well mount up and drive over to take the surrender. It's over.' They climbed aboard the motorcycle combination, and Ziegler set off.[24]

There was a feeling of widespread relief. All had feared a *Gotterdaemmerung* – a fight to the finish – because the victors were close to collapse themselves. SS-Colonel Lippert was as outspoken as ever:

'The British break-out to the south during the night of the 25–26 September was just my luck. My unit would not have been able to withstand a concentrated break-out to the west. The costly battle of the previous few

days had already resulted in gaps in my front line, and there were no further reserves available.'[25]

Harzer's command post staff were elated. SS-Captain Wilfried Schwarz, the Chief of Staff of the 9SS, exclaimed:

'Morale was particularly good at the end. We had actually succeeded in forcing this elite British division to stop, and pushed the remnants back over the Rhine!'[26]

Sergeant Erich Hensel on the other side of the Rhine with the Sperrverband Harzer was equally pleased. 'Morale was high.' For a short period, and for a change, they had 'tasted victory – maybe we will pull through yet!' But the victory at Arnhem was soon tempered with depressing news of further successful Soviet advances in the east.

The cost had been high. Officially released German casualty figures for the whole of the MARKET-GARDEN area were quoted as 3,300, including 1,100 dead. This was very much an underestimate, and, in fact, more than twice as many had died.[27] The evidence was clear to see. Lieutenant Colonel Fullriede arrived on 26 September to visit Niedermeyer, who had taken over Worrowski's battalion of the Hermann Goering Training Regiment. His diary recorded a 'scene of devastation' in Oosterbeek, where

'. . . all around lie dead Germans and Englishmen. The trees are fully decorated with hanging parachutes, with which the English had attempted to resupply their cut off troops. Two of our Panthers [tanks] are also lying there, with their burnt crews inside them.'[28]

SS-Corporal Dombrowski commented 'we had fought non-stop for 10 days and nights. Coffee and Benzedrene had kept us awake. After it was all over we were as exhausted as the British.' Two weary troops from Spindler's SS Artillery Regiment 9. (Fuerbringer Collection)

Operation MARKET-GARDEN was over, and Oosterbeek had been totally ruined. Moeller recorded a similarly dismal impression of that last day:

'A wall of fire shimmering in shades from bright yellow to violet brightened the rainy sky over a long distance. The large gasometer had been hit, and the flames cast a sinister light on a scene of useless destruction.'[29]

The soldiers were totally exhausted. SS-Corporal Wolfgang Dombrowski summed up their situation with a soldier's typical eye for irony:

'We had fought non-stop for 10 days and nights. Coffee and Benzedrene had kept us awake. After it was all over we were as exhausted as the British; we slept and slept. All the Wehrmacht battalions that fought in Arnhem got a special 10-day leave from Hitler. It was our last-ever victory. But not the Waffen-SS. Himmler said we would get our holiday after the Final Victory!'[30]

CHAPTER XXVI

Achievements

It is not possible to destroy overwhelming airborne forces with slight forces, but one can pin him down to secure time to prepare counter-measures.

SS Battalion Commander

General Student's First Fallschirmjaeger Army was a paper tiger at its inception on 5 September 1944. It covered a 75-mile front with only 32 battalions. But within 12 days it mustered sufficient substance to blunt the progress of three Allied armoured corps. Battalions were still forming up on 17 September when it was split in two by three Allied airborne divisions dropped across its rear areas. XXX British Corps, commanded by General Horrocks, brushed aside the single German regiment that bitterly contested the road chosen for the ground advance. By 25 September five major water obstacles, including the Maas and Waal rivers, were overrun and a 65-mile salient driven into German-occupied southern Holland. The bridgehead formed posed a constant threat of a renewed Allied northern thrust, until eventually realised in February 1945. Yet the decision to evacuate Oosterbeek signalled the failure of MARKET-GARDEN. A German collapse had not been precipitated. Most of the operation's planned objectives were never realised: a bridgehead across the lower Rhine was not secured, the north flank of the West Wall was not turned, 15th Army was able to escape and the British 21 Army Group was in no position to drive around the north flank of the Ruhr.

German reinforcements were too few or dispersed to achieve little more than blunt the strategic aim of the Allied operation. IISS Panzer Corps was reinforced by two more divisions: the 9th and 116th Panzer Division 'Kampfgruppen'. Further offensive operations were conducted between Arnhem and Nijmegen, in concert with the 10SS, but achieved nothing. The parlous state of these new reinforcements re-routed from fighting the Americans in Aachen meant that the Corps was obliged to go over to the defensive on 7 October. On 24 September Hitler had ordered the reinforcement of First Fallschirmjaeger Army and the elimination of the Allied salient through simultaneous attacks from Veghel northward. Eventually, 363 Volksgrenadier Division put in a supporting attack along General Bittrich's western flank. But these developments did not occur until the end of the month and were too late. General Meindl's II Fallschirmjaeger Corps struck again from the Reichswald toward Groesbeek, while 15th Army attempted to support him from the west by attacking Grave. Powerful but isolated assaults were launched against the salient until well into October, but to no avail as by this time the British VIII and XII Corps had built up on either side of the corridor. Luftwaffe air attacks, and submarine charges positioned by German swimmers, inflicted only minor damage on the Nijmegen bridge. At around midday on 7 October the Royal Air Force tumbled the Arnhem bridge into the lower Rhine.

This was truly a hollow victory for both sides. Once the bridge was down, the logistic chain nourishing German offensive designs between the lower Rhine and Waal rivers was gone again. They could no longer be realistically pursued. On the same day the Hohenstaufen departed the Arnhem area bound for its belated rest and refurbishment in the Reich. All it had fought for was now destroyed. What was left was denied to the civilian inhabitants who were forcibly evacuated, and systematically looted by the German army during the final winter of the war.

What had been the decisive factors contributing to German success? In the absence of any previous comprehensive survey of the German reaction to MARKET-GARDEN, Allied historians have tended to blame mistakes rather than effective counter-measures in order to account for the failure.

The main factor reducing the impact of the airlandings was not a 'betrayal myth' (now refuted[1]), that SS Panzer formations were pre-positioned to defeat an airborne assault; improvisation and a rapid build-up of force blunted the attacks. This arose from aggressive and swift counter-measures implemented by IISS Corps already located *in situ* and other *ad hoc* combat groups which were rushed to its aid.

German reaction times were astonishing. On 17 September the Allies achieved total surprise, dropping six British and 18 American airborne battalions behind enemy lines in southern Holland, supported by some artillery and anti-tank guns. By midnight, ten to eleven German battalions had assembled in the Arnhem area, mainly because of the IISS Corps concentration,

German reaction times were astonishing. The Allies could not match the German reinforcement rate, here moving to Arnhem.

albeit dispersed in company groups. In the Nijmegen area there had been only two equivalent battalion groups,[2] and only three weak battalions and some flak between Grave and Eindhoven. Within 24 hours this picture was transformed to 13 or 14 battalions in Arnhem, an equal number around Nijmegen and about nine more in the vicinity of Best and Son. By 19 September, 17 battalions had assembled in the Arnhem area, more than 15 around Nijmegen, and 14 were battling against the Americans and advancing British south of Grave. This process continued ebbing and flowing according to casualties and XXX Corps' overland progress until, by 23 September, 27 identifiable Kampfgruppen or battalion groups were operating in and around Arnhem. All this was achieved by improvisation – employing any mode of transport available, whether by road, rail or air. Troops rode to battle in farm carts, wood-burning-powered civilian cars, lorries, and even commandeered fire engines.[3]

German counter-measures were aided by Allied insistence that all offensive air assets protect the airborne landings during the initial critical phase. Although this achieved the aim, the official German Army Group B synopsis of the battle observed: 'During the landings, despite the good weather, German troop movements remained almost completely unhampered.'[4] Trapp's Frundsberg Panzer-grenadier company in Deventer enjoyed an almost exuberant bicycle ride, for once uncharacteristically undisturbed by Allied fighter aircraft, in the race to reach the Arnhem bridge during the afternoon of 17 September.

Swift German reinforcement resulted in an abrupt inversion of odds after the first shock of the airlandings was past. Taking account of casualties, combat ratios on 20 September were three to one in Arnhem in favour of the Germans, two to one against the 82 (US) Airborne Division in Nijmegen-Groesbeek, and almost evens against the 101

(US) Airborne Division being reinforced by XXX Corps as it moved along the corridor. Local German superiority was often achieved because airborne units had to be dispersed to cover 'Hell's Highway' and hold out under pressure until GARDEN grounds forces linked up.

This speed of reaction achieved decisive tactical results. The blocking action instituted by the SS-Kampfgruppe Spindler in the western suburbs of Arnhem during the night of 17–18 September had a crucial effect on the outcome of the battle of Arnhem. Bittrich, Spindler's superior, remarked: 'It was he we have to thank for blocking a steely opponent. Compared to the Kampfgruppe Spindler's performance . . . all other actions in Arnhem should be relegated to a backseat position.'[5] Beginning with two infantry companies of former artillery gunners on 17 September, his Kampfgruppe was quickly reinforced by a further two battalions of SS infantry, assault pioneers and a company of *Reichsarbeitsdienst*. By the time the 1st and 4th British Parachute Brigades were trying to fight through to Frost on the Arnhem bridge, Spindler was defending with two more subsidiary battle groups formed from his own resources – 'Harder' and 'von Allworden'. The force consisted by then of some 20 hastily formed infantry companies varying from SS veterans to navy and pioneer corps personnel who did not know the first thing about infantry fighting. Frost was isolated at the bridge by this successful blocking action, which enabled the Germans to regain the initiative and go over to the offensive, thereby sealing the perimeter from the east. By the end of the battle, the Kampfgruppe had expanded from two companies to three integral battle groups with up to 30 tanks and armoured vehicles numbering some 1,000 men, and held a 2,000-metre frontage around the airborne perimeter. Spindler must have been an outstanding leader to have successfully led such a disparate and *ad hoc* battle group. He was awarded the Knight's Cross on 27 September. Three months later to the day he was killed when his staff car was strafed by a fighter bomber during the Battle of the Bulge.[6]

XXX Corps, advancing along one easily defensible road, was never able proportionally to match this build-up, and achieve the odds ratio necessary for rapid success. More specifically, it was never able to push forward sufficient infantry by ground, or fly them in by air, to secure what were essentially infantry objectives. The weather had an important impact upon this inability to reinforce. On 18 and 20 September ground haze obstructed British take-off airfields, and this was accentuated by poor weather conditions in the Dutch combat zone on 19, 21 and 22 September. After a temporary clear spell on the 23rd, the weather closed in again during the final

phase on 24 and 25 September. Aerial reinforcements after 18 September were piecemeal and indecisive. The build-up race was lost. Three more British battalions and two more American parachuted or air-landed around Arnhem and Son but none reached Nijmegen. This was of crucial significance because Brigadier-General Gavin's 82 Airborne Division lacked sufficient infantry to storm the Nijmegen bridges before the arrival of XXX Corps on 20 September. Two more Polish battalions dropped at Driel on 21 September, but no infantry reached the 82 Division's Overassault drop-zone until 23 September, when three American glider battalions and a further Polish battalion landed. Two Polish battalions landing at Driel caused the Germans to relocate and commit all their reserves in the area – five battalions numbering 2,500 men. This is just one indication of the potential for disrupting the German build-

The Polish parachute landings obliged the Germans to relocate five reserve battalions numbering up to 2,500 men.

A drop nearer Arnhem would probably not have succeeded as they would have been nearer to the main infantry strength of the 9SS.

up that was lost to the Allies due to inclement weather. During the same period of intermittent Allied reinforcement, the Germans, by contrast, raised their numerical stake in First Fallschirmjaeger Army's rear combat zone by an equivalent of 30 battalion groups. MARKET-GARDEN was condemned, therefore, to move in the Allies favour only at XXX Corps laborious pace through the airborne corridor. Progress was made difficult and the road cut on at least two occasions by the sudden deployment of newly arrived German panzer and infantry forces.

Apart from identifying what the Germans felt to be the decisive factors contri-

buting to success, some of the 'myths' surrounding the battle of Arnhem and MARKET-GARDEN have been stripped away by details revealed in this study. There is, in particular, a belief that the British should possibly have jumped nearer the Arnhem bridge – perhaps on the city itself, or at least on both sides of the road bridge to capture it by a *coup de main*. It is unlikely, bearing in mind the geographical dispositions of IISS Corps, that this would have resulted in a different outcome. Such a view is confirmed by an examination of Army Group B's view expressed in a report released five days after the battle. These are spontaneous judgements rather than historic analysis formulated with the benefit of hindsight. 'The enemy's chief mistake,' it discloses, 'was not to have landed the entire 1st British Airborne Division at once rather than over a period of three days.' Nothing was said about the wrong place, apart from the distance dissipating some of the effect of surprise, but it did admit that 'the second chief mistake [was] that a second airborne division was not dropped in the area west of Arnhem', in other words, in the same place to reinforce the first.[7]

SS-Captain Sepp Krafft, a battalion commander faced with the dilemma of what to do on the spot, was initially puzzled at what the objective to these landings could be: the capture of Model's Army Group B headquarters? Deelen airfield or the Rhine bridge?[8] It was not difficult for him writing after the battle to come up with the correct rhetorical answer, but he does make a number of illuminating observations to illustrate his point. Firstly, the thick woodland area enclosing 1st British Airborne Division's drop-zones provided both good concealment and protection for forming up, and a covered approach to the Arnhem bridge. The distance from the bridge was such that it was not the obvious objective. 'Because of the height of the trees in the wood,' Krafft admits, 'the DZ has not been accurately pinpointed.' This was at 1400, immediately after the landings on 17 September, when his battalion was only two kilometres away from the nearest landing-site. So disorientated did his company commanders and reconnaissance groups become in these trees that the initial forays against the landings were ineffective. The woods screening the original British landing-zones provided, therefore, a degree of protection during the crucial forming-up period, and enabled the 1st, 2nd and 3rd Battalions of the Parachute Regiment largely to bypass Krafft during the early course of the fighting. It was Spindler's Kampfgruppe not Krafft's that was to institute the vital

block delaying entry into Arnhem. Although it had imposed important delays, General Kussin's death illustrates that Krafft's battalion had already been bypassed by the early evening of 17 September.

The nearest drop-zones to Arnhem lay north of the city and south at Driel. Flak would not have been the critical factor hindering a successful landing, as estimated by British planners; this would rather have been the presence of the IISS Corps in the immediate vicinity. Their reaction times, if these nearer sites had been chosen, would have been even faster than on the actual drop-zones used. They were in close proximity to the 9SS and not effectively screened by woodland. Apart from Krafft's three companies, there were two more 9SS infantry 'alarm' companies in Arnhem, two more only three kilometres away in Velp, and a further two in Rheden, four to five kilometres away. In fact, the main infantry strength of the 9SS lay along the Arnhem-Zutphen road within easy reach of the city and the nearer DZs. There were about 10 quick-reaction 'alarm' companies within 15 kilometres of the road bridge alone. A drop nearer Arnhem would not have succeeded.

Normandy had highlighted the potentially disastrous effect that a scattered night-landing could have upon the cohesiveness of a divisional-strength airborne assault. The Allies resolved not to repeat this mistake at Arnhem. It is a fundamental principle in airborne operations to land as close to the objective as possible. However, it is likely that the cohesion of any force that had landed upon Arnhem or its immediate environs would have been sorely tested by immediate counter-attacks by veteran infantry units, specifically trained to react swiftly and aggressively against an air-landed enemy. The western drop-zones at least enabled 1st British Airborne Division to land as a whole (if not complete), and form up before being subjected to pressure. This is a particularly vulnerable moment for the air-landed formation, because there is surprise on both sides. Tactical for the defending forces, but the attackers must quickly form up and orientate themselves in unfamiliar terrain. The drop-zones chosen around Arnhem were readily defensible. Capturing both ends of the Arnhem bridge would have posed no greater advantage than holding the more easily-defended northern end. Holding both sides with a split force would have fragmented Frost's strength, and possibly have reduced the length of time that the Allies did hold out.

Frost's capture of the Arnhem bridge was not dependent upon luck but rather on a paralysis of German command, who were uncertain initially of what the enemy's objective could be. SS-Captain Graebner's initial failure to reinforce the Arnhem road bridge security pickets was no different to all the other German assessments at that moment – namely, that some other unit was earmarked to defend it. This failure of command and control was caused by the death of the *Stadtkommandant* of Arnhem, General Kussin, whose job it was to allocate responsibilities, but who nevertheless rode impetuously into a 3 PARA ambush trying to clarify the situation. The forces on the bridge were inexperienced and missed Frost's approach. Thereupon a succession of relieving German units arrived at both ends of the road bridge and blundered into the

SS-Captain Graebner's (left) *failure to reinforce the Arnhem bridge was no different from any other German assessment at that time, namely, that somebody else was earmarked to defend it. General Bittrich* (right) *had ordered him to Nijmegen.* (Fuerbringer Collection)

British resistance with no clear idea of the situation. Control was not re-established until early on the morning of 18 September, when Frost's battalion was already firmly entrenched.

British veterans often pose the question: was there ever realistically a chance to relieve Frost following the sudden Allied capture of the Nijmegen bridge on the night of 20 September? Evidence suggests that the chance was lost to slip a mechanised combat group into Arnhem after the collapse. Between 1900 and midnight there were only security pickets on the road in between Nijmegen and Arnhem, namely at Elst, numbering one to two companies strong. Between midnight and dawn isolated strongpoints had been established, but these too could have been overwhelmed by a determined force. Once again, astonishing German improvisation by the 10SS succeeded in regrouping a force of over two battalions and 16 tanks between 1900 and midnight on 20 September immediately north of Nijmegen. By dawn this force had been thickened to five battalions and 25 tanks and SPs firmly established on a line running through Elst. By then, any attempt to force the road would have been vulnerable to powerful flanking attacks from the east. It was truly a missed opportunity.

This historical analysis of German success in combating a major airborne incursion into a rear combat zone was started very much with a contemporary NATO dilemma in mind. How does one protect the rear combat zone in central Europe against the possibility of massive Warsaw Pact airlandings supported by armoured ground attacks, should a conventional conflict occur in Europe? Much has changed since 1944; are any lessons still relevant today?

One problem facing the armies of the western democracies experiencing population declines, greater affluence and a lessening of threat perception, is where to find the necessary manpower to project a credible conventional response in order to reduce dependence on nuclear weapons. An option examined by some NATO members is an expansion of their Territorial Army forces, to cope with the sort of tasks faced by Student's forces in 1944. Indeed, one interpretation of the German success in MARKET-GARDEN is that regular armoured and airborne formations were deflected from their aim by the employment of Territorial Army soldiers. The Allies had essentially been fought to a standstill by untrained or partly-trained troops that had been quickly formed into *ad hoc* combat groups – *Kampfgruppen* – consisting of 16- to 17-year-old teenagers, or old and infirm men taken from NCO schools and logistic organisations from all three services: army, navy and airforce. Soldiers had been summoned from headquarter staffs, defunct airfields and coastal defence batteries and were required to fight as infantry in units where only an average of 10 per cent had any previous active service experience. SS-Lieutenant-Colonel Walther Harzer was to write 20 years after the battle of Arnhem:

'It is with personal pride that I regard this German victory, because it was achieved not by regular units, but by railway workers, *Arbeitsdienst* and Luftwaffe personnel as well, who had never been trained for infantry work and were actually unsuitable for house-to-house fighting.'[9]

One lesson to be learned is that regular formations are also needed to provide a stiffener or backbone to these formations, in order to achieve success. In the Arnhem context the only truly veteran (or regular) formation in the vicinity was the IISS Panzer 'Corps' undergoing refitting and refurbishment. Both the 9SS and 10SS were only at between 20 per cent to 30 per cent of their established strengths – 2,500 and 3,000 strong respectively. Both units had already been required to send combat groups to bolster the line in southern Holland and possessed virtually no tanks. The corps, resembling more accurately a modern infantry brigade, was dispersed geographically into multiple-company quick-reaction, so-called 'alarm' units. Although at only a fraction of its normal strength, both divisional Kampfgruppen retained a veteran cadre at its core, sufficiently resilient to splinter on untrained elements with some chance of success. This core of survivors from the divisions that had formed only the year before had, nevertheless, received exhaustive anti-airborne training, and they were to prove to be the mainstay of the defence.

What is generally forgotten, however, is the appalling cost in human terms that the commitment of such untrained forces brings. The SS-Kampfgruppe Gropp, an air defence unit employed as infantry, formed up with 87 men on 17 September. By the end of the battle it had only seven men left.[10] Due to shortages, regular forces were rarely relieved in the line and as a consequence were often fought to a standstill. An even higher price was demanded of the inexperienced soldiers in the hastily formed 'territorial' Kampfgruppe. Although such soldiers can be gainfully employed in defence, they are not suited to the more robust, fast-moving and tactically versatile business of the counter-attack. Consequently, casualties were high – far higher than the 3,300 casualties admitted by Field Marshal Model for the whole of the MARKET-GARDEN area on 27 September.

An examination of contemporary diaries and unit returns reveals just how high these may, in fact, have been.[11] Up to ten units identified operating in the Arnhem area claim they suffered up to or in excess of 50 per cent casualties. These were primarily SS units. German battalions inured to high losses in previous campaigns, especially in Russia, retained their cohesion in battle, despite heavy losses, more readily than their Allied opposites. An examination of this evidence, and the probably understated casualties of other units committed in Arnhem of, say, 10 per cent to 15 per cent of the unit total, suggests a casualty rate in Arnhem of 2,500 to 3,000, of which one-third were probably fatalities. This alone almost equals the MARKET-GARDEN official total. J.A. Hey,[12] having researched both British and German war graves in the Arnhem area, has located 1,725 German war dead relating to this period. Working on a norm that deaths generally represent one-third of the total casualty figure, this suggests that total casualties may have been over 5,000. Although not all the deaths may have occurred during the MARKET-GARDEN period, the majority did. Furthermore, those wounded who later died outside the combat zone, or were buried elsewhere (such as General Kussin and his driver and interpreter) are not included.

German casualties suffered in the corridor could be estimated at a low 25 per cent of unit established strengths (as admitted by the Kampfgruppe Walther), which indicated a possible further 3,750 casualties. Taking these together, even at best Model's official figures should be doubled or enlarged even more to a total of 6,000 to 8,000. This statistic makes further sense when it is viewed alongside the depressing Allied totals between 17–25 September. 1st British Airborne Division lost 7,212, the 82nd (US) Airborne Division, 1,432 and the 101st, 2,110. All up, the airborne phase cost 11,850 casualties. XXX Corps incurred an estimated 1,480 and 70 tanks.[13] As both sides were often in the attack a ratio of one German to two Allied dead is perhaps more realistic than official figures suggest. German records are incomplete, but there is little doubt their losses have been understated.

Inexperience demands a high price in war. Would, therefore, an expansion of the western democracies' territorial forces provide a suitable panacea for NATO's future manning problems? Will a less physically resilient and more questioning society be prepared, like the German infantry in 1944, voluntarily to pay such a heavy price?

Army Group B's synopsis of post-operational lessons to be derived from combating airborne forces landed in rear areas is still every bit as relevant to NATO forces today as in 1944.[14] 'An observation net' is required, as part of an 'elementary warning system' which should 'furnish estimates' of enemy air-landed strengths to 'reception centres', which are the unit headquarters located in the rear zone. This is vital, as at least one of von Tettau's units – Sicherheits Regiment 26 – was initially channelled away from Arnhem, investigating bogus landings at Veenendall.

A cohesive command structure is required. Its absence initially cost the Germans the easy capture of the Arnhem bridge, which took over four days to recover. The importance of a mobile reaction force is identified to combat the enemy's 'weakest moments, which are just before and directly after the landings'. Coupled with this requirement is the need to bring heavy weapons to bear as quickly as possible. Swift, aggressive action by commanders at all levels is of paramount importance, as SS-Captain Sepp Krafft was to point out in his post-combat report:

'It is vitally important to attack the enemy immediately with any forces available, not with any hope of destroying him but to disturb and disrupt his preparations for battle. It is not possible to destroy overwhelming airborne forces with slight forces, but one can pin him down to secure time to prepare counter-measures.'[15]

Special 'pursuit groups' were set up in Army Group B's rear combat zone after the landings, commanded by 'an energetic' and capable officer, to produce just the rapidity of response emphasised. In NATO terms this would probably require a helicopter force, as refugees would block roads. Holland did not present this problem to the Germans, as its inhabitants 'stayed at home', waiting to be liberated.

The requirement to bring heavy weapons to bear means essentially armoured vehicles, tanks or SPs. Surprisingly, during the MARKET-GARDEN battles the tank was decisive in a non-traditional area – street fighting – but not along the XXX Corps contested 'Hell's Highway'. Tanks broke the offensive power of 1st British Airborne Division in Arnhem, with the introduction of Assault Gun Brigade 280. However, the terrain between Eindhoven and Arnhem was totally unsuited to the armoured punch mounted by XXX Corps. 1st British Airborne Division's fate was sealed as soon as it was pinned down by superior numbers of infantry, because then enemy tanks could roam virtually at will, systematically reducing strongpoints in the role of SP artillery.

'King Tiger' tanks were invulnerable to anything, apart from high-velocity shot from the few surviving 17-pounder British anti-tank guns keeping them at bay in Oosterbeek. German success against Allied tanks in the corridor was based upon the effectiveness of the 'panzerfaust', simple enough to be operated by novice infantry, yet effective enough at close range to penetrate any Allied tank. Moreover, unlike almost all NATO hand-held anti-tank weapons, it could be fired from cover, and with a good chance of success. This individual capability is not enjoyed by many infantrymen today, who are now largely dependent upon the support of specialist anti-tank platoons employing technologically more sophisticated weaponry.

Model's synopsis of the lessons learned

Tanks broke the offensive power of 1st British Airborne Division in Arnhem with the introduction of Assault Gun Brigade 280, elements here advance down Weverstraat to Oosterbeek.

from MARKET-GARDEN ends on identifying the need to locate quick-reaction forces on the outskirts of towns, so that they are not isolated and trapped in built-up areas by partisan attacks. More importantly, he emphasises that defence measures 'must be realistically rehearsed at least once a month'.

The fundamental tenet to be grasped with regard to the German view of the failure of MARKET-GARDEN is that already identified by the commander of the Frundsberg, SS-Colonel Heinz Harmel. 'Historians,' he remarked, 'have narrow-mindedly concerned themselves [in the past] with Arnhem and Oosterbeek. The Allies were stopped in the south just north of Nijmegen – that is why Arnhem turned

Once the Paratroopers were pinned down by superior numbers of infantry in Oosterbeek, German tanks roamed at will, reducing strongpoints in the role of SP artillery.

out as it did.'[16] Controversies such as whether the British should have jumped nearer the Arnhem bridge pale into insignificance when related to this central point. Quite simply, the Allies were unable to win the reinforcement race. The battles around Arnhem cannot be viewed in isolation. It was merely the final objective along a corridor of minor and major actions fought between the Neerpelt bridgehead and the 'Island' and Betuwe. The battle on the Waal at Nijmegen proved to be the decisive event which, nevertheless, produced a hollow victory. When the British captured the Nijmegen bridge, the Germans already had the Arnhem bridge in their grasp. It was too late for both sides to achieve a decisive

result, and delays imposed in the south spelt the doom of 1st British Airborne Division. The Germans knew it was finished from the moment it was encircled on 20 September. From that moment onwards, Oosterbeek became just another *Kesselschlacht* – a battle routinely to reduce a pocket; a side-show in relation to the crisis being enacted on the Waal. This is why to date it has not had any particular significance in German military histories.

In terms of human suffering, however, it was the most important event shaping the lives of the soldiers who fought it. The human factor is the constant imponderable in battle. This is why, in an attempt to clarify some of the issues, the battle has been portrayed here through the eyes of the German soldiers who participated. Their hardships and those of their other contemporaries in southern Holland did not end on September 26th.

A *Feldwebel* (sergeant) of the 712 Infantry Division wrote as the German line was again pushed back in the Antwerp area:

'28 September 1944. We are again fighting tanks with rifles . . . We report to the commanding officer. A fresh attack is to be mounted – Murder! . . . I go back to my fox hole.

'29 September 1944. Our battalion is now two kilometres back and is to cover the retirement of the division . . . yesterday, before we started off we got canteen supplies: two tubes of toothpaste (not one of us poor swines has a toothbrush on him), one tin of shoe cream (who is still polishing his boots?) . . . I get the order to take an anti-tank section to the road and act as a covering party. It is a suicide order from the start. About five o'clock we hear the noise of tanks coming towards us. One of the monsters comes up behind us. I take up my panzerfaust but the distance is too great. There is nothing left now but to surrender. The Britishers, however, are not taking any prisoners, but open fire on us. Four men are mown down at once. Now another tank rolls up on our left. We run along a ditch. Both tanks are firing all their guns. Running forward quickly in order to get out of the zone of fire, I reach a sheltered spot and lie there exhausted. The tanks pass by . . . I don't know how long all this lasted. I am only surprised at my calmness. We must await nightfall, when the tanks will move away. We are constantly pressing ourselves against the side of the ditch. Now the tanks have reached the company. There will not be much left of our battalion. Who can fight tanks with rifles? . . .'[17]

A final irony was yet to be played out at Arnhem.

CHAPTER XXVII

Postscript – The Final Irony

Where is the fire support? Where are our supplies? Where is our signals detachment and where are the remaining units of the Kampfgruppe?

SS-Captain

As SS-Captain Heinrich Oelkers pushed his dinghy into the current he was filled with a sense of hopeless forboding. They should not be doing this. After what it had cost the British and Poles to cross and recross the lower Rhine, they should not be engaged in the same madness. The supreme irony of the battle of Arnhem was that his battalion was to conduct an assault river crossing over the very feature an entire elite airborne division had failed to secure.

As for many other German soldiers, the fighting did not end on 26 September because 1st British Airborne Division withdrew across the lower Rhine. Although MARKET-GARDEN was past the point of saving, the battle did not climax; it simply petered out, almost unnoticed by some. SS-Junker Rudolf Lindemann recalled after the capture of the Hartenstein Hotel that 'there was no lasting feeling of victory on the German side'. He confided: 'We were glad the Arnhem action was finished, but this was short lived.'[1] The 10SS, fighting between the lower Rhine and Waal south of Arnhem, were faring no better. SS-Colonel Heinz Harmel claimed that '4 October was one of the costliest days the 10SS had suffered since the fighting in Holland started. The vitals of the division had been torn out to such an extent that it was not capable of offensive action in the immediate ensuing period.'[2] The Frundsberg was still contesting XXX Corps advance.

General von Tettau had directed Oelkers' battalion 'to form a bridgehead south of Arnhem over the Rhine, and hold until a defence line north of the river had been established. Strong British forces [were] to be pinned down at the same time to achieve this aim.' His unit was to cross by Castel Doerweth about 2,000 metres south-west of the Driel ferry. Opposing them were units of the 5 Dorsets, later relieved by paratroopers from the 101 (US) Airborne Division. Oelker's Kampfgruppe consisted of a company from Lippert's SS-NCO school 'Arnheim', a company from the *Reichsarbeitsdienst*, another of naval personnel, a fourth from the Hermann Goering Training Regiment, and the fifth, a Luftwaffe company from Fliegerhorst Battalion 3. The attack formed part of IISS Corps' offensive, beginning on 1 October between the lower Rhine and Waal. Newly arrived units from the 9th and 116th Panzer Divisions (Kampfgruppen) attacked from the east, supported by the 10SS. It was anticipated that 363 Volksgrenadier Division would attack in concert from the west under the aegis of a newly established XII SS Corps as soon as it had formed up.

Whatever the grand operational design, Oelkers knew that his assault was merely a feint attack to cloak the main operation. He exclaimed in his diary:

'*Ja* – just about the end! All that this battle group is probably still capable

The crossings took place 2,000 metres south-west of the Driel Ferry (shown here) *across very similar terrain. The operation was a catastrophic failure, a parody of 1st British Airborne Division's experience just over a week before.* (Fuerbringer Collection)

of doing! Preparations continued night and day. Immense problems became apparent; there were no assault pioneers or heavy weapons.'[3]

He was summoned to von Tettau's command post the following day, and sarcastically recorded von Tettau's stated intention: ' "Bridgehead is to be secured and held no matter what the cost" – so read the order!' This was all very well for the divisional staff; he, however, had the practical difficulty of somehow implementing the plan and getting five companies across the river. On 1 October, with 'H' hour approaching,

Oelkers discovered to his dismay that 'there were only four boats; where was the army supplement?' He had no choice but to proceed:

'The first wave crossed over with frightful casualties. Our own artillery did not fire enough and then too wide. I watched this bizarre attempt at an attack whereby some SS men were only able to reach the far bank by swimming and were then immediately engaged in hand-to-hand combat on arrival.'

317

It was a precise re-enactment of the British Dorsetshire Battalion's débâcle that had occurred seven days earlier, in the same spot, but going in the opposite direction. Oelkers decided that the moment had come to cross himself, and he and six others pushed off from the side in a rubber dinghy. The outboard motor refused to start, so they all paddled frantically to the far bank:

'A brave army engineer NCO stayed at the rear of the boat, directing our efforts otherwise we would have drifted off course. He was instantly killed by a shot in the chest. As we neared the bank a machine gun burst hit the dinghy, injuring two men and releasing the air in it. I was lucky – the burst only grazed my knee. Leaping into the water, we attempted to push the riddled boat to dry soil, but failed as we were not able to hang on to it. Unfortunately the dinghy drifted away with our two comrades lying within. I never saw them again.'

The attack had been a fiasco. 'We lay on the muddy bank the entire day, and nobody would go forward.' Their comrades left behind on the north bank attempted to provide fire support. The objective, a brick factory 200 metres from the water's edge was stormed at 2200 under cover of darkness.

'We attacked the objective from the right, something the British had not anticipated. But where were the rest of the troops? Where was the signals detachment?'[4]

Herbert Kessler's Hermann Goering Company now moved forward to run the same murderous gauntlet. He recalled the situation on 1 October, following Oelkers' initial assault:

'In the evening it got livelier. We were ordered across the river. We marched to Castle Doerwerth and lay down 200 metres from the riverside. At midnight I received the order to cross. The pioneers and rubber assault boats are supposed to be already on the bank, ready for us. We move forward. We can't find any pioneers and the rubber dinghies are all shot to pieces. Then up comes a messenger from the rear. "No crossing! The moon's too bright!".'[5]

SS-Junker Rudolf Lindemann had managed to cross in daylight with Oelkers. 'A real disaster,' he recalls. Having captured the brickworks, he set up his mortar position. Oelkers, still unreinforced, was lacking everything. One of his soldiers – Jakabowski – stripped naked and swam back across the river to deliver Oelkers sharp rebuke and orders for the rest of his battalion to get across. 'Finally,' he records in his diary, 'a few sections got across', sufficient to organise a defence ring around the brick factory. Thankfully,

'. . . to our great surprise the first night was quiet. We lay our wounded friends in a brick baking oven. Even then we did not have enough bandages.'

Lindemann from the NCO school 'Arnheim' was more emotionally affected by this minor skirmish than by the whole of the battle for Oosterbeek. The next problem, having established a fragile bridgehead, was to keep it supplied, because, as he recalled, 'enemy machine guns covered the river approaches and mortars the exits. A fast-moving current, moreover, gave the enemy time to bring artillery to bear.' Oelkers had by then even confided to Lindemann that 'the bridgehead is absolutely senseless – we should give it up'.[6] Herbert Kessler would have endorsed this opinion as the pointless blood-letting continued the following day:

'Now it's not bright moonlight, it's suddenly bright sunshine, and we get the order: "Cross at once!" My group was the second to move forward. The first group carrying two rubber dinghies went towards the bank. One dinghy was immediately shot to pieces, the group leader was severely wounded. Those 200 metres to the bank are under heavy artillery fire as well as flanking fire from machine guns. As the wounded group leader was carried past me (he was a friend of mine), I received orders for my group to try it. I jump up, together with my soldiers (about a platoon), run to the rubber dinghy which is still intact, tear down to the bank, and push it into the water, jump into it with three other men, and row it across the river. This all sounds so harmless, but as long as I live I shall never forget that rowing. The shots splashed into the water all around us like hailstones, and how we managed to get to the other side, I don't know to this day. But we did and, still under heavy fire, dug our holes. That crossing in bright daylight was nonsense.'[7]

The next day the situation deteriorated even further. Lieutenant Martin, with the attached Luftwaffe company, lay waiting under heavy fire; 'the men were ready for embarking, but boats not ready' he recorded in his diary on 3 October. They were being constantly harassed by salvoes of mortar and artillery fire, with some twenty to thirty impacts every ten minutes. His company was steadily diminishing under this pounding, 'becoming smaller and smaller'.[8] Oelkers, meanwhile, despaired:

'I am furious with the Regiment, where is the fire support? Where are our supplies? Where is our signals detachment, and where are the remaining units of the Kampfgruppe?'[9]

They were on their way, but could not finally cross until nightfall. Lieutenant Martin wrote on 4 October:

'We finally crossed at 0300. We're with the naval units. Attack starts at 0630. First casualties. 2nd company has withdrawn and I am left alone. Many are left behind. We move to different positions tonight. There are only a few of us left. What's the purpose of all this? I am flank security. Am digging in. The night is cold and stormy.'[10]

His situation mirrored that of Kessler at another point in the same confined bridge-head:

'One didn't dare to get out of the hole, for any reason. I think there were now about 20 of us, with only one machine gun. After we crossed, there were no more reinforcements, because there had been too many casualties.'[11]

Lindemann dolefully remarked that 'the expected Panzer-grenadier counter-attack did not materialise. We heard the tanks but they did not reach us.' For three days the bridgehead was not resupplied. Events were now beginning to resemble the ten-day ordeal, albeit on a smaller scale, that the British paratroopers had endured in Oosterbeek just over a week before. Lieutenant Martin's diary now began to record the progressive deterioration in the small pocket, an ironic postscript to the more publicised drama that had been enacted in Arnhem.

'5 October: Everybody is exhausted. I am a wreck. Received small amount of mortar shells on our positions. Have not had warm food for days. Nothing to drink. The war? Snipers have us pinned down. I have no idea of what is going on.

'6 October: We have been in fox holes since early morning. The road to the factory is covered by enemy mortar and artillery fire. We are along this side of the Rhine. Major Stuks killed at 1700. There is no sense to this. We are all weak.

'7 October: Freeze during the night. Still receiving strong mortar and artillery fire on factory and positions. Many men wounded. Situation hopeless. We just sit in our fox holes and wait. A house on the dam was burned during the night. Two men killed. Combat noises [the relief attempt] from the west. Bombers flying over.'

After ten days there was no further sense in this. Lindemann recalled the struggle his battalion commander had to reverse von Tettau's directive:

'Oelkers said we had to get out of the bridgehead but von Tettau refused. He asked a second time, submitting a written recommendation, but von Tettau said he was 'to hold'. Eventually giving up, Oelkers ordered the bridgehead cleared on his own initiative. Von Tettau attempted to court-martial him for it.'[12]

Only 35 men from Lindemann's original company of 120 made it back to the home bank. Lieutenant Martin was, meanwhile, completely unaware of Oelkers' efforts at the divisional command post on their behalf. He wrote:

'8 October. Am digging my fox hole deeper. Have not washed for five days. Receiving strong artillery fire. Situation very vague. Ration supply is messed up. Argument with Major Merkens. 0115 hit by our own artillery.

'9 October: Washed at medics. Situation restless. Received order to hold bridgehead under all conditions. Shell hit five metres from my fox hole.'[13]

Oelkers had the bridgehead cleared the following day. The operation was successfully carried out. Lindemann admired Oelkers, whom he thought to be 'a very good tactician'. The battalion commander was, characteristically, the last man to leave the bridgehead, in a dinghy which, Lindemann remembers, was 'shot full of holes'. They had made it. When questioned whether he had ever despaired at their situation, Lindemann declared 'we never felt abandoned because of Oelkers' leadership'.

The abandoned positions were checked out by American paratroopers of the 501 Regiment of the 101 Airborne Division. The body of the dead Luftwaffe officer was considered worth searching. As his personal effects were emptied from his pockets and discarded in the bottom of the trench, they came across a diary. They could not understand it, but they took it nevertheless because some of the entries appeared to contain items of military significance. It was passed on to the Regimental Interrogation Team for examination and translation. The bodies scattered about were subsequently buried. The diary belonged to Lieutenant Martin.

Appendices

Appendix A   Orders

IISS Pz Corps

1340 hours   **17.9.44**

WARNING ORDER   **By telephone**

Enemy: Enemy airlandings. Main point of effort identified around Arnhem and Nijmegen.

Tasks:

9SS Pz Div
— Division is to recce Arnhem and Nijmegen.
— Division is to assemble immediately, take Arnhem and defeat the enemy airlandings by Oosterbeek west of Arnhem.
— Absolute speed is necessary. The Arnhem bridge is to be occupied by strong security forces.

10SS Pz Div
— The Division is to assemble, move to Nijmegen and firmly occupy the main bridges, and defend the Nijmegen bridgehead.

IISS Pz Corps

1600 hours   **17.9.44**

CORPS ORDER TO 9SS   **By telephone**

— Harzer's divisional Battle Group is to assemble in the Velp area. From there it is to be prepared to attack the enemy who has landed in Oosterbeek in approximately brigade strength.

1630 hours

CORPS ORDER TO 9SS

— The main body of SS Reconnaissance Battalion 9 is to recce Nijmegen via Arnhem. Smaller sub-units are to recce towards Oosterbeek, and secure the remainder of the divisions move to Arnhem.

(Source: Fuerbringer 9SS-Hohenstaufen)

IISS Pz Corps

1730 hours   17.9.44

CORPS ORDERS   By telephone

Tasks: General Outline

IISS Pz Panzer Corps is to immediately attack and destroy the enemy. The following forces are to be employed:

    Within boundaries in Arnhem: Kampfgruppe 9SS Pz Div against Oosterbeek and the enemy bridgehead north of the Rhine.

    In Nijmegen: Kampfgruppe 10SS Pz Div.

Execution:

Tasks:

9SS Pz Div:
Division is to throw back the enemy which has already penetrated Arnhem by attacking westwards, and eventually down to the lower Rhine.

10SS Pz Div:
Division is to attack the enemy forces that have landed by Nijmegen, take possession of the Nijmegen bridges, hold them, and advance to the southern boundary of the town.

It is particularly vital that the Nijmegen enemy forces are prevented from joining those in the north.

Co-ordinating Instructions:

- Dividing line between 9SS and 10SS Pz Divs is Velp (inclusive to 9SS) the Arnhem road bridge (inclusive to 9SS) and the lower Rhine towards the west.
- The SS Bn Krafft is already in action directly north of Arnhem towards Oosterbeek within 9SS boundaries. Contact is to be established.
- In exchange for SS Reconnaissance Battalion 9 immediately detached to 10SS, SS Reconnaissance Battalion 10, and one battery of Heavy SS Werfer Abteilung 102 (Hvy calibre towed rocket-launchers) is to be moved across and taken under command 9SS.
- Integrated quick-reaction companies under command of 9SS are placed under command of the Comd SS Pz Art Regt 9SS Lt-Col Spindler. Kampfgruppe Spindler is to attack along the main east-west thoroughfares through Arnhem towards Oosterbeek. After reaching the western edge of Arnhem he is to form a blocking line between Krafft's SS Bn attacking in the north, south to the lower Rhine.
- SS Reconnaissance Battalion 10 now referred to as the Kampfgruppe Brinkmann is to attack and destroy the enemy parachute battalion occupying the northern ramp of the Arnhem bridge. This is in order to quickly fight a resupply route to the 10SS in Nijmegen.

(Source: Fuerbringer 9SS Hohenstaufen)

Appendix B The German Order of Battle During Operation Market Garden 17-26 Sep

KEY TO SYMBOLS USED

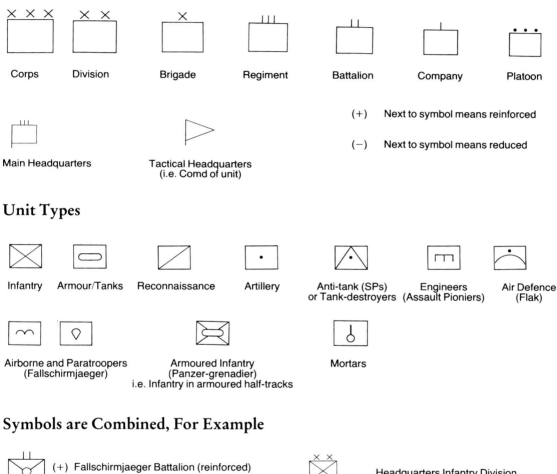

Corps Division Brigade Regiment Battalion Company Platoon

(+) Next to symbol means reinforced

(−) Next to symbol means reduced

Main Headquarters

Tactical Headquarters
(i.e. Comd of unit)

Unit Types

Infantry Armour/Tanks Reconnaissance Artillery Anti-tank (SPs) or Tank-destroyers Engineers (Assault Pioniers) Air Defence (Flak)

Airborne and Paratroopers (Fallschirmjaeger)

Armoured Infantry (Panzer-grenadier) i.e. Infantry in armoured half-tracks

Mortars

Symbols are Combined, For Example

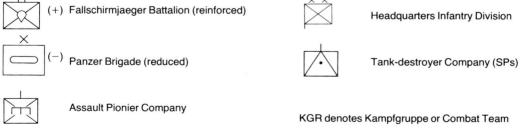

(+) Fallschirmjaeger Battalion (reinforced)

Headquarters Infantry Division

(−) Panzer Brigade (reduced)

Tank-destroyer Company (SPs)

Assault Pionier Company

KGR denotes Kampfgruppe or Combat Team

KAMPFGRUPPE 'WALTHER' NEERPELT BRIDGEHEAD 13-17 SEP 44

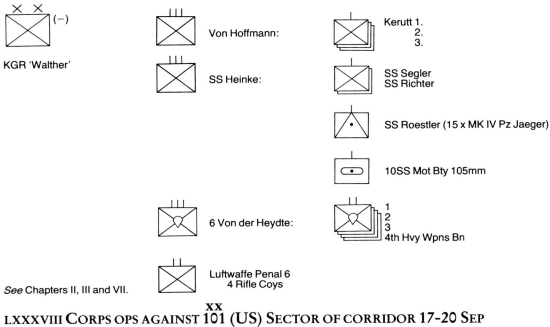

KGR 'Walther'

Von Hoffmann:

SS Heinke:

6 Von der Heydte:

Luftwaffe Penal 6
4 Rifle Coys

See Chapters II, III and VII.

Kerutt 1.
        2.
        3.

SS Segler
SS Richter

SS Roestler (15 x MK IV Pz Jaeger)

10SS Mot Bty 105mm

1
2
3
4th Hvy Wpns Bn

LXXXVIII CORPS OPS AGAINST 101 (US) SECTOR OF CORRIDOR 17-20 SEP

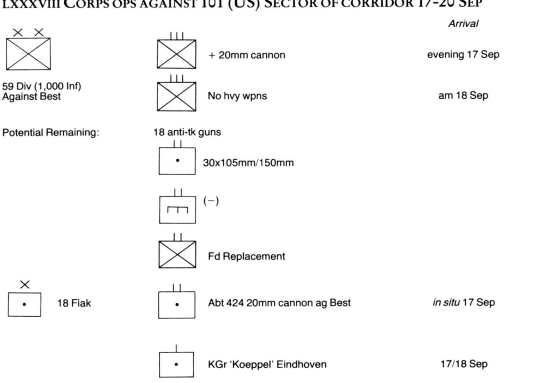

59 Div (1,000 Inf)
Against Best

Potential Remaining:

18 Flak

Arrival

+ 20mm cannon

evening 17 Sep

No hvy wpns

am 18 Sep

18 anti-tk guns

30x105mm/150mm

(−)

Fd Replacement

Abt 424 20mm cannon ag Best

in situ 17 Sep

KGr 'Koeppel' Eindhoven

17/18 Sep

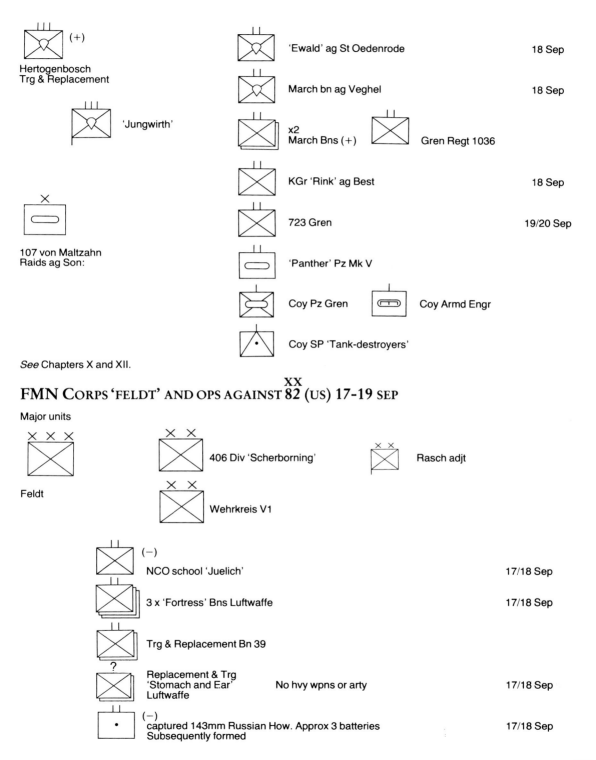

Hertogenbosch
Trg & Replacement (+)

'Jungwirth'

107 von Maltzahn
Raids ag Son:

'Ewald' ag St Oedenrode — 18 Sep

March bn ag Veghel — 18 Sep

x2 March Bns (+) — Gren Regt 1036

KGr 'Rink' ag Best — 18 Sep

723 Gren — 19/20 Sep

'Panther' Pz Mk V

Coy Pz Gren — Coy Armd Engr

Coy SP 'Tank-destroyers'

See Chapters X and XII.

FMN Corps 'feldt' and ops against 82 (US) 17-19 sep

Major units

Feldt

406 Div 'Scherborning'

Rasch adjt

Wehrkreis V1

NCO school 'Juelich' (−) — 17/18 Sep

3 x 'Fortress' Bns Luftwaffe — 17/18 Sep

Trg & Replacement Bn 39

Replacement & Trg 'Stomach and Ear' Luftwaffe — No hvy wpns or arty — 17/18 Sep

(−) captured 143mm Russian How. Approx 3 batteries Subsequently formed — 17/18 Sep

Formed for Attack 18 Sep (from elements of the above. Remainder held line.)

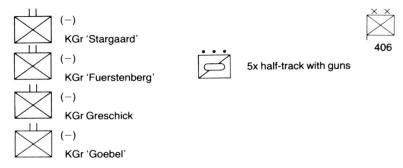

    (–) KGr 'Stargaard'

    (–) KGr 'Fuerstenberg'

    (–) KGr Greschick

    (–) KGr 'Goebel'

5x half-track with guns

406

Circa 3,400 men (?) 5 armd car equivalents. Some Mors & arty

See Chapter X.

NIJMEGEN DEFENCE FORCE 17-20 SEP

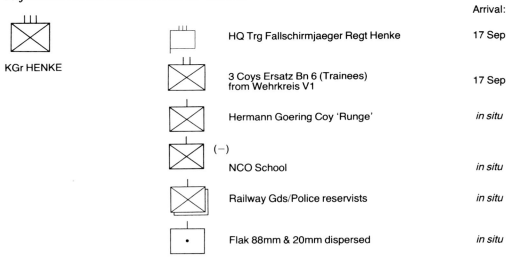

KGr HENKE

Arrival:

		Arrival:
HQ Trg Fallschirmjaeger Regt Henke		17 Sep
3 Coys Ersatz Bn 6 (Trainees) from Wehrkreis V1		17 Sep
Hermann Goering Coy 'Runge'		*in situ*
NCO School (–)		*in situ*
Railway Gds/Police reservists		*in situ*
Flak 88mm & 20mm dispersed		*in situ*

Reinforcements from KG 10SS 'Frundsberg'

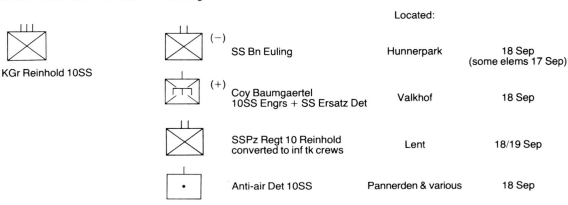

KGr Reinhold 10SS

	Located:	
SS Bn Euling (–)	Hunnerpark	18 Sep (some elems 17 Sep)
Coy Baumgaertel 10SS Engrs + SS Ersatz Det (+)	Valkhof	18 Sep
SSPz Regt 10 Reinhold converted to inf tk crews	Lent	18/19 Sep
Anti-air Det 10SS	Pannerden & various	18 Sep

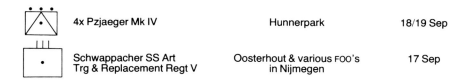

4x Pzjaeger Mk IV	Hunnerpark	18/19 Sep
Schwappacher SS Art Trg & Replacement Regt V	Oosterhout & various FOO's in Nijmegen	17 Sep

See Chapters VIII, XII, XVI and XVII.

KAMPFGRUPPE 9SS DIV ARNHEM AREA 17.9.44

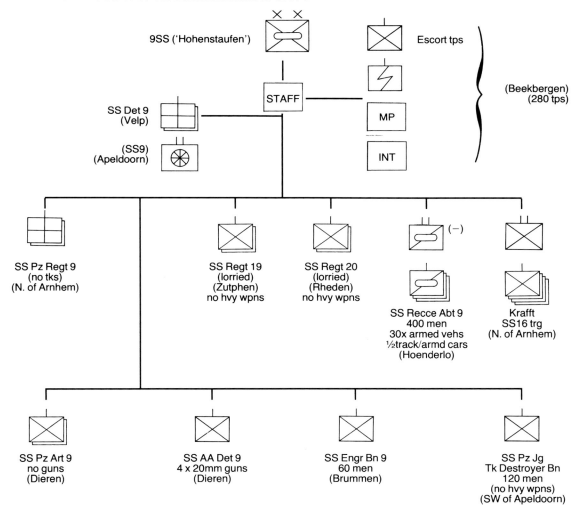

See Chapters III, V, VI and VIII

Circa 3,000 men

Source: *Im Feursturm Letzter Kriegsjahre,* Wilhelm Tieke

Unit history of IISS Panzer Corps.

DIV VON TETTAU 17–18 SEP 44

Forces initially at disposal 1400–2359 17 Sep (See Chapters IX, XIV and XVII.)

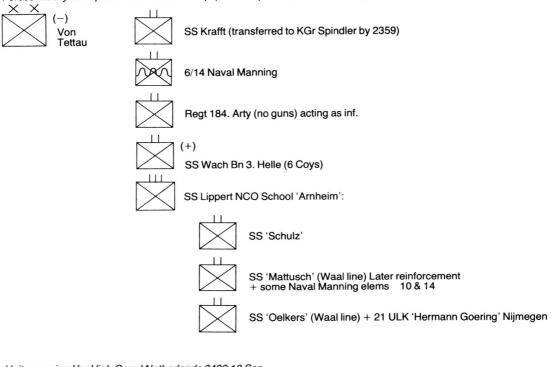

Von Tettau (−)

SS Krafft (transferred to KGr Spindler by 2359)

6/14 Naval Manning

Regt 184. Arty (no guns) acting as inf.

SS Wach Bn 3. Helle (6 Coys) (+)

SS Lippert NCO School 'Arnheim':

SS 'Schulz'

SS 'Mattusch' (Waal line) Later reinforcement
+ some Naval Manning elems   10 & 14

SS 'Oelkers' (Waal line) + 21 ULK 'Hermann Goering' Nijmegen

Units promised by High Comd Netherlands 0400 18 Sep

SS KGr 'Eberwein'

KGr 'Knoche' (Regt HQ & 2nd Bn Sicherheits Regt 26) (+)

Regt 184 (prev. reserve now committed)

KGr 3 Holland Airfield Area (+)

Pz Coy 224. Up to 17 tks. These arrived piecemeal. Mainly French Renaults initially.

Units promised from Trg & Replacement Regt 'Hermann Goering'.

Units in attack by dawn 18 Sep

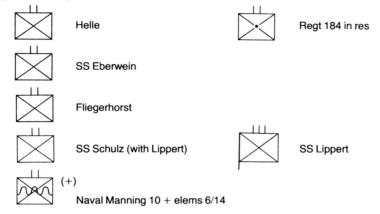

Helle

Regt 184 in res

SS Eberwein

Fliegerhorst

SS Schulz (with Lippert)

SS Lippert

(+)

Naval Manning 10 + elems 6/14

Source: *Gefechtsbericht ueber die Schlacht bei Arnheim,* 17–26 Sept 44.

THE KAMPFGRUPPE 'SPINDLER' 9SS 17–25 SEP 44

17 Sep   *Loc from DZs*

Approx 1700   Pz Arty 9 as inf. circa 120 strong   Dieren 8–9km

Afternoon   (–)   SS KGr 'Moeller'. 60–100 Engrs as inf.   Brummen 10–12km

Midnight (approx)   SS Krafft 4 Coys. Some hvy wpns, circa 440 strong   NW edge of Arnhem

                        (+)   Addit. Quick-reaction 'alarm' tps   Arnhem
                        (?)   and *Reichsarbeitsdienst*, circa 100 (?)

18 Sep   2 further Kampfgruppen formed from reinforcements:

                        (–)   SS Von Allwoerden. Circa 120. Possibly 2xSPs,   S of Apeldoorn 21km
                                      towed PAK anti-tank

                        (–)   SS Harder. 2 Coys of Pz crews as inf, third of log tps   Arnhem Bks with Krafft
                                                                                                     N edge

Early morning

                                      SS Pz Gren Regt 19 (9SS)   Zutphen 15km

                                      SS Pz Gren Regt 20 (9SS)   Rheden 4–5km

329

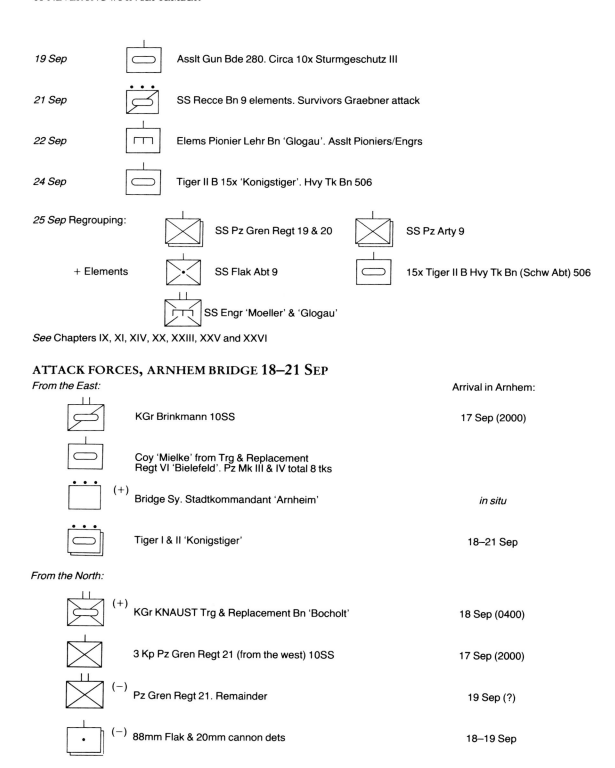

19 Sep — Asslt Gun Bde 280. Circa 10x Sturmgeschutz III

21 Sep — SS Recce Bn 9 elements. Survivors Graebner attack

22 Sep — Elems Pionier Lehr Bn 'Glogau'. Asslt Pioniers/Engrs

24 Sep — Tiger II B 15x 'Konigstiger'. Hvy Tk Bn 506

25 Sep Regrouping:
SS Pz Gren Regt 19 & 20   SS Pz Arty 9

+ Elements — SS Flak Abt 9   15x Tiger II B Hvy Tk Bn (Schw Abt) 506

SS Engr 'Moeller' & 'Glogau'

See Chapters IX, XI, XIV, XX, XXIII, XXV and XXVI

ATTACK FORCES, ARNHEM BRIDGE 18–21 SEP

From the East: Arrival in Arnhem:

KGr Brinkmann 10SS   17 Sep (2000)

Coy 'Mielke' from Trg & Replacement
Regt VI 'Bielefeld'. Pz Mk III & IV total 8 tks

(+) Bridge Sy. Stadtkommandant 'Arnheim'   *in situ*

Tiger I & II 'Konigstiger'   18–21 Sep

From the North:

(+) KGr KNAUST Trg & Replacement Bn 'Bocholt'   18 Sep (0400)

3 Kp Pz Gren Regt 21 (from the west) 10SS   17 Sep (2000)

(−) Pz Gren Regt 21. Remainder   19 Sep (?)

(−) 88mm Flak & 20mm cannon dets   18–19 Sep

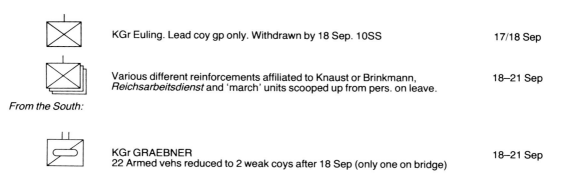

KGr Euling. Lead coy gp only. Withdrawn by 18 Sep. 10SS   17/18 Sep

Various different reinforcements affiliated to Knaust or Brinkmann,   18–21 Sep
Reichsarbeitsdienst and 'march' units scooped up from pers. on leave.

From the South:

KGr GRAEBNER   18–21 Sep
22 Armed vehs reduced to 2 weak coys after 18 Sep (only one on bridge)

Circa Totalled possibly 1,000 men at peak incl. arty and up to 15 (?) Tks.
See Chapters VIII, IX, XV and XVIII.
Source: Fuerbringer, Tieke, Docs, etc.

BUILD UP OF KAMPFGRUPPE 10ss FOR DEFENCE OF NIJMEGEN AND BETUWE 'THE ISLAND' S. OF ARNHEM 18–21 SEP 44

NIJMEGEN DEFENCE FORCE: *Crossed Pannerden ferry following times*

10SS Engr Coy Baumgaertel   Early am 18 Sep

(−) Bn 'Euling' Pz Gren Regt 22   am 18 Sep

KGr 'Reinhold' Tk crews as inf.   pm 18 Sep

Defence of Betuwe after fall of Nijmegen 1900 20 Sep

(−) 16 tks SS Pz Regt 10   Started ni. 18/19 Sep

(−) KGr 'Hartung' Reservists (weak Bn)   19 Sep

(+) SS Pz Gren Regt 22 (1½ Bns)   19 Sep

(−) HQ KGr 10SS   19/20 Sep

HQ (Fwd) IISS Corps   19/20 Sep

Reinforcements for Def Line N. of Nijmegen:

SS Pz Gren Regt 21 (1½ Bns)		Waiting 20 Sep crosses 21 Sept
Hvy Arty Bty SS Arty Regt 10 Flieren		20 Sep
Ferry forces:	Brandt + Munski	18 Sept
	Fla Abt 10 (anti-air)	20 Sep
KGr 'Knaust' departs Arnhem 1200. Elst by 1600		21 Sep
8tks with Knaust 'Panther' Mark IV & III SPs. Possibly Tiger		21 Sep
Remnants Schwappacher SS Trg & Replacement Regt V		*in situ:* 17–21 Sep

See Chapters XVIII and XIX.

DIV VON TETTAU 19–20 SEP 44

North to East (Axis 'Amsterdamsweg' Ede-Arnhem road)

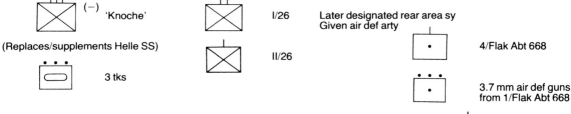

'Knoche'

(Replaces/supplements Helle SS)

3 tks

I/26 — Later designated rear area sy
Given air def arty

II/26

4/Flak Abt 668

3.7 mm air def guns
from 1/Flak Abt 668

+ III air def guns
Fliegerhorst Bn Zaiser

Centre (Axis Ede–Arnhem railway – Wolfheze)

SS 'Eberwein'

Fliegerhorst 'Zaubzer'

South (Axis Wageningen – Heelsum – Oosterbeek)

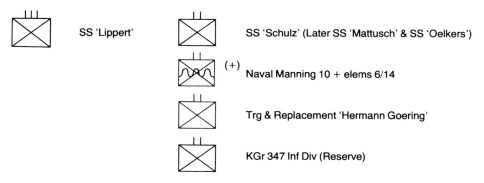

North

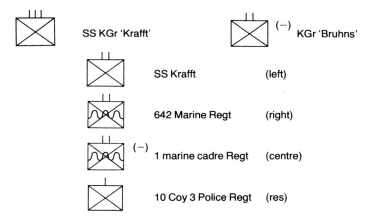

('Putting the lid on the box' – Ede Arnhem rd, then rlwy.)
See chapters XX, XXIII and XXV.

KORPS 'FELDT' 20 SEP
II FALLSCHIRMJAEGER CORPS/406 DIV SPOILING
ATTACK NIJMEGEN HEIGHTS 20 SEP

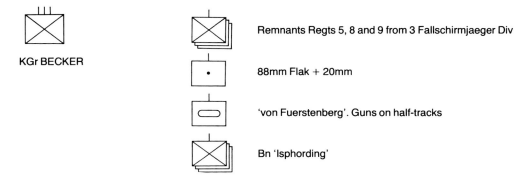

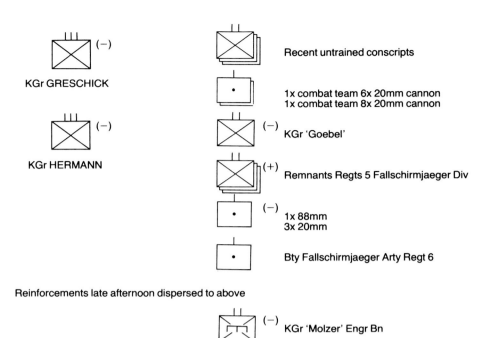

KGr GRESCHICK

KGr HERMANN

Recent untrained conscripts

1x combat team 6x 20mm cannon
1x combat team 8x 20mm cannon

(−) KGr 'Goebel'

(+) Remnants Regts 5 Fallschirmjaeger Div

(−) 1x 88mm
3x 20mm

Bty Fallschirmjaeger Arty Regt 6

Reinforcements late afternoon dispersed to above

(−) KGr 'Molzer' Engr Bn

(−) KGr 'Budde' Fallschirmjaeger Bn

(−) KGr 'Lewin'

XX
Remnants 406 holding line
Source: Kampfbericht Korps Feldt.
See chapter XVI

ATTACKS MOUNTED ON THE AIRBORNE CORRIDOR 22-26 SEPT 44
Attack on Veghel 22–23 Sep

From the East:

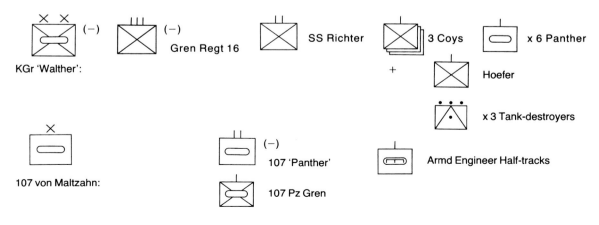

KGr 'Walther':

Gren Regt 16

SS Richter

3 Coys

x 6 Panther

+ Hoefer

x 3 Tank-destroyers

107 von Maltzahn:

(−) 107 'Panther'

107 Pz Gren

Armd Engineer Half-tracks

Reinforcements delayed until 23 Sep:

 'Kerutt'   SS 'Segler'   SS 'Roestel' approx 12–15 Tk-destroyers/SPs

From the West:

KGr 'Huber'

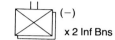 (−)
x 2 Inf Bns

 105 Howitzer

 (−)
1 Coy 559
4x Jagdpanther

Flank and rear protection: (−)
'Zedlitz' rt flank

 (−)
'Bloch' S'Hertogenbosch

6 'Von der Heydte'

 (−)
x 3 Fallschirmjaeger
Bns (incl hvy wpns)

 (−)
1/II 'Finzel'

Attack on Koevering 24–26 Sep

KGr 'Jungwirth'
(4 weak bns +
Tank-destroyers)

 Jungwirth

 Supported by Von der Heydte (*See* above org)

+ (−)
'Bloch' trg bn.

 559 Remnants of 1 Coy

OPERATIONS TO REDUCE THE 'CAULDRON' OOSTERBEEK SEP 20–26 1944

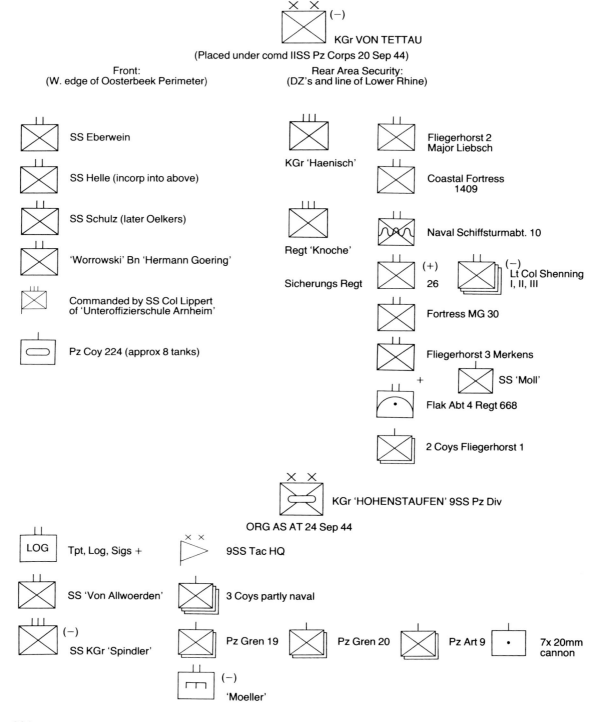

KGr VON TETTAU

(Placed under comd IISS Pz Corps 20 Sep 44)

Front:
(W. edge of Oosterbeek Perimeter)

Rear Area Security:
(DZ's and line of Lower Rhine)

SS Eberwein

SS Helle (incorp into above)

SS Schulz (later Oelkers)

'Worrowski' Bn 'Hermann Goering'

Commanded by SS Col Lippert
of 'Unteroffizierschule Arnheim'

Pz Coy 224 (approx 8 tanks)

KGr 'Haenisch'

Regt 'Knoche'

Sicherungs Regt

Fliegerhorst 2
Major Liebsch

Coastal Fortress
1409

Naval Schiffsturmabt. 10

(+)
26

(−)
Lt Col Shenning
I, II, III

Fortress MG 30

Fliegerhorst 3 Merkens

+

SS 'Moll'

Flak Abt 4 Regt 668

2 Coys Fliegerhorst 1

KGr 'HOHENSTAUFEN' 9SS Pz Div

ORG AS AT 24 Sep 44

LOG

Tpt, Log, Sigs +

9SS Tac HQ

SS 'Von Allwoerden'

3 Coys partly naval

(−)
SS KGr 'Spindler'

Pz Gren 19

Pz Gren 20

Pz Art 9

7x 20mm
cannon

(−)
'Moeller'

336

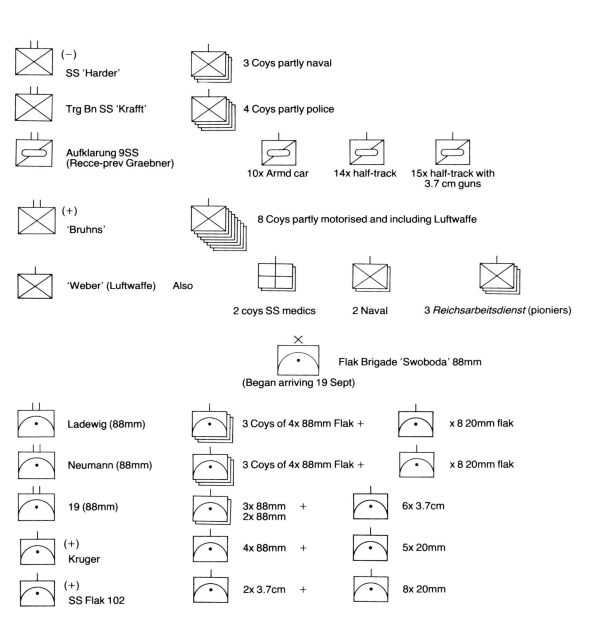

SS 'Harder' (−)

Trg Bn SS 'Krafft'

Aufklarung 9SS
(Recce-prev Graebner)

'Bruhns' (+)

'Weber' (Luftwaffe)   Also

3 Coys partly naval

4 Coys partly police

10x Armd car   14x half-track   15x half-track with
3.7 cm guns

8 Coys partly motorised and including Luftwaffe

2 coys SS medics   2 Naval   3 *Reichsarbeitsdienst* (pioniers)

Flak Brigade 'Swoboda' 88mm
(Began arriving 19 Sept)

Ladewig (88mm)   3 Coys of 4x 88mm Flak +   x 8 20mm flak

Neumann (88mm)   3 Coys of 4x 88mm Flak +   x 8 20mm flak

19 (88mm)   3x 88mm +   6x 3.7cm
2x 88mm

Kruger (+)   4x 88mm +   5x 20mm

SS Flak 102 (+)   2x 3.7cm +   8x 20mm

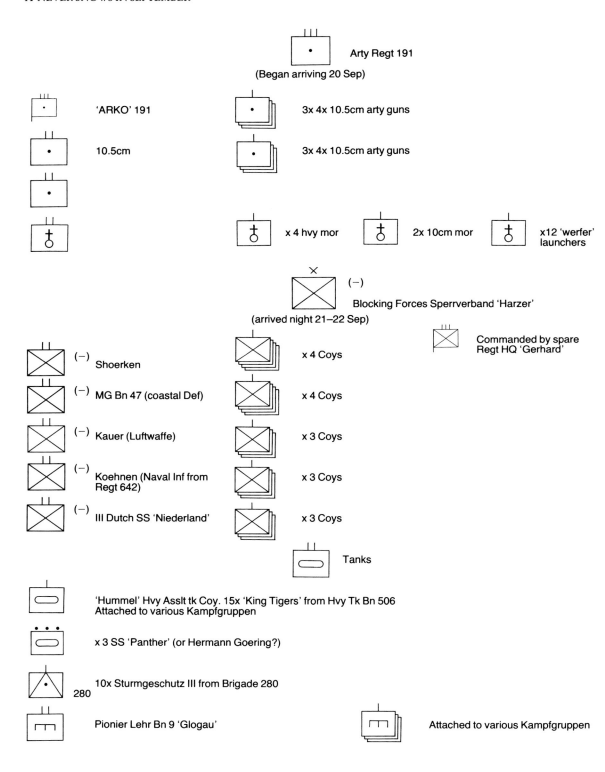

Arty Regt 191

(Began arriving 20 Sep)

'ARKO' 191

3x 4x 10.5cm arty guns

10.5cm

3x 4x 10.5cm arty guns

x 4 hvy mor   2x 10cm mor   x12 'werfer' launchers

(−)

Blocking Forces Sperrverband 'Harzer'

(arrived night 21–22 Sep)

Commanded by spare Regt HQ 'Gerhard'

(−) Shoerken   x 4 Coys

(−) MG Bn 47 (coastal Def)   x 4 Coys

(−) Kauer (Luftwaffe)   x 3 Coys

(−) Koehnen (Naval Inf from Regt 642)   x 3 Coys

(−) III Dutch SS 'Niederland'   x 3 Coys

Tanks

'Hummel' Hvy Asslt tk Coy. 15x 'King Tigers' from Hvy Tk Bn 506 Attached to various Kampfgruppen

x 3 SS 'Panther' (or Hermann Goering?)

10x Sturmgeschutz III from Brigade 280
280

Pionier Lehr Bn 9 'Glogau'   Attached to various Kampfgruppen

Appendix C: A Note on German Casualties During Operation Market-Garden 17-26 Sep 44

Model estimates 3,300 between 17–26 Sep. Compare with following figures:

Arnhem–Oosterbeek 17–26 Sep: Casualty Estimates

	UNIT	REPORTED STRENGTH	CASUALTIES	SOURCE	ESTIMATE
SS (+)	Helle	600	300	Lippert Abschrift	50%[1]
SS	Graebner	400	200	Fuerbringer and diary accounts	50%
SS (−)	KGr Petersen	250	125	C. Ryan	50%
SS	NCO School Arnheim	3,000	480 130 Killed 350 Wounded	Lippert Abschrift	15%
SS	KGr Spindler (includes)	Over 1,000 120 Harder 90 Pz Gren 19 90 Pz Gren 20 60 SS Arty 9	500	Author	50%[2]
SS (−)	Panzerjaeger	120	100	A. Ziegler	83%
SS	KGr Gropp (flak)	87	80	Tieke	92%
SS	KGr Mueller	120	60	H. Moeller Abschrift	50%
	Knaust	200–300	100	Author	33%
SS (+)	Krafft	600+	320 (65 killed 161 wounded 94 missing)	Krafft report	53%[3]
	Von Tettau	3,000– 4,000	10% understatement (300)	Author	Includes NCO School 'Arnheim'

TOTAL   2,565   (understatement as unit records incomplete)

Arnhem-Oosterbeek casualties alone based on this incomplete estimate could be 2,565 compared to Model's 3,300 Market-Garden total.

[1] Attached to NCO School 'Arnheim'   [2] *See* Gropp, Panzerjaeger and Moeller   [3] Although Krafft's own estimate is 62%

J. A Hey *(Roll of Honour, p.98)* has identified 1,725 war dead from the following locations over the same period.

Arnhem	626
Renkum	476
Apeldoorn	131
Rhenen	178
Doetinchem	4
Rheden	137
Utrecht	77
Ede	96
Total	**1,725**

Therefore the total casualty list (fatalities x 3 for wounded and missing) could be as high as 5,175 for the Arnhem area.

Market Garden Corridor 17–26 Sep: Casualty Estimates

	UNIT	REPORTED STRENGTH	CASUALTIES	SOURCE	ESTIMATE
(−)	KGR Walther includes	Approx 10 bns at 300 each 3,000	750	Schacht	25%
	107 Von Malzahn				
(−)	10SS Frundsberg	3,000	750	Author, Tieke and Harmel (estimate)	25%
(−)	Feldt	Approx 20KGr 300 each 6,000	1,500	Author	25%
(−)	59	1000 Inf and 5 Fallschirm-jaeger Bns 3,000	750	Author	25%
	TOTAL		3,750	(Rough estimate as records incomplete)	

Total German casualties for Market-Garden 17–26 Sep could therefore be:

Arnhem-Oosterbeek	2,565 or 5,175
Corridor	3,750
Total	**6,315 or 8,925**

This almost doubles or trebles the estimate assessed by Field-Marshall Model on 27 Sep 44.

Sources

Published Sources

BOOKS

Bauer, Cornelius,	*The Battle of Arnhem* (Stein and Day, New York 1967)
BBC	*War Report – D Day to VE Day* (BBC Ariel Books, 1985)
Bernhard, Herbert,	*1945. Die Entscheidungsschlacht am Nieder Rhein* (Verlag Buchhandlung Dambeck-Wesel, 1976)
Carell, Paul,	*Invasion – They're Coming!* (Harrap, London, 1962)
Creveld, Martin van,	*Fighting Power. German and US Army Performance 1939–45* (Greenwood Press, USA, 1982)
Critchell, Laurence,	*Four Stars of Hell* (Jove Books, 1987)
Dollinger, Hans,	*'Kain, wo ist dein Bruder?'* (Fischer, Frankfurt am Main, 1987)
Fuerbringer, Herbert,	*9SS-Panzer-Division. Hohenstaufen 1944: Normandie Tarnopol-Arnhem* (Heimdal, 1984)
Goerlitz, Walter,	*Model-Strategie der Defensive* (Limes Verlag Wiesbaden, 1975)
Haupt, Werner,	*Rueckzug im Westen 1944* (Motorbuch Verlag, Stuttgart, 1978)
Hey, J.A.,	*Roll of Honour. Battle of Arnhem 17–26 Sep 1944* (Society of Friends of Airborne Museum Oosterbeek, 1986)
Kamman, Willi,	*Der Weg Der 2. Fallschirmjaeger Division* (Schild-Verlag GmbH, Munchen, 1972)
Kamman, Willi,	*Die Geschichte des Fallschirmjaeger-Regiment 2. 1939 bis 1945* (Druckhaus Goldhammer Scheinfeld, 1987)
Keegan, John,	*Six Armies in Normandy* (Jonathan Cape, 1982)
Kuhn, Volkmar,	German Paratroops in World War 2 (Ian Allen, 1978)
Maassen, G.H.,	*Oosterbeek Destroyed 1944-45* (Meyer a Siegers b.v., Oosterbeek Holland, 1980)
MacDonald, Charles B.,	*The Siegfried Line Campaign. The US Army in World War 2* (The European Theatre of Operations, Washington, 1963)
McKee, Alexander,	*The Race for the Rhine Bridges 1940, 1944, 1945* (Stein and Day, New York, 1971)
Powell, Geoffrey,	*The Devil's Birthday. The Bridges to Arnhem 1944* (Buchan and Enright, London, 1984)
Ryan, Cornelius,	*A Bridge Too Far* (Hamish Hamilton, London, 1974)
Schramm, Percy E.,	*Kriegstagebuch des Oberkommandos der Wehrmacht. Band IV 1 Januar 1944–22 Mai 1945.* (Bernard and Graefe Verlag fuer Wehrwesen-Frankfurt am Main, 1961)

Seeman, Gerhard von,	*Die Ritterkreuztraeger 1939–45* (Verlag Hans Henning Podzun)
Shulman, Milton,	*Defeat in the West* (Coronet, 1973)
Sims, James,	*Arnhem Spearhead* (Imperial War Museum, 1978)
Swiecicki, Marck,	*With the Red Devils at Arnhem* (Maxlove Pub Co Ltd, London, 1945)
Tessin, Georg,	*Verbaende und Truppen der Deutschen Wehrmacht und Waffen-SS 1939–45 (Biblio Verlag, Osnabrueck, 1973)*
Tieke, Wilhelm,	*Im Feursturm Letzter Kriegsjahre. IISS-Panzer Korps mit 9 und 10SS Division Hohenstaufen und Frundsberg* (Munin Verlag GmbH, Osnabrueck, 1975)
Winterstein, E.M. und Jacobs, H.,	*General Meindl und seine Fallschirmjaeger* (Bundes Deutscher Fallschirmjaeger Braunschweig).
Witte, Gerhard,	*Ein Bild des deutschen Soldaten am Beginn des sechsten Kriegjahres. Aus 'Panzer Operationen'* (Gerd Niepold Mittler und Sohn, Bonn, 1987)
Zeno,	*The Cauldron* (Pan Books, 1968)
Korthals Altes, A,, Margry, K., Thuring G., and Voskuil, R.,	*September 1944* (Derde Druk, De Haan, 1984)

PERIODICALS

Anon	'Die Schlacht von Arnheim aus der Sicht der Luftnachrichten-Truppe', *Der Freiwillige* (Schneider)
Harmel, Heinz,	'Die Frundsberg in Nijmegen', *Der Freiwillige* Sep 1956 (Schneider)
Heck, Erwin,	'September 1944. Operation Market-Garden', *Der Freiwillige* 12/84 1/85 (Schnieder)
Hinz, Lothar,	'Unser Einsatz am Niederrhein 1/22: Die 6. Unteroffizierschule der Luftwaffe. I, II and III, *Die Weissen Spiegel,* DNK (Donth)
Kern, Erich,	'Der Faire Kampf um Arnheim' (Schneider). Anon periodical
Kessler, Herbert,	'Kaempfe im Raum Arnheim', *Die Weissen Spiegel* 2/85, 5/85, 6/85
Kershaw, Robert,	'The Kampfgruppe Spindler in Arnhem September 1944', *World War 2 Investigator,* Nov 1988
MacKay, E.M.,	'The Battle of Arnhem Bridge', *RE Journal* Dec 1954, pp 305–325
Schwarz, Wilfried,	'Persoenliches aus Arnheim – vor 40 Jahren', *Der Freiwillige* 10/84 (Schneider)
Sixt, Friedrich,	'Abwehrschlacht in Westdeutschland'. Die 3. Fallschirmjaeger-Division im Herbst 1944, *Der Deutsche Fallschirmjaeger* DNK (Donth)
Student, Kurt,	'Arnheim Letzter Deutscher Erfolg', *Der Front Soldat* 1952, Nos 5,6,7,8 and 9. Also *Der Deutsche Fallschirmjaeger* 1964 No 9 (Donth)

Volz, Heinz,	'Fallschirmjaeger Regiment von Hoffman', *Der Deutsche Fallschirmjaeger* 2/55 (Donth)

Unpublished Sources

DOCUMENTS

Anlageband Heeresgruppe B.	Ic. Meldungen 1.9.44-30.9.44
Boeree, Lt Col Theodore,	'Fragen an und Antworten von Bittrich', 24 March 54
Heydte, Oberst von der,	'Kaempfe des Fallschirmjaeger-Regiments 6 mit amerik. Fallschirmjaegern in Holland im September 1944.' (Freiburg) Ms-C-001
Kriegstagebuch Nr 1 des Befehlshabers Abschnitt III und Korps Feldt 9.8.44–19.12.44	Div Scherbening. Anlagen und Kriegsgliederung (Bundesarchiv) (handwritten).
Kriegstagebuch Stab General Kommando LXXXVIII AK	16.9.44–27.9.44 (Bundesarchiv)
Krafft, SS Sturmbahnfuehrer Sepp,	SS Pz Gren A.u.E. Btl 16 in den Kaempfen bei Arnheim 17.9.44–7.10.44
Lippert, SS Standartenfuehrer M,	Abschrift. Der handschriftlichen Aufzeichnungen des ehem. Staf. M. Lippert letzter Kommandeur der SS-Unterfuehrerschule Arnheim (Schneider)
Luftwaffe, Oberkommando der,	Einzelnachrichten des Ic Dienstes West der Luftwaffe. Nr 76/80 8 Okt 44. Neuerkenntnisse ueber den Einsatz Allierter Fallschirm-und Luftlandtruppen.
Oberkommando der Heeresgruppe B,	'Erfahrungsbericht ueber die Bekaempfung und Vernichtung der 1. engl. Luftlande-Division im Raum westlich Arnheim' (Schneider)
Offical War Histories	Narratives (Military); Section D Chapter V Advance from the river Seine to the Siegfried Line and the battle for Arnhem Aug 29–Sep 30 1944: Book III Operation 'Market-Garden' (ref CAB 44:254)
Rasch, Major,	Abschrift. 'Meine eigenen Erlebnisse in den letzten Kaempfen zwishen Maas und Elbe, (Schneider)
Reinhard, Helmuth,	Commitment of the 406th Division Against the Allied Air Landing at Nijmegen in September 1944'. Questions posed by Historical Div US Army 7 Dec 50
Schacht, Gerhard i.G.,	Abschrift. 'Die Kaempfe der Gruppe 'Walther' vom 13.9.44 bis zum 12.10.44 in Sued Holland (Bundesarchiv)
Schuster, Oberstleutnant a.D. Kurt	'The 85th Infantry Division Feb–Nov 1944. MS B-846, National Archive, Washington

Schwappacher, SS Hauptsturmfuehrer,	Abschrift. 'Kampfbericht der V/SS-Art. Ausb. u. Ers. Regt bei den Kaempfen um Nijmegen 29.9.44 (Schneider)
Sitter, H.,	Bericht: Kaempfhandlungen Sept-Okt 1944 Holland-Belgien. Merzig 15.3.72 (Donth)
Tettau, von,	Abschrift. 'Gefechtsbericht ueber die Schlacht bei Arnheim 17-26.9.44' (Bundesarchiv).

CORRESPONDENCE, INTERVIEWS AND DIARIES

Brandt, Albert,	Abschrift ueber 10SS Pz Pi Btl. 'Frundsberg'. Brief 22.2.55 an Harmel. (Schneider)
Damaske, Heinz,	Bn Adjt I/22u. II/21 10SS Pz Div Frundsberg. Correspondence. Die Kaempfe in Belgien und Sued Holland September 1944. Die Einsaetze der Kampfgruppe Richter. Nov 82. Einsatz von Kampfgruppen der 10. Pz Div 'Frundsberg' waehrend der Kaempfe in Sued Holland im September 1944. Niedernhausen Oct 82.
Dombrowski, Wolfgang,	SS Rottenfuehrer 2 Kp. Pz Pi Btl 9SS Correspondence and interview 23 Oct 87.
Enthammer, Joseph,	Lieutenant Artillery. Interview 15 Jun 87
Euling, Karl-Heinz,	SS Hauptsturmfuehrer, Btl comd. Copies of correspondence and maps (Schneider).
Flavell, James,	Lt pl comd 2 PARA. Interviews Staff College battlefield tours Arnhem, May 87/89
Fuerbringer, Herbert,	9SS. Extensive correspondence and documents
Fullriede, Fritz,	Oberstleutnant 'Hermann Goering' Division. Abschrift Tagesbuch 31.8.44–27.12.44
Hackett, J.W. DSO MBE MC,	Comd. 4 Parachute Brigade copy of diary
Harmel, Heinz,	Generalmajor der Waffen SS a.D. Comd, 10SS 'Frundsberg'. Interview 27 Oct 87. Correspondence and maps. Die 10SS Pz Div 'Frundsberg' im Einsatz von Juni bis November 1944.
Harzer, Walter,	SS Obersturmbahnfuehrer Comd 9SS. Unit memorandum. Dutch source.
Hensel, Erich,	Feldwebel. Div Nachrichten Kp. Interview 4 Jun 87.
Kaebel (Kracht), Karl-Heinz Dr.	Pz. Schuetzen: 6 Pz Ers. Rgt 'Bielefeld'. Photographs and copies of correspondence.
Lindemann, Rudolf,	SS Junker. SS Unteroffizierschule 'Arnheim'. Interview 11 Jun 87
Moeller, Hans,	SS Hauptsturmfuehrer. Pz. Pi. BH 9SS. Correspondence and Abschrift. 'Die Schlacht um Arnheim-Oosterbeek. Der Einsatz des Pionier Battalion 9 Hohenstaufen vom 17. bis 26 September 1944. (Sep 78)
Mueller, Paul,	SS Rottenfuehrer. Pz Gren Regt 20. 9SS Pz Div. Abschrift 'Arnheim'.

Oelkers, Heinrich,   SS Btl Comd. 'Kampf um Arnheim-SS Unterfuehrerschule 'Arnheim'. Auszug aus Aufzeichnungen aus einem Tagebuch.

Powell, Geoffrey,   156 PARA 4 Bde. Interviews Staff College battlefield tours Arnhem, 1987/89.

Schwarz, Wilfried,   SS Hauptsturmfuehrer. Div Ia. 9SS. Interview 16 Sep 87.

Sixt, Friedrich,   Transcript of interview Aug 54

Trapp, Rudolf,   SS Rottenfuehrer 3 Kp 21 Pz Gren Regt 10SS Frundsberg. Abschrift and interview 17 Sep 87

Ziegler, Alfred,   SS Rottenfuehrer. Panzerjaeger Abt 9SS. Interview 23 Nov 87. Abschrift 'Einsatz Arnheim', Bamberg 1976

Notes on the Text

CHAPTER I   THE FRENCH ODYSSEY
1. Figures: Tieke pp 282–283, Keegan p 313.
2. Joseph Enthammer interview, 15 Jun 87
3. H. Dollinger p 274
4. Wilfried Schwarz interview, 16 Sep 87
5. General Meindl und seine Fallschirmjaeger. Ernst Martin Winterstein/Hans Jacobs pp 203-204
6. P. Carell, p 274
7. Fullriede diary, 31 Aug 44. Nijmegen Archive.
8. Alfred Ziegler interview 23 Nov 87.
9. Wolfgang Dombrowski interview, 23 Oct 87

CHAPTER II   STAND AND FIGHT
1. *US Army in World War 2* p 122. 'The Siegfried Line Campaign'. Charles B MacDonald.
2. Arnheim Letzter Sieg pp 4-5. Kurt Student.
3. Kammann, W., *Die Geschichte des Fallschirmjaeger – Regiment 2* pp 182-3.
4. M. Shulman, *Defeat in the West*, p 232.
5. *US Army in World War 2*, p 232.
6. Erich Hensel interview, 4 Jun 87.
7. Lt Heinz Volz, *Fallschirmjaeger Regt von Hoffman* (Archiv Donth), and Schacht *Die Kaempfe der Gruppe 'Walther' vom 13.9.44 bis 12.10.44 in Sued Holland.*
8. Von der Heydte, *Kaempfe des Fallschirmjaeger – Regiments 6 mit amerik. Fallschirmjaegern in Holland im September 1944.*
9. *US Army in World War 2*, p134.

CHAPTER III   ALL QUIET ON THE WESTERN FRONT
1. Wolfgang Dombrowski interview, 23 Oct 87.
2. Official War Histories: Narratives (Military); Section D Chapter V. P 30 para 17.
3. *Ibid*, 67
4. *Arnhem Spearhead*, James Sims p 28.
5. Rudolf Lindemann interview, 11 Jun 87.
6. Krafft, Sepp, 'Pz. Gren. A.u.E. Btl 16 in den Kaempfen bei Arnheim. 17.9.44–7.10.44'.
7. Record of Interrogation PA Helle. Dutch original.
8. Fullriede diary, 13 Sep 44.
9. Harmel interview, 27 Oct 87.
10. Sources are fragmentary. Tieke's estimate p 301.
11. Moeller, Hans, *Die Schlacht um Arnheim – Oosterbeek. Der Einsatz des Pionier Btl 9 Hohenstaufen vom 17. bis 26 September 1944.*
12. Official War Histories Narratives pp 64–65.

13. Harmel, interview 27 Oct 87.
14. Heinz Damaske, correspondence and account of Kampfgruppe Richter, p 6.
15. Kriegstagebuch Stab Gen Kdo LXXXVIII. AK 16.9.44 Abschrift 719 ID. KGr Chill (85ID) Beurteilung der Lage 16.9.44. Schacht *Kampfgruppe Walther* p 8.
16. Official War Histories Narratives, p 30.
17. Heinz Volz, '*Fallschirmjaeger – Regiment von Hoffman*'.

CHAPTER IV   PORTRAIT OF THE GERMAN SOLDIER IN HOLLAND SEPTEMBER 1944
1. Alfred Ziegler, interview 23 Nov 87.
2. Wolfgang Dombrowski, interview 23 Oct 87.
3. H Lippert 'Abschrift' handwritten account.
4. H. Volz article.
5. *Die Geschichte des Fallschirmjaeger Regt 2*, Willi Kammann, p 182 and 186.
6. Von der Heydte document.
7. M. Shulman quote p 270, *Defeat in the West*.
8. POW interrogations quoted M. Schulman p 268.
9. *Ibid* p 271.
10. Interviews Ziegler and Dombrowski, 23 Nov and 23 Oct 87.
11. M. Shulman, p 212.
12. Gerd Niepold. *Panzer Operationen* p 137. Article by Gerhard Witte.
13. Martin van Creveld, *Fighting Power*.
14. H. Dollinger, p 264.
15. Fullriede diary (Nijmegen Archiv).
16. Martin van Creveld, p 87.
17. The section on 'beliefs and concerns' is based upon an annex to Niepold's *Panzer Operationen*, entitled 'Ein Bild des deutschen Soldaten am Beginn des Sechsten Kriegjahres' by Oberst A. D. Gerhard Witte. This is in effect a sociological survey of 12 Pz Div on the eve of the collapse of Army Group Centre on the Russian Front. It has been supplemented by interviews and the other quoted sources to adapt its implications to the situation faced by the German soldier in Holland in 1944.

CHAPTER V   THE LANDINGS
1. Quoted Erwin Heck, *September 1944. Operation Market-Garden*.
2. H. Kessler, *Kaempfe im Raum Arnheim*.
3. Ziegler, interview 23 Nov 87.
4. Volz. *Fjg – Regt von Hoffmann*. Note that German summer time was one hour ahead of British GMT.
5. Quoted from Lt Martin's diary in Laurence Critchley's *Four Stars of Hell*, Ch 26. The unit identified by Critchley is incorrect. Further research suggests Lt Martin was part of Luftwaffe Fliegerhorst Battalion 3 commanded by Major Merkens.
6. Kurt Student, *Arnheim. Letzter Deutscher Erfolg*.
7. Kriegstagebuch Korps d. Kav. Feldt and Stab Gen Kdo LXXXVIII Army Corps entries for 17.9.44.
8. Letter to his battalion commander Major Oswald Finzel (Archiv Donth).
9. Abschrift M. Lippert.
10. Ziegler, interview 23 Nov 87.
11. *The Battle of Arnhem*, C. Bauer, quoted p 92.

12. Moeller Abschrift.
13. Model, *Strategie der Defensive* (W. Goerlitz). This is a more plausible account than that more often offered, with Model, panic-stricken, dropping his personal belongings from his suitcase on the steps of the Hotel Tafelberg, later used as a British dressing station. Model had maintained his composure often in far worse situations on the Russian Front. As John Waddy of 156 PARA later treated for wounds in the hotel related to the author, 'There were and are no steps in front of the hotel.' More significantly, no maps or signs of its previous military use by the Germans were found on occupation by the British. Model's staff, as ever, were thorough.
14. Enthammer, interview 15 Jun 87.
15. Trapp, interview 17 Sep 87.
16. H. Bernhard, *1945. Die Entscheidungsschlacht am Nieder Rhein*, p 14.

CHAPTER VI   DRIVE INTO THE TEETH
1. Krafft report.
2. Moeller Abschrift.
3. Kriegstagebuch Korps Feldt und Stab Gen Kdo LXXXVIII A.K. 17.9.44.
4. Fullriede diary 17.9.44.
5. Kriegstagebuch Stab Gen Kdo LXXXVIII A.K. 1925 hrs 17.9.44
6. Krafft report.
7. 'Die Schlacht von Arnheim aus der Sicht der Luftnachrichten – Truppe', *Der Freiwillige* Jun 75.
8. P. Mueller Abschrift: 'Arnheim'.
9. Div Ia 9SS Pz. Div. Interview: 16 Sep 87.
10. Ziegler, interview 23 Nov 89.
11. Dombrowski, interview 23 Oct 87.
12. *See* Note 13, Chapter V.
13. Based on Model, *Strategie der Defensive* (Walter Goerlitz), pp 8–9.
14. H. Fuerbringer, pp 425–426. A reconstructed operational order is given at Appendix A.

CHAPTER VII   SMASHING THROUGH THE CRUST
1. Volz, *Fallschirmjaeger Regiment von Hoffmann*.
2. Von der Heydte account.
3. H. Damaske, '*Die Kampf in Belgien und Sued Holland Sept 44.*
4. Schacht, *Die Kaempfe der Gruppe 'Walther' vom 13.9.44 bis zum 12.10.44 in Sued Holland*.
5. Bericht: 'Kaempfhandlungen Sep – Oct 1944 Holland – Belgien'.
6. Kriegstagebuch Stab Gen Kdo LXXXVIII Corps 18.9.44.
7. Von der Heydte account.
8. Kriegstagebuch Stab Gen Kdo LXXXVIII Corps 0852 18.9.44.
9. *Ibid* 1318 hrs. 18.9.44.

CHAPTER VIII   MARCH! FOLLOW THE SOUNDS OF SHOOTING
1. Trapp, interview 17 Sep 87.
2. Moeller Abschrift.
3. Dombrowski, interview 23 Oct 87.
4. Lt James Flavell, interview Staff College tour of Arnhem, May 1987.

5. Tieke, pp 319–322.
6. Quoted from A. McKee, *The Race for the Rhine Bridges*, p 176.
7. *See* Appendix A.
8. McKee, p 176.
9. Trapp, interview/account.
10. Enthammer, interview 15 June 87.
11. Harmel, interview 27 Oct 87.
12. Rasch Abschrift 'Meine eigenen Erlebnisse in den letzten Kaempfen zwishen Maas und Elbe.'
13. *US Army in World War 2*, MacDonald, p 163.
14. Harmel, *Die Frundsberg in Nijmegen, Freiwillige* Sep 1956.
15. Harzer. Boiree Questionnaire.
16. It is likely these soldiers were the advance guard of the battalion Euling accompanied by engineers.

CHAPTER IX   ARNHEM. THE PENDULUM SWINGS

1. Krafft's report.
2. Its organisation is shown at Appendix B.
3. Tieke, p 318.
4. Signal. *Wie es Wirklich War – Arnheim*. Erwin Kirchhof. See photograph on p 105.
5. Ziegler interview, 23 Nov 87.
6. Moeller Abschrift.
7. *See* Note 2.
8. Lippert Abschrift.
9. Based on remarks taken from Lippert's Abschrift, Oelkers' diary and Rudolf Lindemann's interview of 11 Jun 87.
10. *See* chart at Appendix B.
11. Abschrift Von Tettau. 'Gefechtsbericht ueber die Schlacht bei Arnheim 17. – 26.9.44. 1350 hrs 17.9.44.
12. *Ibid* 1350 hrs.
13. Army Gp B 2315 hrs.
14. 'Gefechts bericht' Div von Tettau 0400. 18.9.44.
15. Lindemann, interview 11 Jun 87.
16. H. Kessler, Die Weissen Spiegel, 2/1985.
17. Lindemann, interview 11 Jun 87.
18. Lippert Abschrift.

CHAPTER X   SCRAPING THE BARREL

1. Anlageband Heeresgruppe B. Ic Meldungen 1–30 Sep 44. 2330 hrs 17.9.44.
2. Student. *Arnheim Letzter Deutscher Erfolg.*
3. Kriegstagebuch LXXXVIII Korps. 2014 hrs 17.9.44.
4. Student, *Arnheim Letzter Deuscher Erfolg.*
5. Kriegstagebuch LXXXVIII Korps 2355 hrs 17.9.44.
6. *Ibid*. 1845hrs 18.9.44.
7. *Ibid*. Beurteilung der Versorgungslage 18.9.44.
8. *Ibid*. Beurteilung der Lage 18.9.44.

9. Rasch. 'Meine eigenen Erlebnisse in den letzten Kaempfen zwischen Maas und Elbe. I. Groesbeek'.
10. Commitment of the 406 Div against the Allied Air Landings at Nijmegen, Sep 44 (MS C-085 Washington).
11. *Ibid.*
12. Figures based upon reports Kriegstagebuch Korps Feldt 9 Aug – 19 Dec 44. Entries for the period 17/18 Sept 44. 2300, 0730 and 1220 hrs. *See also* 'Meindl'. Winterstein and Jacobs p 211.
13. 406 Div. MS C-085 Washington.
14. Rasch account.
15. 406 Div. MS C-085 Washington.

CHAPTER XI   TAKE THE ARNHEM BRIDGE

1. Anlageband Heeresgruppe B. Ic Meldungen. Fernmundliche Orienteerung durch II SS Corps K/Ic 18.9.44. Fernspruch Ostuf Richter II SS Corps 1315.
2. Harmel, *Die Frundsberg in Nijmegen.*
3. Trapp, account and interview 17 Sep 87.
4. C. Ryan, *A Bridge Too Far*, p 229.
5. James Sims, p 56.
6. *Ibid* p 57.
7. Comments passed during interview 16 Sep 87.
8. Mauga. Quoted Fuerbringer, *9SS Panzer Division. Hohenstaufen*, p 430.
9. The picture of the attack has been recreated by H. Fuerbringer's *9SS Hohenstaufen* pp 428–30 and Maj. E. M. MacKay's *The Battle of the Arnhem Bridge*. Royal Engr Journal Dec 1954 pp 305–25. Further information has been provided by the Schwarz interview of 16 Sep 87 and some conjecture. For many years it was believed that Graebner's body was never recovered and that he may indeed have leaped into the Rhine. More recent evidence suggests that his remains may have been recovered first to Arnhem where they were later transferred to the German Military Cemetery in Ysselstein. (Schneider 10SS Archiv).
10. Schwarz, interview 16 Sep 87.
11. Kracht, letter 9 May 1980. Kaebel-Kracht correspondence to author.
12. *Ibid* dated 14 May 1984.
13. Interview, Harmel 27 Oct 87.
14. J. Enthammer, interview 15 Jun 87.

CHAPTER XII   SCHWERPUNKT IS SOUTH!

1. Harmel, *Die Frundsberg in Nijmegen*, Freiwillige Sep 56.
2. Harmel, interview 27 Oct 87.
3. *Ibid.*
4. Schwappacher. Abschrift: 'Kampfbericht der V/SS-Art. u. Ers. Regt. bei den Kaempfen um Nijmegen 29.9.44.
5. *See* Appendix B for Nijmegen Defence Forces.
6. Letter to Harmel 22.2.55. (Archiv Schneider).
7. Schwappacher report and Anlageband Heeresgruppe B. Ic Meldungen 1915. 19 Sep 44.
8. Harmel, *Die Frundsberg in Nijmegen*, Freiwillige Sep 56.
9. Kriegstagebuch LXXXVIII Korps. 0950 hrs 19.9.44.

10. *Ibid.* 1500 and 2000 hrs 19.9.44.
11. *Ibid.* 2100 hrs.
12. A. McKee, *The Race for the Rhine Bridges*, p 138.
13. Student, *Arnheim Letzter Deutscher Erfolg*.
14. McKee, p 138.
15. Kriegstagebuch LXXXVIII Korps. 'Lagerbeurteilung'. 19 Sep 44.
16. Official War Histories: Narratives; Section D Chapter V, p 118.
17. Tagesmeldung Gen Kdo LXXXVIII A.K. 2110 hrs 20 Sep 44. Account supplemented by Student *Arnheim Letzter Deutscher Erfolg*, eyewitness reports and photographic evidence.
18. *Die Kaempfe der Gruppe 'Walther' vom 13.9.44 bis zum 12.10.44 in Sued Holland*, pp 14–15.
19. *Ibid.*

CHAPTER XIII THE IMPACT ON GERMAN SOIL

1. Korps Feldt. Kriegstagebuch Nr 1 17.9.44
2. *Ibid*
3. *Ibid.* Signal Ia/8259/44. 18.9.44
4. H. Bernhard, *1945. Die Entscheidungsschlacht am Nieder Rhein*, p. 15
5. *Ibid.*
6. C. Ryan. Quoted *A Bridge Too Far*, pp 230–31.
7. Milton Shulman, *Defeat in the West*, pp 266–67.
8. L. Hinz, 'Unser Einsatz am Nieder Rhein', *Die Weissen Spiegel*.
9. From material taken from H. Bernhard *1945. Die Entscheidungsschlacht am Nieder Rhein*.

CHAPTER XIV ARNHEM. THE PENDULUM SWINGS BACK

1. Bittrich. Boiree 'Fragen an und Antworten von General Bittrich'. 24 Mar 54.
2. Lippert Abschrift.
3. *Ibid.*
4. *See* organisation of Kampfgruppe von Tettau at Appendix B.
5. 'Die Deutsche Wochenschau'. Film 735/42/1944.
6. *See* stills from the 'Wochenschau' report.
7. Material also from John Waddy 10 PARA. UK Staff College Tour of Arnhem 11 May 87.
8. Material based on C. Bauer, *The Battle of Arnhem*, p 145, and Record of Interrogation of Helle, Naumann and Fernau by Lt Col Th. Boiree.
9. Gefechtsbericht von Tettau. 1520 hours 18 Sept 44.
10. Lippert Abschrift.
11. Lindemann, interview 11 Jun 87.
12. Schwarz, interview 16 Sep 87.
13. Moeller Abschrift.
14. *See* German order of battle at Appendix B.
15. *See* sketch of para advance Utrechtstrasse.
16. Moeller account.
17. Mueller, Abschrift, 'Arnheim'.
18. Moeller Abschrift.

19. Dombrowski, interview 23 Oct 87.
20. Ziegler, interview 23 Nov 87.
21. *See* plate on p 105.
22. Ziegler, interview 23 Nov 87.
23. *Ibid* and Abschrift: 'Einsatz Arnheim'.
24. *Ibid.*

CHAPTER XV   BLASTING THE BRITISH OUT – THE ARNHEM BRIDGE
1. Enthammer, interview 15 Jun 87.
2. Schwarz, interview 16 Sep 87.
3. *A Bridge Too Far*, C. Ryan.
4. *Ibid*, p 319.
5. Trapp, interview 17 Sep 87.
6. Harmel, interview 27 Oct 87.
7. *A Bridge Too Far*, C. Ryan p 319.
8. Kracht material taken from series of letters written by Dr H. Kabel-Kracht 9.10.84/ 9.5.80/14.5.84 and photographs passed on to the author.
9. Trapp's experiences as related in his written account supplemented by an interview conducted with the author on 17 Sept 87.
10. Enthammer, interview 15 Jun 87.

CHAPTER XVI   HOLD ON THE WAAL
1. Arppe's film 590/2332. Traced Bundesarchiv Koblenz. Bild 101 Numerischer Index der Kriegsberichter Heer und Luftwaffe 1-451. Band 2/16.
2. List of plates from note 1 and examples shown with text.
3. Text supporting photographs based upon original research and Kriegstagebuch Nr 1. Korps Feldt 18–20 Sep 44.
4. Order Div Scherbening (406 Div) Nr 6. 19.9.44.
5. *US Army in World War 2*, pp 168–169, Charles B. MacDonald.
6. Kriegstagebuch Korps Feldt 0925 hrs 20.9.44.
7. Charles B. MacDonald p 178.
8. Primary sources for the counter-attack by II Fallschirmjaeger Corps 20 Sep are: Kriegstagebuch Nr 1 Korps Feldt 18–21 Sep 44. 'Abwehrschlacht in West Deutschland: Die 3. Fallschirmjaeger Div. im Herbst 1944' by Gen. Lt. Friedrich Sixt. (Article Donth Archiv.) 'Gen. Meindl und seine Fallschirmjaeger.' Winterstein a Jacobs pp 211–217.
9. Euling letter to JW Schneider 18 Jun 79.
10. *Ibid.*
11. Harmel, interview 27 Oct 87.
12. Charles B. MacDonald p 175.
13. Schwappacher account.
14. Harmel, interview 27 Oct 87.
15. Schwappacher, report 29.9.44.
16. Zonnenstahl's map *see* p 196.
17. Harmel, interview 27 Oct 87.
18. 1700 hrs Zwischenmeldung II SS Korps 20.9.44. Anlageband Heeresgruppe B.
19. Charles B. MacDonald p 179.
20. Schwappacher report 29.9.44.

21. *Ibid* p 3.
22. *Ibid* p 3.
23. Harmel, interview 27 Oct 87.
24. Schwappacher, p 4.
25. Charles B. MacDonald, p 182.
26. Harmel, *Die Frundsberg in Nijmegen, Der Freiwillige* Sept 56.
27. Correspondence (Schneider) 18 Jun 79.

CHAPTER XVII   PUTTING THE LID ON THE BOX
1. 'Gefechtsbericht' von Tettau 19.9.44.
2. *With the Red Devils at Arnhem*, Marek Swiecicki, p 26 (Maxlove Pub Ltd 1945)
3. Krafft Int report. The Enemy Para 2 (0).
4. Gefechtsbericht von Tettau. 1545 19 Sep. Note the difference in British summertime.
5. *Ibid.* 19 Sep 1600.
6. Krafft Pz Gren A.u.E. Btl 16 in den Kaempfen bei Arnheim 17.9.44/7.10.44.
7. Ziegler, interview 23 Nov 87.
8. Krafft, report 20 Sep 0600 hrs.
9. *Ibid.* 20 Sep 0830 hrs.
10. Gefechtsbericht von Tettau 20 Sep 0900–1500 hrs.
11. *Ibid.* 20 Sep 1830 hrs.
12. Schwarz, interview 16 Sep 87.
13. Lippert Abschrift.
14. Krafft, Int report. The Enemy 2. (c).
15. Lindemann, interview 11 Jun 87.
16. *Ibid.*
17. Lippert Abschrift.
18. Lindemann, interview 11 Jun 87.
19. Alfred Ziegler, interview 23 Nov 87.
20. British movements during this chapter based on the detailed comments and grid references contained in Hackett's personal diary of events.

CHAPTER XVIII   HOLLOW VICTORIES
1. Anlageband Heeresgruppe B. 2015 hrs 20.9.44.
2. Telephone conversation quoted Charles B. MacDonald p 182.
3. Schwappacher, report p 4.
4. Diary entry 27 Sep 44 after interviewing survivors from the 'Kompanie Runge' which had just returned to German lines.
5. SS-Capt Brandt. Letter to Harmel 22.2.55. Archiv Schneider.
6. Schwappacher, report p 6.
7. Letter to Archiv Schneider 18 Jun 79.
8. Escape account based upon the extract published in the 'Frundsberg-Errinerungsbuch'. Quoted Tieke pp 342–45.
9. Schwappacher, p 4.
10. Harmel, 'Die Frundsberg in Nijmegen', *Der Freiwillige*, Sept 56.
11. Harmel, interview 27 Oct 87.
12. Trapp, interview 17 Sep 87.
13. Enthammer, interview 15 Jun 87.

14. Trapp, interview 17 Sep 87.
15. Kabel-Kracht correspondence, 14 May 84.
16. Enthammer, interview 15 Jun 87.
17. Anlageband Heeresgruppe B. 1100 hrs. 21.9.44.
18. According to Tieke, p 349.
19. Enthammer, interview 15 Jun 87.
20. Sims p 88–9, *Arnhem Spearhead*, Imperial War Museum. 1978.
21. Interview Staff College Battlefield Tour Arnhem, 11–12 May 1987.
22. Sims p 88.
23. Trapp was particularly scathing about the film 'A Bridge Too Far' during the interview. 'The film,' he said, 'got it all wrong, making us look like parade ground soldiers!.'

CHAPTER XIX   THE MISSED OPPORTUNITY
1. Kabel-Kracht correspondence 14 May 84.
2. Harmel, 'Die Frundsberg in Nijmegen', *Der Freiwillige*, Sep 56.
3. Letter to author 18 Feb 88.
4. Harmel, interview 27 Oct 87.
5. Brandt letter to Harmel 22.2.55.
6. Harmel, 'Die Frundsberg in Nijmegen'.
7. Tieke, p 346.
8. Brandt letter to Harmel 22.2.55.
9. Harmel, interview. 27 Oct 87.
10. *Ibid*.
11. Kabel-Kracht correspondence 14 May 84.
12. *Ibid*. 9 May 80.

CHAPTER XX   THE WITCHES CAULDRON
1. Fuerbringer, p 447.
2. Befehle fuer Tageseinsatz 19.9.44. 3. Jagddivision. Abtl. Ia Br. B. Nr. 2/44 geh. v.18.9.44.
3. Trapp Abschrift.
4. 'Werfergruppe Krosta' anon article English text.
5. Ziegler, interview 23 Nov 87.
6. Fuerbringer pp 446–447.
7. Recorded 20 Sep 1944, p 203, *War Report. D Day to VE Day* (BBC Ariel Books 1985).
8. Macdonald, p 199.
9. H. Kessler, 'Kaempfe im Raum Arnheim', *Die Weissen Spiegel*, 2/85.
10. Lawrence Critchell, *Four Stars of Hell*, quoted p 160.
11. Kessler, *Die Weissen Spiegel* 2/85, 5/85.
12. Gefechtsbericht ueber die schlacht bei Arnheim'. Div von Tettau. 0040 hrs 21 Sep.
13. *Ibid*.
14. Critchell, p 160.
15. Kessler, *Die Weissen Spiegel* 2/85, 5/85.
16. Fullriede diary 21 Sep 44.
17. Kessler, *Die Weissen Spiegel* 2/85, 5/85.
18. Fullriede diary 21 Sep/24 Sep 44.
19. Gefechtsbericht von Tettau. 1050 hrs and 1145 hrs 21 Sep.

20. Kessler 5/85.
21. Fullriede diary 21 Sep 44.
22. Gefechtsbericht von Tettau 1020 hrs 21 Sep 44.
23. Moeller. 'Die Schlacht um Arnheim-Oosterbeek. Der Einsatz des Pionier Batallion 9 Hohenstaufen vom 17. bis 26. September 1944.'
24. Compiled from Gerhard von Seeman, *Die Ritterkreuztraeger 1939–45*. Mathes was also posthumously awarded the Knights Cross for Arnhem. Verlag Hans Henning Podzun. Also *Verbaende und Truppen der Deutschen Wehrmacht und SS 1939–45*, Georg Tessin (Biblio Verlag Osnabrueck, 1973).
25. Betr: 'Gliederung der Kampftruppen'. Abt. 1a. Kno./Sch. Div Gef St. 9SS Div Hohenstaufen 25 Sep 44.
26. Moeller Abschrift.
27. Dombrowski, interview 23 Oct 87.
28. Moeller Abschrift.
29. Ziegler, interview 23 Nov 87 and Abschrift 'Einsatz Arnheim'.

CHAPTER XXI   THE CRISIS

1. Rudolf Trapp, interview 17 Sep 87.
2. Lippert Abschrift.
3. C. Bauer, *The Battle of Arnhem*, p 219.
4. Compiled from 'Abschrift 9SS 'H' Abt. 1a Kno/Sch. Betr. Gliederung der Kampftruppen. Div. Gef. Stand den 25 Sep 44'.
5. Hensel, interview 4 Jun 87.
6. Kracht-Kabel Dutch correspondence 14 May 84.
7. Hensel, *Op cit*.
8. Harmel, interviews by Gen Lt A.D. Friedrich Sixt, Aug 1984.
9. Trapp, interview 17 Sep 87 and Abschrift.
10. Hensel, interview 4 Jun 87. Harmel, 'Die Frundsberg in Nijmegen', *Der Freiwillige* Sep 56.
11. Tieke, p 351.
12. Anlageband Heeresgruppe B Ic Meldungen. Abendmeldung IISS Pz Corps. 1750 Ostf Richter. 43 Wessex positively identified by 23 Sep.

CHAPTER XXII   CUTTING THE CORRIDOR

1. Kriegstagebuch LXXXVIII Corps. 1130 uhr 21.9.44. Original translation refers to the attack directions as from north and south, meaning more accurately NW and SE. To avoid confusion this has been corrected to read from 'east' and 'west'. (Author).
2. *Die Kaempfe der Gruppe 'Walther' vom 13.9.44 bis zum 12.10.44 in Sued Holland. V. Der Angriff auf Veghel am 22/23.9.44*, Schacht.
3. There is some debate whether this could have been the SS Kampfgruppe 'Heinke'. H. Damaske argues convincingly it was his own unit: IISS Pz-Gren Regt 22 also from the 10SS Frundsberg.
4. LXXXVIII Corps KTB 1850 hrs 21.9.44. (Also Charles B MacDonald, p 189.) And Lagebeurteilung 22.9.44 Fernspruch 1930 hrs 21.9.44.
5. MS-C-001 Kaempfe des Fallschirmjaegersregiments 6 mit amerik. Fallschirmjaegern in Sued Holland in September 1944. 2. Der Angriff des Falljschirmjaeger rgts. 6 bei Schijndel.

6. H. Damaske, Abschrift *Die Kaempfe in Belgien und Sued-Holland September 1944*, 30 Nov 82.
7. Official War Histories: Narratives Sect VII. Para 68. Sept 22. Also MacDonald, pp 188–89.
8. Official War Histories. *Ibid*.
9. Damaske Abschrift.
10. Official War Histories. *Op cit*.
11. *Race to the Rhine Bridges*, A. McKee, p 209.
12. Damaske Abschrift.
13. Von der Heydte. MS-C-001
14. *Ibid*.
15. Kriegstagebuch Kdo LXXXVIII Korps 1210 hrs 23.9.44. Response 1216 hrs.
16. Von der Heydte. *Op cit*.

CHAPTER XXIII   THE INVESTMENT OF OOSTERBEEK
1. Kessler, 'Kaempfe im Raum Arnheim', *Die Weissen Spiegel* 2/85
2. Von Tettau. 'Gefechtsbericht ueber die Schlacht bei Arnheim'. 1900 hrs 21 Sep.
3. Harmel, interviews. Gen Lt A.D. Friedrich Sixt Aug 1954, p 57.
4. Von Tettau. 0906 hrs and 0930 hrs 23 Sep 44.
5. Lippert, Abschrift.
6. Von Tettau. 1330 hrs 22 Sep.
7. Interview 23 Oct 87.
8. Von Tettau. 2120 Fuerbringer p 454.
9. Von Tettau. 2210 hrs 22 Sep.
10. *Ibid*. Tagesmeldung 1900 hrs 23 Sep.
11. Interview 11 Jun 87.
12. Diary quote p 160 L. Critchell, *Four Stars of Hell*
13. Hoffmann. 'Ln-Die Geschichte der Luftnachrichtentruppe' Bd II. Quoted from 'Die Schlacht von Arnheim aus der Sicht der Luftnachrichtentruppe'. *Der Freiwillige* Jun 75.
14. Moeller Abschrift.
15. Von Tettau. 1345 23 Sep.
16. Diary quote p 161. L. Critchell.
17. Interview 23 Oct 87.
18. Ic Meldungen 2115 22 Sep and Morganmeldung IISS-Korps 23 Sep 1944.
19. Krafft. Kampfbericht. 1330 hrs 17 Sep 44.
20. Fullriede diary 1–2 Oct 44.
21. Interview 23 Oct 87.
22. Interview 15 Jun 87.
23. Interview 11 Jun 87.
24. Interview 23 Oct 87.
25. Interview 11 Jun 87.
26. P. Mueller, Abschrift and letter to author 29 Oct 87.
27. Interview 15 Jun 87.
28. Mueller *op cit*.
29. Moeller Abschrift.
30. Interview 23 Oct 87.
31. Divs Befehle Nr. 15. von Tettau Gef. St. den 22 Sep 44.

32. Gefechtsbericht von Tettau. 1900. 21 Sep 44.
33. *Op cit* Befehle Nr 15. Anlage 5. 22 Sep 44.
34. Figures derived from photographic research, and the eyewitness and diary accounts recorded in this book. For example, Bittrich (Boiree interviews) speaks of 8 French Renault tks and 20 Sturmgeschutz employed. 24 Mar 54.
35. Harzer interview. Sixt.
36. Written in novel form under the pseudonym 'Zeno' in *The Cauldron* (Pan Books), pp 201–203.
37. Gefechtsbericht von Tettau 2250 24 Sep 44 and 0515 25 Sep 44. The report further stated that despite having been requested and agreed at HQ Netherlands, the arrival of the Goliaths 'was delayed for so long' that 'they were not used in the operation'.

CHAPTER XXIV   THE FINAL CUT: KOEVERING

1. Kriegstagebuch LXXXVIII Korps. 1725 and 2055 23 Sep 44.
2. Model to von Rundstedt 1300. 24 Sept 44. Quoted MacDonald p 197.
3. *Die Kaempfe der Gruppe 'Walther' vom 13.9.1944 bis zum 12.10.1944 in Sued Holland,* Anhang A. Fernsprechtaeuschung in Bakel.
4. *See* Charles B MacDonald p 194.
5. Kriegstagebuch LXXXVIII Korps. 1915 and 2025 23 Sep 44.
6. L. Critchell, *The Sand Dune Fight,* pp 138–142, from *Four Stars of Hell.*
7. Official War Histories: Narratives para 71. 'The Third Cut in the Nijmegen Corridor'. (6) 24 Sep – on 30 Corps Axis.
8. Kriegstagebuch LXXXVIII Korps Tagesmeldung 1945 hours 23.9.44.
9. *Ibid.* 0445 hours 24 Sep.
10. Von der Heydte account.
11. Official War Histories: Narratives: d. 25 Sep on 30 Corps axis.
12. Kriegstagebuch LXXXVIII Korps 1055 25 Sep 44.
13. *Ibid.* 1700 hours 25 Sep 44.
14. *Ibid.* 1720 hours.
15. *Defeat in the West*, Milton Shulman, p 270.
16. H. Sitter. Merzig. 15.3.72 Bericht: 'Kampfhandlungen Sep–Okt 1944 Holland–Belgien'.
17. Kriegstagebuch LXXXVIII Korps 0812 Hours, 1008 hours 26 Sep 44.
18. *Op cit*, H. Sitter. He was wounded between 26 Sep–3 Oct, 'I don't know exactly'.

CHAPTER XXV   THE END

1. Von Tettau 'Gefechtsbericht' 0515 hours and 0610 hours 25 Sep 44.
2. Moeller Abschrift.
3. Lippert Abschrift.
4. These were: 4x15mm, 30x105mm, 2x10mm, 12x15mm, 12x75mm field guns, 20x88mm and 20x105mm Flak in the field role and 10x12mm mortar. Fuerbringer, p 458. In some instances, eg 15mm, the calibres were equal but the wpn systems different.
5. Harzer, interview. Sixt.
6. Krafft, report 25 Sep.
7. G. Powell, interview Staff College Arnhem battlefield tour May 1987.
8. Kessler, *Die Weissen Spiegel,* Nr 2/1985.
9. Lindemann, interview 11 Jun 87.
10. Harzer, Unit Memorandum.

11. Moeller Abschrift.
12. Krafft 2. Der Feind (a) (b).
13. Lippert Abschrift.
14. Critchell, p 161.
15. 'Gefechtsbericht'. von Tettau 1400 25 Sep and 0903 26 Sep 44.
16. Kessler, *Der Weissen Spiegel*, 2/85.
17. Hensel, interview 4 June 87.
18. Moeller Abschrift.
19. Harzer. Unit Memorandum (Dutch source).
20. Kessler, *Der Weissen Speigel*, 2/85.
21. Lindemann, interview 11 Jun 87.
22. Ziegler, 23 Nov 87.
23. Moeller Abschrift.
24. Ziegler, interview 23 Nov 87.
25. Lippert Abschrift.
26. Schwarz, interview 16 Sep 87.
27. Tagesmeldung A Gp B 0220 hours 27 Sep 44. *See* Chapt XXVI and Appendix C.
28. Fullriede diary 26 Sep 44.
29. Moeller Abschrift.
30. Dombrowski, interview 23 Oct 87.

CHAPTER XXVI ACHIEVEMENTS

1. C. Bauer, *The Battle of Arnhem*. Chapter: 'The Mystery of the Hohenstaufen Division', pp 37–89.
2. German battalion groups varied in strength between 300 to 600 men with some heavy weapons. They were *ad hoc* organisations, normally referred to as 'Kampfgruppen' because of their weak strengths.
3. Figs based on von Tettau, Korps Feldt, LXXXVIII Corps, unit records and diaries. The average size of a battalion was probably 250–300 men.
4. Erfahrungs Bericht ueber die Bekaempfung und vernichtung der 1. engl. Luftlande Division im Raum westlich Arnheim. Oberkommando der Heeresgruppe B. 10 Oct 44 1) Beurteilung des Feindverhaltens.
5. Boiree interviews Bittrich. 24 Mar 64. Fragen an und Antworten von Gen Bittrich.'
6. RJ Kershaw, '*Kampfgruppe Spindler in Arnhem Sep 1944*', *World War Two Investigator, Nov 88.*
7. Erfahrungsbericht. Army Gp B. 1.10.44. 1) and 2).
8. Krafft Kampfbericht. 1330 hrs 17 Sep 44.
9. *Race for the Rhine Bridges*, A. McKee, p 285. Stein and Day, NY, 1971.
10. Tieke, pp 359–60.
11. *See* Appendix C.
12. *Roll of Honour. Battle of Arnhem 17-26 Sep 1944*, compiled by JA Hey (The Society of Friends of the Airborne Museum Oosterbeek, 1986). Appendix C. German War Dead.
13. HQ Br. Abn Corps-Cabinet Office Historical Section. Quoted MacDonald p 198.
14. Erfahrungsbericht Army Gp B.
15. Krafft G2 Bericht. h. 'Der Feind'.
16. Harmel, interview 27 Oct 87.
17. Milton Shulman, *Defeat in the West*, pp 270–271.

CHAPTER XXVII POSTSCRIPT – THE FINAL IRONY
1. Lindemann, interview 11 Jun 87.
2. Friedrich Sixt: Harmel Bericht 'Die 10SS Pz Div im Angriff 1–4.7.44'.
3. Oelker's diary, 30 Sep 44.
4. *Ibid*. 1 Oct 44.
5. Kessler. Quoted A. McKee p 297.
6. Lindemann, interview 11 Jun 87.
7. Kessler *op cit* 9 298.
8. Lt Martin diary. 2/3 Oct 44. Critchley p 262.
9. Oelker's diary, 3 Oct 44.
10. Lt Martin 4 Oct. Critchley p 262.
11. Kessler, *op cit*, p 298.
12. Lindemann, interview 11 Jun 87.
13. Lt Martin *op cit*, p 263.

Index